INNOCENT UNTIL

INTERROGATED

GARY L. STUART

INNOCENT UNTIL

INTERROGATED

The True Story of the
Buddhist Temple Massacre
and the Tucson Four

THE
UNIVERSITY
OF ARIZONA
PRESS
TUCSON

The University of Arizona Press
© 2010 Gary L. Stuart

www.uapress.arizona.edu

Library of Congress Cataloging-in-Publication Data

Stuart, Gary L., 1939–
  Innocent until interrogated : the true story of the Buddhist
temple massacre and the Tucson four / Gary L. Stuart.
    p. cm.
  Includes bibliographical references and index.
  ISBN 978-0-8165-2924-7 (pbk. : alk. paper)
  1. Murder—Investigation—Arizona—Maricopa County. 2.
Judicial error—Arizona. I. Title.
  HV6533.A6.S78 2010
  364.152'309791776—dc22
                                    2010006814

✿

Manufactured in the United States of America on acid-free,
archival-quality paper containing a minimum of 30 percent
post-consumer waste and processed chlorine free.

15 14 13 12 11 10   6 5 4 3 2 1

The fascination that the police have for the thief is manifested by the thief's temptation to confess when he is arrested. In the presence of the examining magistrate who questions him, he is seized with giddiness: the magistrate speaks gently to him, perhaps with kindness, explaining what is expected of him; practically nothing: an assent. If only once, just once, he did what was asked of him, if he uttered the "yes" that is requested, harmony of minds would be achieved. He would be told, "That's fine," perhaps he would be congratulated. It would be the end of the hatred. The desire to confess is the mad dream of universal love; it is, as Genet himself says, the temptation of the human.

—*Jean-Paul Sartre*

Contents

Illustrations

Author's Note

The temple murders and the related murder of Alice Marie Cameron are heavily documented. They spawned more than five hundred thousand digital records and six thousand pages of court transcripts, pleadings, motions, and opinions. Long before the trial began, file cabinets all over Phoenix accumulated the official reports from dozens of agencies, public and private individuals, and more than fifty lawyers. There are thousands of still photographs, hundreds of audiocassette tapes, scores of videos, and an incalculable number of private images in the hands of the lawyers, investigators, witnesses, suspects, victims' families, journalists, and authors involved in the cases. It took more than four years to resolve the criminal and civil litigation. Even with all of that, some of the facts are not only unknown, they are unknowable.

Just how many young people in West Phoenix knew who the real killers were before their apprehension is unclear. Some estimate the number at a handful; others at a dozen or more. However many there were, none of them came forward voluntarily to help solve the crimes. The number of people who investigated, analyzed, reviewed, prosecuted, defended, judged, consulted, and managed the criminal and civil cases spawned by the ten murders likely extends to the thousands. And yet, despite their prodigious efforts, no one can say with certainty exactly what happened inside the temple on August 10, 1991, or at Alice Marie Cameron's campground twenty miles away and six weeks later.

The first two chapters in this book are a reconstruction of the basic story from the forensic evidence, the confessions of the killers, the recollections of those who knew them, and the opinions of experts who second-guessed everyone, including one another.

The remaining chapters, particularly the courtroom scenes and interrogations, necessarily present only a small part of the reality. I conducted more than fifty personal interviews and read the entire trial and appellate records in the cases. I reviewed three years of print and broadcast news coverage and read the police reports and the transcripts of all custodial interrogations and official interviews.

In addition, I downloaded the digital discovery exchange between prosecutors and defense lawyers into an ISYS database containing digital files from Maricopa County Sheriff's Office, the Maricopa County Attorney's Office, and nonprivileged files from various defense lawyers. I examined the exhibits admitted in evidence in the Doody trial, along with original court pleadings.

This book is an excerpted and condensed narrative of what happened. The full truth lies in the interrogation transcripts, police reports, trial testimony, pretrial depositions, exhibits, and sworn affidavits. To make sense of that mountain of documentation, I eliminated redundancy, translated legal jargon, and tried to clarify the narrative. While all the stated facts are true, the opinions and legal interpretations in this book are strictly my own.

INNOCENT UNTIL

INTERROGATED

A CIRCLE OF DEATH

1

On Saturday, August 10, 1991, temperatures in Arizona's Valley of the Sun were predicted to climb to 113 degrees Fahrenheit. By 10:00 a.m. the little thermometer at the Buddhist temple called Wat Promkunaram registered 94 degrees. Like everything else at the temple, the thermometer was a simple indicator of impermanence and change. Plain and unadorned, it was a metaphor for the way the monks lived, worked, and worshipped. The current temperature was merely a truth at a given time. Change was inevitable, for better or worse, as the days and the seasons unfolded. The monks lived in the moment and accepted the passage of days, weeks, seasons, and years without much fuss.

Luke Air Force Base sits some twenty miles west of the center of Phoenix. The hungry sprawl of America's fifth-largest and fastest-growing city peters out near the base. Wat Promkunaram is a mile farther west, surrounded by the large irrigated plots and well-kept farmhouses that make up the little community of Waddell, Arizona. Cotton farms and bean fields flourish here, nourished by precious Colorado River water carried by a 336-mile canal snaking east through the desert. While the Thai monks at the monastery meditate and withdraw, fighter pilots in training head for the Barry M. Goldwater Bombing Range, an area roughly the size of Connecticut. There they practice dropping smart bombs and engaging in air-to-air combat. The roar of F-16 fighter jets taking off and landing about 150 times every day pummels the temple grounds, but little else intervenes in Wat Promkunaram's pastoral tranquillity.

That August, shimmering heat waves formed a dancing, translucent barrier around the tall concrete-block wall enclosing the temple and its five acres of vegetable gardens and meditation paths. The white, red-roofed single-story building was—and still is—home and meditation center to monks, nuns, acolytes, and bell ringers. The wall was not for protection; two wide paved driveways broke its continuity and gave easy access to the parking areas used by the four hundred or so members of the third-largest Thai Buddhist community in the United States.

Between the driveways was the wall's one distinguishing feature: a forty-foot section, painted white, on which bright red letters announced "Wat Promkunaram, Buddhist Temple of Arizona."

In 1991 Chawee Borders, a fifty-one-year-old Thai woman married to an American serviceman, lived in Waddell, near both the temple and the air force base. For her, August 10 began as a typical Saturday: as her husband put on his uniform and left for his job at the base, she dressed modestly to go to the temple. That morning she was to drive her friend Premchit Hash, another immigrant from Thailand, to the temple, where they would cook lunch for the monks. Women members took turns cleaning the temple and providing the monks' meals. The work was an honor, a small service they could do as part of their faith.

Borders had belonged to the temple since her arrival in Arizona in 1976, and she knew some of its residents well. Today she and Hash would fix rice and vegetables for three longtime acquaintances: Phra Pairuch Kanthong, their abbot since 1982; Surichai Anuttaro, the abbot's closest colleague since 1985; and Boonchuay Chaiyarach, who had transferred to Wat Promkunaram from a temple in the Netherlands a few years before.

Another old friend was Foy Sripanprasert, who, like Premchit Hash, had followed her daughter from Thailand to Arizona some time ago. Just recently, in her seventies, Foy had decided to become a nun. She was a happy woman, quick to laugh, devoted to the temple. The only woman living there, she had a tiny sleeping alcove off the kitchen, well apart from the monks' private quarters.

Foy's seventeen-year-old grandson, Matthew Miller, had just joined her at the temple to spend part of his summer vacation immersed in Buddhism, as other young men had done before him. Come September, he would let his shaved hair grow back and start tenth grade at Agua Fria High School.

Borders was still getting to know Chalerm Chantapim, who had come from Thailand about a year before. The two newest monks she hardly knew at all: Siang Ginggaeo had recently replaced the temple's former bookkeeper; Somsak Sopha had arrived just a few days ago. And there was a visitor. She thought he was a relative of the abbot's. Pairuch had brought him back from a trip to Thailand six weeks ago. He was only twenty-one, maybe a good companion for Matthew. His name was Chirasak Chirapong, but Borders and her friends just called him Boy.

At about 10:40 a.m., Borders dropped off Hash near the front door and went to park her car. The women were used to the shudder and roar of the fighter jets but were relieved, as always, to be inside the concrete walls of the temple compound.

The door was locked, and Premchit Hash had no key, so she walked toward the back of the building, where she found an unlocked door near the kitchen. Removing her sandals at the threshold as tradition dictated, she carried her grocery bags into the kitchen, then went into the main hall of the temple and propped open the double doors for her friend.

Chawee Borders saw that the ground around the building was flooded with water and wondered why. Had the monks forgotten to turn off the irrigation system? She also wondered where everyone was. There was no one tending the garden, no one walking on the paths, and no one at the door. The lack of activity made her uneasy.

But the women had come to serve the monks, not to question them. While Hash put water on the stove to boil for rice, Borders laid a bouquet of fresh-cut flowers in front of the statue of the Buddha in the main hall, then headed for the car to get the rest of the groceries. One of her questions was answered when she passed the open door to the sitting area and saw the monks, in their orange robes, lying on the floor. She guessed they were praying.

When the meal was almost ready, Borders thought she heard a telephone ringing. She moved quickly to the pay phone near the kitchen, only to find that its cord had been cut, the two ends dangling at odd angles against the whitewashed wall.

At that moment, with the dead phone in her hand and her unease turning to fear, Borders noticed that something else was very wrong. One of the people on the floor was wearing white. It had to be Foy Sripanprasert, the temple's only resident nun, lying there with the monks. This was forbidden.

Alarmed, Borders looked closer. The monks lay face down on the carpet in a rough circle, their heads toward the center. They could have been praying or sleeping. Yet most had their hands clasped above their heads, an uncomfortable position for sleep and an odd one for prayer. Borders called out to them, telling them to get up and eat.

Then she saw the blood. Pools of it. A shudder later, she began to recognize individuals in the array of bodies. She knew them all. Along with the abbot and the other monks and Foy, she now recognized Matthew Miller and the young visitor everyone called Boy. They were all so still.

Not the quiet of sleep; not the serene stillness of meditation. Borders had never seen death this close, and her heart sent a scream up to her throat.

Beginning to sob, Borders ran to the kitchen and told Hash they had to get help. As though being chased by what Borders had seen, the friends ran barefoot to their car and drove quickly to a nearby house to find a phone.

The houses were generously spread out in the old farming community, the nearest house almost two hundred feet from the temple's wall. That neighbor's dogs scared the women, so Borders drove on to the second house.

Joe Ledwidge opened his door to find two Asian women crying so hard that he couldn't understand their words. Something had happened at the temple, he thought; maybe one of the monks was having a heart attack. He hustled the women into his white pickup truck and went to find out.

Ledwidge would later describe what he saw as an execution. One look was enough. He rushed home, shouting for his wife to call 911. After the call, he drove Borders and Hash back to the temple parking lot, where the three of them sat in his truck and waited for the police.

Wat Promkunaram is in one of Arizona's "county islands." While larger communities like Phoenix and Glendale have their own police departments, smaller towns like Waddell contract with their counties for law enforcement. Accordingly, the dispatch center for the Maricopa County Sheriff's Office (MCSO) took all 911 calls from Waddell.

The dispatch operator logged in Mrs. Ledwidge's call at 11:09 a.m. "911 Emergency," she answered.

"Yes, emergency at the Buddhist temple," the caller began. Screams were audible in the background, but the voice on the phone was steady.

The operator made a note of the address shown on her call screen and sent an automatic signal to all patrol cars in that area, advising them of "unknown trouble." She told Mrs. Ledwidge the police were on the way.

Then another voice came on the line, heavily accented, high pitched and shrill. This was Chawee Borders. "Hi, lady?" Borders began. "I'm got a membership in the temple. I come feed them lunch today."

The operator didn't understand her. "You can do what?"

"I come feed them lunch today, my monk. They all die the same place."

Asked for details, Borders sounded frantic. "No, I don't know. Nobody answer. I see blood all over. Come see, please officer. Please! Now! Go see now."

News of the grisly discovery Chawee Borders and Premchit Hash had made that morning soon radiated through the Valley of the Sun. Arizona, the last of the lower forty-eight to be granted statehood, had its first mass murder. By 11:45 a.m., radio coverage was widespread; for the rest of the day, TV stations featured the story as breaking news. The first print account came the next morning, when the *Arizona Republic* devoted much of its Sunday front page to Borders's first glimpses of the horror that had turned Wat Promkunaram, a place of peace, into a place of blood.

The first officer at the scene, MCSO deputy Don Wipprecht, slid into the temple's parking lot at high speed at 11:21 a.m. Seeing a white Ford pickup in the lot, he radioed in its license number, then waited in his car for backup. It was a short wait. Deputies P. Ellis, G. Sanchez, and T. Lopez pulled in at 11:23; Sgt. A. Hosford a minute later; and Lt. Ron Reyer, the shift commander, soon after Hosford. Before long, the temple would be crowded with deputies, forensic investigators, technicians, and most of Sheriff Tom Agnos's command staff. At this moment, its only occupants were the dead.

While Sanchez, Lopez, and Reyer secured the perimeter, Hosford, Wipprecht, and Ellis entered the building. Ellis went in from the west side near the kitchen; the other two used the double doors in the east wing that Premchit Hash had propped open for Chawee Borders.

Hosford and Wipprecht found themselves in a fifty-foot-square room, the temple's main hall. The window shutters were open, allowing the harsh light of a hot desert day to flood in. Bright white walls supported a high cantilevered ceiling from which hung large ceiling-fan chandeliers. At one end of the room was a kaleidoscope of color and pageantry: an alcove six feet deep and twenty-five feet wide housing a life-size golden statue of a seated Buddha. The statue sat eight feet above the floor on an altar festooned with statuary, pictures, flower arrangements, candles, and religious symbols. Flanking the alcove were narrow doorways providing access to the kitchen and the dining and sitting areas. The main hall also held the temple's money tree, with dollar bills dangling from its branches like leaves.

Glancing around this place of worship, the men saw nothing that seemed disturbed or out of place. Even the money tree appeared to be untouched. But this was not the time for a detailed search. To their left, through the entrance to the sitting room, Hosford and Wipprecht saw exactly what Borders and Hash had seen: bodies on the floor, arrayed like logs floating in a pond of blood. As the officers gingerly stepped through the door, more victims came into view. Wipprecht tried to count them, but he was so agitated by the grisly scene that he kept losing track and having to start over. His sergeant was having the same trouble. Eventually they counted nine victims.

Deputies would later recall that the stench of the crime scene made them gag. A trace of stale cigarette smoke hung in the air. The other, overpowering stink was one a cop never gets used to—the acrid mixture of gunpowder and clotting blood. Nine innocent people had been slaughtered here; nine lives blotted out.

As Hosford and Wipprecht stood near the doorway, their passage blocked by the prone victims, Ellis appeared on the west side of the dining-sitting area. He needed backup to search the south wing, the sleeping quarters. To join him without touching the bodies, Wipprecht had to walk across a sofa. Nearly there, he lost his balance and braced his hand against a door, a detail he was careful to include in his report. Cautiously moving down the hall, he and Ellis noted that the rooms had been ransacked but found no additional victims and no suspects.

Meanwhile Hosford stayed in the sitting area. Knowing it was hopeless, he went through the routine of checking the victims for signs of life. No need to touch them to feel for a pulse; gunshot wounds gaped in their skulls, and lividity was obvious in their toes. Crowded into the small space, hemmed in by furniture, they lay face down, shoulder to shoulder. The fallen bodies formed a strangely orderly pattern, a rough oval, with the monks' tonsured heads close together in the center. Arms, hands, and elbows touched in many places. Almost all the victims had their hands above their heads, fingers tightly interwoven. Their feet were bare, and the monks' vivid orange-and-saffron robes seemed to blanket the cluster of bodies.

Those who know Buddhist doctrine feel sure that from the moment the killers stormed into the monastery, the monks and the nun began to withdraw into a state of inner peace in which all impulses toward resistance dissolved. Taking refuge in the Buddha, they removed the armor of life. But the two young men, lacking their elders' discipline and experience, must have felt desperate fear. And the nun, however accepting of death for herself, must have been terrified for her grandson.

The victims' last words, how they faced their fate, and how the death knell sounded for them are, to this day, known only to their killers. Only the murderers can still see the flash of muzzle fire and hear the thud of bullets ripping through flesh and bone. Most of us will never be able to fathom the depravity that allowed the invaders to annihilate nine unresisting human beings. Even so, we are not completely in the dark about what happened at the temple that August night. Much of the true story of the murders and their aftermath eventually came to light.

Forensic evidence found at the crime scene established that there had been at least two invaders. Ballistics testing identified two weapons fired from different vantage points. One was a Marlin or Revelation .22-caliber rifle; the other was a 20-gauge shotgun. These weapons, more suited to hunting small game than to a life of crime, indicated that the killers were not professional criminals. FBI profilers, called in to help with the investigation, deduced from the attackers' apparently aimless acts of vandalism—spraying fire extinguishers in the sleeping quarters, carving the word "Bloods" on the wall—that they were young and stupid.

Investigators estimated the time of the initial break-in as somewhere between 10:00 p.m. and midnight. Some of the monks were already in the sitting area. The invaders rousted the others from their sleeping rooms and shoved them into the cramped L-shaped space formed by the dining table, two couches, and a loveseat. The six monks, the young visitor, and the teenaged acolyte were ordered to kneel down facing one another. Passive by both culture and training, the monks laced their fingers together behind their heads as commanded and knelt on the edge of the unknown.

At some point, possibly while pillaging the sleeping rooms, the intruders discovered an elderly woman, the nun. They wedged her into a space at one end of the oval, where she, too, knelt with her hands behind her head and faced her longtime friends. Like the others, she was barefoot. Unlike the saffron-robed monks, she wore plain white cotton: a long shirt over ankle-length pants.

For the next hour or so, the invaders took turns guarding the residents and ransacking the sleeping rooms. They upended mattresses, knocked over simple tables, pulled drawers out of chests, and swept everything off shelves. The temple's safe was in plain sight, but they needed its key. Evidently the monks revealed nothing about the key's whereabouts; they maintained their silence, and their safe remained intact.

Although those bedrooms held all the monks' earthly possessions, from a thief's point of view, there was little to steal. The loot, investigators would later learn, amounted to less than three thousand dollars in cash, two stereos, six inexpensive still cameras, a low-end video camera, a pair of binoculars, and a bullhorn.

Not only did the invaders never crack the safe, they left the dollar bills hanging on the temple's money tree. But however haphazard they were as thieves, they proved to be thorough as murderers. The one holding the rifle moved around the oval, behind the kneeling, defenseless victims, and shot them, one by one, in the back of the head.

A single rifle shot, though enough to be fatal, was not enough to satisfy the killers: one monk had three bullet wounds in his head; most of the victims had two. Several were hit by close-range shotgun blasts as well. According to the autopsy reports, each .22-caliber bullet ground its way through the base of the skull, penetrated the occipital bone, and in some cases settled in the foramen magnum, through which the spinal cord drops down from the cranium into the spine. Some of the shots were fired with the tip of the rifle barrel only inches away from the victim's scalp. The locations of the spent shell casings indicated that the rifleman circled the room, moving methodically from victim to victim. This was no frenzied, panic-driven burst of gunfire, but a cold-blooded massacre.

Showing a lack of concern about evidence, the killers left cartridges scattered on the bloody carpet and among the bright robes. Investigators found seventeen .22-caliber casings and three spent shotgun shells. Oddly, although ballistics indicated that all the .22 casings were fired from the same weapon, the casings were of two types. Ten were .22 shorts and the other seven were .22 long rifle rounds. Whoever loaded the rifle knew little about the weapon. Furthermore, the 20-gauge shotgun was loaded with birdshot, which, as any gun owner would know, was not the ammunition to take to a murder. Used on humans, it would wound but not kill.

While the victims were still alive, the holder of the shotgun sprayed birdshot into the crowd. Even though this shooter did not kill anyone, it was not from lack of effort, as the forensics made clear. One monk's kneecap was blown almost completely off. Another monk had many pellet wounds in his head, neck, and upper back. Several victims suffered what the medical examiner called "multiple grazing wounds." The locations of the 20-gauge shell casings left at the scene indicated that the shotgun was fired from very close range. The blasts, while not lethal, must have been utterly terrifying because of their sound. The pop of a .22 rifle sounds like bumping your car into the garbage can as you back out of the garage; the sound of a shotgun is more like getting hit by a semi once you get on the highway. As a weapon of terror, the shotgun has no peer.

Although the temple murderers left no witnesses, they did leave many clues—the spent casings, footprints, the letters carved into the wall—that would eventually tie them firmly to the crime scene. But before that day came, the shameful way the Arizona legal system dealt with the state's first mass murder would add a new layer of blood to what had been a place of peace.

Wat Promkunaram remained a locked-down crime scene from August 10 through August 16. As one day melted into the next, with no relief from either the temperature or the media, pressure mounted on the Maricopa County Sheriff's Office to release the temple to its members. The victims' families and the rest of the close-knit Buddhist community wanted to hold funerals, which could not happen until the grieving members returned to their temple. On the morning of August 16, deputies took down the crime-scene tape.

A new abbot, Winai Booncham, came from California to live at Wat Promkunaram. Along with new monks sent from monasteries around the country, he worked hard to scrub away the coal-black bloodstains on the sitting room carpet.

All the victims except Matthew Miller and his grandmother were flown back to Thailand for cremation, but a three-day ceremony for all nine was held at Wat Promkunaram. A memorial altar honored the dead. Speakers talked about having only the present moment. Focusing on that solitary moment in time, when all concerns are taken away, allows Buddhists to let go of the person who has died. Many devout Buddhists believe in a form of reincarnation. Often, as they see it, in the first moments after a person's death, there is a silence of the mind, in which the "mind made body" can start to name things. These first few seconds, while new things come into being, are a time of silence.

As is standard procedure for funerals of murder victims, a few detectives attended the ceremonies in both countries. In Arizona, team members snapped photos and ran camcorders at the temple on the chance that the killers would return to the scene of their crime. In Thailand, they simply listened and watched for any sign that this horrific crime had been more than a local event. (One of the murderers did indeed return to the temple, briefly on the day the bodies were discovered and again for part of the three-day funeral. But he went unnoticed by the investigators.) As time passed, the photos and videos gathered dust in the sheriff's cabinets.

Fifteen years later Winai Booncham, still the abbot of Wat Promkunaram, again prepared for a ceremony to commemorate the nine murder victims. By that time, the annual event had become a major gathering for Buddhist monks from all over the United States. The simple memorial altar had been replaced by a permanent structure in the courtyard. At its base, lotus flowers floated in a lily pond. Above the pond rose a triangular pillar, its three sides holding plaques commemorating Foy Sripanprasert, Matthew Miller, and Chirasak Chirapong. The pillar supported a hexagonal platform with plaques for the six murdered monks. Behind these plaques lay small portions of the monks' ashes, the rest of which had been scattered in the ocean off the coast of Thailand.

Before the 2006 memorial service, Booncham talked with *Arizona Republic* reporter Angela Cara Pancrazio about his old friend Pairuch Kanthong. His memories of Kanthong were still vivid and fresh. The two had come to America together as young monks, one assigned to Arizona, the other to California. They had talked often in life, and Kanthong's death did not really change that, as he began to appear in Booncham's dreams. Even after fifteen years, Booncham said, "Before I do anything at the temple, I ask Pairuch to help me."

Not all the abbot's dreams were pleasant. Sometimes he saw the murders. "I see my friend. I see what happens in my mind. And how my friend suffered before he died." But when asked whether he held a grudge against the killers, Booncham quoted one of Kanthong's most treasured Buddhist sayings: "Don't brood over the past."

Pancrazio noted that Buddhists understand and expect death: "You are born, you serve, but eventually you will be gone." A temple member qualified that statement. "It was time for them to go," she said, then added, "It's still not the right way to go."

THE SHERIFF'S TASK FORCE

Tom Agnos, a highly respected police officer and a former commander with the Phoenix Police Department, was elected sheriff of Maricopa County in November 1988. Most of his predecessors as sheriff had been good men in cowboy boots who enforced the law from a small-town perspective. Agnos ran for the office as its first professional law enforcement officer, promising to bring in modern techniques and upgraded standards. And he lived up to his promises. Among other things, he is credited with increasing admission requirements for new deputies.

Sheriff Agnos was at home, recovering from open-heart surgery, when Chief Deputy John Coppock called him to report the killings at Wat Promkunaram. Weak from the operation and busy with postsurgical rehabilitation, Agnos could not head the investigation himself. And a crime of this magnitude would require far more manpower than the Maricopa County Sheriff's Office (MCSO) could provide. After talking to his field commanders, Coppock and George Leese, Agnos chose Captain Jerry White to assemble a task force to track down the killers.

White was a hard-driving veteran officer, the longtime commander of the MCSO's narcotics, vice, and gambling divisions. For just three months, since May 1991, he had also headed the homicide, arson, and vehicular crime units. At six feet three and 240 pounds, White was a formidable presence. He had earned a reputation for quick, impulsive decision making and dogged faith in his own decisions—and for instant retaliation on those who strayed from his command positions. A colleague described him as "beyond stubborn."

White picked the MCSO's top homicide detective, Sgt. Russell Kimball, to manage the task force's day-to-day operations. This assignment meant Kimball would be working closely with White for the first time.

The original plan was to limit the Maricopa County Multi-Agency Task Force to experienced homicide detectives and narcotics officers, but, as happens in many multiagency efforts, it did not turn out that way. The group quickly became an unwieldy collection of men and women from a dozen different, and often competing, agencies. Most of the members from outside the MCSO were experienced homicide investigators. Most of the MCSO deputies were from White's narcotics unit, reflecting the internal thinking that the temple killings must have been drug related.

The task force became as contentious as the United Nations. The collaborating agencies were intensely competitive. While most of the other agencies were "big city," the MCSO was still a primarily rural organization, accustomed to handling traffic, drugs, and highway issues "out in the county." The outside officers were "police," but those from the MCSO still held the old-time title of "deputy sheriff." In the task force, the deputies were paired with officers and agents from the FBI, the Drug Enforcement Agency (DEA), the Immigration and Naturalization Service (INS), Arizona's Department of Public Safety (DPS: the state police), the Phoenix Police Department, the Tucson Police Department, and the Office of Special Investigations (OSI) at Luke Air Force Base.

Thai interpreters, along with State Department staffers in Washington, were also designated as task force members. FBI profilers and experts from other national agencies logged in as special resources and consultants. A specialist in Asian gangs was found at the Arizona DPS. The Phoenix police department assigned three full-time officers to the task force. Eventually, the Tucson Police Department and the Pima County Sheriff's Office also became involved. The Maricopa County Attorney's Office served as legal adviser. Before long the task force had swelled to 226 people, including 56 full-time detectives.

White's new organization operated like a separate police department. It set up headquarters on the fourth floor of the Maricopa County Superior Court's East Court Building in Phoenix. By mid-September it had taken over the entire floor. It held its first meeting on August 13, 1991, three days after the murders. Before the group was effectively disbanded in the spring of 1992, its members had interviewed more than 1,800 people and sorted thousands of telephone calls into two categories: real leads and dead ends. For a fateful length of time, it was hard to tell which was which.

The spilling of so much blood in such a holy place created a profound need for retribution—and, from many quarters, a demand for death to the murderers. Meanwhile, Arizona's Buddhist community sought to maintain balance among the chaos of the investigation and the media's fixation on the crime. Like most of the world's major religions, Buddhism teaches forgiveness. Perhaps more than some other religions, Buddhism actually cultivates forgiveness. Buddhists are encouraged to let go of the past and make a fresh start. Forgiveness cannot be forced, but for those brave enough to open their hearts, forgiveness began to emerge.

The task force's lawyers, detectives, technicians, psychologists, and administrators lived by a less forgiving code. They put immense energy into the business of catching the killers. In ever-expanding circles, detectives moved outward from Wat Promkunaram searching for clues. The search took them from the far west side of Phoenix to South Tucson, California, and even Thailand. After a disgracefully long interval, it would bring them back to their starting point, in the neighborhoods around the temple and Luke Air Force Base.

As the team moved from conference rooms and blackboards out into the field, some members answered phones at the tip line set up to take calls from the public. Some interviewed temple members. Others collected evidence, searched for guns, and coped with intense interest from the media. Kimball sent a team to canvass a two-mile area around the temple; he ordered every farmhouse, home, store, and vacant lot identified, checked, and cleared. Clerks, detectives, and technicians busied themselves checking the criminal histories of hundreds of names that came up. Secretaries and clerical workers transcribed interviews and typed, reviewed, collated, and distributed faxes, phone slips, teletypes, interoffice memoranda, and officers' reports. Team members searched local and state databases for similar cases and assigned names and addresses to the scores of license plate numbers, tips, and rumors that poured in. They sorted through phone books, lists of confidential informants, and outstanding warrants for information about pawnshops and "other fencing," trying to track the small items the killers had taken from the temple. The investigation was hugely expensive. In the first month, the team logged one hundred thousand dollars in overtime pay—and turned up no promising leads.

Duane Brady, the MCSO's public information officer, worked valiantly to manage the barrage of attention from local, national, and international media. He announced a reward fund of seventy-five thousand dollars. The news media broadcast this impressive number widely, although the actual balance of the fund depended on donors and never rose above ten thousand dollars. The financial disparity turned out to be irrelevant: despite hundreds of leads, no one ever received the reward.

Sheriff Agnos tried his best to keep his detectives focused on solving the crime while responding to the insatiable demand for news. He kept the press on what Kimball called a starvation diet, trying to limit the number of details about the killings released to the public. Kimball said later, "The sheriff wanted a media blackout. . . . The only time we released anything to the media was when we wanted something publicized." Nevertheless, between mid-August and mid-October, more than three hundred print stories and several thousand broadcast reports on the temple murders were disseminated. Media outlets gathered and spread rumors about the case, the criminals, and the victims. Hard evidence and solid leads were slow to develop, but scuttlebutt and loose tips were abundant. As usual with sensational crimes, speculation ran high: alleged sexual affairs by one of the murdered monks; dark hints about the Asian heroin trade; fifth-hand stories about secret caches of gold bullion buried on temple property.

Kimball, in an article published in the *Phoenix Magazine* in October 1993, noted the amount of raw data assembled by the task force: "4.2 million words . . . contained in 36,000 pages, in 72 hard-bound books . . . more than 60,000 bits of telephone information in a computer system to do link charts." Seven computer programs were developed to manage the mass of information. Kimball also listed "700 photographs taken, [and] 2,100 items of evidence, from guns to tennis shoes to tapes." Perhaps the most astonishing number in his account is the 300,000 latent fingerprint examinations that were made in an effort to crosscheck the twenty-one people identified as potential suspects. Officially, each potential suspect was logged into the computer system as an "investigative lead."

Gregg McCrary and Tom Salp, profilers with the FBI's Behavioral Science Unit, flew to Arizona from their headquarters in Quantico, Virginia, and examined the crime scene. Profilers use findings from behavioral science research, along with computer models and their own expertise at interpreting evidence, to form deductions about the likely characteristics of unknown criminals. Task force members carefully preserved the crime scene for agents McCrary and Salp, who arrived three days after the murders. McCrary later described their work on the temple case in his book *The Unknown Darkness: Profiling the Predators among Us* (2003).

At the temple, the profilers looked for insights about both the dead and their killers. "As each victim was murdered," McCrary wrote, "the remaining victims had to know they were about to die, and it appeared that they had all accepted their fate peacefully." He pointed out a possible exception: one monk had received grazing shotgun wounds on his arms, "which indicated to us that he may have raised his arms in a defensive manner and perhaps tried to resist. But he was the only one."

"It was chilling," McCrary commented. "Here were monks, who were probably more spiritually pure than most of us will ever be, calmly accepting their destiny, absorbing the utter depravity in their midst. Accepting one's own murder is quite un-American."

As for the murderers, the two guns fired from different positions indicated at least two shooters. Cigarette butts from two brands reinforced that conclusion. Assuming that the monks did not smoke, McCrary took the number of cigarette butts as evidence that the killers had spent considerable time at the temple. To the profilers, the weapons "looked like guns and ammunition that a kid got out of his father's hunting collection, just whatever happened to be lying about." To McCrary, this evidence, plus the depleted fire extinguisher and the crude carving on the wall, almost screamed the killers' likely profile: "disorganization, youth, and stupidity."

In its early stages, the investigation followed several threads that had nothing to do with McCrary and Salp's profile of the probable killers. The task force was under intense pressure to find a quick solution to the murders. Rick Sinsabaugh, an MCSO detective deeply involved in the case, later recalled the effect of that pressure: "We were going off in all directions at ninety miles per hour with our head up our ass."

One of those directions involved investigating the lives of the victims in the hope of gaining insight into their murderers. This process, called "victimology," sometimes generates useful investigational leads. In this case, however, close looks at the victims' backgrounds yielded few leads, and none that proved relevant. Many temple members were questioned, but none provided any helpful information. These killings were not only unanticipated, they were virtually unthinkable. The monks were generous people and good neighbors. Local residents appreciated their quiet ways; temple members attested to their willingness to listen to problems and to help at any time. The temple doors were never locked during the day, and what little the monks had, they willingly shared.

The abbot, Phra Pairuch Kanthong, was thirty-six years old; his young visitor was only twenty-one. The other monks were in their thirties and forties. Matthew Miller, at seventeen, was the youngest victim; his grandmother Foy Sripanprasert, at seventy-five, was the oldest. Nothing in any of their backgrounds explained why they had been targeted, much less why they had been murdered so brutally. Nothing about them or the way they lived seemed likely to attract violence, and they had no known enemies.

Besides gathering information about the victims, the task force was also pursuing some of the same rumors that the media were disseminating. For example, the victims' ties to Thailand, along with the execution-style murders, raised the possibility that the crime might be a contract killing connected to drugs. A brisk international trade in heroin thrived in Thailand, as in other parts of Asia. Drug-sniffing dogs reportedly reacted to two areas in the temple, a file drawer in the abbot's bedroom and a section of carpet near the altar in the main hall. But no traces of illegal drugs were found in the temple or on its grounds, and none of the victims had any record, or had ever been suspected, of drug trafficking. And to the profilers, the temple killers seemed sloppy and disorganized—characteristics that contract killers never display.

Gang activity, with or without a drug connection, was another possibility. The task force looked into Asian gangs as well as other gangs that operated in Arizona. Because of the word "Bloods" carved on the temple wall, the investigators devoted considerable attention to the well-known rivalry between the Bloods and the Crips. As would later become clear, that was exactly what the killers wanted them to do. Officers removed the wall and confiscated it as evidence.

While the task force processed data and assessed forensic evidence, a rumor floated in that one of the monks had had an affair with another man's wife. Revenge was always a likely motive. A neighbor had seen a red and white late-model Ford Bronco near the temple at around 7:00 a.m. the day after the killings. Detectives speculated that the vehicle might belong to a jealous husband—or perhaps to a kid with too much money.

On August 23, detectives from the MCSO and the INS interviewed Chawee Borders about the monks' "personal lives, habits and relationships amongst themselves and others"—information that, according to the detectives' written report, was difficult to acquire because of "the extremely quiet and reserved nature of the Thai community." Borders denied having heard any hints of drugs at the temple or gang involvement among temple youth, but she did recount gossip about a romantic relationship between the abbot and a woman congregant.

Another theory of the crime was racial or religious hatred. Hate crimes were rare in Arizona, but these Thai monks had settled in the conservative farming community of Waddell quite recently, within the last three years. Most locals were longtime residents or military families connected to Luke Air Force Base. Racism or religious intolerance was a plausible motive for the killings. This possibility alarmed the government of Thailand and Buddhists around the globe, fueling keen international interest in the murders.

Then there was money. Could a burglary gone bad have led to such violence? A Buddhist monastery seemed an unlikely target for thieves. The attackers had stolen from the temple, but they had also left valuable items untouched, including the dollar bills on the money tree. As far as the investigators could determine, all that had been taken were a few cameras and some personal belongings from the monk's sleeping rooms—objects that could easily be traced if they turned up in pawnshops. To the FBI profilers, the bungled burglary was one more indication of inexperience and lack of intelligence: youth and stupidity. But at this stage, the investigation was still "going off in all directions."

As the task force looked for killers, local Buddhists tried to put the suffering of their friends out of their minds and focus on the present. Buddhist temples, like many other churches, are full of candles. One temple member said the murdered monks had died like candles in a strong wind. The investigation, according to another member, was like a whirlwind in a dying breeze—going nowhere. After an entire month of searching for clues and finding none, Sheriff Agnos and his team probably agreed.

One month after the massacre, on Monday, September 9, task force investigators were painfully aware that their "task" was completely unaccomplished. To Sheriff Agnos's and Captain White's dismay, after thirty days their team was no closer to identifying the killers than it had been on day one. More than five hundred "real" leads had come in (along with countless dead ends), but not one had produced a viable suspect.

A day later the dismay was gone, replaced by excitement. September 10 brought two new leads, logged in as numbers 510 and 511. In the end, one of those leads would break the case; the other would break the task force itself.

Lead 510 emerged from a report filed in the Office of Special Investigations at Luke Air Force Base. Two young men named Rolando Caratachea and Johnathan Doody had been stopped twice while driving on the base, on August 20 and 21. Caratachea had a Marlin .22-caliber rifle in his car. The base security officer looked at the rifle and checked out Caratachea and Doody, then returned the gun and forwarded his report to the OSI. The rifle was the type identified as the murder weapon, but the OSI at Luke was not on the list of agencies to be routinely notified of developments in the case. And at that time, ten days after the killings, the task force had not yet released information about the weapon to all law enforcement agencies.

Eventually, when the OSI learned that the task force was looking for .22-caliber Marlins, an officer checked back through their files and found the report, which by then was twenty days old. He thought it might be significant, since the base was only a mile away from the temple, so he called the task force.

Sgt. Kimball sent MCSO detective Rick Sinsabaugh to track down the rifle. Sinsabaugh found Caratachea at his workplace, an upscale restaurant called Le Gourmand in the suburb of Litchfield Park. Caratachea seemed to assume the MCSO was looking for a stolen weapon, and Sinsabaugh did not set him straight. They went to Caratachea's apartment to get the gun. When handing it over, Caratachea commented that it needed cleaning because a friend had borrowed it and returned it dirty. Asked to name the friend, he said he didn't recall.

Sinsabaugh planned to send the rifle to the state crime lab, where, like all the other rifles and shotguns the team collected, it would be compared with the bullets and shell casings from the crime scene. But by the time he got back to the East Court Building, the fourth floor was buzzing about a more exciting lead, and processing one more weapon suddenly seemed far less important.

Earlier that day, the Tucson Police Department had informed the task force about a strange phone call. A man who gave his name as John had called with a tip about someone named Kelsey Lawrence, a patient at the Tucson Psychiatric Institute, who had been talking about "some kind of murders that happened in Phoenix at the Buddhist temple." Kimball assigned this lead to DPS officer Larry Troutt and MCSO detective Don Griffiths, who set off for Tucson to find out what Lawrence knew.

For the task force members, gathered in the conference room for the latest update, the stalled investigation was suddenly moving again.

The entire group felt new energy, a surge of adrenaline. Lead 511 gave them a chance, at last, to interrogate an actual informant and possibly even a real suspect. This understandably overshadowed lead 510; after all, you can't interrogate a gun.

Instead of moving forward on both leads at once, the task force literally set aside Caratachea's .22 Marlin rifle: Sinsabaugh placed it behind an office door, where it would languish until October 21 before anyone remembered to send it to the Arizona DPS crime lab for ballistics testing.

In the interim, the team had a live suspect named Kelsey Lawrence to interrogate.

THE MAN WITH MANY NAMES 3

Lead 511 began with an anonymous call to the Tucson Police Department. With the tape recorder running, Officer Brad Starr answered the phone.

The caller said he had heard a guy talking about the murders at the Buddhist temple in Phoenix. He added that the guy had "a Bronco or a Blazer, something like that, and I remember watching on the news a while back they said that someone did drive off in a Bronco or a Blazer."

The caller refused to identify himself to Starr; later he would give his name as John. He said the man they should talk to was Kelsey Lawrence, who had tried to commit suicide and was now in the Tucson Psychiatric Institute.

Before transferring the call to an officer assigned to the temple murders, Starr assured the caller that the phone line was "non-taped"—the first of many lies that would be told to suspects in the case. Starr quickly corrected himself—"I mean a non-traced line"—but other investigators would not be so scrupulous.

This particular suspect, as would eventually become clear, was telling plenty of lies of his own. It would be many hours before the investigators learned that both John and Kelsey Lawrence were false names, or that the anonymous caller and the man he had implicated were the same person: Mike McGraw, known in his South Tucson neighborhood as Crazy Mike. And it would be much longer before they realized that this big break in their case was nothing of the kind.

Transferred to Detective Tom Garrison, the caller repeated his story, coming up with more details each time Garrison asked a question. This time the Blazer or Bronco was beige or dark brown and "supposedly a stolen one." The guys "went to Phoenix to party . . . and everybody got kind of pretty wasted, and then they went ahead and did something stupid."

Lawrence, the caller said, had checked into the psychiatric hospital because he was having "a real hard burden thinking about, you know, killing somebody and stuff, that he just wanted to get his head straight with God and everything." In describing Lawrence, he gave significant details at odd moments, as in this exchange:

"How much did he weigh?"

"I don't know. He is kind of a stocky guy."

"Oh really?"

"Yeah, he carries a gun."

After Garrison tried several times to persuade him to give his name, "just the first name," the caller finally offered "John."

Garrison's other attempt at persuasion failed: John refused to meet with him, saying he was too busy. His excuse was an odd one to give the police. "I got a drug buy going on."

Near the end of their conversation, Garrison announced that officers were on the way down from Phoenix to talk to Kelsey Lawrence. "Oh shit," John said. "Are you serious?"

At the Tucson Psychiatric Institute, DPS officer Troutt and MCSO detective Griffiths asked for Lawrence. At 7:35 that evening, they began their interview with the suspect, or what some of their colleagues would later dub "the chat with the nut."

They were waiting in a conference room, a concealed tape recorder turned on, when nurse Sally Carroccio brought in the patient she knew as Kelsey Lawrence. After the introductions, Troutt said, "Why don't you have a seat?" He suggested a nearby chair, but Lawrence chose a more distant perch. "More comfortable over here," he explained.

Troutt told Lawrence they were police officers and asked if he knew a man named John, who had called them about him. Lawrence replied that John had called him too. "I guess somebody had told him that I was involved in some bullshit. I don't know what it is."

Unaware that the suspect was playing a multilayered game with the police, Troutt assured him, "I'm not playing games with you." John, he said, had told them that "you wanted to talk to us about the temple situation in Phoenix." Here Lawrence told the truth. "I don't know anything about the temple thing in Phoenix." But he got over that tendency very quickly. As the task force would gradually discover, Crazy Mike McGraw knew only what he made up.

When Troutt mentioned the temple murders, he got a strong reaction. "Oh, no, no, no, no, uh, I don't, I don't, I don't do murders, dude."

Lawrence gave vague answers, dodging around Troutt's questions. After half an hour he said, "You by chance don't have a recorder or something on, do ya?"

Troutt, in turn, dodged the question. "No, uh, yeah, we're not going to play any games with you, not at all. If you need to talk to us, we'll damn sure listen."

The game playing continued on both sides. Asked if John was a friend of his, Lawrence played coy. "I don't know, I know a lot of Johns."

"We're talking about the John that's talked with you on the phone today."

"There's two of them that called me today."

Troutt got the interview back on track. "You were in Phoenix on August the ninth?"

In fact Lawrence had been at work in Tucson that day, but the task force would not check on that crucial fact until a week later. He said yes, he'd been in Phoenix, but claimed he didn't recall anything about the temple: "I was pretty much passed out."

After Troutt said nine people had been shot, probably in a robbery that went bad, Lawrence's memory improved. He recalled that he had stayed in the parked Bronco while his friends went into a building, and after about forty-five minutes, "everybody started running, and they were just like really, um—"

Troutt helped him along. "Excited?"

"Yeah."

Lawrence rambled on about worries that the guys might have done something he couldn't remember. "Well," Troutt told him, "let's see if we can help you clear this up in your head."

The detectives helped him locate the temple on a map and showed him a drawing of its floor plan. They asked about people, times, places, distances, and conversation among the eight men he said were in the Bronco and the Blazer. As for the building, he vaguely remembered a door that had "not stained glass but glass," and "two white doors." Only much later did it occur to investigators that this description matched images broadcast by every TV station in the state.

Suddenly Lawrence remembered that after leaving the building, they had stopped at a house, where two guys "took the black bag directly inside." This was the first mention of any bag, black or otherwise, and Troutt wanted to know more. Lawrence said the house was on Moreland, but he had no idea what was in the bag.

He said "the black guy" had a gun and was "kind of calling the shots." Griffiths asked if the black guy had said why they were going to the building.

"No."

"Oh, but you got a pretty good idea now, though?"

"Well yeah, from what you told me earlier."

That answer didn't satisfy Griffiths. "What do people normally go to buildings with guns for?"

"Well, usually to shoot people's kneecaps off, I know that."

When Troutt asked about weapons, Lawrence listed a sawed-off 12 gauge, a Glock, and a 9mm Beretta, then added, "I had a gun that night too. I didn't use it or anything like that." His was a 380 auto.

The murder weapon wasn't on the list. Troutt hinted, "So you've got one shotgun, and all handguns? No rifles?"

Lawrence's reply, vague at first, took on detail as he spoke. "There may have been a rifle in that Blazer, 'cause it was like he had, um, the hooks inside the Blazer, and I recall seeing it back up there, and I think it was a rifle, looked like a thirty-aught-six or maybe a thirty-thirty."

Late in the evening Lawrence had an idea. "If I went up there or something, you know, and retraced the path that we went, I figure I could retrace it pretty good." His offer fit perfectly with the officers' plan to take him into custody and drive him to Phoenix for a more intensive interrogation.

According to the official summary of the case by MCSO detective Pat Riley, Troutt and Griffiths decided to move the interview to task force headquarters because "information provided by Lawrence necessitated further investigation." As Riley put it, Lawrence asked "if there was 'Blood or Bloods' found on a wall anywhere in the temple."

But this question does not appear in the transcripts of Lawrence's taped interrogation, and Troutt himself gives a different version. He reports that he walked Lawrence to his hospital room, where Lawrence asked, "In your case, is there some kind of writing in blood or something like blood on the floor or wall?" Troutt notes, "This was the first indication of information coming close to the temple murder crime scene that was not available in the news media."

That the killers had carved "Bloods" in a wall in the temple had been withheld from the media. Troutt apparently interpreted Lawrence's question about "writing in blood or something like blood" as a close-enough reference to the carved word and thus as evidence that Lawrence either knew the killers or was one of them. On the strength of this supposed inside information, Troutt and Griffiths took Lawrence to Phoenix.

Lawrence was an inpatient in a psychiatric hospital; there were formalities to go through first. Carroccio, the nurse, phoned his doctor. The doctor spoke to Carroccio, then to the patient, then to Troutt. He told Troutt that Lawrence was free to sign himself out and said he had never heard Lawrence mention the temple murders.

Before releasing the patient, Carroccio gave him what Troutt called "an anti-depressant drug." "According to her," Troutt noted, "it would take the edge off during the drive to Phoenix." As Troutt and Griffiths transported their informant and suspect to headquarters, they may have been surprised at how readily he had agreed to the trip. Little did they know, he couldn't wait to step up to the big time in Phoenix.

A hundred years had passed since the last time an Arizona sheriff's posse had mounted up and ridden hell-for-leather in search of desperadoes. In the evening hours of September 10, the MCSO deputies and other task force officers felt that, in the tradition of their frontier predecessors, they were hot on the trail of the outlaws who had killed the monks.

They gathered in the main conference room of their fourth-floor headquarters. The deputies, in their western-style uniforms, blended well with the government setting, the steel desks, haphazardly organized yet starkly efficient. The entire headquarters had an air of something cobbled together in a hurry. What had been a vacant floor a month earlier was now a hodgepodge of mismatched straight-backed chairs, folding tables, and government-issue executive swivel chairs, freshly oiled. No squeaky wheels were allowed in Captain Jerry White's outfit. Rehabbed file cabinets bore freshly printed labels befitting a multiagency task force.

Team members gossiped, reread dead-end reports, and waited impatiently for the treasure trove of information that might be coming up Interstate 10 from Tucson. Sgt. Kimball briefed the deputies, officers, agents, sergeants, and detectives, plus two high-ranking command officers, on the likelihood of a major break in the case.

Technicians had installed audio-recording devices in three of the rooms designated for questioning suspects. Each recorder was hardwired to a monitoring room, where task force brass and prosecutors could listen to interrogations as they progressed. The recorders were not high-quality equipment. The tapes they produced were scratchy and sometimes inaudible.

By the time of the first trial in the temple case, two years later, the MCSO would accumulate more than five hundred audiotapes. Each would be painful to listen to and embarrassing to the officers involved. Some of the revelations on the tapes were true, at least in part. But most were products of the will of the interrogators rather than the honesty or culpability of the suspects.

Charles E. O'Hara, author of the massive text *Fundamentals of Criminal Investigation*, had long been one of America's most influential authorities on investigatory techniques. From 1956 through the mid-1980s, tens of thousands of police officers considered his book their bible. O'Hara defined the job this way: "A criminal investigator is a person who collects facts to accomplish two goals: To identify and locate the guilty party, and to provide evidence of his guilt."

Task force members thought that at last, thirty days after the temple murders, they had accomplished the first of these goals. As it turned out, however, although they had located a suspect, they had not yet identified him. As for evidence of his guilt, they had only his own self-incriminating but self-contradicting statements.

At 1:15 a.m. on Wednesday, September 11, Troutt and Griffiths arrived at headquarters with their prize suspect in tow. Seven interrogators would take turns questioning Lawrence over the next three days. He would be given short breaks, new clothes, a hotel room, and food—as well as a great deal of information about the crime and many hints about what the interrogators wanted him to say. Everyone on the team "helped" him search his memory, and expand it, to solve the case. He was a gold mine of misinformation, and his questioners were eager prospectors.

Escorting Lawrence to an interview room, Troutt set the stage for the next three days. "Just sit down, relax, if you need to lay on the floor, lay on the floor. Give me a little bit of time so I can talk to these folks and go over everything that we talked about in Tucson. A couple of them will probably come in and you can start from the beginning and go back over it with them. Tell the truth as you know it. If you can, try and recall the details that we need."

When Troutt returned at 1:45 a.m., he had to wake Lawrence. "Oh, man," Lawrence said, "I should never have took those drugs." Troutt introduced two new interrogators: MCSO detectives Tom Shorts and Pat Riley.

As Lawrence told it, he had been laid off from his job at the McCullough Corporation—a chainsaw plant in Tucson—on August 7. On August 9 he had been fishing at Lakeside Park when "everybody agreed to go cruisin' around to Phoenix and party." The new version of his story had only four guys, not eight. In his first hour with Shorts and Riley, Lawrence changed not only the number of guys but their ethnicity, their positions in the Bronco, and their weapons.

Before going to the temple, he said, they drove to Camelback, where "we ride ATCs [all-terrain cycles] and stuff like that." In response to a question from Riley, he specified that he meant Camelback Mountain. "That's the place. Anyone would know about that." Then they did more driving, "way out in the boondocks," until they came to "this, uh, church house-like building."

Pressed to estimate how far the building was from the mountains, he replied, "Like I said I was pretty sloshed, so, you know, I, I don't know. I couldn't be honest with you about that." But he was clear about what got him sloshed: they left Tucson with three or more cases of beer and some wine coolers; in Tempe or Mesa, they bought a case of Bud Light.

At one point Lawrence started drawing an imaginary map on the wall, gesturing as he talked. "We were on bumpy dirt roads. . . . And then this was like a big, empty field, uhm, we went in like this, turned, and there's this building right here."

Shorts offered to get him a piece of paper.

"No, I'd be lost."

Riley said, "You're doing a good job on the wall."

In the parking lot, Lawrence said, everybody else got out and went into the building. He stayed outside because "the black dude told me, 'Hey, go park that truck—you jerk—somewhere else.'" While he was smoking a cigarette and listening to Dave Pratt on 98 KUPD on the Bronco's radio, he heard "a bunch of ruckus in there, like things breaking, and . . . like three loud bangs."

Riley asked about the timing. "It was bang-bang, and then bang, and a buncha shit going all over the place like somebody was ransacking it or, you know how you get pissed once in a while when somebody starts exploding shit and it makes a bunch of noise? It sounded just like that, and everybody just came pouring outside really quick."

Responding to hints, Lawrence willingly expanded his story in many directions, but there was one scene he kept refusing to write. Over and over he dodged questions about what the men said after they left the building. Some of his evasive maneuvers showed that, despite all the contradictions in his narrative, he had a firm memory for certain details.

Back at the hospital, Lawrence had mentioned stopping at a house on Moreland, where two people took a black bag inside. He had said nothing else about the bag. Now, hours later, in a new location with new detectives, he brought it up again.

Riley asked, "What'd they tell ya?"

Instead of answering, Lawrence offered a distraction. "What happened was that—no, the black bag that came into my view, that went to this house on Moreland."

Riley fell for it, asking for details. Lawrence provided them. The bag was "like canvas but like jean, jeans, you know"; it measured about three feet by two; it had three straps and a long zipper.

"Okay," Riley said, "and this black guy came out with that?"

Again the reply was not an answer. "The black guy and some other guy walked into the room, like, he was like really pissed off . . . and he said somethin' about, 'Oh, well, you know, it's sad, happened—but it happened.'"

Now and then Lawrence seemed to notice his own incoherence: "I fucked up with somewhere along here"; "I'm kinda losing myself." But the moments of self-awareness didn't change much. "I'm just trying to think the way it was supposed to be going good, man, and make somethin' up there. I think I made a jump myself tomorrow."

The next time Riley asked about the men's conversation, Lawrence came up with another distraction. "I left my cigarettes in the truck. And I went to go back and get them. And I opened the door." With a storyteller's instinct, he paused and cleared his throat before announcing, "There's like blood, on the door . . . on the inside too." He said the black guy told him, "You better get your fuckin' ass to the car wash and make that fuckin' thing sparkle."

As before, the distraction worked. Riley moved on to other topics.

Lawrence claimed the group had driven to California after the murders. Riley wanted details, but with Lawrence, details were seldom stable. He changed his story of the trip from one car to two, from three guys to six, from one day to three, and from remembering a little to remembering nothing.

As Tuesday night became Wednesday morning, Lawrence offered a new excuse for his foggy memory. "I want to wait for this medication to wear off; that way my head will be straight. They gave me a pill up there." And later, "I just want to wait until morning until my head's completely clean."

"We understand that you been medicated," Riley told him, "and, you know, we don't have any problem with that. We want to get as much information . . . as fresh as it is right now in your mind." Then he went back to the question Lawrence had been sidestepping. Had the guys talked about what happened inside "this, what you're calling church?"

In reply, Lawrence finally recalled some conversation—and finally gave the detectives a name. "While on the way, Danny, he said they talked."

Riley reminded Lawrence that he had told Troutt or Griffiths about "somebody specific doing something."

In spite of the ambiguity, Lawrence seemed to know exactly what Riley wanted. "Yeah," he answered, "it was like logos or some kind [of] weird design with the blood."

While Riley and Shorts questioned Lawrence, other team members ran background checks. Kelsey Lawrence, as far as they could tell, had no criminal history—but also no driver's license, no address, and no social security number. In law enforcement parlance, he was a ghost. During a break in the interview, Captain White and Sgt. Kimball chided Riley for questioning somebody without knowing who he was.

Back in the interview room, Riley said, "The biggest milestone to overcome right now, is to know who we're talking to. . . . And I'm not convinced that Kelsey Lawrence is you."

Lawrence lobbed the implied question back at him. "Well, who am I supposed to be then?"

"I tell you what. Who is John?"

"John's pretty much of a dweeb."

"What's John's last name?"

"I have no idea. I don't know him."

Peppered with questions, Lawrence admitted he'd used "nicknames," mentioning Shepherd, Kelley, and Brian, which he said were first names. As for last names, "I try not to fuck with those. I in fact get those mixed up."

Riley asked if he had ever been arrested before. "Yeah, once. Speeding ticket."

"What did you use when you got arrested?"

"I used, uh, Michael Lawrence McGraw on that one."

The task force would eventually determine that the man Troutt and Griffiths had extracted from the Tucson Psychiatric Institute really was Michael Lawrence McGraw. But not yet. Now he said that his true date of birth was March 4, 1967, but that he sometimes used June 1, 1954. He said he was unsure of his social security number, but later in the interrogation he rattled it off. He said his car was a brown '79 Camaro, but when asked what name it was registered under, he said it belonged to a friend. "I use it a lot though."

Riley gave a long speech with a short point: if Lawrence lied about his identity, they'd have a credibility problem. He finally said, "I would assume that you got a driver's license."

Oddly, this was the first time any of the four investigators thought to ask the suspect about something as straightforward as a driver's license. Perhaps the oversight didn't matter, because the suspect answered, "No, I don't." He said he'd never had a license and wasn't sure he even had a birth certificate. Fishing for a birth date, Riley asked, "Okay, you were born?"

McGraw kept it simple. "Yes, I was."

After more probing, he said he'd been born in Phoenix. He gave his mother's name as Nancy and his father's as Smiley Lawrence. He said he had two sisters and gave them names that turned out to be pure fiction. Riley and Shorts kept asking whether Kelsey Lawrence was his "true name," his "legal name," his "born given name." The answers were evasive. "That's what I've used, yes"; "I never actually use my born given name." At last he capitulated. "To be honest with you, it's Michael."

"Okay. And your born middle name would be what?"

"Lawrence."

"Lawrence? And your born last name is?"

"I didn't have a middle name. I was just Michael Lawrence."

"And you just go by Kelsey?"

"Well, I've used Kelsey Lawrence for, like, years now."

Thinking they now knew who the suspect was, Riley and Shorts pushed "Michael Lawrence" to name the guys he had hooked up with in the park.

McGraw talked around the question, then said, "I didn't get any real names."

Shorts was incredulous. "You spent three or four days with 'em, you know, traveling across California, you gotta know names."

Riley added, "You gonna hang around with these people that you don't even know?"

"Why not?" McGraw said. "I go to bars and do it."

Later Riley asked directly, "Did you kill these people?"

The answer was equally direct. "No."

"Okay, you say no. I'll take your word at that."

McGraw's response must have surprised the detectives. "No," he said, "don't take my word at that."

Riley's next words captured, in a revealing if inadvertent summary, the way he and his colleagues conducted interrogations. "Kelsey, all I can do at this point is listen to what you have to say and base what you have to tell me on what I know about what happened."

It had been a long night, and Riley and Shorts needed a break. Before they left the room, Shorts made a standard argument—that unless Lawrence talked first, the other guys would put the blame on him. McGraw's reply foreshadowed the direction his story would take in the hours ahead. "They're not gonna come to you and say that. . . . I'm gonna take you to them."

Riley returned with Troutt in place of Shorts. The first voice recorded was Troutt's. "Hey, Kels. How ya doing, bud?"

McGraw complained, "Now I feel like I'm being tried like I'm a criminal."

"Well, I hope you don't take that attitude, that's not the point. You're the man with the information." Ignoring McGraw's attempts to interrupt, Troutt gave a lecture. It ended, "We're talking about a crime, so we gotta talk criminal-type talk. Just hang with it and do the best you can."

McGraw said he wanted to help, but "I feel, like, that I'm being the criminal." He repeated that he'd been plastered and on drugs the night of the murders. And now, he added, "you got me to the point where it's like, I'm trying to think as hard as I can, but I can't."

Troutt told him Riley "knows where he's taking you."

Where Riley took him was back to the question of names. "You don't just talk to somebody as 'hey you, hey dude.' . . . There's a name that goes with that face. And you know these people."

"No."

Trying to break through this obstinacy, Troutt asked, "You got some concerns about getting burned later on?"

"Yeah, I do." He didn't want his "name to slip out somewhere."

Riley reassured him. "We told you that wouldn't happen. What more can we do to convince you that it won't happen?"

"Kelsey," Troutt said, "we're talking about nine murders. The loss of nine lives. Bubba, if you got information we can protect ya. . . . You gotta let it go—you told me that you wanted to work with us."

McGraw looked up at Troutt, who had been standing since he came in, and echoed the question Troutt had asked him when they first met. Like a cordial host, he asked, "Why don't you have a seat?"

McGraw's hospitable invitation signaled a significant shift in the interrogation. He was now ready to name names, and he began as soon as Troutt sat down. "One of the guys' names is Peter Sherfield."

As if an internal dam had broken, the names poured out—some imaginary, others of McGraw's South Tucson neighbors. Riley kept quiet while Troutt encouraged the flood of details. McGraw said Sherfield drove the Blazer, which was probably stolen: "He's pretty much into auto theft." One of his passengers was Mark Nunez.

McGraw claimed to have been in the back seat of the Bronco. Asked who was with him, he paused, then named Victor Zarate. In Phoenix the Bronco picked up Robert and Tony Torres. The Blazer also took on new riders, a Mexican named Leo Bruce and a white guy named Craig. Bruce, McGraw said, "runs a lot of dope."

In Phoenix the guys "fucked around for a little bit and then we went over to that church, Budapest church." Aside from the creative variation on "Buddhist," McGraw's memory seemed to have improved markedly. He described the building, the location of both cars, and the route they took. Then his vagueness returned. "I guess something happened or something, and the shots rang out, a bunch of things started—"

"Come on," Troutt said, "don't do that to me. . . . Don't start the 'Uh, I guess something happened.' Explain it to me."

"Three shots rang out." He said the guys stayed in the building for maybe forty-five minutes. Leo was wearing a trench coat and had the shotgun. McGraw now identified the black guy, the leader in his tale, as Peter Sherfield. When the guys came out, they were "mumbling like something seriously happened," but they didn't talk about it until later, back at the house.

At the hospital McGraw had told Troutt and Griffiths the house was on Moreland. Then, on the drive through Phoenix to task force headquarters, he had pointed out a house on East Culver Street, near Moreland but on the opposite side of the Red Mountain Freeway. Now Troutt asked, or rather stated, "You feel real confident that the house you showed me tonight coming in here is the house you guys went to."

"I'm almost sure, yeah."

That brief exchange would lead to a search warrant for the house on East Culver, a long interrogation of the homeowner—and a lawsuit against the MCSO, the Arizona DPS, and DPS officer Larry Troutt.

For now, McGraw had plenty to say about what went on in the house. "There's a black bag. Peter and this other guy went in the room. Peter started yelling and screaming—got pissed off, came out, threw the bag. . . . Walked across and got his crack pipe, smoked crack, and now all of a sudden his eyes start gettin', I don't know, like the devil, and they all, he looked at me like . . . I fucked up or something."

Troutt asked if Sherfield had "admitted to killing anybody in that church."

"Yeah, he did."

Riley asked what he said.

"That they didn't really think it was gonna go like that, but it happened, and it was fucked, you know, they had to die."

Troutt prompted, "You still haven't told me that he said he killed anybody."

McGraw gave Troutt what he wanted. "Peter said he shot a little girl."

"He shot a little girl? And what else?"

"To—and someone that was next to 'em, he didn't say who it was."

At one point McGraw mused, "You know, this is strange. These are friends that I grew up with, man."

Riley asked, "These guys never done anything like this before?"

Again McGraw probably surprised the detectives. "Hell, yeah. They've all done it before."

He called Peter a hard-core killer. Peter, he said, belonged to the Crips, the others to the Bloods, but McGraw wasn't a gang member. "I don't go running around, I try to stay by myself."

Going back to McGraw's elusive mention of something on the temple walls, Riley asked about "the blood, or writing, or logos or something."

McGraw said Peter had talked about "logos or a design, on one of the walls." Asked several times what the logo was, he insisted that he hadn't seen it. "I never left that truck."

When Riley gave him a hint, asking about "blood, or Bloods," McGraw's response was both evasive and obscure. "The blood was used by Peter Sherfield. And he had a good degree of blood in paint."

Soon after that dead end, McGraw declared, "I don't care how far this goes, just as long as I'm not going to be drug in the mud and fucked over."

"That's not our intention at all."

"You can't guarantee that, though."

"Well," Riley answered honestly, "for me to sit here and guarantee anything to you, would be somewhat misleading on my part." But, he added, "We're not gonna leave ya hangin' high and dry."

"I need some serious sleep now," McGraw said. He had been awake for more than twenty-four hours.

"Well, we're gonna take care of that. Let me ask you this. Are these guys that we already talked about—"

McGraw didn't let him finish. "I know where every one of 'em lives." He gave Sherfield's address and said Nunez lived in the same neighborhood.

Troutt chimed in with some positive feedback. "Doing a good job, Bud. Came here to work and you're working! I appreciate it."

The interrogation continued for another hour. During a five-minute break, Troutt asked McGraw if he was "John," who had called the Tucson Police. McGraw admitted it. He also apologized for lying and for waiting so long to name the suspects.

Riley was supportive. "You got a conscience, Kelsey, and that's important."

"You don't understand how I live. They're friends. I just didn't want to give up my friends because—well, I shouldn't say friends now because of the position I'm in."

Troutt asked, "But when you talk about guys that are capable of doing something like this, are they friends?"

"Not now."

Troutt and Riley had more questions about McGraw's identity. At the address he gave them, the manager had never heard of him. The phone number he provided had been disconnected. He now gave them his full name, Michael Lawrence McGraw, and his social security number. But he asked them to keep calling him Kelsey Lawrence.

Explaining why he used aliases, he claimed he had been a police informant, working under cover to catch a ring of car thieves. He had used his real name, and it "was like leaked out, to like every prison." Because of the leak, "a lot of people, they think that I'm a narc, and that, you know, I feed cops information left and right."

McGraw had been feeding these particular cops information all night long, but they still wanted more. Troutt launched the next topic. "I want to find out as much as you know [of] what occurred inside that church."

McGraw suggested they try "hypnosis . . . if you want it like perfect details." Troutt dismissed the idea. Then suddenly, as if hypnotized after all, McGraw began to come up with details. A concrete sidewalk with a railing and a fence. Shrubbery on one side. A dirt road, bumpy with little rocks. A grassy field or farm next to the road. A telephone pole on the corner. A white block wall. Windows, no lights on inside.

He said he got out of the Bronco to look at the building's doors, lit up a joint, and listened to the radio. He heard two loud shots. "Peter came out and he had blood on him. On his pants, on his shirt, on his hands and foot." On the drive back, Peter said he had killed a girl.

Asked "what guns went in there," McGraw answered, "Well, mine went in."

"With you?"

"No, I didn't go in."

"Okay, who did you give your gun to?"

"I gave my gun to Leo."

McGraw said Peter had the rifle, a bolt-action type. A few minutes later, Troutt came back to this, asking if Peter used a bolt-action rifle.

McGraw mocked him. "Don't you guys know what kind of weapons were used?"

Troutt said he did know, but "I don't want to tell you what my weapons are. I want you to tell me what your weapons were. This is getting into that thing of detail, detail; that I can look at the detail of your situation, the detail of our situation, and tell you whether or not they merge. The goal was for me to tell you, 'Yeah, Kelsey, I think you guys were at our church,' or 'No, I think you were somewhere else.'"

"Well, so far, do we match on each other's church?"

"In places we do, yeah, in other places it's sketchy. We need to work on detail—"

"Yeah, details rule the day."

Troutt was not convinced that McGraw had stayed outside the temple. "My feelings are, that you probably were inside, that you're still worried about gettin' burned and gettin' hung on this deal. You need to get that out of your system so you can just let go. You're still not breathing full; you're kind of half-breath."

McGraw agreed that his chest was tight. He paused and fidgeted: "crumbles a cup," the transcript notes. Then he said, "I wasn't in the building. And that's the God's honest truth. I wish I knew exactly what, what exactly went on in that place."

By this time the sun was well up in the sky, and both interrogators and suspect were exhausted. After another short break, Troutt had good news. "We're going to take you to get some sleep."

"Where at?"

"We're talking motel."

"Motel? Be cool."

In fact Troutt would ask many more questions before McGraw got anywhere near a bed. But the suggestion—or perhaps his exhaustion—made McGraw less wary. Answering the next series of questions, he at last placed himself inside the temple.

"When you guys got there," Troutt asked, "there were people there?"

"Yeah."

"Outside?"

"No, they were inside still."

"What did these people look like?"

"Asian people."

"What were they dressed like?"

"Like gowns and uh, stuff."

Troutt hinted, "Any gold color on any of them?"

"Almost like they mixed colors, you know, like Hawaiian dress like." Then McGraw changed his mind. "It didn't look like that, looked more like a gown, white gown, or red."

"What color hair did they have?"

"A few of them had grayish hair and some had black, straight long black."

This was the crucial moment: the crime itself. "So Peter got there to the temple and started questioning these people. . . . So then what happened?"

"He was telling people to lay down on the floor." Then McGraw tried to retreat to vague summary. "They ransacked the place big time."

But Troutt had him. "So, Kelsey, if you weren't in there, how are you telling me that he made them all lay down and things like that?" No response. "Give it up to me, Bub," he urged.

Bub gave it up. "I kind of took a peek inside."

Tired though he must have been, Troutt didn't miss a beat. "Tell me what you saw."

"I saw these people laying down. At first he told everybody to get on their stomachs and lay down. I thought he was just gonna slap somebody or something, whatever." As if reliving the scene at the temple, McGraw began to cry.

"What did you see him doing?"

"He was kicking people; said 'Answer me, answer me, talk; tell me where the fuck it's at.'" McGraw did not know what "it" was.

"You did not see him shoot anybody?"

"I just peeked inside, I didn't get a good view of anything at all." Immediately he revised that answer. "I went inside and maybe saw fear in their eyes."

McGraw said Peter "came by this one old lady . . . he just slapped the shit out of her so fuckin' hard. Then my heart went out to her, but"—he sobbed—"I can't do that, okay? . . . It was my fault they died."

"Nah, it wasn't," Troutt assured him. "Chances are you'd just been laying on the floor with 'em."

Asked how many guys did the shooting, McGraw said four. Asked how the old lady answered Peter, he said, "She didn't talk broken English."

"What ethnic group, what nationality was she?"

"Indian maybe." More sobbing. "I could have stopped it somehow, but I didn't. And these people died because I didn't go in there."

Troutt asked, "You are convinced that that was our temple, aren't you?"

"Yes."

After more tears, more guilt, McGraw elaborated on that answer. "Oh yeah, I don't have a doubt that it wasn't the church. I firmly believe that's what happened."

"Kelsey, I'm leanin' real convinced it is our church, too. . . . Can you give me any more information that will help me go find these folks?"

"I know where they live." McGraw's next few speeches were equally cooperative. "I can take you to 'em all." "I can give you descriptions." "I'll give you anything you want." He added, "I was so afraid of Peter Sherfield that night."

Soon he became less responsive and said, "I'm tired, I'm tired."

Troutt offered to take him to the motel for a few hours of sleep. "I need you to have a clear head when you do this so that you're as accurate as you possibly can be on these descriptions."

But then Riley took over, ignoring Troutt's comment that McGraw needed time to regroup. He began, "If you're in there and you saw the things in there, that's fine, and we can deal with that,"

"I wasn't in there."

That wasn't the right response. Riley reminded McGraw of what he had told Troutt. "You looked in and you saw, or some of the activities. . . . Your ability to see—"

McGraw cut him off. "My ability to see was a mistake. It was, it was, it was a big fuckin' mistake I made, fucking—" Whatever he might have said next dissolved into sobs.

The sixth and final tape of Mike McGraw's interrogation started with a creative riff that even Riley, who seemed eager to believe McGraw, found hard to credit.

Riley asked if the group had left fingerprints in the temple. McGraw said no.

"Why's that?"

"They were wearing socks over their hands as gloves."

"Socks, you mean socks you wear on your feet?"

"Socks." Some of them, McGraw said, wore powdered gloves stolen from a Tucson hospital.

Riley wanted to know which guys wore gloves. "Peter had gloves on. He had one glove on and he had one sock; he took it off. He told the old lady sittin' there, 'I should take one of the statues and beat the fuck out of you with it.'"

Next McGraw said Peter wore black gloves. Leo Bruce had socks on his hands: "Dallas Cowboy socks. That's his favorite team." And Mark Nunez "doubled up on the rubber gloves, put powder on 'em."

Riley abruptly abandoned this line of questioning. "Who had the shotgun inside the temple?" No response. "Come on, Kelsey, you know. The reason you can't tell me, Kelsey, is I think you had the shotgun."

"I didn't."

Pressed hard for an answer, McGraw fell back on an earlier accusation. "Leo had the shotgun."

Later McGraw asked, "I'm in your custody, aren't I?"

Troutt ducked that question. Nowhere on the tapes of McGraw's first day of interrogation had anyone read him the *Miranda* warnings. (According to Troutt's report and Riley's case summary, Troutt read him his rights in the car during the drive to Phoenix.)

"Well," Troutt said, "you're going to a motel where in, we're going to be there for probably two or three days. . . . And are you in our custody? Yeah, you're under our wings, definitely."

Some time after that, McGraw said, "I am so fucking shit-faced right now."

Troutt responded, "Washed out, huh, tired?"

"Washed out, tired, sad."

"You'll get a real good idea about [what] law enforcement's all about when this is over. It's tough work—it's hard work."

As if to show what he already knew about law enforcement, McGraw reversed their roles and questioned Troutt. "How many people in here be put away? How many for murder, murder charges? That actually stuck?"

Troutt should have felt a shiver of foreboding at that last phrase. "I haven't worked that many murders," he said.

McGraw had another question. "Do you have any doubts that I lied—had anything to do with murders?"

He seemed to need solace, and Troutt offered it. "I don't think you're a shooter. I think you could fool me, I've been fooled before, but I don't think so. I don't see it in your eyes. You have an enormous amount of remorse. You're carrying some heavy, heavy guilt."

With that, the grueling interrogation came to a temporary end. Another officer entered the room and introduced himself. "How ya doing? I'm Gary Labenz." Then he asked, "What's your name?"

"Kelsey," said Mike McGraw.

At 8:30 a.m. on Wednesday, September 11, thirteen hours after Troutt and Griffiths began their talk with "Kelsey Lawrence," Detective R. M. Minner checked himself, Labenz, and McGraw into the four-star Sheraton Hotel in downtown Phoenix. McGraw ate a room-service breakfast, then fell asleep, but not for long. Shortly after 1:00 p.m. he was back at task force headquarters for more interrogation.

McGraw spent the next two days helping the task force extract confessions from the guys he had named as his partners in crime. On September 11 he took a tour of Phoenix to retrace their route to the temple and later a tour of Tucson to point out where they lived.

One of his escorts on the Tucson tour, MCSO detective Al Tamala, reported that McGraw, fearing that the Tucson police would "identify him as a snitch," asked for something to hide his identity. Tamala gave him a red handkerchief, which he tied around his face, covering his nose and mouth. When the police car pulled up to a group of "Mexican males," the red handkerchief must have been a dead giveaway. Tamala noted, "I heard the word 'snitch' being yelled. We immediately left the area." They got back to the Sheraton at 3:30 a.m. on September 12.

McGraw also identified his old friends in photo lineups: cards showing photographs of a suspect and five other men of similar age and ethnicity. He did not recognize Robert Torres, Tony Torres, or Peter Sherfield, but he picked out Mark Nunez and Leo Bruce and said they had been "there that night." At 4:45 a.m., when McGraw was sleeping after his excursion to Tucson, detectives woke him to look at photos of two men named Victor; he identified the one of Victor Zarate.

No one knows what McGraw expected to gain from the story he told the task force. Many people at the time assumed he was after the reward; others considered him a sensation seeker. He did get some new clothes out of the deal: at his request, the deputies bought him underwear, a t-shirt, socks, shoes, sweatpants, and a toothbrush.

On September 13 McGraw was given his new outfit, but later that same day he had to trade it for a standard-issue inmate's jumpsuit. At about 4:00 that afternoon, McGraw "was advised that he was under arrest and subsequently taken to court for his initial appearance."

In three days of interrogation and other assistance to the task force, McGraw never invoked his right to remain silent. The tapes, which provide no evidence that anyone read him the *Miranda* warnings, also demonstrate that remaining silent was not in his nature: McGraw clearly loved to spin a tale.

Despite McGraw's eagerness to talk, the interrogators repeatedly threatened that if he refused to give them details, the men he had implicated would do the same to him. Then it would be their word, their collective word, against his. He would never be able to stand up against accusations, so he might as well admit that he had been inside the temple with the others.

The interrogators also emphasized over and over that being in the temple "doesn't make you a shooter." This simple distinction—shooter versus accomplice—was meant to lull McGraw into believing that confessing would not bring him terrible punishment. Legally, though, the distinction made no difference whatsoever. Both shooters and their accomplices face first-degree murder charges. More often than not, they get the same sentence—as would prove to be all too true in the temple murder case.

Wat Promkunaram Buddhist Temple of Arizona in 1991

An aerial view of the Buddhist temple in 1991

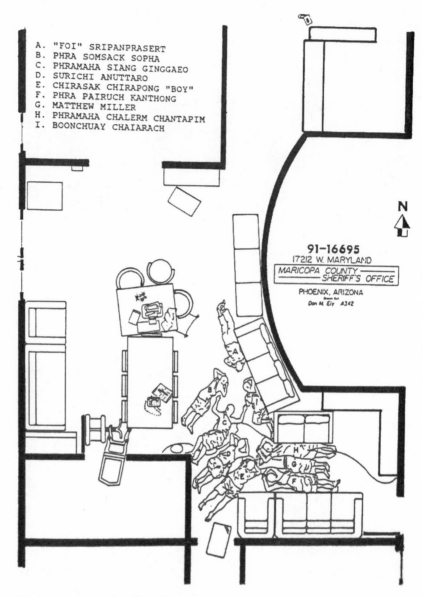

A. "FOI" SRIPANPRASERT
B. PHRA SOMSACK SOPHA
C. PHRAMAHA SIANG GINGGAEO
D. SURICHI ANUTTARO
E. CHIRASAK CHIRAPONG "BOY"
F. PHRA PAIRUCH KANTHONG
G. MATTHEW MILLER
H. PHRAMAHA CHALERM CHANTAPIM
I. BOONCHUAY CHAIARACH

N

91-16695
17212 W. MARYLAND
MARICOPA COUNTY
SHERIFF'S OFFICE
PHOENIX, ARIZONA
Don M. Ely   A342

Maricopa County Sheriff's Office crime scene diagram, a *State v. Doody* trial exhibit

VICTIM	AGE SEX\RACE	OCCUPATION	CAUSE OF DEATH	MANNER OF DEATH	LOCATION OF WOUNDS	WEAPON USED	IDENTIFIED BY
A SRIPANPRASERT, FOI	75 FEMALE ORIENTAL	NUN	GUNSHOT WOUND TO HEAD	HOMICIDE	RIGHT OCCIPUT, OVER VERTEX, PELLET WOUNDS OVER LEFT ARM	RIFLE SHOTGUN	KAMCHAD HIRANRAT
B SOPHA, SOMSAK	46 MALE ORIENTAL	MONK	GUNSHOT WOUNDS HEAD AND NECK	HOMICIDE	RIGHT SIDE NECK, RIGHT OCCIPUT	RIFLE	KAMCHAD HIRANRAT
C PRRAMAHSIANG, GINGGAEO	35 MALE ORIENTAL	MONK	GUNSHOT WOUNDS HEAD AND NECK	HOMICIDE	RIGHT OCCIPUT, RIGHT SIDE NECK GRAZE-LEFT HAND, LEFT FOREARM, LEFT SUPERIOR SHOULDER AND BACK	RIFLE SHOTGUN	KAMCHAD HIRANRAT
D ANUTTARO, SURICHAI	33 MALE ORIENTAL	MONK	GUNSHOT WOUNDS TO HEAD	HOMICIDE	RIGHT FRONTAL LOBE RIGHT CHEEK	RIFLE	KAMCHAD HIRANRAT
E CHIRAPONG, CHIRASAK	21 MALE ORIENTAL	CIVILIAN	GUNSHOT WOUND TO HEAD	HOMICIDE	MID-OCCIPUT	RIFLE	KAMCHAD HIRANRAT
F KANTHONG, PAIRUCH	36 MALE ORIENTAL	MONK	GUNSHOT WOUNDS TO HEAD	HOMICIDE	TOP OF SCALP, NECK BASE OF SKULL	RIFLE SHOTGUN	KAMCHAD HIRANRAT
G MILLER, MATTHEW LEE	17 MALE ORIENTAL	NOVICE MONK	GUNSHOT WOUNDS TO HEAD	HOMICIDE	ABOVE RIGHT EAR, POSTERIOR PORTION OF SKULL	RIFLE	KAMCHAD HIRANRAT
H CHANTADIM, CHALERM	33 MALE ORIENTAL	MONK	GUNSHOT WOUNDS TO HEAD	HOMICIDE	3 SHOTS TO POSTERO-OCCIPITAL AREA OF HEAD	RIFLE	KAMCHAD HIRANRAT
I CHAIYARACH, BOONCHUAY	37 MALE ORIENTAL	MONK	GUNSHOT WOUNDS TO HEAD	HOMICIDE	TO THE HEAD, SUPERFICIAL WOUND OF HEAD, RIGHT ARM, LEFT BUTTOCK	RIFLE SHOTGUN	KAMCHAD HIRANRAT

Maricopa County Sheriff's Office victim chart, a *State v. Doody* trial exhibit

Michael Lawrence McGraw arrest photo

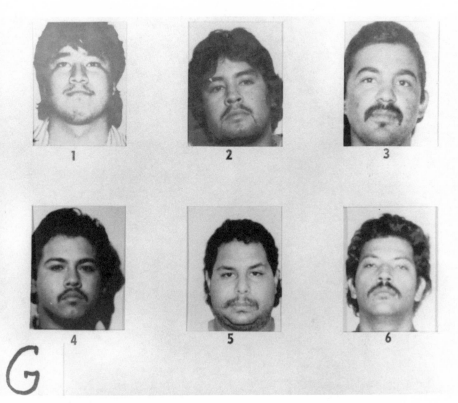

G

Michael Lawrence McGraw photo lineup card

Leo Valdez Bruce arrest photo

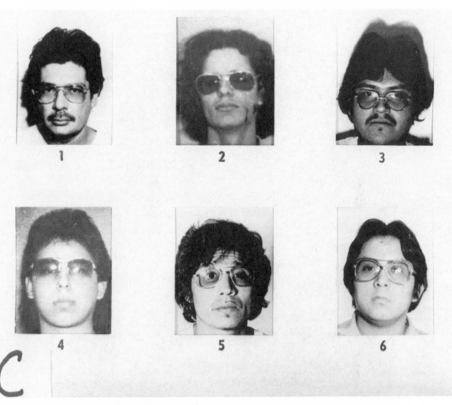

C

Leo Valdez Bruce photo lineup card

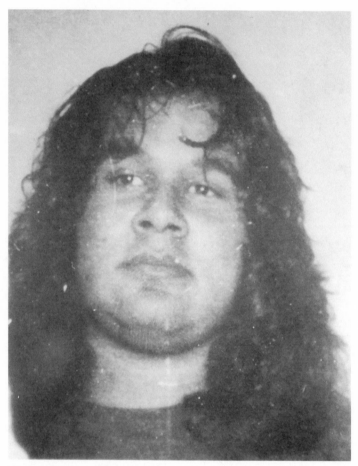

Marcus Felix Nunez arrest photo

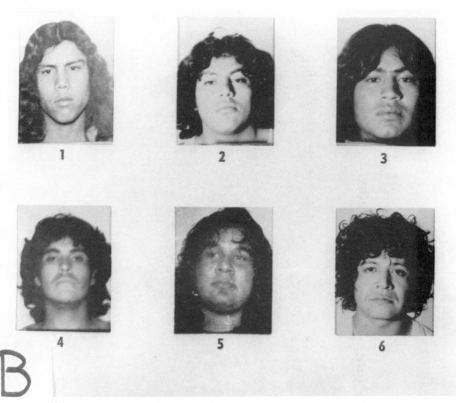

1 2 3

4 5 6

B

Marcus Felix Nunez photo lineup card

Dante Parker arrest photo

Dante Parker photo lineup card

Victor Perez Zarate arrest photo

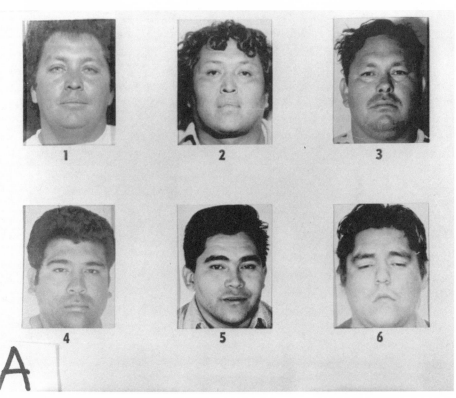

Victor Perez Zarate photo lineup card

The prop room used in interrogating the Tucson suspects. The butcher-paper chart shown in the photo below hung on the wall directly in front of the chairs where the suspects were seated.

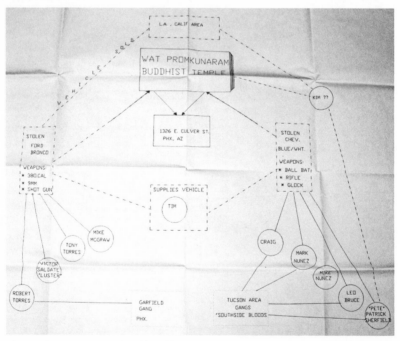

The Maricopa County Sheriff's Office butcher-paper chart displayed in the prop room

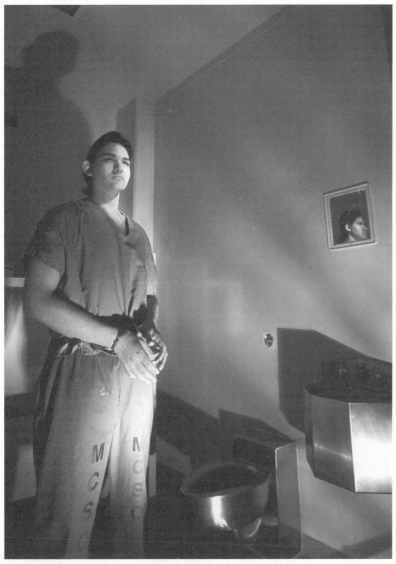

Photo of Alessandro "Alex" Garcia published in *GQ* 64, no. 1 (January 1994).
(Photo copyright Max Aguilera Hellweg)

Rolando Caratachea, October 1991

Johnathan Doody, October 1991

A WAITING LINE FOR CONFESSIONS

4

Once Mike McGraw began to spill out names and locations, the search was on for everyone he implicated. The Arizona Motor Vehicle Department's database yielded addresses and driver's license photos. Task force members and Tucson Police Department SWAT teams went to South Tucson to pick up the suspects. While McGraw was still talking, his neighbors and former friends were being tracked down and driven to Phoenix.

On the fourth floor of the East Court Building, the mood at midday on Wednesday, September 11, blended high anticipation, uneasy confidence in McGraw's ramblings, and the thrill of the chase. Interview rooms were hastily outfitted with hidden microphones. Room 469, known as the prop room, got a video camera and a display of information about the case: documents describing the crime scene, photographs of the victims, a floor plan of the temple, and on one wall a large chart, drawn on butcher paper, connecting the men McGraw had named with the guns and vehicles he claimed they had used in the murders.

The first suspect picked up was Patrick "Pete" Sherfield, portrayed by McGraw as the group's terrifying leader. Tucson police officers staked out Sherfield's house until he came outside, and he agreed to accompany them to Phoenix. Officer Troutt and Detective Griffiths began interrogating him shortly after 1:00 p.m., just a few hours after McGraw first gave his name.

Sherfield said he seldom went to Phoenix, and he denied knowing anything about the murders. Later he told Troutt, "My baby godbrother, come to think of it, said he was in Phoenix." His godbrother's name was Dante Parker. He added that Parker's trip to Phoenix had been the previous May, not in August. The detectives were more interested in what he told them next: his identification had been stolen a while back, and he suspected Parker of taking it. Parker, he said, had a bad temper, owned a .22-caliber automatic handgun, and had been in prison in California on a gun charge. The detectives bought his suggestion that Parker was the one they wanted.

Mike McGraw showed as much flexibility about Sherfield's name as he had about his own, saying that "all the information he had provided investigators so far regarding Peter Sherfield actually applied to Dante Parker."

The case reports do not say why the task force so readily believed Sherfield's claim of innocence. None of the other suspects' denials would get such respectful treatment. He first said he had been home alone with his wife on the evening of August 9, then changed his mind and claimed he had gone to a birthday party. The documents do not mention confirmation of either alibi—and strong alibis did not protect the other young men fingered by McGraw.

For whatever reasons, the investigators released Sherfield and started searching for his godbrother. They would have two other suspects in custody and under interrogation before they found Parker.

At suppertime that Wednesday, Marcus Felix Nunez was alone at home, expecting his mom any minute. Just nineteen, a student at Pima Community College, he still lived with her. Marky, as friends called him, was a big guy, tall and heavy, but mild mannered and shy. Outgoing in small groups, he could be nearly invisible in larger ones, in spite of his size. He didn't make new friends easily, but his old ones stuck by him— or at least they had until now. His family situation was complicated. The woman he called Mom was actually his grandmother, who had adopted him when he was a child. His biological mother and her husband also lived in the house. And Mike McGraw, busily blabbing Marky's name to the police, was his first cousin.

It wasn't his mom who came to the door. Instead, at 6:27 p.m., the Tucson SWAT team burst in. With only a bewildered teenager to subdue, they declared the house secured by 6:34. Four more officers, including MCSO sergeant Mike Mitchell, went in and found the suspect handcuffed and lying face down on the living room floor. They helped him to his feet and told him they were taking him to Phoenix. Nunez asked what it was about, but Mitchell said detectives in Phoenix would answer his questions. He asked them to leave a note for his mom, and Mitchell did so.

Shortly after 8:00 p.m., Kimball logged Nunez in at task force headquarters and noted his social security number, home address, and phone number. Those few facts were all the investigators knew about him apart from the accusations of his voluble cousin. In interview room 466, deputies removed Nunez's handcuffs and gave him a rubber band so he could put his long, curly hair in a ponytail. Kimball assigned MCSO detective Pat Riley and FBI agent Gary Woodling to question him.

Before starting the questioning, Riley took Nunez to the prop room, which was designed to "help" the suspects recall their roles in McGraw's version of the temple murders. Kimball later wrote that the prop room was the FBI's idea. Anyone who spent time in that room learned a great deal about the temple murders—details that, the investigators would claim, only the killers could have known.

A video camera recorded events in the prop room, without sound. Riley watched on the monitor as Nunez studied the information on the wall and looked closely at the photographs of the victims. According to Riley, Nunez was in the prop room only "one to one and a half minutes." But Nunez's interview did not begin until 8:55 p.m., forty-five minutes after Kimball logged him in. It is possible that Nunez had longer than ninety seconds to study the information displayed in the prop room.

Back in room 466, the only furniture was three metal-framed chairs: "no desks, tables, or other furniture." Nunez's chair was against one wall. Riley and Woodling sat facing him, one toward each side; Nunez had to turn his head to look at them.

At the beginning of the interrogation, Riley had to read the suspect his rights. He told Nunez, "There's some formality things that I need to take care of. For your interest, my interest, everybody's interest. . . . I'm sure you've heard of this on TV and everything, when it's blown out of proportion . . . it's called a *Miranda* warning, and I'd like to read that here to you real quick. . . . You have the right to be silent, anything you say can be used against you in a court of law. You have the right to the presence of an attorney to assist you prior to questioning, and to be with you during questioning if you so desire, if you cannot afford an attorney, you have the right to have an attorney appointed for you prior to questioning. Okay, did you understand all of them?"

"Yes."

The *Miranda* decision is far more than a "formality thing," but Riley's dismissive approach was a common technique to discourage suspects from invoking their rights. The staging, prop room evidence, uncomfortable chairs, and tone of Nunez's interrogation were typical of the way the task force would treat all the Tucson suspects. Every officer took part in the staging and role playing designed to squeeze out confessions and keep suspects from consulting lawyers.

Nunez told them he was a premed student and already had a degree in laboratory science. He had been arrested for drunk driving when he was fifteen and now didn't drive at all, didn't even have a license. He hadn't been to Phoenix for two or three years until the previous Sunday, when he'd come up for a Van Halen concert.

He said he knew a black guy in Tucson named Pete, and when asked to name his friends mentioned, among others, Leo, Randy, and "this real close friend of mine, Dante Parker, that's who I DJ with." He explained to the puzzled detectives: "Disc jockey with him, like [at] parties."

Half an hour into the interrogation, Nunez asked, "Am I under arrest?"

"Um, no," Riley said. "As far as my conversation with you here right now, I'm not placing you under arrest. What I want to do is talk with you, you know, about these things and get these things ironed out."

It was true that Nunez was not yet under arrest in the formal sense, as in "I arrest you for the crime of murder." But he was certainly in custody. Suspects rarely realize that it is custody, not arrest, that triggers the obligation to give *Miranda* warnings.

"Basically," Riley said, "what I wanted to discuss with you is a case of murder."

"A murder."

"Yes, a murder. In fact, several murders."

"I don't know nothing."

Responding to that denial, Riley introduced a circular argument that would come up again and again: the very fact that the police were questioning a suspect meant he must be involved in the crime. Riley's first use of it was subtle. "We normally don't go knock on people's doors . . . unless we have a feeling that they seriously have either some information to give to us or maybe possibly some involvement in the matter. . . . I know that you have some information that can assist us in the investigation."

The tactic may have worked. "Well," Nunez replied, "what do you want to know?"

Leo Valdez Bruce woke up on Wednesday, September 11, with the ordinary concerns of a man working two jobs to make ends meet. He reported for work at the Custom Shutter Shop by eight sharp. He'd held that job for two years without missing a day, assembling window shutters and installing them in customers' homes. After putting in eight hours there, he went to his second job, starting racing dogs at Tucson Greyhound Park. As usual, he left the track at 11:00 p.m. and drove the five miles to his apartment in South Tucson.

At twenty-eight, Leo was the oldest of the guys McGraw claimed had committed the crime, but in his mug shot he looks barely out of his teens. The picture shows him with long hair, oversized aviator-style glasses, and a t-shirt printed with a skeleton, a shotgun, and the phrases "Cold Steel" and "Hot Lead." In normal circumstances, Bruce looked handsome and vibrant. He was quick to smile, laughed more than he cried, and enjoyed his busy life.

Eleven hours after McGraw identified Bruce in the photo lineup, Sgt. Mitchell and Deputy Mike Adams were surveilling Bruce's apartment, waiting for him to come home. At 11:30 p.m. they saw a 1977 Oldsmobile approaching. A radio check of the license confirmed that it was Bruce's car.

Bruce parked in the lot and headed toward his front door. Encountering armed officers so late at night didn't worry him, even though these two had unfamiliar-looking uniforms. South Tucson had plenty of drugs and other trouble, so the police were often in the neighborhood, but they never bothered with him. He didn't use drugs or hang around with anyone who did. He turned toward Mitchell, who told him to put his hands on his head.

Mitchell reports what was, for the MCSO and the task force, a textbook arrest. He handcuffed Bruce and told him they were taking him to Phoenix to speak with detectives. When Bruce asked what it was about, Mitchell pretended not to know.

The arrest was not textbook for any other police agency at the time, in Arizona or elsewhere. State law required that Bruce be taken immediately to the nearest magistrate in Pima County, the county where he was picked up. Instead, he was ordered into a police car and driven through the night to Maricopa County without being told why.

Bruce was quiet during the two-hour ride. His habitual acceptance of authority, from his family, from his bosses, was simply transferred to the officers. When they told him he had to go with them, he did. When they told him they didn't know why he was wanted in Phoenix, he believed them. That same pliant acceptance would define him for the next two days.

Kimball put Bruce in interview room 426 and assigned FBI agent Robert Casey and MCSO deputy Dave Munley as the first team to tackle him. They got started at around 2:30 a.m. on September 12.

Munley told Bruce that he and Casey were investigating the temple murders. When Bruce said he'd heard about the crime, Munley got serious. "Let me just get something straight here right now, okay? Everything I tell you is going to be the truth. . . . We're not going to feed you any lies. Everything that we're going to tell you is fact. Okay? And I'd appreciate it if you would do the same."

With no idea of the ordeal he was about to face and no way to know that Munley had just told an outright lie, Bruce responded, "No problem."

Soon after that Munley read Bruce the *Miranda* warnings and asked, "Do you understand those rights?"

Here the transcript notes, "Bruce answered 'yea.' . . . However, the answer did not record." The interrogators reviewed drafts of the transcripts; this helpful note was probably added by Munley or Casey.

Casey urged Bruce to talk now, "before other people come in and start telling a story, naming you. . . . You haven't told us much yet, but we'll take your word for it."

Casey and Munley had no intention of taking Bruce's word for anything. He said he hadn't been to Phoenix since the previous fall, when the Dallas Cowboys played the Cardinals. Casey responded, "What would you say if we told you that we know that you were up here and involved with some people in a deal that went down over here?"

"I'll have to see the proof."

"You'll have to see the proof? You don't look like you're too sure yourself." This challenge—that Bruce didn't "look too sure"—would be repeated over and over through the night.

Asked if he knew anyone named Victor, Bruce mentioned his brother-in-law and then Victor Zarate. Asked if he had a friend named Mike, he answered, "Yeah, I used to," but said he hadn't seen McGraw for about five years. He admitted owning a .22 rifle. He said he had learned about the temple killings from TV and the radio.

Munley wanted to know if he'd ever discussed it with anyone. Bruce said, "Me and a guy at work, the manager, we discussed it. . . . I don't see why people should make other people go through what they went through."

"What do you think they went through?"

"Well, they say some kind of a massacre or something."

Routine interrogations are conducted in a Q&A format—question and answer. The temple case was different. Because the investigation of Arizona's first mass murder was so media oriented and so politically dangerous, the task force brass had approved Kimball's plan to secretly tape interrogations. Knowing that the brass, ensconced in the monitoring rooms, were listening to every word, the interrogators may have been more confrontational than usual. As Kimball later put it, every deputy was on display. Accordingly, the Q&A format often gave way to A&D— accusation and denial.

Casey and Munley launched a blitz of accusations and insinuations, bombarding Bruce with words while he sat in silence. Casey echoed Riley's circular argument. "We just didn't wake up and open the newspaper one day and, you know, pick your name out or throw a dart at a dartboard and say come down and pick you up. There has been some statements and information given and that has checked out. . . . We did not drive you a hundred miles up here in the middle of the night for no reason whatsoever."

All the words in this portion of the transcript are from Casey and Munley. Bruce said nothing except an occasional mutter that the typist rendered as "Unintel."

Kimball would recall Bruce as one of the most patient people he had ever met. He could sit there and listen to long, repetitive speeches from detectives who had their minds made up about his guilt. He did not confront them; he just listened. Sometimes he held out his arms, palms up, to convey his complete lack of understanding of what in the world they were talking about.

The barrage of accusations went on for four or five hours. Bruce said innumerable times, "I wasn't there." When he clammed up, Munley and Casey must have wondered if they would ever break him. Again Casey said, "You're not sitting here for no reason."

Bruce finally spoke. "Well, I know that." But, he went on, "I wouldn't do anything like that."

Casey was a bulldog. "We believe otherwise. And we have a whole packful of information, you know, that leads us otherwise."

Their goal for the coming hours was to make Bruce himself believe otherwise.

Dante Parker, Peter Sherfield's "baby godbrother," spent Wednesday night at his girlfriend's apartment and was up early on Thursday, September 12. He was going to school to learn air-conditioning and refrigeration, and he had an exam that day. At age twenty-one he lived in South Tucson with the elder Sherfields, who had raised him and whom he considered his mom and dad. Muscular and dark skinned, with a strong forehead and close-cropped hair, Parker was a serious man who carried himself with an air of bravado.

Before the investigators could find Parker, he found them. His mom gave him a phone message from the Tucson police. Returning the call, Parker agreed to wait at home for Sgt. Ron Zimmerling. At 8:15 a.m. Zimmerling drove up, and Parker left the house to talk to him. He was dressed for school, where he planned to go right after their conversation.

Instead, Zimmerling turned Parker over to DEA agent Al Reilly and INS agent Phil Bonner, who drove him to Phoenix. Conversation in the car ranged over "sports, professional football, social dating, a prior jail term in Folsom Prison, and Parker's future employment."

When Parker mentioned Folsom Prison, the task force already knew about his criminal record. Following up on Sherfield's hints, they had extracted it from a national database. They learned that he had been in prison for burglary as a juvenile and was currently on parole. They also found a warrant for his arrest for violating parole by leaving California.

Kimball assigned Parker to MCSO detectives Pat Riley and Wayne Scoville. At 11:27 a.m., in interview room 467, Riley and Scoville began the carefully orchestrated campaign to get him to confess.

As he had with Nunez the night before, Riley started off with *Miranda* and carefully downplayed it. "It's not anything to get you all excited or, you know, intimidate or anything like that. All it is, is to let you know what's up and protect your, protect our interests and everything . . . so don't let this ruffle your feathers or anything like that, it's just a formality that we have to go through." He read the required warnings and asked, "Do you understand these?"

"Yeah."

"Okay. Any questions about those at all?"

Parker's answer is inaudible on the tape. In place of words, the transcript includes a stage direction: "shakes head side to side." Similar notations are scattered throughout Parker's transcripts, probably added by Riley or Scoville when reviewing the typists' work.

Early in the interrogation Parker said nothing but an occasional "Yeah." His first substantive statement asserted his innocence. "I don't know nothing about this, the only thing I know about the, the temple murders is from what happened on TV."

If one of Riley's principles of interrogation was "We wouldn't be questioning you if you weren't guilty," another was "If two or more people tell the same story, it must be true." He explained the second principle to Parker. "People can't individually create a scenario in their minds, and telepathically convey it to somebody else. . . . The only way a story can be the same is that those people were there and they experienced it."

Riley claimed that the investigators' method was to talk to a lot of people and use their answers to paint a picture. "We talk to three, four or five, ten, twenty, a hundred people if we have to . . . and it's kinda like a jigsaw puzzle that you put together, that whenever you get a piece of information you put it in that puzzle, then it starts to paint a big picture." From talking to people, he said, they knew Parker had information about the murders: "You were actually there."

"That's the thing," Parker responded. "I don't know nothing about this case. Where am I in this big picture? 'Cause I don't know."

"You're actually right in the middle of it," Riley said. He went on, "It's not a very comforting sensation knowing the things that you know in having been there . . . 'cause it wasn't pleasant, I know that, it wasn't pleasant at all."

Parker echoed Riley's favorite word. "Okay," he said. "You tell me."

Victor Perez Zarate, the last of the five Tucson suspects to be interrogated, was not accosted by armed officers in the dark of night. Instead, like Dante Parker, he called the police himself. In fact he called them twice: his cell phone cut off the first call, so he went to his parents' house and used a landline.

MCSO sergeant Pat Cooper took his call at 2:05 a.m. on Thursday, September 12. Zarate said he had heard the police were looking for him and wanted to know what was going on. Officers picked him up in Tucson at about 3:00 and delivered him to MCSO headquarters in Phoenix, in handcuffs, around 5:00 a.m. But his formal interrogation would not begin until nearly twelve hours after he was taken into custody.

On arriving at headquarters, Zarate was briefly questioned by Captain White, the task force commander. White mentioned "the killings of the Buddhist priests." Zarate denied knowing anything about that and told White he'd never been to Phoenix. White showed him some photographs; Zarate picked out Leo and Mark. He also recognized a man named Victor and told White they might have picked up the wrong Victor.

After the meeting with White, Zarate apparently did a lot of waiting. The next record of his activities is at 12:05 p.m., when he was placed in a lineup and both McGraw and Nunez identified him as a participant in the temple murders. It may be that no one had time to question him in the intervening hours. Many detectives were involved in interrogating McGraw, Bruce, and Nunez. Even Parker, who arrived at headquarters several hours after Zarate, was questioned before him—possibly because, being black, he fit McGraw's description of the murderers' ringleader. Zarate's first interrogators, detectives Riley and Scoville, were with Parker until shortly before they joined Zarate. As Kimball later commented, there was a waiting line for confessions that day.

By the time Zarate's interrogation finally began, at 2:16 p.m., he must have been awake for more than thirty hours—just right by MCSO standards. He was in interview room 466, where Nunez had been the day before.

Riley began with the *Miranda* warnings, prefaced by his usual dismissive remarks. Zarate said he understood his rights and had no questions. Riley asked if he knew why they wanted to talk to him.

"Well, I think Mr. White told me something about the, uh, Buddhist priests or something like that."

Factual questions followed. Zarate lived with his mother but sometimes stayed with his girlfriend; he had worked at Tucson Greyhound Park for eight years; he paid child support for three kids and was about to have another one with his girlfriend.

Riley abruptly, if obscurely, returned to the topic of the crime. "What we're trying to understand, as is, well, everybody else down the line, the whys and wherefores and everything, the why and how everything happened the way they did, and to be able to understand an explanation, or to have a reasonable explanation as to how things happened. Things like this aren't black and white . . . and the end result isn't always planned or intended."

Zarate seemed to understand this speech. He said, "That's what Mr. White was telling me, the same thing."

His next words were the first of scores of firm denials he would utter before the interrogation ended. "I don't know . . . what you guys are talking about, 'cause I was in Tucson." He added, "And I worked that night, too."

Riley and Scoville ignored this mention of Zarate's alibi, as they and their colleagues would ignore his more and more desperate assertions of it in the next eleven hours.

Hours before Zarate's interrogation began, Detective Riley said to Mark Nunez, "You were in fact in Phoenix with some friends on a given day."

"Oh, I was seen here?"

"Well, yeah, you were."

Nunez started to respond. "I could—well, no, I'm sorry to interrupt."

Riley was equally polite. "The easiest thing to do is probably just to see if we can hammer out what you might have been doing during those days and those weeks, and see what you can remember about them. Would that be fair?"

"Yes, that sounds fair."

On Tuesday, August 13, Nunez had registered for his classes. He wasn't sure about the weekend before. He usually partied with his friend Javier. "I think we might have had a party, you can call Javier on that one and see. . . . But I drink, I drink a lot on the weekends . . . honestly I can't tell you what I did."

Riley brought up Dante Parker again, and Nunez contradicted what he'd said about his close friend and fellow DJ. Now he said he'd seen Parker but had never partied with him. He didn't hang around with "what you'd call gangsters, you know, crack dealers."

Riley jumped on that. "You must have a suspicion that Dante's a gangster."

"Yeah, well he, he seems intelligent but he has that little . . ." Nunez's voice trailed off.

He had never seen Parker carry a gun and didn't think he used drugs. He'd also never seen him in a car; Dante got around on a bicycle. Asked about gangs, Nunez implied that both he and Parker were assumed to be Bloods because of their neighborhood. "You know, they feel 'He's a Blood because he's from South Park.'"

Up to this point Nunez had been responsive and made regular eye contact. But when Riley steered the conversation back to the crime, he "became noticeably nervous, agitated, and began looking down to the ground when answering questions." Riley took these changes as signs of guilt, and his own tone changed as well.

"Let me explain a few things to you," Riley said. "This murder involved more than one individual, I'll go ahead and tell you that. I know that you, Mark, you were actually present. . . . I'm not saying that you killed anybody—"

"I, I—"

"Hold on, hold on, hold on, but you were present, okay. Wait, let me finish. I know that, and I wouldn't tell you that if I didn't know that for a fact."

"I don't know what the hell you're talking about, this murder."

"Mark, Mark, Mark, Mark, Mark. That's not true."

Riley repeated his circular argument. "I wouldn't be pointing a finger or saying that Mark Nunez was at a given place if he wasn't there." To get the "complete picture," they had to talk to everyone involved. "It's like a jigsaw puzzle, you know, when you're putting pieces in a puzzle, and this little straight piece that doesn't fit. . . . We don't want somebody else, Mark, later on down the line, to start filling in little pieces."

"I don't know what the hell you are talking about."

Little changed in the next half hour. Riley alternated short jabs with slightly longer questions. Nunez said "I don't know what you're talking about" seven times, plus "That can't be," "I wasn't here," and "I'm telling the truth."

Then Riley's paragraphs stretched into full monologues, and Nunez began to weaken under the barrage of words—which was, after all, the point of Riley's technique. Firm denials gave way to "I don't know" and a plaintive "What's going on?"

Riley insisted, "You do know, yes you do. Because you were there. . . . You were there with these other people having a good time. Like you say, you go drinking on the weekends, that's where all this started."

"Was it on a weekend?"

Noticing Nunez's uncertainty, Riley said, "You have an obligation, and you have to tell us what you saw, or what you heard. And Mark, you can't tell me that you don't know what I'm talking about."

"I must have been drunk, I don't know."

Riley ran with this hint of capitulation. "You probably were, 'cause you said yourself that you go drinking, and you have a good time on the weekends. There's nothing wrong with that. . . . But when you're with these people and they go and do the things that they did—they killed a bunch of people, you know that because you were there—that is some serious stuff." His tone shifted from stern to reassuring. "We can make it better by explaining what happened and make sure these people can't hurt anybody else. You don't want them to hurt anybody else, do you?"

"I'm trying to remember if I was there. I must have been drunk but I'm trying to remember."

"I can ease that thought," Riley offered. "I know you were there."

Agent Casey tried using psychology on Leo Bruce. "You don't seem like you're convinced that you're telling the truth. You seem like something's bothering you."

"Something like this—wouldn't you be nervous?"

Munley said, "Let me tell you about the judge and jury, okay? They're gonna look highly upon a person who is going to stand up there and tell the truth." Casey reinforced the point. "The other people will get up there and tell the truth. They're gonna be the good guys."

"In other words, I'm the bad guy?"

"No. . . . This is an opportunity for you to tell your side of the story."

"There is no story. I told you the truth."

Casey dismissed that answer. "There's already been statements taken and there's already been evidence matched up."

In fact there was no evidence, matched up or otherwise. The task force had nothing but McGraw's inconsistent story. But lying to a guilty man is a time-honored technique, and Munley and Casey clearly considered Bruce guilty. Keeping the suspect high on sugar and low on sleep was another good technique: Casey left the room to get Bruce a can of soda pop.

Meanwhile, Munley worked on Bruce. "We talked to all your friends," he said. "All your friends."

Bruce saw through that lie. "Which ones? Because all my friends were at work at the track today."

By now, Bruce had long forgotten the *Miranda* warnings. Looking back years later, he said it never occurred to him that the "right to silent part" meant he didn't have to answer questions. He thought it was some kind of court thing that didn't apply in jail, and jail is where he thought he was. He recalled being too scared to do anything but sit there. He had no idea that his questioners were required to let him have a lawyer if he requested one. Besides, he had faith in the justice system and thought they couldn't do anything to him because he was innocent.

Casey returned with the soda pop and a new question. "What do you know about this guy Mike McGraw?"

Bruce said McGraw "spends a lot of time in those correctional homes and stuff. . . . He had his problems and I don't want to be involved with him."

Asked if he knew McGraw's friends Dante, Peter, and Patrick, Bruce said the only one he had heard of was a black guy named Peter. Asked about Mark Nunez, he said he knew him from around the neighborhood. He didn't know anyone named Craig or Robert Torres or anything about a Blazer or a Bronco.

As Bruce kept up his denials, many of his answers were the kind a lawyer, if he had had one, might have recommended: short yes-or-no replies without elaboration or qualification. And he showed notable stubbornness, as in the following exchange with Casey.

"We got statements and we got evidence and the vehicles. . . . You are one of the eight people that was in the Bronco and the Blazer that went to the church when the deal went down. And you've got to tell us—"

"I wasn't there."

"—absolutely got to tell us."

"I wasn't there."

"I could see it in your eyes, man."

"I wasn't there."

"You know, we're talkin' about a serious, serious deal here."

"I was not there."

Of all the interrogations of the Tucson suspects, Dante Parker's was the longest and the most invasive. It lasted more than sixteen hours and filled twenty-one audiotapes. The official transcript is about the size of the average John Grisham novel. Seven officers worked in shifts to keep the questioning going. Their goal was to get Parker to paint a detailed picture of the temple murders—one that matched the one painted by Mike McGraw.

If Parker didn't explain what happened, Riley said, the others would "paint that picture for you completely." He added, "Most people are not going to paint a pretty picture, they're gonna paint the ugliest picture possible 'cause that's what they want to believe." As for him and his colleagues, "We deal with truth. We're not gonna go with what one person says and hold that as gospel, but there are a lot of people, three, four, five, a hundred people if necessary, to find out stories about what happened and piece those together with everybody else, and if all those stories make sense and they're all the same then it's gotta be the truth."

Scoville told Parker, "You're one of the last persons that we talk to, right? We already know the majority of the story. . . . There's no doubt in our mind that you were there."

"But that's the thing."

"That's not the thing."

"That's the thing. . . . I was with Rene. I didn't do anything."

Riley and Scoville shifted into accusatory style, hammering Parker with allegations while also feeding him information about the crime they insisted he had committed. The next hour of questioning followed this pattern: accusations from Riley and Scoville; firm denials from Parker.

Riley made colorful threats: "If you don't take the chance right now to explain to us the way things are, you are going to get slam dunked in the final end." "You're gonna sink real fast. They're gonna tie a lead weight on your feet and you're gonna go all the way to the bottom and you are not gonna be able to come back up."

Parker's answers were consistently aloof and detached. He provided a detailed alibi. He had spent the entire weekend with his girlfriend, Rene, and her roommate could confirm this. He hadn't been to Phoenix at all since moving back to Tucson from California in March. He was not a member of the Bloods. He "wasn't with nobody in Phoenix that night."

"You're the only one saying that, 'cause everybody else is saying 'These are who was there and Dante is one of them.'"

"New one on me."

"How about a Ford Bronco," Riley asked. "You ever been in one of those? You were that night."

"I don't know nobody, no Ford Bronco."

"Sure you do, you went to California with the damn thing after this thing happened."

"I ain't been in California since I been here."

As if he'd been waiting for this cue, Sgt. Kimball opened the door just long enough to announce, "The guy in the separate room just gave up where the vehicle went after the murders." Kimball made this up, just as other officers made up other supposed revelations, to convince the suspects that everybody was snitching on everybody else. But Parker simply repeated, "I never been in California since I been here."

A few minutes later Riley made a threat far more direct than slam dunks and lead weights. He imagined what jury members would think about the one suspect who refused to confess. "These other guys seem like decent people that screwed up, they admit it, they're sorry. . . . This other guy over here, he don't give a shit. . . . Do we throw him in prison for the rest of his life, or . . . maybe we send him to the gas chamber?"

When Parker just sat there, Riley changed tack. "Am I all fucked up when I say that I believe you're sorry about what happened, you didn't mean for it to happen?"

That got a response. "Don't know what happened, that's what I'm trying to tell you."

Riley fed Parker some names. "What's Leo gonna say? Did I just pull that name out of a hat? No. You want me to give you another one?"

Parker said the only Leo he knew was fat and black. Scoville offered a second name. "What's Mark gonna say?"

"A white boy Mark?" Parker asked. "I know a Mark and I know Leo." But he didn't "hang with them."

Riley snapped, "There's an explanation of why this thing happened, and you're gonna let them paint that picture for you, Mr. Bad Ass."

Mark Nunez could not hold out against the interrogators' certainty. When Riley told him, "I know you were there," he wavered. "I don't, don't know. I don't remember that."

"What can I do for you, Mark?"

"Name names."

"Well, Mark, I could give you all the names in the world, I could lay out all the facts to you about what happened."

Nunez asked for "type of car or something."

So Riley laid out one fact. "One of the vehicles is a Bronco." Later Nunez would ask about the other one, and Riley would answer, "Chevy Blazer." In the months ahead, Nunez's knowledge of these details would be taken as evidence of his guilt.

Soon Nunez had a question. "If I remember, what's going to happen to me?"

Riley said, "What happens to you is entirely up to you. . . . Did you kill anybody?"

"No, I couldn't even think of anything like that."

Nunez's deepening confusion became evident in an exchange about the prop room. Riley asked if he remembered "that room with information on vehicles."

Nunez responded, "We only take pictures of Chinese people beat up."

"Did you see anything else? Did it have any effect on you?"

"Made me sick, yeah."

"I still don't think you necessarily had a part in murdering those people. Is that right?"

"Those are the people?"

At one point Riley took the focus off Nunez, asking who he thought would be capable of "something like this."

Nunez still sounded disoriented. "And he would not be capable of not remembering. It seems I for one, would want to believe." Soon he was babbling. "I know remember I don't remember if I did anything I will remember that's not true." He was also doubting his own innocence. He wanted to remember, "but if I did, but I know I ain't that positive that I'm not involved."

The suspect's waning confidence was good news for the interrogators. When Nunez pulled himself together, Riley's frustration was obvious.

Nunez said he didn't remember going to Camelback Mountain with a bunch of people.

"The hell you don't, you were there."

"I wasn't."

"Mark, you were. Christ, you tell me all these things, 'No I wasn't, no I wasn't.' You were. I can give you little bits and pieces here, trying to stir your memory, but I'm not gonna feed you the whole thing."

The next time Nunez said he knew nothing about the crime, Riley made a direct accusation. "You're lying to me." He added, "It offends me because I'm trying to be reasonable with you."

Nunez tried to be reasonable with Riley. "I know I didn't do anything. . . . I don't know what happened. I don't know where Lakeside Park is at, I don't know about a Bronco, I don't know about Leo."

Woodling claimed that Nunez had already named people involved in the murders. "We didn't provide names, you came up with a name."

Nunez corrected him. "You asked about Leo. He said do you know a Leo."

Riley conceded that one. "Well, whatever, Mark, you're probably right." Then he returned to a standard theme: if Nunez didn't tell them what happened, other people would control what happened to him. "Gosh, I mean that isn't fair, that isn't fair to you."

The friendlier tone seemed to sap what was left of Nunez's strength. "What can I do, what can I do? I'll do anything. What can I do if I don't know anything?" From desperation, he moved toward cooperation. "I wish you would give me some idea of what's going on."

Riley asked, "Why do I need to tell you things that you already know?"

"Well, tell me what I already know and then maybe I can help you out with that."

The more firmly Leo Bruce stuck to his story, the harder Casey and Munley pounded him. "We found four people that say you were in Phoenix at a church. And those people said that you were in a Blazer, and that you went inside the church, and that you know what happened inside there. . . . You were there."

"No I wasn't."

Casey tried sympathy. "Right now you're the only one saying it your way in this whole mess . . . you're gonna just have to give in and say 'I'm gonna say what happened.' Just get it off your shoulders, man." He imagined Leo standing alone saying "no no no" while everyone else declared he was guilty.

Munley reinforced Casey's message. "You are alone, Leo."

"I am," Bruce agreed.

Munley invited him to come in from the cold. "It's time to join the team. It's time you tell the truth, Leo."

"I can't join the team when I was nowhere around here." Bruce clung to his alibi. "How could I be around here when I was at work?"

The task force would not get around to checking Bruce's alibi until ten days later, but a lack of information didn't inhibit Munley. "Leo, don't you know that we know your employers? . . . We found out all about you before dragging your ass all the way up for—"

"What do you know about me?" Bruce asked the question three times before he got a response. The response he eventually got was a classic example of coercive custodial interrogation. If the interrogators could get Bruce to focus, not on what he actually remembered, but on what McGraw said he had done, he might break.

Munley went first. "I'll tell you what we know about you. You were involved with the incident at the temple. Plain and simple. . . . You're gonna go down hard because everyone else is gonna put the shit on you. . . . The smartest thing for you to do right now is to get it off your chest, like your friends did."

Casey chimed in. "We know about the Bronco and the Blazer. And we know about the church and we know about the guns. . . . And we know you were there, Leo. We absolutely know."

Bruce could only repeat, "Like I said, I wasn't there."

"All we got to do is find the right button to convince you that the best thing for you to do is absolutely just tell the truth about what happened."

But truth, in hard-core custodial interrogation, is not the goal. The goal is confession. As for the means to that goal, as Casey put it, they just had to find the right button. Confessions—especially false confessions—emerge through cracks in the human psyche, and Bruce's psyche was beginning to crack.

DPS agent Richie Martinez walked in unannounced, looked at Bruce, and said, "That's him." Then he walked out again. Bruce had no way to know that this was another time-honored technique, a psychological ploy.

"That was a DPS gang investigator from Tucson," Casey said, then kept talking as if no one had interrupted. "Okay, about these other names, Mike McGraw, Nunez, Dante, Peter Sherfield, Victor, and these other guys. You got, you know, dead human beings over here. . . . Look, if you stayed outside, tell us that. Tell us that now, you know, tell us what happened now. Tell us."

But Bruce said nothing. Mute suspects are a good cop's bad dream. Silence is the enemy. If you can't overcome a suspect's silence, then you won't draw the "queen of proofs": you won't extract a confession.

Bruce must have begun to realize that Casey would never accept his innocence. "All right," he said, "go on with it."

Casey went on—and on—with it, but Bruce's answers didn't change. "I wasn't there. I don't know what happened."

At around 4:30 a.m., Casey suggested a break. He and Munley were ready for a rest. As for Bruce, he'd been awake for more than twenty hours, worked two jobs, and faced down authority figures who refused to believe a word he said. Even the sugar and caffeine supplied by the task force were wearing off. The brass wanted Casey and Munley refreshed and Bruce worn down. They decided it was time to remind him of the details of the crime, and they assigned Sgt. Pat Cooper to do the reminding.

First, to prove that his friends "had in fact been arrested," Cooper handed Bruce that day's newspaper, which had a front-page story about the arrests. Bruce handed it right back, saying he had no need to read it because he wasn't involved.

Next Cooper conducted Bruce to the prop room, where Bruce looked closely at the photographs of the victims in life and in death. Cooper called his attention to other information displayed on the walls, including the chart that listed Bruce and the other suspects. After about five minutes Casey appeared, and the next half hour of Bruce's interrogation took place right there in the prop room. This room was not wired for sound, and Casey, as an FBI agent, did not submit written reports to the task force, so the only record of what happened during that half hour is Cooper's terse summary: "Mr. Bruce made no statements which implicated himself with the murder and did not associate himself with the case."

Riley tried a new threat on Dante Parker. He said they'd pick up the woman Parker had named as his alibi and ask her to take a polygraph test. "What is she gonna do when she fails? What is she gonna do when she goes to jail for lying to us?"

"But that's the thing, it's the truth."

"No it's not. So what you're saying is you don't care about Rene?"

"Oh, I do care about her."

"Well, obviously not."

Again Riley threatened that if Parker didn't cooperate he might get the gas chamber. "I don't say that to scare you, Dante, but in this situation that's a real possibility." (In fact the gas chamber was *not* a real possibility; Arizona's method of execution was lethal injection.)

Scoville said they weren't against him: "We're here to help you out."

"Yeah, but you're trying to help out the wrong person. I don't know, you're trying to help out the wrong person."

"I'm sure we're not." Scoville warned Parker, "This is your opportunity. . . . On down the road it's too late."

"You're not giving me an opportunity, 'cause I wasn't the one that did it."

Later Scoville asked if Parker had heard of premeditated murder. Parker said no.

"Premeditated murder is the worst kind—'I planned it, I went in and killed 'em.'" As Scoville explained it, premeditation was "go in there to do this," as opposed to "go in there and it happens." If Parker understood that difference, Scoville said, he'd come clean.

So far nothing the interrogators had thrown at him had cracked Parker's psyche. "Oh, I understand," he replied. "But there's nothing to come clean with."

Scoville favored a style of questioning reminiscent of children yelling, "Did so!" "Did not!" Now he and Parker exchanged twelve consecutive accusations and denials.

"You're not standing up for what you know."

"I'm standing up for what I know."

"You're standing up for what you wish were true."

"I'm standing up for what I know is true."

"No you're not." And so on.

At last Scoville varied the pattern. "We have people who are implicating themselves, who are saying otherwise."

"Then fuck them, man," Parker retorted.

"That's right, you keep that attitude and you go to court, okay, but when you're sitting in prison don't come crying to me."

"I ain't gonna cry to nobody, man."

That response inspired Scoville to an even longer series of accusations in the same style, this time about whether Parker was "being a man."

Parker stuck to his story, but the fast-paced verbal blows were wearing him down. His anger began to give way to a mixture of defiance, fatalism, and gallows humor. Answers like "I'm standing up for what I believe" gave way to darker ones: "If I have to die, I'll go out dying, let the motherfuckers know that I didn't pull any of this bullshit." "I'm not scared to die . . . Why not, I'm gonna die one of these days. So if I get to the gas chamber, electric chair, then fuck it; I'll just have to live with it, right?"

When Parker reverted to earnest denials, Riley cut him off. "I didn't do nothing wrong," Parker said. "I didn't do nothing at all. I don't know nothing—"

"Dante, it's a whole box full of jury people that you gotta convince. . . . You're not convincing us, you're not gonna convince them."

"If you all won't believe me they won't either, I don't care."

"You don't care what happens to you for the rest of your life?"

"If it's gonna happen, let it happen."

Parker sounded like a man who had given up hope.

Riley asked Victor Zarate about the second weekend in August. Confident of his alibi, Zarate readily talked about his job. He never took Fridays or Saturdays off, and he could prove it. "I got my check stubs here too, that I worked." He looked through the stubs and said, "Ooh, yep, these the ninth."

Getting back to the crime itself, Riley began with a cordial good-cop tone and one of his favorite similes. "It's just like putting together a jigsaw puzzle . . . either the piece fits or it doesn't fit . . . you go and you talk to these people and they tell you bits and pieces of the story and you piece those things together. You put 'em together and you try to make a picture."

Zarate matched the amiable tone. "Pat, but like I told you, I wasn't in Phoenix, nothing like that. I was at work, and I basically do the same thing every weekend."

Later Riley tried another technique he had used on McGraw. "Nothing that we've been told so far indicates that Victor had anything to do with killing anybody, okay? But it does indicate that Victor, unfortunately, was at a place that he probably did not want to be, when all this stuff was going on. . . . What we don't know is what exactly your involvement in that whole process was—"

"No, no way—"

"—at this temple when this thing happened."

"Oh, no, no. I swear to God, I was not out of town."

"Well, you were, though."

Scoville spoke up. "We're not saying . . . that you killed anybody, all right?"

"But you guys did say that I was there, which I wasn't there." Zarate still had faith in his alibi. "If you look up on my work and everything you'll see that that's true. It will prove that."

Scoville didn't want to hear it. "Do you ever drink, Victor?"

"I do once in a while, yeah."

"Did you ever drink enough that you forget?"

"No."

"There's no chance that you were there and you forgot?"

"No way. No."

Riley recycled the principle he had explained to Parker: two people couldn't tell the same story "unless they experience it." He didn't mention the possibility that two suspects might tell the same story because detectives had fed them the same details.

Scoville, too, soon recycled a technique he had used on Parker: his "Did so—Did not" style of arguing. Zarate said, "I'm serious. Like I said, I was not there."

"No, you're not serious."

"Yes, I am very serious."

"You're not serious at all." And so on.

Scoville told Zarate that his boss said he hadn't worked that night. This was a lie: the task force had not yet talked to Zarate's boss. Scoville followed it with another lie: that Zarate's girlfriend had not confirmed his alibi. He painted a grim scene of Zarate on trial. "She's going to testify against you, holding your little baby, and . . . say, 'He wasn't home.'

She'll be crying. You're going to have all your friends tell everybody that you were there."

Ignoring the part about the crying girlfriend, Zarate protested, "Leo Bruce would never tell you that I was there, when I was not there."

Scoville speculated about why Victor's friend and girlfriend would both say he was involved in the crime if he was innocent. "Are Leo and your girlfriend seeing each other?"

"No, no."

"So they're not plotting this against you. The whole world's not plotting this against you."

"No, something, something's wrong here."

"Yeah, you're right. Something's wrong and it's you."

Three hours into the interrogation, Riley took Zarate out into the hallway to be photographed. Meanwhile, Detective Griffiths walked Leo Bruce down the hall. The suspects did not speak, but Riley noted "definite eye contact" between them.

According to Riley, seeing Bruce left Zarate visibly shaken. When the questioning resumed, he had a "distraught look" and seemed about to cry.

"I don't know why my friends pointed at me," Zarate said. "I don't have no idea why . . . . I never did nothing to them."

"They were there," Riley told him.

"That's where I'm lost." Zarate did sound distraught. "Everybody says I was there. And I say I wasn't there. I wasn't there, I don't know what else to say. I don't know what else to do. I'm telling the truth. I don't know what else to say. Everybody's against me."

"What are you afraid of?"

Zarate described his plight in a nutshell. "I'm afraid of something I didn't do."

The rest of Scoville and Riley's initial stint with Zarate was a relentless barrage of accusations. For Zarate, it must have been a nightmare. He was lost in a maze, and every path he took led to "guilty."

For example, Scoville challenged him, "Give me one thing that will make me believe you, anything."

Zarate tried desperately. He had worked that night. "It doesn't matter, you had plenty of time to be up here." He was with his girlfriend. "Nah. She says you weren't there." His boss would vouch for him. "He doesn't remember seeing you."

"You can't give me anything," Scoville scoffed. "I guarantee you can't give me anything because you were there."

"I was not there."

"The only thing that you can give me is the truth."

"That's what I'm giving you."

"You're a hundred miles away from the truth, partner. And you're going downhill fast. Remember when I told you, your time is running out on you?"

"Yes, yes, yes."

"It's running a lot faster than you think it is."

Trapped though he was, Zarate did not collapse. Realizing that Riley and Scoville were getting nowhere, Kimball ordered them to stand down and sent in an interrogator with a very different style. Sgt. Pat Cooper took over questioning Zarate at about 6:30 p.m.

Twenty or so hours before Cooper introduced himself to Zarate, room 466 still held Mark Nunez, and Riley was feeding him bits of information. Riley said Nunez had been in the other vehicle, not the Bronco. Dante and Leo and some other dude were with him.

Nunez asked, "Leo what?"

"Bruce."

"Leo Bruce was in the car?"

"Yeah."

As Riley and Woodling hammered at him, Nunez sounded less and less sure of himself. "I don't remember what happened that weekend. I told you, I told you, I told you." "I need to call Javier and ask him if I was with him that weekend. And other than that I don't know what's going on. I don't know what to tell you. I pray to God, I wish I did."

Riley mocked him. "You? Pray to God? What is He going to think?"

Instead of wilting under the sarcasm, Nunez seemed to rally. "I know for a fact, I didn't do nothing wrong. . . . You're blaming me for something I didn't do."

"I'm not blaming you for something you didn't do."

"Oh, you're blaming me for seeing something I didn't see."

"So why do you keep going back to that you didn't do anything wrong?"

"Well, because I'm stuck here where I shouldn't belong. I should be home in bed right now, getting ready for school tomorrow."

Woodling said Nunez couldn't control what happened at the temple.
"I wish I [had] control over *this* situation. I'm not worried about *that*
situation 'cause I was not around to have any control of it." Nunez added,
"I'm not that stupid, I'm not that irresponsible."

By this time Riley and Woodling were finishing each other's thoughts
like a long-married couple. Riley spoke first. "It doesn't take an irresponsible person to kill somebody."

Woodling: "It does take an irresponsible person to witness someone
being killed, to know about a murder."

Riley: "It takes an irresponsible person, though, to not to tell what
they know."

Nunez held firm. "I don't know anything."

Woodling introduced a new threat. This refusal to talk must mean
that Nunez had "more than just knowledge"—that he was one of the
killers.

Nunez heard the threat loud and clear. "I'm scared, I don't know where
to go, I don't know what to do, what to say. And you're telling me I know
something I don't know. And I don't—how is that supposed to feel? . . .
to feel your gut busted and out of school and stuff . . . not knowing what's
going on and someplace out of town and blamed for something that you
weren't there, or didn't do."

Nunez may have been wavering, but he wasn't ready to break. He
made the same clear denial that Leo Bruce would repeat endlessly in
room 426: "I wasn't there."

Just then the brass sent in MCSO sergeant Mark Mullavey to shake
up the suspect. He opened the door and asked, "Is he fucking with you?
These other people say . . . he was there with the rest of them. Said he was
blinking his lights, the whole nine yards." Having delivered that ominous
if puzzling news, the sergeant disappeared.

Mullavey's mission was an instant success. Nunez wailed, "I can't
believe this." And a moment later he surrendered. "On my word I can't
remember . . . you must be right, I must have been there."

From the prop room, Sgt. Cooper returned Leo Bruce to room 426 and
handed him over to his next interrogator: not a team this time, just DPS
agent Richie Martinez, who had made a brief appearance earlier.

Martinez began with a sympathetic approach, saying he wanted details because "if you are innocent, and you don't have any involvement, it's got to be real easy to check out."

As if relieved at this apparent willingness to consider his innocence, Bruce answered readily as Martinez took him back over his work schedule and his daily routine. In fact, Martinez had little interest in those details and even less interest in checking out Bruce's alibi. In police parlance, Martinez was a "fresh face." Sometimes that's all it takes—a new, unfamiliar interrogator—to turn denial into confession. Martinez's assignment was to break through Bruce's defenses and replace "I wasn't there" with "I did it." Accordingly, he soon switched from sympathy to the accusatory style Bruce had already endured from Casey and Munley.

Both interrogator and suspect seemed exhausted; much of their three-hour conversation was incoherent. At one point Martinez told Bruce, "I'm like you. I can hear by looking at you at all, I sense that you're a man, looking at you with my eyes, and looking at you with my ears, yeah. At least you've been working on it, you don't smell too bad, but I don't have to listen to the scent too light. I hear one thing, I see one thing too, you know."

Whatever language Martinez was speaking, by this time Bruce was speaking it too. He replied, "I'm the kind of guy who's big on the eyes, I guess. My eyes, they're wandering now, like, in a box."

Nearing the end of his shift in the interrogator's chair, Martinez left the room to consult with the brass, and Bruce fell asleep on the floor. The next sound on the tape is Martinez saying, "You're taking a little break here, huh? It's already 8:50 in the morning, time for work. . . . You said you had a gun in your house."

Bruce shook himself awake to face a new day filled with old questions. Still not realizing that he had a right—or any reason—to remain silent, he said, "I have a rifle."

After more questions, Martinez summed up, "It should be in the linen closet, in the corner. . . . It's a semi-automatic, .22 Marlin, tri-fold, long rifle? What color is the shot?"

"Dark color, with a light part to it."

"Okay. I'll check it out."

Bruce surely hoped finding the gun would convince the police that he was telling the truth. Martinez believed it would be the clinching evidence against Bruce: the murder weapon.

With Martinez's departure, Leo Bruce disappeared from the tapes for approximately twelve hours, though his interrogation continued. When taping resumed, Bruce would be a changed man, dramatically different from the one who had insisted, "I wasn't there."

In room 467, Dante Parker held his own through another childish argument with Scoville, which ended when Riley broke in to say, "You're boiling up inside."

"Because I'm pissed off man," Parker agreed. "Wouldn't you get pissed off if you was being accused of something you didn't do?"

Parker said he had a bad temper. Scoville commented, "Now you're telling the truth. . . . Bad enough to kill somebody."

"No, no, no, no, no. I couldn't kill nobody, never could and never will."

Scoville brushed that off. "We both know you did it."

If they were that sure, Parker responded, they would have arrested him. But instead they "just got me in for questioning."

"Do we."

"Well, arrest me then."

"We're just talking to you now, okay? Listen, we know you did it because we been talking to other people. We have evidence, the same stuff the jury's going to have." Scoville said the only thing they didn't have was "what's in your head."

"Nothing in my head about this, man, nothing. If there was, I would have turned myself in."

"Oh, you would?"

"I couldn't live with no guilt of killing nobody."

Scoville had an answer. "The cold-blooded person that went there to kill these people could live with it."

"I'm not a cold-blooded person."

"That's the way you're coming across to me, and that's the way you're going to come across to everybody else."

Riley headed off what might have become another Scovillean shouting match. "What are you gonna say to your mom, Dante, when she asks you why?"

"She knows I ain't do this."

At the end of tape 4 of Parker's interrogation, Scoville declared a break. He and Riley would soon move across the hall to begin interrogating Victor Zarate.

During the break, Parker met his next team of interrogators, MCSO detective Rick Sinsabaugh and DPS officer Larry Troutt. They took him to the Madison Street Jail, where he appeared in a lineup. Both Nunez and McGraw, viewing the lineup, picked out Parker and said he had been at the temple during the murders.

Sgt. Cooper did something no other interrogator had done: he let Victor Zarate know about the secret microphones. "Do you know everything we say is being recorded right now? . . . We are going to play to a jury, in your trial, your first-degree-murder trial, they're gonna hear every single lie that you did."

"Yeah, but I was not lying to you guys. I never lied."

A bit later Cooper executed a planned maneuver. "Let me play something for you. You know Bruce's voice pretty good, don't you?" He produced a small tape player and played a brief excerpt from Bruce's interrogation. The recorder in Zarate's room picked up only the interrogator's voice saying something about panicking and shooting; the suspect's replies were "Unintel." But Zarate must have been able to hear them. He exclaimed, "That's not Bruce's voice."

"This is Bruce's voice. Bruce told us that he's got the .22. You know how many hours it took for him to say that? About nine hours of talking, before he finally let that go."

Zarate said he didn't know anything about it, and Cooper hit back hard. "You're lying right to my face, Victor."

"No. I'm not lying to you, sir."

"Bullshit."

"No, sir, I didn't murder anybody."

"Bullshit. Bullshit."

Zarate gathered his innocence around him like a suit of armor. Hour after hour, Cooper banged away at him as if swinging a mace. Every time, Zarate took the hit, gritted his teeth, and repeated that he had nothing to do with the murders. And every time, Cooper countered with some variation on "Why would Bruce lie?"

Zarate apparently shared Bruce's faith that an innocent person does not need a lawyer, even when accused of a crime. He told Cooper, "I come up here to tell you the truth without a lawyer or anything, but I wanted to get this thing straightened out because I had nothing to do with those murders."

By this time Zarate had been in police custody for more than sixteen hours. If he had truly understood his *Miranda* rights, he would long ago have demanded to see a lawyer. Instead he tried yet again to explain himself rationally.

To Cooper, even Zarate's reasonable tone was a sign of guilt. A truly innocent person, he maintained, "would be going fucking bananas. Demanding things, that we were lying and had the wrong person. You're not doing that. You're a classic textbook case of someone who's just holding down until the end."

"I'm not no textbook person. I'm telling you the truth."

Like the other interrogators, Cooper spoke in various voices, from righteous accuser to sympathetic helper. At one point he lectured on the complexity of the investigation: sixty officers working on the case full time; 510 leads that didn't pan out; crucial information withheld from the press. Then came lead 511, from a person who told them things that "only the killer or someone the killer had talked to" could have known. "That 511th lead," Cooper said, "is what brought you into this room today. And I am telling you from experience of those 500 leads that you are guilty."

At other points he attacked. "Do you know the part that absolutely disgusts me about you, Victor? That the . . . seventy-one-year-old woman who worked, wouldn't hurt anything, is dead now because of people like you. That fucking disgusts me. And the part that pisses me off the most . . . is knowing that you can sit there and just lie your ass off over and over again saying that you weren't even there."

If Cooper's purpose was to get an emotional reaction, he succeeded—but the suspect still didn't go bananas. He said, "No, I'm not lying to you. I'm about to lose my temper. I'm going to lose my temper."

"Well, do something, Victor," Cooper urged. "Give it up."

Zarate kept his temper after all. "I was not there that night, sir. I was not there. I don't know nothing about it."

Zarate began to shift around in his chair and stopped making eye contact. Though Cooper must have welcomed these signs of agitation, he chided the suspect. "What are you fidgeting for? Why can't you just look at me . . . instead of your eyes tweaking back and forth and fidgeting all over your chair?"

"'Cause you don't believe what I'm telling you."

"Victor, I haven't believed you for one minute."

Cooper made it clear that Zarate would be stuck in that chair until he confessed. "If it takes three more teams of people coming in here, new faces, we'll do it. And you're going to keep lying to every one of them until one time you're going to say 'It's not worth it' and you're going to start talking—"

"I'm not lying to nobody, sir."

"Say it right to my face, right now. 'I'm not lying.' Just say it to my face without fuckin' moving your eyes and moving around in your chair."

Zarate complied. "Sir, I didn't do it."

"Fine," Cooper said. As if fed up with Zarate's earnest words, he got up and moved toward the door. "You take some time, Victor. Enjoy yourself sitting here, okay?" He left Zarate alone for nearly forty minutes.

Cooper's actual reason for leaving was a mandatory meeting. At about 8:00 p.m., task force members gathered in the conference room for a "full-scale debriefing." After two days and nights of bustling activity, with the interview rooms overflowing and officers working around the clock, Captain White called the meeting to bring everyone up to date on what everyone else had learned. Interrogators described techniques that were working, dead ends, breaking points. Detectives compared "the activities and knowledge levels of the remaining suspects, including Zarate." "Several sources," Cooper reported, "not only implicated Zarate but placed him in crucial positions during the shooting." White ordered Cooper to go back in and get a confession.

Mark Nunez now believed he might have been at the temple the night of the murders, but he had no memories of it. Over and over he said he couldn't remember.

"No," Riley insisted, "it's that you don't want to."

For Nunez, one type of desperation was giving way to another. At first he had been desperate to make Riley and Woodling believe him; by this time he was desperate to end his ordeal. With no understanding of his *Miranda* rights, he thought the only way to end it was to give the interrogators what they wanted. "I would if I could. Don't you think I would get myself out of it so I could go home? I want to go home so bad it hurts."

But desperation did not spark recollection. Riley tried to help, reminding Nunez of Mullavey's brief earlier visit. "About you blinking your lights. . . . Does that jog your memory at all?"

Nunez wanted more hints. "What kind of vehicle was it?"

Here Riley identified the second vehicle—"Chevy Blazer"—and threw in a few other details as well. "Both it and the Bronco were stolen in Tucson before you guys left Tucson and came to Phoenix. You and seven other people. . . . And everybody ends up out at this one particular place and you're in this Blazer. . . . Am I making sense to you right now?"

"Yes—no."

Woodling asked what Nunez wanted from them.

"Tell me what's going on?"

"We already told you what's going on. What do you want from us?"

"I want you to believe me that I wasn't there."

"I can't do that."

Asked if he owned a gun, Nunez answered with an emphatic no—and perhaps with a joke. "My mom would shoot me if I ever had a gun."

Tape 4 of Nunez's interrogation ends here. There must be a gap in the taping: when tape 5 begins, Nunez is in the middle of talking about a dream, and Woodling is the only interrogator in the room.

Nunez didn't remember much about the dream. "Just me being lost. . . . I don't belong."

Woodling played the shrink. "Don't you think your conduct of this symbolized . . . that you may be wanting, you want [to] talk about this?"

"Maybe. I wish I could, but I don't know what to tell you."

For several minutes Woodling offered encouragement, praising Nunez for trying to protect his future by going to college, saying he knew it was "real real hard" to admit something like this.

Suddenly Nunez said, "I remember seeing things."

"It's just you and me here," Woodling assured him, "and nobody else."

"We were out," Nunez began, but his voice trailed off.

"You wouldn't forget this," Woodling said. "You may temporarily, but then you would remember." He reminded Nunez of the evidence in the prop room. "If you saw those pictures, you wouldn't forget that."

Nunez finally agreed with Woodling's suggestion that he'd been out with Dante. Woodling called Dante "a bad dude," then said, "Okay. You don't have any control over this guy. . . . You're going down the road, well, where did ya go?"

"Maybe I was there," Nunez replied. "Maybe that night . . . he did something or mentioned something that I was committed to. And I didn't dream of it."

Woodling must have thought he could smell it now: a confession seemed moments away. He urged Nunez to say more.

Nunez did say more, but not what Woodling wanted. "I freed Charles Manson."

"You like freaked out. . . . Charles Manson situation?"

"No. I mean I let him loose, of jail. And he went crazy, he choked these people, and I had to shoot him."

Charles Manson was apparently too much for Woodling, who soon left the room. Riley reappeared with more questions, but he got nowhere. Riley and Woodling had worked on Nunez for three hours, from about 9:00 p.m. to midnight, without breaking him. Now Riley "came out of the interview and told [Kimball] that he simply couldn't go on anymore." Kimball sent in two fresh faces, himself and Sgt. Mullavey.

Leo Bruce was picked up at 11:30 p.m. on September 11, and his interrogation did not end until around midnight on September 12. So, after a long day at his two jobs, Bruce was interrogated for roughly twenty-four hours. He later recalled those hours as much worse than the ten weeks he spent in jail.

Interrogators can often identify a single breaking point, the moment when a suspect stops resisting and becomes willing to confess. When Bruce reached his breaking point, the tape recorder was not running. Tape 4 of his interrogation was not followed by tape 5. Approximately twelve hours passed before taping resumed, and when it did, the numbering started over. The rest of Bruce's eleven tapes are numbered 1 through 7, and their transcripts are labeled "Enhanced": "Tape #1—Enhanced," and so on.

While the first four transcripts are full of denials, the seven Enhanced transcripts contain only admissions: a detailed and apparently voluntary confession. During those untaped twelve hours, something prompted Bruce to make a complete about-face, from "I wasn't there" to "I did it."

The only evidence of what so thoroughly broke Leo Bruce is a report by Detective Griffiths. According to Griffiths, he went to talk to Bruce at about 9:15 a.m., and they were alone together for more than four hours.

In those hours, Griffiths noted just one moment when Bruce seemed to move toward a confession. When Griffiths told him the shotgun hadn't killed anyone at the temple, Bruce seemed to get an idea. "Not saying I am, but what if I was the shotgun shooter? What would happen to me?"

But then he said he didn't know if he was the shooter. "I don't remember being there. I don't remember what happened." Tears ran down his cheeks, and he took off his aviator glasses to wipe his eyes.

Griffiths asked Bruce about everything he did on Friday, August 9, from getting out of bed to watching TV at home after his second job. Bruce stopped there, saying he didn't remember anything later that night.

At about 1:30 p.m., Detective Todd Bates joined Griffiths. Bruce had now been awake for more than thirty hours. An hour after that, the interrogators gave him a Coke to keep him going—and made a breakthrough.

Griffiths retraced Bruce's day, eliciting more details than before. His alarm clock played music; he hit the snooze button to sleep a little longer; then he got up and took a shower. This time his memory did not go blank when he described getting home from work. Instead, he told a dramatic story.

Marky—Mark Nunez—came over and invited him to go out and party. He did go, taking his rifle for protection. They got into the backseat of a Ford Bronco. A Hispanic guy Bruce didn't know was driving, and a black guy ("later identified as Dante Parker," Griffiths wrote) was the front passenger. On the freeway going north, the Bronco began following a Chevy Blazer. Bruce drank at least six Budweisers in the car.

They pulled into a parking lot, and everyone but the driver got out. Mike McGraw and three or four other guys climbed out of the Blazer. Asked if Victor Zarate was one of them, Bruce said, "No, I did not see him."

The others entered the temple, and soon Bruce went in to see what was happening. Hearing a woman scream, he walked toward the sound and saw "bald men in monk suits," some standing, others kneeling. They looked "extremely scared." There was another scream, then a shot that sounded like a small-caliber weapon and a blast like a shotgun. Running back outside, he heard more shots, about fifteen from the small-caliber gun and two from the shotgun. Minutes later, the rest of the guys came out.

In the Bronco they drove straight back to Tucson. Bruce didn't know if anyone talked during the trip: "scared shitless," he wasn't listening.

At about 5:00 p.m. Griffiths and Bates took Bruce down the hall to be photographed. They walked past a black man and asked if Bruce knew him. Bruce didn't know his name but said he had been in the Bronco that night. Griffiths noted, "Bruce was told the subject's name was Dante Parker."

Fortified with more Coke and a Snickers bar plus a promise of pizza, Bruce gave the interrogators another breakthrough. It happened after Griffiths and Bates told him they had learned from other interviews that he was the shooter. As they pushed him to admit it, he "hung his head and tears came to his eyes."

Griffiths reported the pivotal moment this way: "I stated to Bruce, 'You shot those people, didn't you,' to which Bruce replied softly, 'yes' and tears came down his cheeks which he wiped away with his hands. He was then asked who he shot and he replied, 'All of them.'"

With that victory, the interrogators called a break and let Bruce have his pizza and a Sprite. In the hallway they passed Victor Zarate, who was being photographed. After seeing his friend, "Bruce broke down and started to cry."

Back in the interview room, the detectives were ready to start over with Bruce's alarm clock, but he told them that "up to the point where Marky Nunez came to his apartment, nothing in his statement needed to be changed." The changes he did make were major ones. Rather than staying outside when the others entered the building, now Bruce went in with them—and he was armed. "He carried the rifle in his right hand with the barrel pointed down. He told us the reason he took the rifle inside was to 'scare somebody.'"

In the temple he encountered a woman, who screamed. Then he saw the monks. "He yelled at the monks to kneel down . . . he was afraid because the woman kept screaming and then he began to shoot them. . . . He shot all of them in the back of the head and did not know how many times he shot each one."

After this confession, according to Griffiths, Bruce seemed relieved. His interrogators went off to consult with the brass, and "Bruce was allowed to lay down on the carpeted floor for almost two hours before being inter-viewed again."

When Sinsabaugh and Troutt began to question Dante Parker, Sinsabaugh played good cop, claiming he didn't see Parker as a cold-blooded killer, "but when I don't get the right responses, that bothers me." Troutt took the role of bad cop, speaking alternately with Sinsabaugh as if in a well-rehearsed routine. He played the family card, implying a threat to Parker's brothers, Peter and T. C. Sherfield. "We got Peter back. . . . They're picking up T. C. now."

Peter Sherfield had steered the task force toward Parker, but Parker did not retaliate in kind. "My brothers ain't got nothin' to do with this." Strong as he sounded in that assertion, the danger to his family penetrated his defenses. A moment later he gave the interrogators their first glimpse of victory. "I was drunk, and I was passed out . . . and I woke up at home." But he quickly returned to flat denials: "I wasn't there."

One portion of the tape has more pauses than voices. It seems Parker asked to use the bathroom, and once in there, he wanted to stay. The only audible words for several minutes are Sinsabaugh's "Come on out, Dante."

When Parker did return to the interview room, he refused to talk. The transcript typist noted one silence as "pause" and two as "long pause." Eventually Parker said, "I didn't have nothing to do with it, man. Why say anything further?" If he had really understood his *Miranda* rights, he might have saved himself right then by asking for a lawyer. Instead, he clammed up again.

Sinsabaugh tried a few conversational gambits. "It's fourth quarter, Dante. Fourth down, goal to go." Long pause. "The guns, everything. It's all coming together." Pause. Only one of his openings got any response. "My other question is, did you plan this?"

"I didn't plan nothing."

Troutt resumed threatening the Sherfields. He claimed that if Peter told them he didn't do it, "we'll let him say it one time and he goin' to jail." And that "there were eight of them and they're saying T. C.'s the eighth." Troutt was making this up: no other suspect, not even McGraw, had mentioned any Sherfield but Peter.

Parker still didn't talk much, but he held his own. To Sinsabaugh's threat that his lies would get him into "a world of shit," he retorted, "I'm already in a world of shit. I ain't got nothin' to lose."

Sinsabaugh gave a sermon. "Whether you believe it or not I give a shit about ya. And that's no bullshit because the fucking blood in you is just like the fuck in me. We're all the same. Regardless that I'm white and [you're] black, I've served with black guys in the Marine Corps. We had a code of fucking honor too. . . . All we're asking, Dante, is get your shit straight, man. . . . I just want to make sure that this wasn't pulling any triggers, my man, and that's the only thing I—"

Parker cut him off. "I guarantee you it wasn't pulling no triggers."

"How do I know that, Dante, when you're lying to me about other things?"

Troutt urged, "If T. C.'s not involved in this, man, give it up."

And Parker gave it up. "Leave T. C. out of it," he began. "T. C. don't have anything to do with this. Peter either." Troutt and Sinsabaugh heard the implicit offer: if they left his brothers out of it, he would put himself in it. The family card was about to win the game.

Sinsabaugh asked again, "Did you pull the trigger?"

Parker repeated, "I didn't pull no trigger."

"But you were there?"

Parker had now been in custody for fourteen hours and under interrogation for more than ten. On the tape, his next three words sound more like the gasp of a beaten man than the confession of a guilty one—but on hearing them, Sinsabaugh and Troutt must have given each other mental high fives. This time Parker did not repeat, "I wasn't there." Instead he answered, "In the car."

Riley, in his summary of the case, notes this victory without mentioning how hard the interrogators worked to get it. "At approximately 10:00 p.m., Parker ultimately admitted that he was at the temple the night of the murders." The battering exchange of accusation and denial is omitted; threats and coercion are scoured from the record. From the summary alone, no one would ever know that Parker's collapse occurred during a bruising give-and-take that became a give-and-give-more.

Resuming Victor Zarate's interrogation after the full-scale debriefing, Sgt. Cooper changed his tactics. For the first time he tried sympathy and compliments. The goal was still to provoke an emotional response, but now, rather than anger, the emotions he wanted were love and shame.

"You've led a very good life and you should be proud of where you are, and you've got a woman that truly loves you right now. You've got a child about ready to come into this world. . . . Your girlfriend is being talked to. She loves you very strongly." He added, "I am sure you are probably hurting for her. And how she's going to take it and how your mother is going to take it."

Cooper made an offer. If Zarate told the truth, they'd let him talk to his girlfriend and his mother "to put them at ease emotionally." He asked if Zarate wanted to change his statement.

"No."

So much for sympathy. Cooper needed yet another tactic. He asked if Leo Bruce was Zarate's closest friend. "Leo's pretty close," Zarate agreed.

"So if Leo was to talk to you, you would understand that Leo is not lying or tricking you?"

"If he tells me I guess I'll believe him." He had known Leo since third grade.

"That's a long long time," Cooper replied. "I wish I had a person I really liked like that. It's hard for a police officer to stay in touch with people from that long ago." He asked, "Why would Leo say that you were there?"

"I don't think that Leo has got his head straight right now."

"Leo's probably got his head straighter than he's ever had it in his life." Cooper's good-cop tone vanished, and the subsequent exchanges must have deepened Zarate's nightmare. For example:

"I had nothing to do with it. . . . I only told you about two hundred times."

"It doesn't matter whether you tell me one time or three thousand times."

"I don't know what else to tell you 'cause that's the truth."

"Tell me the truth."

"I been telling you the truth. . . . You don't believe me, you believe everybody else except for me, and now I'm stuck like this. I'm the only one that's been telling the truth and I don't know why."

"Every detective is trained to monitor body movements, and it's all a science, and you are doing things that tell me that you're having a hard time acknowledging the truth."

"If you were in my spot, saying what you're saying to me, you would be very nervous, very scared and unpredictable."

"There's one difference, though. If I didn't commit the murders, I would not have tolerated this as long as you have."

That jab made Zarate think of a lawyer again. "I don't know the legal system, I don't know if I can just tell you to get me a lawyer or whatever. . . . I don't know if I can make a phone call."

Cooper ignored the not-quite-direct request for information. "That's because you're not a hardened criminal."

"And if I can get a lawyer, which maybe he can come and do something, I don't know, 'cause I can't even afford a lawyer with the little bit of money I make, I'll have to get one appointed or whatever."

"They took the time to read you your rights? Correct?"

"Yeah, yeah."

"They also took the time I'm sure to tell you—"

"I tell you guys everything that I know and that's nothing. . . . I'm going to tell my lawyer the same thing."

Then Zarate seemed to contradict himself. "I want to straighten everything out . . . that's why I don't want a lawyer. I just might as well tell you guys everything that I know and everything that I don't know."

"When you go to court and you can't afford to hire an attorney, you know that they are going to give you an attorney."

"Yeah."

Might a more sympathetic listener, or one more concerned about respecting the suspect's legal rights, have interpreted Zarate's words as a request to consult a lawyer? Of course. Anyone in law enforcement would have recognized these statements, however poorly worded, as an invocation of Zarate's rights.

Perhaps to distract Zarate from his legal status, Kimball and White decided it was time to give him a tour of headquarters.

Kimball walked in and delivered a lecture about what Zarate was up against. Tucked into the middle of the lecture was its major point: "The last liar here gets the death sentence." Kimball also said, "One of the last people that we had to roll just rolled, and that's Dante. And I'm going [to] take you in and show you what I meant."

Kimball was Zarate's escort, with Cooper and Riley tagging along. The tour was intended to convince Zarate that he might as well confess because everyone else already had. The first stop was room 471, where they showed him the equipment used to track the interrogations. Each monitoring room, in Cooper's words, "was manned with a detective and was position[ed] next to the actual interview room."

The detective in room 471 was monitoring Dante Parker's interrogation. Troutt's threats had "broken" Parker shortly before, and he was now adding details to his confession. According to Cooper, Zarate heard Parker say, "'Victor's got the Bag,' referring to a black bag . . . removed from the temple." Questioned about this, Zarate "provided no additional or useable information."

Next stop was an office where Mark Nunez, whose second day of interrogation had ended several hours earlier, was asleep on the floor. Then, in another monitoring room, Kimball and Zarate listened in on Leo Bruce. By this time, Bruce was again being taped, giving his Enhanced interview. Zarate "appeared to be deeply depressed and/or distraught upon hearing Bruce's voice." Considering that reaction a good sign, Kimball and Cooper returned Zarate to room 466 and left him alone to think.

Returning after ten minutes, Cooper found Zarate on his knees. Offered another moment of privacy, Zarate replied, "It's okay, I want you to be here when I say it." He intoned, "As God is my father, as God is my witness, I tell this man the truth, about this killing. I have no involvement or nothing to do with this, and that's the God's honest truth. . . . Please take my soul. Amen."

"Nice touch, Victor," Cooper jeered. "But it ain't gonna work."

Nearly twenty-four hours before Zarate would see Mark Nunez sacked out on the floor, Kimball and Mullavey took over Nunez's interrogation.

The two sergeants were the task force's best tag team. They had perfected the technique of promising that if a suspect was straight with them, they would be straight with him. Suspects almost invariably took this promise as a way out of the trap they were in. Nunez certainly took it that way. Shortly after the new team entered the room, he began telling the story they wanted to hear. As Kimball put it, "Within five minutes, Nunez was incriminating himself."

Kimball urged Nunez to "lay it all out for us."

And Nunez began to lay it out. "Okay. I remember, I don't remember how I got up with them, I just remember being with them and looking around, going to a house."

Kimball talked to Nunez like a friendly uncle. "You've never been involved in anything like this before, have you? . . . We have a little bit of empathy for what you might be going through right now. We also have a little bit of an understanding of how hard it is for you to get it out. But you have to get it out."

Trying to please, Nunez answered questions about Parker and mentioned a Cuban named Tony. But he said Leo Bruce had not been at the church that night. There were other guys, but he didn't know them.

Kimball combined disbelief with encouragement. "Mark uses 'I can't remember' when Mark really means 'I can't do it, I feel I can't do it.' We know you can."

Mullavey asked, "Have you been treated fairly since you've been here?"

"Yeah."

"Yeah. We're going to continue treating you fair and square. . . . We need you to commit to us that you're going to be on the level with us. Just tell us who was there and then we'll get past it and we'll go on."

Nunez named Mike, Dante, Leo, Tony, Victor "or something like that," and a man he thought was named John Jones.

Inch by inch, Kimball and Mullavey nudged Nunez toward their view of what must have happened—the temple murders as scripted by Mike McGraw. At one point Kimball asked, "Why were these people killed?"

"I don't know, man."

"Yes, Mark, you know why these people were killed . . . tell me what you now know happened."

"People got killed." This compliant echo would later be treated as an admission of guilt.

"What kind of people got killed? Were they Anglo, were they black?"

"They were small like from India."

Kimball pounced. "How in the fuck do you know what the people look like, if you're outside?"

The response didn't tell him much. "Because they were small."

Kimball and Mullavey spent hours pressing for details to fit McGraw's story. Nunez told them he had stayed in the car while six or seven guys had gone into the church. They'd been wearing coats, dark sweaters, and light-colored gloves. Mullavey, thinking of August in Arizona, said, "Coats and sweaters. Do you know if it was hot?"

"That day, I guess it must have been. One of them I seen wear a big jacket."

"Who did you see in a big jacket?"

"Uh, Victor or Mike and the other guy . . ." Nunez's voice became inaudible on the tape.

Either his muttered words specified Victor, or Mullavey made an assumption. "Why do you think that Victor had a big jacket on?"

"Because he had a big gun."

"Big" was typical of Nunez's vocabulary for describing firearms. He said Dante's gun was black. Presented with a multiple-choice question, he decided it was an automatic rather than a revolver. Someone else had "a brighter gun." One weapon was left in the vehicle with him: a "small, little gun, like a twenty-two almost."

More multiple choice. "Pistol, revolver, automatic—what?"

"Pistol."

Though Kimball and Mullavey worked Nunez to the bone, they never got him to confess going inside the temple or killing anyone himself. What they did extract was a story about what might have happened while he sat in the Bronco listening to the radio. Pushed to guess how long the men had stayed in the church, he said, "A couple of songs," then revised his answer to "a whole song."

Asked if he'd heard gunshots, Nunez answered, "I'm sure I did, I know what they sound like. They sound like pops."

"Did you hear different kinds of gunshots?"

"I heard a boom."

"How many booms did you hear?"

"Uh, two or three."

Mullavey wanted to know what the men were carrying when they came out. The guns, Nunez said. Mullavey repeated the question, making it clear that he wanted a different answer.

Nunez seemed to be improvising. "It's a purse . . . like a box." He didn't see what was in it, but "I would guess money."

Mullavey asked how much money.

"A lot."

"What's a lot?"

"Couple grand."

"Who told you that?"

"I'm guessing."

"What's your guess based on, did you see money?"

"No. I figure they wouldn't rob anybody for a couple hundred."

Soon after that exchange, Mullavey halted Nunez's interrogation for the night. In the final minutes, Nunez asked, "Are you going to arrest me?"

"Are we going to arrest you right now? Ah, no." But, Mullavey continued, "because of the integrity of this investigation, we do not want you to go home tonight, so, what do you say to us putting you up in a hotel. . . . Take a shower, get a good night's sleep, we'll sit down, maybe we'll talk a little bit more tomorrow." He corrected himself. "Talk a little bit more today, it's already 2:10. Would that be okay with you?"

"Will I go home tomorrow?"

"I don't know if you will go home tomorrow or not. . . . Let's see how tomorrow goes, okay?" Mullavey added, "We don't want you to talk on the telephone . . . just because of the investigation. Mom knows that you are with the sheriff's office."

"Did she call here?"

"I think she's called here and asked about you. . . . We'll make arrangements to get in touch with her as soon as we can."

Mullavey left, and an Officer Dunn entered the room and introduced himself. Pulling out a pair of handcuffs, Dunn told the young man who had not been arrested, "This is just a formality right now, we are going to take them off when we get there."

Apparently the task force brass saw nothing wrong with extracting a murder confession and then telling the suspect he was not under arrest. Nor did they see anything unconstitutional in putting him up in a hotel on the condition that he not call anybody. Given the way his transfer to the hotel was accomplished, in handcuffs and under armed guard, it is little wonder that Nunez felt he *was* under arrest.

As it turned out, Nunez had no time for phone calls and little time for sleep. Checked into the Sheraton at 3:45 a.m., he showered and fell into bed. Around 5:00, Detective Munley dropped by and woke him for a twenty-minute conversation. At 7:30, other deputies woke him to take fingerprints and photographs. This time he stayed awake, refusing food but ordering orange juice from room service and using the new toothbrush offered by his guards.

By 11:30 Nunez was back at headquarters, where he spent much of the day waiting for detectives to find time to question him. The next portion of his interrogation did not begin until 5:25 p.m. The half-hour session was not taped; Mullavey's report is the only record of what was said. According to Mullavey, he "re-advised Mr. Nunez of his rights per *Miranda*." Then he pressed Nunez to specify who had been in the Bronco. Nunez named Tony, "Dante Parks," and Leo Bruce. If Mullavey's report is accurate, this was the first time Nunez had implicated Bruce. The previous day he had eventually agreed that "Leo" had been at the temple, but he had consistently denied that it was Leo Bruce. As for "the Blazer and/or Suburban," Nunez named Victor Zarate as the driver and said the passengers were Mike McGraw, Pete Sherfield, and a man known as C. C., or Crazy Craig.

Nunez was the first of McGraw's dominoes to fall. His capitulation gave the task force ammunition to use against the other suspects. Bruce, Parker, and Zarate were still being spoon-fed McGraw's story; now they would also be expected to swallow Nunez's supposed corroboration of that story.

Detectives Griffiths and Bates had pushed Leo Bruce to his breaking point and beyond—but his confession was not yet on tape. Just before 9:00 p.m. they ushered him back to his wired interview room to begin the Enhanced portion of his interrogation.

On the Enhanced tapes, Bruce is a changed man. His voice, rusty and anguished before, is now smooth and free. But the standard answer from the first four tapes—"I wasn't there"—has disappeared completely. His new standard answer is an acquiescent "Yeah."

With the audio recorder running, Griffiths made an effort to authenticate Bruce's ambiguous waiver of his *Miranda* rights, about which the typist had noted, "the answer did not record." Griffiths read the warnings again. "Do you understand these rights?"

"Yeah."

"Will you voluntarily answer our questions?"

"Yeah."

"I want you to just go ahead and start at the very beginning again . . . when you woke up on Friday, August 9th."

Bruce didn't respond. Griffiths offered, "You want me to go ahead and start for you?"

"Yeah."

Griffiths reminded Bruce of the smallest details. "You hit the snooze button, listened to music . . . finally rolled up out of bed about 7:15. And then you took your shower; why don't you go ahead and pick it up here."

Bruce spoke as if reciting memorized lines. "Took a shower, got—took my shower and got ready, got in my Buick and left for work at 7:40. . . . Got to the Custom Shutter Shop where I work at. Do I have say that all over?"

Bates chimed in. "Okay, we got that part, skip that part."

Bruce said Nunez had picked him up at 9:30 Friday night. Marky didn't tell him where they were going, just invited him to go partying. He took along his rifle for protection. Again as if reciting by rote, he said, "I get my gun, then into a Bronco, I was behind the passenger." Mark was with him in the back, a Hispanic guy was driving, and a black guy sat in front. On the freeway going north, a Blazer passed them, and they followed it.

"Okay, what happens then?"

"Then go up to the church."

They parked in a lot. Bruce didn't see any people at the building. Of the guys, the only one he recognized was Mike McGraw. Two of them were black; the rest were Mexicans. They all wore dark clothing but no masks or disguises.

Bates wanted to know what Bruce took into the temple.

"My .22."

"Meaning that you were going in there and do what?"

"Just to get somebody a scare and that's it."

"Chances are," Griffiths said, "if you got a gun . . . there are some other folks there that have got guns also. Isn't that true?" No answer.

"That would be the logical thing to think, wouldn't it?"

"Yeah."

"Yeah, I would think so. When these other folks that we would logically think would have some guns, chances are that they probably did have some guns."

"Yeah."

Bruce would not say he had *seen* other guns. Bates asked, "Nobody else had anything to scare anyone with?"

"If they did, they hid them pretty good."

As the story neared the actual killings, the untaped rehearsals paid off. Griffiths and Bates kept their questions short, and Bruce answered readily. The climax of his Enhanced confession took only a few minutes.

"It all happened fast. It was real fast."

"Okay. What happened?"

"The shooting happened."

"What started it?"

"The lady screamed."

"Why did she scream?"

"From fear."

"How long after that . . . does the shooting take place?"

"About a minute, if not less."

"During that minute what do you personally do? Are you saying anything to these people?"

"No."

"Didn't you tell me in an interview, that you told them to kneel down?"

"After."

"After the minute is over? Okay. Did they do that?"

"Yeah, except first, one man."

"Did anybody else say anything?"

"No. Everybody scream and stuff."

"Who was screaming?"

"The people."

"Many of the monks?"

"Yeah."

"Are they pleading with you guys?"

"I figure they were. I would say yes."

"Okay. So what do you do then?"

"Start pulling the trigger—"

"How many times did you pull the trigger?"

"Until they run out."

"And how many rounds would that have been?"

"About thirteen, fifteen, somewhere in there."

"Thirteen to fifteen. Was everyone shot by that time?"

"Yeah."

There it was, a tidy confession to nine murders. But when prodded to add details, Bruce faltered. He didn't remember which victim he shot first or where he was standing when he pulled the trigger. Griffiths tried to jog his memory. "Did you just stand in one spot, did you have to move, how did that part work?"

The next few remarks are inaudible on the tape. The transcript notes that Bruce, Bates, and "?" all spoke. The questioners may have been reminding Bruce of his programmed answers—but there is no way to know.

Then Bates said clearly, "So you moved? Were you in front of people or in back of them?"

"In back."

"So where were you shooting them?"

"In the back of the head."

Again, when Bates wanted specifics, Bruce couldn't produce. "Going back to the guy that was standing up, do you remember when you shot him?"

"No."

"Did you make him kneel down before he was shot or was he still standing?"

"I was scared, I wasn't thinking, it just happened."

Bates tried a simpler question. "How long would you say from the very beginning, the first shot was fired, until you fired the last one?"

Here the typist noted a "long pause." Finally Bruce spoke. "No more than a minute. No more than that."

Troutt and Sinsabaugh were ready to build on Dante Parker's admission that he had been "in the car." Troutt urged Parker to tell them what happened, "step by step."

"But see," Parker said, "I don't know what step by step because I wasn't inside the temple with them." This insistence that he had stayed outside was a natural response to the interrogators' technique of suggesting to each suspect that he was less guilty than his friends. McGraw and Nunez had responded the same way.

Troutt and Sinsabaugh were determined to get Parker to place himself in the murder room. They had discovered a surefire way to keep him talking: whenever he showed signs of resistance, Troutt threatened his brothers. Now Troutt played that winning card again. "I believe Peter was there."

"Who brought up Peter's name? Peter don't bother nobody."

As Parker gradually told it, the group that drove to Phoenix that night included Victor, Leo, Mark Nunez, Tony, Mike McGraw, Craig, and a black guy he knew only as Blood. Convinced by McGraw that "the black guy" was the ringleader, the interrogators figured either Parker or his brother must have planned the crime. First they accused him of doing the planning himself, but he denied it.

"No, no, 'cause if I would have planned it nobody would have got hurt."

Troutt said, "If you didn't plan it then there's only one person that did. Peter."

"No, I don't think so."

"Well, everybody says it's Peter. If not, you planned it, Dante."

Slowly, Parker did begin to present himself as the planner, though not of the murders. "All I told 'em was . . . if somebody comes in just hit 'em in the head, knock 'em out, or pull them to the side. And I told 'em, 'Man, there shouldn't be no need for no shooting up these people.'"

Once he got started, Parker told the investigators more than any other Tucson suspect did. He also piled inconsistency upon inconsistency, but to the task force brass, inconsistency didn't matter at that time. What mattered was that they now had enough to sustain an indictment.

Parker's reward was a few hours of sleep—very few. Sgt. Mitchell, who had taken both Nunez and Bruce into custody, was assigned to escort him to the Sheraton. Mitchell and Deputy G. D'Agostino checked Parker into the hotel at 4:30 a.m. on Friday, September 13; by 10:30 a.m. Parker was back at headquarters.

That morning Parker faced another round of questioning by his original interrogators, Riley and Scoville. Riley asked if he still understood the *Miranda* warnings, and according to the transcript, Parker "nod[ded] his head yes."

Riley told him a couple of points were still unclear. "Can we talk about those real quick?"

It was not quick. The first two tapes of the day were devoted to a supercharged effort to get Parker to implicate Peter. Sinsabaugh and Troutt had pressured him to confess by implying that he could keep his brothers out of it. Now, just a few hours later, Riley and Scoville pressured him to put Peter right in the middle of it.

But Parker kept resisting. So the brass, namely Captain White, took action. Just before noon, when Parker said yet again, "I don't know who planned it," White burst into the room.

"Dante, I'm Captain White. Okay, I'm in charge of the task force that's been working this situation." White wanted Parker to identify the guy he called Blood. "I know who it is, but I got to hear you tell me who it is."

"I don't know who it is."

Taking it as a given that Blood was Peter Sherfield, White said, "Dante, he gave you up." He claimed Peter had told them, "My godbrother, Dante, he's the one that did it."

White stayed for half an hour or so, adding his authority to the attempt to break Parker on this last point. His long speeches were reinforced by contributions from Riley and Scoville, all with the goal of nailing Peter. Finally White asked again, "It was him, right, Dante?"

Parker made no sound, but the transcript notes, "Shakes his head up and down."

"That's what I thought," White said. "Let him get some rest, the man is worn out. . . . Thank you, Dante." Mission accomplished, the captain departed.

To get Victor Zarate up off his knees, Sgt. Cooper said, "Let me show you something over here," and fed him some information. What he showed Zarate may have been a chart like the one on butcher paper displayed in the prop room, or perhaps it was just a list of suspects. "This is lead number 511 that I was talking to you about. You can disregard all this stuff. Do you know Craig? . . . You know Mark?"

Zarate focused on one name on the list, saying, "That's not my last name." (The prop room chart listed "Victor Saldate" and gave "Luster" as an alternate surname.)

Cooper brushed that aside and told Zarate this was his final chance to give them the truth. Once he was entered into the criminal justice system, it would be too late. "You will be booked into jail, you will be officially charged. There will be no opportunities for you to discuss anything, with any of the county attorneys or anybody else."

"Okay."

"Okay, and you have nothing more you want to say?"

"No."

Cooper left the room, but if Zarate thought the interrogation was over, he was soon disappointed. Returning, Cooper announced that Bruce had "given a full and total confession and he is going to come over and talk to you. Leo's even told us where the weapons were. . . . Now we've got the murder weapon and the person who admitted the murder."

"I'm glad you found it," Zarate answered. "It won't have no fingerprints of mine."

Cooper took on a badgering tone. "You're the only one that's gonna take a death sentence. Do you realize that? Because you're the only one that's not going to say the one little thing that will bring it down to a life sentence." And moments later, "You're a big man, I'm real impressed. I'll be there for your trial, mister."

Either Zarate's reply was utterly naïve, or Cooper's sarcasm was contagious. "Please be there. Maybe you can help me out."

"I'll help put you in prison. I'll help put you in the gas chamber, mister. That's where my help's gonna come."

When Zarate again said he knew nothing about the crime, Cooper decided to educate him: he took him to the prop room. But the field trip accomplished nothing. Back in room 466, Zarate simply reiterated, "I had nothing to do with that."

"Bullshit."

"People dying like that. No way."

"The people were fucking murdered. They didn't choose to die like that."

"I feel sorry for those people but I had no part—"

"You should feel remorse for the rest of your fucking life."

Asked what he thought of Leo by now, Zarate replied, "Leo doesn't seem to be that type that could do something like that."

"He's going to tell you he did it."

"He can tell whatever he wants, but I was not there. Poor Leo."

With Cooper getting nowhere, the brass sent in replacements. First Riley took over, but he made no progress. After a time Mullavey relieved Riley. He introduced himself and asked Zarate, "You scared?"

"Yes sir, real scared."

Mullavey claimed he'd just been talking to Leo. Zarate said, "I was not there and I did not see Leo there that night so I don't know what Leo had to do with it."

"Would he lie about something like that?" Mullavey asked.

However strong his faith that the truth would protect him, Zarate understood what the task force was doing to the suspects. "I don't know what Leo would do right now. You guys got him probably all scared over there. You guys probably make him say something that wasn't true. You guys try to make me think to say things that ain't true. You guys put things in my mind that are not, that not even exist."

Soon Bates led Bruce into the room. The plan, as Cooper described it, was for Bruce to tell Zarate he had confessed so that Zarate would "reconsider his denials." What actually happened was quite different.

Zarate repeated, "I don't know nothing about this. I was not there."

Mullavey turned to Bruce. "Is that true or false?"

"That's true," Bruce said.

Bates protested, "That's not what you said on tape a while ago."

When Zarate insisted he hadn't been out with Leo for years, Mullavey again addressed Bruce, "Is that true?"

"Correct," Bruce said.

Bates whisked Bruce out of the room; Riley stayed to give Mullavey a hand. Zarate enjoyed a moment of vindication. "See, I told you guys, I was tellin' you guys the truth."

Then Mullavey explained it away. "Your buddy was trying his best to save face . . . not to let you realize that he turned on you."

Minutes later Zarate said, "Please give me a lawyer now. I have no other words to say to you."

The reply came from Riley. "Victor, the only thing I have left to say to you is you are under arrest and you are going to jail for first degree murder, nine counts." But Riley *always* had more to say. "I've been trying to convince you that, hey, now is the time—"

Zarate interrupted. "I'm not change my story for nobody. My story is safe and my story is right—"

Mullavey broke in. "We're not going to talk to you anymore. You want to talk to us, you tell us you want to talk to us, otherwise it's over." And yet even Mullavey couldn't stop talking. "You're going to jail for first degree murder, nine times, regarding the monks in that temple. Think about it. You have handcuffs on now. It is not a game."

"I didn't say it was a game. I've been trying to tell you my part, sir."

"We know your part. We wanted you to tell us the truthful part, and you chose not to." Here the transcript notes, "Conversation stops."

According to Cooper, Zarate invoked his rights at about 1:15 a.m. After that, he was "formally placed under arrest and handcuffed," then "escorted to a secondary office to await transport to a detention facility."

Leo Bruce had portrayed himself as the killer of all nine victims, but he balked at implicating anyone else. Detective Bates asked him what the other guys were doing during the shooting.

"They're stunned."

"Does anyone else use a weapon?" No answer, but Bates went on as if Bruce had said yes. "What kind of weapon was that?"

"A loud one."

"You know what a shotgun sounds like, don't you?"

"I just know they're loud."

"How many times did you hear this loud gun?"

"I have no idea, just wanted out."

Griffiths took a turn. "Leo, how many people do you remember shooting?"

"Probably all of them."

"Did anybody else shoot anybody?"

"No."

Bates asked, "Why did you shoot everybody if you wanted to get out so bad?"

Bruce's answer matched Agent McCrary's FBI profile of the temple killers. "Stupidity."

After the shooting, Bruce said, nobody talked; they just got in the trucks and left. He denied overhearing any conversation on the drive back to Tucson.

Griffiths didn't give up. "Nine people don't die and, and you drive all the way back to Tucson, and there's not a conversation about what just went on. . . . We need to know what you guys talked about."

After more questioning, Bruce finally agreed that the men had talked in the Bronco. But he said only, "They all had mixed feelings."

"What kind of mixed feelings?"

"That it shouldn't have happened like that."

"But what else are they saying? Are they questioning you about it?"

"No."

"You are the shooter, right? In essence, did they ask you why you did that?"

"No."

Bates pointed out, "The conversation's not gonna convict you, you know. The shootings may, but the conversation—we just want to know what the mindset was going home. When you said they had mixed feelings, what did you mean?"

"It shouldn't of happened."

"Who was saying that it shouldn't have happened?"

"Me."

During the long interrogation, Bruce had named, or had answered "Yeah" when the detectives named, Mike McGraw, Mark Nunez, and

Dante Parker—but not Victor Zarate. Griffiths was determined to get that final name.

"You would lie for Victor, wouldn't you?"

"No."

It was Bates who lied. "Victor is telling us that you were there."

Bruce continued to deny that Zarate had been at the temple. Griffiths continued to insist that he had. Neither backed down. "Don't try to mislead me," Griffiths said, "Just say, 'Don, I'm not going to tell you.' Be honest with me."

Demonstrating that he had no understanding of his *Miranda* rights, Bruce replied, "That would be incriminating myself, won't it?" He was weakening, as his next answer showed. "Maybe he did, went in, after everything was going on, and I didn't see him."

Nunez had said Zarate carried the "big gun"; Griffiths and Bates wanted confirmation. Bates spoke as if Bruce had already put the shotgun in Victor's hands. "So the first time you saw the shotgun was when he had it inside, when you heard the noise?"

"When I heard the noise—"

"Victor was holding the gun at that time, correct?"

Bruce caved in. "Yeah."

"Say that louder for me."

"Yeah."

At this success, Griffiths began the closing ceremonies. "We have to go out and talk to our bosses. . . . We'll be back to let you know what's going on for sure, probably just a couple more questions and that's it."

At about 12:30 a.m., when Bruce had been in custody for nearly twenty-five hours, two deputies handcuffed him and escorted him to the Sheraton Hotel.

After Captain White's triumphant departure from room 467, Riley and Scoville wanted Dante Parker to confirm his wordless admission of his brother's involvement. But now Parker said, "He didn't do it."

Scoville and Riley alternated lines like duet singers. "Come on, Dante." "Tell us, tell us about Peter." "Come on, Dante."

Parker was singing a different song. "Nothin' to tell about Peter."

At that, White rushed back in and asked, "What's wrong?"

Scoville put it in a nutshell. "Peter wasn't there now."

White sounded disgusted. "Ah, there's no use for you now. You're gonna waste it now."

Riley and Scoville spent all of tape 19, the better part of an hour, trying to get Parker to implicate Peter. They said Peter was still talking to them. "He's going to tell us he was there, and he's going to tell us who planned it. And when he does that, your chances are over."

Parker wanted to hear Peter say it in person, but Scoville told him, "We're not going to put you two together."

"Well, how come I can't sit face to face with him?"

The truth was that Peter was *not* still being interviewed; he had exercised his *Miranda* rights and would not talk to the task force without a lawyer. Riley and Scoville needed the fictional version of Peter as leverage against his godbrother. Scoville said, "He isn't going to talk with you sittin' there, just like you wouldn't talk with him here." But, he added, "he's already given you up and he's going to give you up again."

The ploy worked, eventually. Near the end of tape 19, Riley said, "You call him your brother; he says, 'No, he's not my brother.' He's playing you. He doing a damn good job of it, too. You can't tell me that you're not smart enough, Dante, to keep him from doing that. I think you're smarter than Peter."

Parker gave in. "Peter planned it. That's all I'm saying."

It is unclear why the investigators pushed Parker so hard to implicate Sherfield—just as it is unclear why they so readily believed Sherfield's implication of Parker. Roughly twelve hours after this "admission," Troutt interviewed Sherfield a second time, with his lawyer present. Troutt read the *Miranda* warnings and took Sherfield through his alibi again, but he did not confront Sherfield with Parker's reluctant accusation, let alone take him into custody.

Riley noted the outcome of Parker's two-day interrogation. "Parker was advised that he was under arrest and was taken immediately before Judge Ronald Reinstein of the Maricopa County Superior Court for an Initial Appearance. Parker was then booked into the Maricopa County Jail."

Victor Zarate's refusal to talk without a lawyer lasted only half an hour. Confined in the secondary office, he banged on the door and told Deputy

Danny Gonzales he wanted to see Cooper. Instead of continuing to exercise his right to remain silent, Zarate gave the task force another chance to break him.

Cooper and Riley reinstalled Zarate in room 466. Cooper made it official. "By law we can't talk to you unless you're telling us right now that you want to talk to us. Is that correct?"

Zarate burst into speech. "Yeah, I want to talk to you guys about what was going on, and maybe these guys do got the wrong guy, 'cause this guy does look like me, and the only ones that I've seen is Leo and Marky, and I don't know if Leo and Marky can identify me, exactly you know, because Leo walked in here and told me I was not there."

If that opening was not entirely coherent, Zarate soon pulled himself together and showed a clear understanding of what the task force was doing to him and his friends. When Cooper told him Bruce had done the killings, he said, "I don't believe it was Leo." He went on, "You guys almost made me think that I did it, but you know what, I didn't do it . . . you guys almost made me switch my mind."

The suspect had just demonstrated high self-awareness, but the interrogator did not follow suit. Cooper replied, "I'm not gonna let you say things just because I want to hear it."

Zarate made another cogent comment. "Something is wrong with this whole investigation. . . . People are lying." Later he came back to that thought. "I don't know why people are lying."

Cooper was so close to the truth that, unlike Zarate, he couldn't see it. "They're lying to save their lives right now," he said, then quickly corrected himself. "That's what it started off to be, but people aren't lying right now, Victor."

"You got all these people scared. . . . You guys have me scared, shaking and everything."

"Murdering other people will have the tendency to get people scared."

"Yes sir, that's why I'm trying to correct everything. I don't know exactly what happened because I was not there."

"Dante says you were there."

"I never met Tante. I never heard of that Tante name before in my life until right now."

Cooper repeated, "Dante."

"Dante? I don't think that I heard that name before."

"He knows you."

Granted this second chance, the brass gave it everything—and every-one—they had. Gonzales joined Cooper and Riley, then took over from them for an hour, speaking to Zarate in a mixture of English and Spanish. Scoville made a brief reappearance. Cooper was in and out. Detective Gary Labenz took a turn. Troutt showed up with a few tough questions. And the brass sent in their best closer, Rick Sinsabaugh, known for his skill at extracting confessions from reluctant suspects.

None of the rotating teams of inquisitors got anywhere with Zarate. This suspect made even Sinsabaugh look like a rookie.

Zarate's final tape, tape 15, deserves to be inducted into the Interrogation Hall of Infamy. He was hammered by four officers, Sinsabaugh, Troutt, Labenz, and Cooper. At times room 466, with its three chairs, must have been bursting at the seams—especially when Troutt brought in Dante Parker.

Sinsabaugh didn't introduce Parker, just said, "This guy's done a lot of hard time . . . he's been around."

Everyone shut up and waited for Zarate's reaction; the transcript notes a long pause. Finally he broke the silence. "I don't know you, dude. You ever see me?"

"No," Parker answered. "Your buddies said something, dude."

But when Zarate asked again, he got the opposite answer. "Have you seen me?"

"Yep."

Sinsabaugh joined the conversation. "He's already picked you out, my man."

This meeting of supposed partners in crime was the last straw for Zarate. After Sinsabaugh and Parker left, Troutt tried to pick up the questioning, but Zarate stopped him. "No, that dude read my rights, man, and I want no part of it."

So the interrogation fizzled to an end. As Gonzales led Zarate out of the room, the tape picked up his voice one last time. "I'm just saying, man, you know, I'm innocent."

As the only suspect who had not confessed, Zarate was not invited to enjoy the task force's hospitality at the Sheraton. Instead, at approximately 9:00 a.m. on September 13, he was booked into the Maricopa County Jail on nine murder charges.

RECANTATIONS AND INDICTMENTS

5

At lunchtime on Friday, September 13, Agnos, White, and the rest of the task force brass had reason to feel like celebrating. Four confessions on record: an impressive outcome for three hectic days. True, Victor Zarate had not confessed, but he was tucked away in a jail cell with time to reconsider his denials. The other suspects were still at headquarters, but they would soon appear before judges and join Zarate in the Maricopa County Jail.

It was the county attorney's office that brought the long interrogations to a close. As Kimball later put it, "Fearing claims of coercion due to the length of time the Tucson suspects were being interrogated, prosecutors demanded that the suspects either be booked or released. Five were taken to jail, including Victor Zarate, who did not confess. Would never confess."

If any task force members were superstitious, that afternoon's events confirmed their belief that Friday the thirteenth was unlucky. The case that seemed so neatly sewed up at noon began to unravel before suppertime.

In Mark Nunez's brief and busy first stay at the Sheraton, he had followed Sgt. Mullavey's instruction not to make any phone calls. His second night in the hotel was apparently uninterrupted, and on Friday morning, after his orange juice, he called home and spoke to both his grandmother and his mother. During the half-hour conversation, according to the deputy guarding him, he "cried several times and was visibly upset." Strengthened by the call, Nunez—the first of McGraw's unfortunate friends to confess—would soon become the first to recant his confession.

By early Friday afternoon Nunez was back at headquarters, stashed in an empty office to be available for more questioning. When Sgt. Mullavey went in to ask what his sister knew about the murders, Nunez changed the subject. "I lied to you last night," he said. "I wasn't there, I'm not involved." Nunez asked to talk to an attorney; Mullavey stopped talking and left the room.

Under interrogation, Nunez had been unsure what he had done on August 9, and the detectives had convinced him he must have been too drunk to remember. But his mother's memory was clear, and so was her voice as she spoke up to the authorities who had her son in custody. He had been in Tucson that night; she had seen him at 8:00 p.m., at midnight, and again at 3:00 a.m., when he came home from the Over 50s Club and woke her by cooking a steak.

Romelia Duarte was Nunez's biological mother. After his birth, she had moved away, leaving the baby with her own mother, who adopted him. Duarte later came back to live in the family house in South Tucson. Talking to detectives, Mark called her his mother-slash-sister. From the time of his arrest, Duarte became her son-slash-brother's most vocal champion.

Duarte was also Mike McGraw's aunt, and she knew very well how her nephew, Mark's cousin-slash-accuser, had earned his nickname, Crazy Mike. Interviewed by the task force, she described McGraw as mentally disturbed and a compulsive liar, though intelligent and streetwise. She also said he had told her not to worry, "that nothing was going to happen to the persons he named, and that when it is all over he would be rich."

Duarte rallied her neighbors in South Tucson. On Saturday, September 14, and again the following Monday, neighborhood residents protested the arrests of Nunez and the others. Protesters carried signs reading "Wrongfully accused, minorities used as scapegoats," and "Innocent until proven guilty, not guilty until proven innocent." Duarte prepared a statement referring to the jailed men as "sacrificial lambs." Demonstrations were also held on the steps of the state capitol in Phoenix.

Javier Cuesta, the friend Nunez usually partied with, turned out to have been out of town on the weekend of the murders, so he could not give Nunez an alibi. But he had plenty to say about all the suspects but Parker. "Leo is a real crybaby." "Victor, he's probably pissed off as hell." Mark, he said, was "real quiet"; "he don't know how to express himself a lot." As for McGraw, Cuesta's information might have saved the task force months of useless effort, if only anyone had listened to him. "Mike is schizoid," he said. Mike's story was "one big hallucination." Mike had pulled tricks like this all his life: "stolen cars, burned houses down, shot guns . . . and every time he's done something, he always involves people in the neighborhood." So the neighborhood did not believe McGraw's story about the temple murders, and residents were "mad and frustrated" because the men McGraw had named were in jail. "They read all that's going on, and they feel like [the suspects] are convicted already."

Witnesses confirmed Romelia Duarte's statement that Nunez had been at the Over 50s Club the night of the murders. The task force brass ignored his alibi and kept investigators searching high and low for evidence to corroborate his confession.

Meanwhile, county attorneys presented their case against Nunez to a grand jury. Like a trial jury, a grand jury is composed of citizens called to do their civic duty. Unlike a trial jury, the grand jury functions in secret. It examines evidence presented by a prosecutor, and it can issue an indictment, which is handed up to a court. Through this process, suspects can be bound over for trial without any chance to hear the evidence against them or to present evidence in their defense.

The grand jury duly indicted Nunez, and he was locked up in the Maricopa County Jail to await his trial. He would be confined there for seventy-one days.

After getting Leo Bruce's Enhanced confession on tape, the task force had granted him, too, a respite at the four-star Sheraton. Deputies D. Zebro and D. Chrissinger checked him in at 12:45 a.m. Bruce slept until 7:00 a.m., then ordered blueberry pancakes from room service. (Chrissinger reports that he also ordered "sausage, 3 patties" but was too full to eat it. Whether the deputies ate the sausage themselves or let this taxpayer-funded food go to waste is not recorded.) After breakfast Bruce phoned his mother and talked for about ten minutes. At 1:15 p.m. his escorts delivered him to headquarters.

Detectives Griffiths and Riley joined Bruce to tie up loose ends in his confession. But the minute they walked in, Bruce announced that "he wanted to make some corrections in his statement."

A night's sleep, a hearty breakfast, a talk with his mom—something had changed Leo Bruce overnight. He now declared that his story was true only up to the point when Marky Nunez came to his apartment. Because of the "pressure you guys were putting me under," he had made up the rest, using information from the prop room. Now he remembered he had an alibi for the night of the murders: he had been at his friend Brenda's place, and several people could vouch for him.

The detectives quickly ended that conversation and went to find out what had caused this about-face. Griffiths questioned Zebro and Chrissinger, who told him about Bruce's phone call but said they didn't know what he had said because they didn't understand Spanish. Later, when the press asked what had made him recant his confession, Bruce said his mother had urged him to go back to the police and tell them the truth.

Bruce had not offered his alibi during his first seven hours of interrogation because he was too busy denying involvement in the crime. He later explained the omission with a question: Since they wouldn't believe him about *not* being at the temple, why would they believe him about being at work? He had not offered the alibi during the untaped twelve hours of his interrogation because of the same exhaustion and hopelessness that had induced him to give the inquisitors what they wanted. And he had not offered it in his three-hour Enhanced interview because he had been concentrating on reciting the false confession Griffiths and Bates had elicited from him between tapes.

The task force brass did not believe Bruce's recantation, but once he changed his statement and provided an alibi, the team was forced to investigate, rather than just interrogate. MCSO detectives Gary Eggert and Munley went to Tucson and took statements from Bruce's friends and employers, who confirmed the alibi. Bruce had been at Brenda Collins's place that Friday night, August 9. He had gone to Joey Looper's house for a spaghetti dinner, then back to Brenda's, where he had stayed until about 1:00 Saturday morning.

Glenn and Peggy Armentrout, Bruce's bosses at the Custom Shutter Shop, told investigators he had worked eight hours for them on August 9. They described him as a quiet person, very dependable, "a follower and definitely not a leader." At the Tucson Greyhound Park, supervisors and co-workers praised his work ethic, his personality, and his reliability. No one who knew Leo Bruce thought he was capable of murder—except, apparently, his neighborhood acquaintance Crazy Mike McGraw.

Ballistics testing, which the investigators expected to clinch the case against Bruce, instead dealt it a major blow. The state crime lab determined that Bruce's Marlin .22-caliber rifle, found in a closet at his mother's house, was not the murder weapon.

The task force learned something else about Bruce when they got around to checking his criminal record. He had never been suspected of, arrested for, charged with—let alone convicted of—any crime. As Bruce said years later, his one and only involvement with the police was when they took him to Phoenix and "made me say I did something that I couldn't ever have done."

Like Mark Nunez, Leo Bruce was indicted by grand jury. And like Nunez, he spent seventy-one days in the Maricopa County Jail.

For Dante Parker, Thursday, September 12, had been a very long day followed by a very short night. Picked up at 8:15 a.m., driven to Phoenix, interrogated until around 3:00 a.m., he didn't leave for the Sheraton until 4:00 Friday morning. After a stop at Jack in the Box for a patty melt and a large 7UP, he and his escorts reached their room at about 4:30, and he was in bed by 4:45. Up at 8:30 a.m., he ordered a room-service breakfast of scrambled eggs, bacon, toast, and orange juice, then made two phone calls "to unknown persons." At 10:30 a.m. he was taken back to task force headquarters.

Parker, too, was indicted for the temple murders, but his indictment did not come from a grand jury. Instead, the county attorneys presented their case against him in a preliminary hearing before Judge Ronald S. Reinstein. According to the *New York Times*, "Officials refused to say why Mr. Parker's case was handled separately, or if the grand jury had declined to indict him." Parker's court-appointed attorney, Stanley Slonaker, suggested another reason for the hearing: he thought the prosecutors wanted to avoid burdening a grand jury with the large number of alibi witnesses he planned to call on his client's behalf.

At a preliminary hearing, unlike a grand jury proceeding, defendants have the right to be present, to hear the evidence against them, and to present evidence in their defense. In Arizona the burden of proof at such a hearing is light. The prosecutor only has to establish probable cause that a crime was committed and that the defendant committed the crime.

Parker's hearing began on September 23, ten days after his arrest, and lasted nearly two weeks. Slonaker represented him; three assistant county attorneys represented the State. Eight detectives testified. Friends and neighbors took the stand to describe Parker's life in Tucson. In Slonaker's "offer of proof" concerning Parker's alibi, he proposed to call thirty-one witnesses. Judge Reinstein allowed him to call six.

Despite Slonaker's long list of witnesses, establishing an alibi for Parker was not an easy task. Under interrogation, he had claimed that he spent the night of the killings with his then girlfriend, Rene. Detective Riley had used threats against Rene as one technique to induce Parker to confess, asking "Don't you care about Rene?" and "Do you want to see her go to jail?" When investigators tracked her down, Rene told a different story. She said she had dated Parker for about a month, but only in May and June. On August 9 she had been with her new boyfriend.

Other witnesses were willing to give Parker an alibi, but their memories were vague. The *New York Times* quoted typical testimony from the hearing. "'I'm not sure what night it was,' said one witness from Tucson, 'but I seen Dante Parker.'" Two such witnesses, Carmen Bell and her mother Dwennia Tillman, told Slonaker that Parker had attended a taco party at their house on August 9. After Slonaker filed his list of witnesses with the court, detectives interviewed Bell and Tillman and warned them of the penalties for giving false testimony. The women then declared that their taco party had been on a different weekend, and that they had not seen Parker on August 9 after all.

After the lengthy hearing, Judge Reinstein decided that the evidence against Parker (which was only his confession and the supposed corroboration of it by the other suspects) did amount to probable cause, and bound Parker over for trial. The judge set a trial date of December 16, 1991, which court insiders considered wildly unrealistic. They knew the prosecution would ask for the death penalty, and they knew it would take at least two years to prepare for a capital trial in such a major case. Like Bruce and Nunez, Parker remained in the Maricopa County Jail for seventy-one days.

Having jailed Victor Zarate without getting him to confess, the task force had more work to do. With this suspect, their interrogation techniques had failed. Now they began the real police work: the search for hard evidence that would convince a judge to let them keep Zarate in custody.

On September 13, the same day Zarate was jailed, Detective Shorts and Sgt. Bart Goodwin interviewed his girlfriend, Denise Mills, at the trailer Zarate shared with her and her children. Shorts called Mills "very uncooperative." She told them firmly that Victor worked nights at the dog track, including Fridays, and that every night for the past eight months he had come straight home to her after work. Shorts was dubious because Mills "had no documentation to back this statement." Mills also insisted that she did not allow guns in her home because of her children, and that she had never seen Zarate with a gun.

The next day, in the early evening, the task force executed search warrants on Mills's trailer and Zarate's parents' house. At the trailer, no one was home, and the door wouldn't budge, so Sgt. Cooper ordered Detective C. Lewis to get in through a window. Lewis reported, "As I pried upward on the window, the glass pane cracked but did not break out. I was able to gain entry through the opening I had created without further damage." Items confiscated from the trailer included a black jacket, a meat cleaver found under a bed, sandals, and "a greeting card in a red envelope addressed to Denise Mills and signed by Victor Zarate."

At the senior Zarates' place, Detective Sinsabaugh and others confiscated several pieces of possible evidence, including "a small dark green Buddha statue." The statue was trucked to Phoenix—along with Zarate's photo ID from the Arizona Department of Racing, a roll of undeveloped 35mm film, a black Raiders cap, a bill for some jewelry, tennis shoes, an aluminum baseball bat, two pairs of scissors that appeared to have blood on them, and a handwritten note in Spanish. This evidence was duly processed, but except for the statue, none of it seemed remotely incriminating to anyone but Captain White.

If the investigators could tie the little statue to the temple, or to a motive for the crime, they might persuade a judge to keep Zarate in jail even if he still refused to confess. On September 15 Detective Gonzales interviewed the suspect's parents, Maria and Victor Zarate. Mrs. Zarate said she had never noticed any statues in Victor's room. Mr. Zarate said he didn't know what Victor kept in his room, then asked if Gonzales was referring to "the Buddhist statue." If Gonzales thought the suspect's father had just contradicted himself, he was soon disappointed. Asked how he knew about the statue, Mr. Zarate explained that he had seen it mentioned in the search warrant log. He added that reading the log was the first time he'd heard about the statue.

That same day, the MCSO brass took the statue to the temple to see if anyone there recognized it. An impressive delegation—Captain White, Lt. P. J. Yale, and sergeants Riley, Kimball, and Mullavey—visited Wat Promkunaram, where temple members had assembled to talk to them. Riley showed the figurine to Chawee Borders, the woman who had discovered the bodies. He reported, "She immediately grabbed it from me and clutched it to her chest while also breaking down into tears." Then she "grabbed ahold of Capt. J. White and wept upon his shoulder. Mrs. Borders wept for several seconds and was very visibly shaken at what she saw. This exchange of emotions also resulted in Captain White's eyes tearing up."

After Borders calmed down, she said the statue had belonged to the abbot, Pairuch Kanthong. She had seen it many times in his room at the temple's former location, where she had cleaned the monks' living quarters. After the temple's move to Waddell four years before, women were no longer allowed to enter the monks' rooms. So she had not seen the figurine for the last four years, but she was sure it was Pairuch's.

Borders's statement linked Zarate to the temple. It was welcome news for the task force commanders, but they needed more than that to keep him in jail without a confession. They got a court order from a justice of the peace and served it on Zarate in the jail on September 17. By this time he had hired a lawyer and was savvy enough to insist on talking to him before agreeing to anything at all. He spoke to his lawyer on the phone, then complied with the order, which allowed them to draw two vials of blood from his right arm and collect hair and skin-cell samples. As it turned out, none of these matched the evidence taken from the crime scene. There were also no fingerprints or shoe prints that placed Zarate at the scene. The shoes, caps, and other personal items confiscated from Zarate's two homes proved to be just that—personal items. The only possible piece of incriminating evidence remained the "small dark green Buddha statue."

It was not enough. Four days after his arrest, Zarate was unceremoniously released. On September 20 he called headquarters to ask when he could get back his truck, which had been seized by investigators. Sgt. Cooper met him at the DPS lot and let him inspect the truck. Zarate found damage to the locking bracket for a storage box. Cooper noted that "the bracket had been forcibly removed during the search process" and told Zarate how to file a damage claim. "However, Mr. Zarate indicated that he would not file a claim and that he 'just wanted to get on with his life.'"

The task force wasn't ready to let him get on with his life—the brass hadn't given up on nailing him. On September 27, Lt. Yale showed the figurine to an antique dealer, David Adler, who said it was "a souvenir or good luck piece rather than a religious article. It is believed that rubbing the object's belly brings good luck." In November, Agnos ordered an independent evaluation of the statue. FBI special agent Gary Woodling consulted Henry Triesler, a local collector of "art-quality and antique Buddhas." Triesler announced that the Buddha from Zarate's house was not a Buddha at all, but a Hotei, "a figurine of a Chinese folk god of happiness." Not only that, but it was "of crude quality and little value." It was not likely to have been the treasured property of a Thai Buddhist monk.

The team also checked Zarate's alibi. He claimed he had been at work the night of the murders, and his girlfriend confirmed that statement.

But a loved one's alibi evidence is always suspect. Detective Gary Eggert went to Tucson to interview Zarate's co-workers and look for evidence at the dog track. He collected various forms, programs, and work schedules, along with a videotape recorded on the night of the murders, August 9. Part of Zarate's job was to start dog races, and under Arizona's rigorous public wagering rules, the races had to be videotaped. Screening the video for Eggert, the track manager pointed out Zarate at the starting gate just before the day's fifteenth race, at 11:02 p.m. The written documents confirmed that Zarate had been on duty that night. Here was clear proof that he could not have been committing murder a hundred miles away.

The tape and the work records got Zarate out of jail, but they did not end the search for evidence against him. More than two months later, Detective R. M. Minner checked the videotape out of the property room and had a copy made for headquarters, where he watched it with Kimball and Yale. Unlike Zarate's boss, they cherished doubts that the man on the tape was Zarate. Minner acknowledged that the tape "shows an individual similar in size and shape to Victor Zarate Jr. starting the dog race." But, he concluded, "At no time is the race starte[r] shown close enough for me to positively identify him."

Thus the investigation of Victor Zarate ended with a whimper. Despite the prodigious outpouring of manpower and the intense effort to extract a confession, the task force ended up with nothing whatsoever to connect him to the temple murders.

Being locked up did not put an end to Mike McGraw's storytelling. According to the Phoenix newspaper *New Times*, he talked to several reporters from the jail, "insisting upon his innocence and spilling out quotes." Although his public defender, Charles McNulty, warned him not to discuss the case, McGraw made more than a dozen phone calls to the *New Times* alone. The paper's reporter, Philip Martin, quickly realized what kind of witness the task force had found at the Tucson Psychiatric Institute. Martin wrote: "Interrogation? Mike McGraw does not have to be interrogated. He spews out information, whether or not you want to hear it."

Nor did being locked up make McGraw's stories consistent. Months later he would still be offering investigators tantalizing new details about the temple crimes—for example, claiming that he and the other men had posed for a photograph in front of the temple, holding their guns and a Phoenix newspaper dated August 9. From the jail he told a different tale.

In a jailhouse interview with the *Arizona Republic*, he proclaimed, "This has now turned into like a political case, and we're like political prisoners." He confided in the *New Times* that interrogators had coached him, telling him, "Do this and say this and whatever we say, you repeat back to us." They had also made "intense physical threats." "They, like, coerced this confession out of me. They kept me up, they kept all of us up, and told us that if we'd admit we were involved they'd let us go."

South Tucson residents were rumored to be furious with McGraw for implicating other guys from the neighborhood. McGraw denied this, telling *New Times* that "his old neighborhood pals [were] eager to see him." Eager to see him or not, his acquaintances were unanimous in telling the task force not to trust Crazy Mike. Romelia Duarte called him a compulsive liar. Javier Cuesta called his story one big hallucination. Under interrogation, Victor Zarate called him "the biggest liar of all," and Leo Bruce said, "he had his problems and I don't want to be involved with him." Even McGraw's sister, Gina, knew better than to trust him. She told him in a letter sent to the jail, "I love you, Mike, you're my only brother. You've done lots of stupid things in your day, but everyone knows you're no killer. But also everyone knows you like to open your mouth about things that you don't know about. . . . If you said what they said you said, I know you're lying, Mike."

The task force's own investigation of McGraw's criminal record turned up reports that while in prison in 1988, he had made one outlandish claim after another: he had information on an escaped fugitive; he knew people on the outside who were dealing guns and explosives; his own brother-in-law was putting out contracts on people; "something big was going to happen on the streets"; he was a former California highway patrolman and needed protective custody because there was a contract out on him.

With so much evidence that McGraw was a talespinner, and so little evidence that he and his friends had been anywhere near Wat Promkunaram on August 9, why were the task force brass so determined to consider McGraw a reliable witness? To skeptics—inside or outside the investigation—who pointed out that he was a psychiatric patient, the brass had a ready answer: McGraw was hospitalized because of suicidal guilt over killing the monks. The task force maintained that McGraw had known crucial details about the crime and the scene, but in fact he had learned many of those details from the interrogators. Here is just one example:

Troutt: "Did he have them laying on their stomachs? Face down? Hands up to their side?"

McGraw: "Yeah."

From exchanges like this one, the task force brass concluded that McGraw had an insider's knowledge of the murders.

In addition, Detective Riley, who wrote the search warrant affidavit based on McGraw's interrogation, edited McGraw's statement to fit the facts of the crime. For instance, where McGraw said the victims had been wearing mixed colors like Hawaiian clothing and a white or red gown, Riley changed it to a woman dressed in white and men dressed in orange robes.

Riley's reconstruction of events in his official summary of the case provides some hints about why the task force so readily bought into McGraw's bizarre story. McGraw's confession was collective: that is, he said much more about his former friends than about himself. His accusations of their foul deeds somehow softened his complicity. His eagerness to confess somehow made their claims of innocence blasphemous.

Over three days of interrogation interspersed with star treatment at a posh hotel, Crazy Mike convinced even himself that he and the others were guilty of a gruesome mass murder. His narrative was disjointed, but the overall plot made a kind of sense—the pulp novel kind. A gang of gun-toting drug dealers from Tucson, led by a violent psychopath, planned to rob a sacred temple of exotic treasures but ended up slaughtering nine innocent Buddhists.

For McGraw, the story ended there, but the investigators added a few chapters of their own. Enter the heroes, dedicated enforcers of the law. At first the scumbag perpetrators swore they had nothing to do with the crime. Then expert interrogators, with skill, patience, and teamwork, demolished the denials and broke all but one of the five suspects, thus giving birth to the media moniker "the Tucson Four."

Except for McGraw's statement—a bizarre, contradiction-ridden tale spun by a man with many names who called in his tip from a mental hospital—and their own confessions, there was no evidence against the Tucson Four. Their alibis checked out. Even McGraw, who did not offer an alibi, proved to have one: he had been at work when the Blazer and the Bronco were supposedly on the road to Phoenix. But the Four had confessed, so unlike Zarate, they had to stay in jail. Fortunately for them, once they were booked into the Maricopa County Jail, their fate was taken out of the clutches of the county sheriff and his task force and placed in the hands of the county attorney. Nevertheless, Mike McGraw, Mark Nunez, Leo Bruce, and Dante Parker would spend the next ten weeks of their lives behind bars.

THE FORGOTTEN
MURDER WEAPON

6

Leo Bruce's rifle was not the only .22-caliber Marlin semiautomatic collected by the task force. One of the others was lead 510, the rifle Detective Sinsabaugh had confiscated from Rolando Caratachea on September 10. Overshadowed by lead 511, Mike McGraw's elaborate narrative, that weapon sat in an office at headquarters for weeks, both out of sight—behind a door—and out of mind.

Attention did not turn to the other confiscated guns until after the Tucson defendants recanted their confessions, when the state crime lab reported that Bruce's gun could not be the murder weapon. Caratachea's rifle was not submitted to the lab for testing until October 21. On October 23 Sgt. Kimball got a call from ballistics expert Bill Morris, a heads-up on what the next day's official report would say: Caratachea's rifle had fired the .22-caliber casings found at the temple. Suddenly, if belatedly, lead 510 became the investigators' primary focus.

Back on August 20, a few minutes after the security officers at Luke Air Force Base had first seen the rifle in the trunk of Caratachea's car, they stopped another car, driven by Johnathan Doody, who said he and Caratachea were visiting the same friends in base housing. When Sinsabaugh interviewed the boys on September 10, both mentioned a third friend, Alex Garcia. All three lived in Glendale and went to high school in Avondale, towns in Phoenix's western suburbs near the air force base and Wat Promkunaram.

Sinsabaugh also gathered two bits of information that would later take on significance: Caratachea claimed that someone had borrowed his gun in August and returned it stained and dirty; Doody said his brother David had lived at the temple as an apprentice monk until shortly before the killings.

Thus what Sinsabaugh learned on September 10 connected all three boys to the temple: Caratachea through his gun; Doody through his brother; and Alessandro "Alex" Garcia through Caratachea and Doody. David Doody's name was added to the long list of people to be interviewed in the future, but Sinsabaugh's report, like the confiscated rifle, was forgotten in the excitement over the talkative Mike McGraw.

By coincidence, David Doody and his father were being interviewed at task force headquarters when the ballistics report arrived. Sinsabaugh had invited them to headquarters in the hope that David would be able to identify property stolen from the temple.

In the young acolyte's eyes, Wat Promkunaram was full of treasures. Sinsabaugh reported, "David informed us that there were enormous valuables in the temple. He said the monks always kept a large amount of currency on their person attached to their robes. One of the monks showed David a solid gold Buddha approximately six inches tall which was extremely valuable." To the disappointment of the investigators, David did not recognize any of the items confiscated from the Tucson suspects. But his interview did provide other information.

Master Sergeant Brian Doody, David's father and Johnathan's stepfather, had been sent to Colorado for training from mid-June to mid-August 1991. On his return, Johnathan had moved out of the house to live with friends. In September Brian had been transferred to Falcon Air Force Base, also in Colorado, and the family had relocated with him—all but Johnathan, who wanted to finish high school in Arizona.

David had lived at the temple that summer from mid-June until late July. Johnathan had visited him there regularly, often with one or more friends. On Friday night, August 9, David recalled, his brother had not come home. David thought he had stayed with Alex Garcia.

On October 25, the day after receiving the ballistics report on Caratachea's rifle, the task force set out to find its owner. At the apartment in Glendale where Sinsabaugh had picked up the gun six weeks earlier, he now asked Caratachea to accompany him to headquarters.

Caratachea's official interview began in room 467 at 3:53 p.m.; it would not end until nearly eighteen hours later. Sinsabaugh and Troutt were his first interrogators, with Sinsabaugh doing most of the talking. Caratachea chewed Copenhagen tobacco and asked for a Dr. Pepper. Sinsabaugh fetched the beverage plus "something to chew" for himself; he joked with Caratachea about sharing a cup as a spittoon.

Sinsabaugh read the suspect his *Miranda* rights, the juvenile version because Caratachea was seventeen. He interspersed the reading with conversation about future plans. Caratachea responded that he did understand his rights, he did want to join the navy, and he did not want a parent or guardian present during questioning.

After an hour or so, Caratachea named the friends who had borrowed his rifle that summer: Johnathan Doody and Alex Garcia. He said he wasn't sure why they wanted it, maybe for shooting at targets or road signs. They'd been practicing making silencers out of potatoes, and he said he'd seen a couple of carved-out potatoes in their car when they'd picked up the gun, plus a sandwich bag full of .22-caliber rounds.

Doody and Garcia kept the gun for two days. When Caratachea got it back, there was tape around the barrel, and the butt was scratched up. That pissed him off.

Caratachea hadn't lived with his parents since a fight with his dad early in the summer. He'd lived in his car, then stayed with a girl named Amanda, and in September he had rented an apartment with Doody and Mike Myers. He and Myers had kicked Doody out at the end of the month. "He almost made us lose the apartment 'cause he wouldn't come up with money. He was working at the commissary, but he'd blow it . . . he never saved any of it for the rent." Doody, he said, now lived with the Garcias, Alex and his parents.

Alex hadn't been around lately. He had run away with his girlfriend, Michelle Hoover, and since they'd been caught, no one had heard from him "because his dad kicked his butt." As for Doody, he didn't have many friends. "He's like a nerd or something, I don't know. He keeps to himself basically."

Sinsabaugh asked if the boys had friends in Tucson. Caratachea didn't know. He also didn't seem to know where Tucson was. "It's northeast here in Arizona, isn't it. Eastern."

When Sinsabaugh asked if Doody and Garcia had been doing any burglaries, Caratachea said they'd shown him some cameras, including one that made videos, and had told him they'd "jumped some people for it." "But I know that they were lying, just trying to make themselves look big."

Sinsabaugh waited about two hours before mentioning the temple murders. Caratachea said he didn't know any Buddhists, and he didn't know what nationality the temple members were. He didn't know Doody's nationality, either. "His mother is Oriental. I don't remember which of the Orients he belongs to." Neither Garcia nor Doody had ever talked to him about the temple.

From all the questions about his rifle, Caratachea figured that "the Buddhists" must have been killed with a .22. He tried to get Sinsabaugh to be direct with him. "Tell me something, when you checked the ballistics on my gun, did they match the ones at the temple?"

Sinsabaugh tossed the question right back. "What do you think, Rollie?"

He didn't think they matched. The gun belonged to him, so if the ballistics had matched, "that would of been evidence right there, and you could of taken me in. Why would you wait around?"

Ducking the question about the delay, Sinsabaugh told him that the ballistics identification was definite. "That's the gun, Rollie."

Caratachea said he hadn't killed anyone. "Okay, then, since that's the gun, the only person that had used it . . . was Johnathan Doody and Alex."

After Caratachea declared that Doody and Garcia had borrowed his rifle, officers were dispatched to pick them up. Caratachea said they would probably be at the football game that night. Doody would be marching with the ROTC honor guard.

MCSO detective Pat Riley and FBI agent Gary Woodling went to Agua Fria High School, in Avondale, and waited in the stadium parking lot until Doody came out. Riley drove him to headquarters, leaving Woodling at the school to keep looking for Garcia.

At headquarters, Sgt. Kimball greeted Doody and said he looked sharp in his ROTC uniform. Kimball sent him to room 424, where Riley and MCSO detective Dave Munley started questioning him at 9:25 p.m.

According to Riley, room 424 was well lit, with a comfortable temperature, three padded chairs, and "a hidden microphone for recording purposes." The room may have featured padded chairs, but, as Doody's lawyer would later complain, it had no table or desk, nothing a tired teenager could lean on.

Doody said he had never heard of the *Miranda* warnings. Before reading them, Riley minimized their importance, just as he had with Nunez,

Parker, and Zarate. "It's not meant to scare you or anything like that." "It's something that's for your benefit, as well as for ours."

Then, instead of reading Doody his rights, Riley talked about ROTC. Doody said he was in charge of the honor guard and the color guard. The color guard carried the flag, and the honor guard carried the rifle. It was fun, "except when you drop the rifle."

Several minutes later, when Riley finally read from the juvenile *Miranda* form, Doody said he understood his rights and was willing to talk to the detectives. As for whether he wanted a parent or guardian present, he said, "It doesn't matter."

Riley and Munley took Doody through his changes of address. That summer he had lived with Moses, then with Rollie and Mike, and now with Alex. In Doody's version of why he had moved out of Rollie and Mike's apartment, they weren't getting along, and Rollie had started doing something illegal, "like selling something."

Asked where they could find Garcia, Doody said he'd be at home. "He got grounded."

"He got grounded? What did he do?"

Doody laughed. "Ran away with a girl." They had taken her parents' truck and gone up north somewhere.

Doody had known Alex for about three years; he'd just met Rollie that summer. He and Rollie had been friends at first, before Rollie's "attitude problem."

"So who's your best friend right now?"

"Ah, Alex, and ah, yeah, I'd say Alex."

Doody said he had first heard about the temple murders at work. He worked at the commissary on the base, and "a lot of Thai ladies" worked there too. That Saturday the ladies all got up to leave, and he asked them why. Then his mom stopped by on her way to the temple. She was going there to find out what had happened, but she told him to keep working.

His brother had lived at the temple until about three weeks before the murders. Their mother visited him often, and also went to the temple to cook and clean for the monks. Johnathan went once a week or so, picking up David's dirty laundry and taking David American food he missed, like hamburgers from McDonald's. Sometimes Alex or another friend went along. The monks would invite them into the kitchen and offer water or soda or ice cream. David was usually sitting on the couch and watching TV.

Doody said he didn't know the monks, but he knew Boy. Boy's parents had sent him here from Thailand to get him away from a gang or something. He wanted a Terminator cup from Subway, so Doody got him one. When he handed it over, "we already drunk the soda and he asked us what happen to the soda."

Munley brought up Doody's future plans. He expected to go to college and then join the air force or the navy. Since he was five, he'd wanted to be a pilot, but now he was "kinda like conflicting" between becoming a pilot and joining the air force search and rescue team. He knew about search and rescue from being in the civil air patrol. "You're just out there with a radio and basically a map and a compass . . . there's no one around you to tell you what to do, and you got something to do that somebody depend upon you to do. It's a lot of fun."

He'd met his girlfriend, Vickie, in ROTC, and they'd been going out about eight months. But he didn't want to get married until he was a junior in college, "or as soon as I get into the service."

Doody denied ever using or borrowing Caratachea's rifle. Riley left the room briefly, and when he came back he implied that he had just talked to other suspects. He launched a lecture featuring one of his standard metaphors, the jigsaw puzzle. This time the piece that didn't fit was Doody's denial that he had ever "been in possession of" Caratachea's gun.

"Well," Doody said, "I've never borrowed it from him, but maybe Alex have."

Questioned about the night of the murders, Doody contradicted what his brother had told Riley twelve hours earlier. He said he had spent the night at home. He and his friend Brandon went to a movie. Afterwards he dropped Brandon off, got home around midnight, said hi to his mom, and went to bed. On Saturday he got to work by 11:00 and didn't hear about the murders until early afternoon.

Riley asked if he knew what happened to the monks.

"Just basically what the news said. That they went over there drunk or something like that and tried to commit burglary, something like that."

In his next lecture, Riley's tone was earnest and friendly at first but darkened as the sentences accumulated. Someone had thrown "a bad piece into that puzzle." Doody was lying. They knew he had information about the rifle and the temple, and they needed to hear it. He asked again if Doody and his friends had ever borrowed Rollie's rifle.

Doody gave him an answer of sorts. "I don't recall, but I think I remember Alex borrowing it, but I don't recall it at all."

Riley tried a new topic. Had the guys ever tried to make homemade "attachments or things like that for guns"?

That got Doody talking. "Alex had this book on trying to make a silencer and he wanted to try it out on an Uzi but the problem is he couldn't get ahold of an Uzi." Rollie gave Alex "this idea about a potato," but they hadn't tried it; they thought it was stupid. Then he said the book wasn't Alex's; it was his. "I have a whole bunch of a collection of books like combat survival."

Getting back on track, Riley asked several more times about borrowing Rollie's rifle. Doody kept saying he didn't know.

As both Riley and Munley hammered him with words, Doody stopped responding in any way. Riley wrapped up the series of monologues. "It's so important for you to tell us. I mean you have to tell us. You have to. Believe me, once we get past this milestone, it's gonna be so much easier."

Munley varied the metaphor. "Just gotta get over that hill. . . . You just have to open up and let us know what's in your head."

"Maybe it'd be easier," Riley said, "for me to [ask] you just this one thing. Who was with you?"

At last Doody spoke. "Me and Alex borrowed the gun for two days."

Shortly after 9:00 p.m., Caratachea learned that Doody was talking to investigators. Sgt. Mullavey stuck his head into room 467 just long enough to announce, "J. D. says that [Rollie] knew what was going on."

Mullavey was lying, but Caratachea didn't know that. He exploded. "Get that motherfucker over here. Let him say it to my fuckin' face."

Sinsabaugh tried to calm him down, then responded in kind. "Are you forgetting that you pulled a trigger and killed a fucking monk?"

"No, I didn't." Caratachea said he went to church; he believed in "Thou shall not kill." "I don't have it in me to kill somebody. I have it in me to beat someone's ass, but I don't have it in me to kill."

Describing Doody and Garcia, Caratachea painted a picture of classic high school misfits. "They don't have many friends at the school, they don't have any friends at all." As for Doody, "A lot of people make fun of him because he's oriental. Anybody that's in the ROTC, he's high in command, behind his back they make fun of him, to his face they make fun of him." "That's why I never thought J. D. had it in him to kill," he added. "Because he didn't do anything to people who made fun of him, all he did was just take it."

Sinsabaugh scoffed. "It takes no fucking nerve to kill, cowards kill."

"Well, J. D. is a coward."

Caratachea's shouting could be heard far beyond his interview room. Kimball came in to cool him down and to give Sinsabaugh a short break.

Kimball encouraged Caratachea to trust Rick, "one of the most compassionate and understanding detectives we have." Caratachea said he did trust Sinsabaugh. But he was furious that Doody had (supposedly) implicated him in the crime. "Let that motherfucker in here and I'll get the fucking truth, I'll beat the fucking shit out of him." Letting him beat up Doody, he argued, would "get the fucking truth out quicker, instead of trying to beat it out of him with words."

Kimball left, Sinsabaugh returned, and suspect and interrogator were soon buddies again. To lighten the mood, Sinsabaugh let Caratachea try on his straw hat and told him, "You look good in a hat."

"I look good in anything," Caratachea said with a laugh. "Except behind the bars."

Caratachea's good humor diminished when Mullavey reappeared to lecture him about lying, and it vanished when Captain White came in and said, "I just talked with your mom."

The suspect was not pleased. "Couldn't it have waited until after this was done?" "Then my name would of been cleared . . . and she wouldn't have to be worried."

White didn't try to reassure him. "You're right," he said, "the lady is worried to death." She was coming to headquarters, and he wanted Caratachea to do some hard thinking. "Rollie, this is not a joke. It's serious to you, it's serious to your mom."

When White left, Caratachea was simmering again. He boiled over when Mullavey said, "If there's information, you've got to give it up."

"I already did," Caratachea shouted. "Can't you get that through your fucking head?" He screamed and kicked the wall.

Mullavey was stern. "Quiet down." Sinsabaugh took a softer approach. "Hey, knock it off, Rollie, don't do that."

The anger quickly gave way to tears. "I didn't want my mom to know. I go day to day wondering if she is going to live or whether she is going to die, and she doesn't need any more pressures." He insisted, "Everything I've been telling you guys is the truth. I just wish you guys would understand that."

Later Sinsabaugh asked about people Doody and Garcia ran around with. Caratachea asked who had been arrested. Hearing the names might "kick something in my memory." Maybe he had seen them at school.

They didn't go to his school, Sinsabaugh said—they were from Tucson. "This is what I'm trying to figure out. Your gun gets tied in with some guys from Tucson. Don't make fucking sense."

Sinsabaugh had that right: it made no sense at all. But the task force brass still took Mike McGraw's meandering tale of booze, drugs, and murder as gospel. If the Avondale boys had committed the crime, they must have done it with the guys from Tucson.

Doody's admission that he and Garcia had borrowed the rifle must have felt like progress to Riley and Munley, and to their audience in the monitoring room. It was the only progress they made for some time. Doody said he wasn't sure when they borrowed it, maybe in June. And they didn't shoot it because it wasn't loaded. Anyway, Rollie had lent his guns to other people, such as one of the ABL gang—the Avondale Barrio Locos.

Munley urged Doody to tell the truth about the crime. They had heard other versions; now they needed to hear "what J. D. has to say." For the next twenty minutes, J. D. said nothing whatsoever.

Riley and Munley filled the silence with long harangues. Reading this part of the transcript is a numbing experience; the accusations and admonitions blur together as they must have done in Doody's mind at the time. Now and then the detectives paused for replies. Getting none, they went on, in Caratachea's apt phrase, trying to beat it out of Doody with words.

A multitude of words later, Riley got back to the murder weapon. "Did you have that rifle when those people were killed?"

That got an answer. "We gave it back to him about, I don't know, before it happened."

Doody retreated to silence for several more minutes, and when he did speak, he changed the subject. "Rollie . . . are you aware that he used to be in a gang?"

The diversion worked, and Doody became talkative. He mentioned several members of the ABL, including a leader named George who drove a Monte Carlo SS. He recounted an incident at the Whataburger restaurant involving someone throwing soda at a windshield and a guy named Jason waving a sawed-off shotgun. His point was that George might have borrowed Caratachea's gun: George and Rollie left the Whataburger with Rollie's rifle in a bag, after which the rifle "was never seen for quite a while."

Then Doody hinted that Caratachea was involved in the murders. He said he didn't know who had killed the monks because he didn't inter-act with Rollie anymore. He recalled that after the murders Rollie sud-denly had money for rent, but then said the money was probably from selling speed. He claimed that Rollie had "told me and Mike that he's killed somebody before or seen somebody killed before." Asked if Rollie or Mike had any new property after the crime, he listed a stereo system, a dual tape player, and a boom box that played tapes and CDs. Asked about jewelry, he said Rollie had lots of rings that he wore "like a brass knuckle" to beat people up.

Soon he fell silent again. Riley and Munley gave more speeches—no response. Doody spoke only when Riley switched to short, blunt ques-tions. "Okay, did you kill anybody at that temple?"

"No."

"Okay, were you at that temple the night these people were killed?"

"No."

Back in September, when Sinsabaugh had first talked to Doody, Garcia had been with him. As Riley now told it, Garcia had gotten in Sinsabaugh's face, saying he didn't "want Rick talking to you unless he's there." Why would he say that, Riley wondered, unless he was trying to look after Doody or keep him from saying something to the police?

"But see," Doody said, "Alex is like my big brother."

Captain White escorted Sheila Caratachea into Rollie's interview room. "Talk to your mom," he said. "Go through this with your mom and with Rick here, and get it taken care of." After he left, it became clear that he had carefully prepped the mother to contribute to the son's interrogation.

She briefly took over the questioning. "Who did you lend your gun to, Rollie?"

"J. D."

"Who's J. D.?"

"The oriental dude who was staying with us?"

"You lent the gun to him for how long?"

"Two days."

Later she had more questions. When he got his gun back, "Wasn't no blood, no nothing else on it?" When he recalled something sticky and brown, she commented, "Dried blood is brown." White's coaching was most evident when she asked if J. D. might "know the people from Tucson." Her next words may have revealed the captain's current theory. "So he set it up to get the gun to use it for that? For them?"

"That's what I figure," her son agreed.

Sheila Caratachea soon went home for the night, and Sinsabaugh got a briefing about Doody's interrogation. Back in his chair, he asked about the Whataburger.

As Caratachea told it, some of his friends had left a party to get something to eat at the Whataburger. A guy threw ice on Angel's car, and Angel came back to the party for reinforcements. "Just the big guys," including Caratachea, Doody, and Jason, went with him. In the parking lot, a guy pulled out a baseball bat, so Jason pulled out a sawed-off shotgun. Then a car alarm went off. "We thought it was the cops, we split, and that was it."

Caratachea's moods varied widely as the hours passed, but he kept a high opinion of himself throughout. He said his nickname was "Shakespeare," because "I'm a con artist, I have my way with words. . . . I can make the average person believe anything I want to." Laughing, he bragged that he "could probably convince them that it rained up."

Sinsabaugh joked, "I hope you're not doing that to me."

The conversation turned to a gang Caratachea and Jason had formed, the AM (After Midnight) Posse. He called it "our club at the time we were doing the burglaries." There had been about twenty members, but the Posse had "been dead ever since we got arrested." Caratachea had been arrested for burglary in May and again in July.

Sinsabaugh asked what Caratachea's friends drove, but Jason's Nova and Angel's Nissan Sentra weren't the answers he was looking for.

"You know anyone who's got a Bronco? Or seen a Bronco or Blazer?" Caratachea couldn't think of anyone.

A knock at the door summoned Sinsabaugh to another conference. Returning, he asked, "Did you arrange for some weapons and meet somebody at Whataburger?" He mentioned the ABL gang.

Caratachea denied ever being with an ABL member at Whataburger, then took it back. He'd gone there once with a guy named Ray, after a party given by Kenny, "a black dude who lives out by me."

"That's the kind of stuff I need," Sinsabaugh said. He wanted details about the black dude. Caratachea described Kenny, then volunteered that he'd seen a black Bronco at the party, or maybe a Blazer. At the party there were a lot of gangsters "fronting rags, colors." Blue rags for the Crips, yellow for some other gang, and "brown which is Mexican." Asked if he had met anyone from a Tucson gang, he said no.

After the party Caratachea had stopped at Whataburger to "eat something to sober up some." People were sitting there bullshitting, and he talked to them. He insisted that the talk was not about guns.

Just before 2:00 a.m., Captain White called Sinsabaugh out of the room and gave him a new assignment, temporarily halting Caratachea's interrogation.

White sent Sinsabaugh to join Riley, Munley, and Doody in the room with the three padded chairs. His mission was to get Doody to talk.

But nothing changed. Sinsabaugh tried lectures. No response. All three detectives jabbed at the suspect with quick questions. Nothing. Munley tried "Do it for Vickie" and "Tell us what you fear." Riley tried "Let us help you." Sinsabaugh tried "Make a stand" and "Trust me on this one." Doody sat in silence.

Sinsabaugh stopped asking about the case; he just wanted Doody to open his mouth. He asked a very simple question. Did Doody remember talking to him before? "Do you remember, yes or no?"

"Yes."

Success at last. Sinsabaugh ran with it. "You remember my name? Yes or no, do you remember my name?"

"Yeah."

"Okay, what's my name?"

"Richard Sinsabaugh."

"Well, why is that so hard? I'm here for ya, you got to talk."

The back-to-basics technique worked. Doody remained taciturn, but he occasionally answered a question. Asked what he was afraid of, he said he wasn't afraid *of* anybody; he was afraid *for* somebody. After more questions, he named Vickie.

Sinsabaugh tried to take advantage of this new volubility. "Did you kill anyone there, Johnathan? Look me in the eye, yes or no, did you kill anyone there?"

"No."

"You were there though, Johnathan, right?" No response. He repeated the question again and again. Silence. "Answer me, answer me, Johnathan. Johnathan, answer me. Answer me." Finally, on the ninth repetition, he got the answer he wanted.

"Were you involved?"

"Yes," Doody said.

The one-word concession did not herald any outpouring of admissions. Instead the lopsided interrogation continued, with Sinsabaugh combining long strings of questions with pleas—and demands—for answers.

Eventually he did get another significant reply. Asked if Alex was with him at the temple, Doody first said, "I can't."

"Nine people were killed and you're saying you can't. Johnathan, I'm here with ya, you can. Was Alex with ya, I know Alex was with ya, you're not telling me nothing I don't know, was Alex with you?"

"Yes."

But then fourteen questions in a row—variations on "Was Rollie involved?"—got no response at all. Sinsabaugh returned to the basics. "Say something, say something, Johnathan, come on, man, this is ridiculous, say something. What's your name? What's your last name?"

"Doody."

"Okay, what's so hard about that? Speak up. . . . What's your last name?"

"Doody."

Soon after that exercise, Sinsabaugh introduced a new topic. "Who knew the guys in Tucson? . . . At least talk to me, say something, say 'I don't know.' . . . Who knew the guys in Tucson?"

"I don't know," Doody said obediently.

Alex Garcia was at home, where Doody said he would be, but officers did not pick him up until they went to his parents' house with a search warrant at 2:30 a.m. on Saturday, October 26. Roused from sleep, Juan Garcia gave them permission to take his sixteen-year-old son to headquarters.

MCSO detective Brian Sands and DPS officer Larry Troutt drove Garcia to the East Court Building, where Kimball put him in room 428, the room next to Doody's. White and others prepared to listen in, and the interrogation began at 3:29 a.m.

Sands noted that Garcia was sixteen, in tenth grade, and getting Cs and Ds, then read him the juvenile *Miranda* warnings. Unlike Riley, he added no deprecatory remarks. Garcia said he understood his rights and didn't want his parents or guardians present "at this point."

Apparently the walls at headquarters were thin. Garcia asked, "Johnathan Doody's next door, right?" Troutt said they'd just have to put those voices out of their minds—but for the next two hours, Garcia would continue to hear his friend through the wall. As would later become clear, he listened closely.

Troutt wanted to know who he hung out with. "Johnathan," Garcia said. "He's the only one I know."

"Is Johnathan your best friend?"

"Yeah, at this point, yeah."

He also knew Mike Myers and Rollie Caratachea, but just to talk to. He and Doody had met in ROTC. They used to spend more time together, but now Garcia was usually with his girlfriend. When he refused to give the girlfriend's name, Troutt gave it himself: Michelle Hoover.

Troutt informed Garcia that they were investigating the temple murders, and Sands asked when he had first heard about them. Garcia said it must have been the next day, on the TV news. At first he and Doody hadn't talked much about the crime except for hoping "the murderer wasn't still around." After they heard the killers had been caught, they started "watching some news."

Troutt and Sands wondered why the crime didn't mean more to Garcia, given its seriousness and his connection to the temple. "To me?" Garcia said. "I don't know . . . you hear about, you know, murders and all this other stuff on the television, you know, you really don't care for it anymore."

The next time Caratachea's rifle was mentioned, Garcia was the one who brought it up. Troutt asked what Doody and Garcia did on the day of the murders. Garcia described a get-together at Amanda's house, Rollie's friend Amanda. He and Doody went there in Doody's Mustang. "We just walked in and we saw everybody and then [I] remember I talked to Rollie, you know, we use his gun."

Troutt asked about the conversation with Rollie. Garcia replied, "Me and Johnathan wants to know if we can use your gun." He recalled driving around with Doody "when I had Rollie's gun, or we had Rollie's gun." Some guys in another car were "being dicks," so he "fired a couple shots in the air." They had borrowed Rollie's gun just that one time; he hadn't seen it since.

Kimball opened the door. "Got some big developments," he announced. Sands followed him out of the room to hear the news.

At around 4:00 a.m., Captain White interrupted Doody and Sinsabaugh with a message about the guys from Tucson. "We've got people that we know did the shooting."

White's point was that Doody could talk without fear of retaliation: the bad guys were already in jail. But in making that point, he revealed a theory of the crime that deflected blame away from the Avondale boys. Doody would soon make use of that second message.

"That's our captain," Sinsabaugh said as White disappeared. "If you can't trust a captain, who in the hell can you trust?" He decided he and Riley would sit back and let Doody tell the story. "Just go ahead, Johnathan. Just start talking."

Doody did start talking, though his first words were not what White and his men wanted to hear. "There were no connection with the people from Tucson."

Then he began to offer information about the temple murders. "I don't know who did the killing," he began, but he provided plenty of other details. Perhaps building on White's hint that someone else had done the shooting—or perhaps simply because English was not his first language—he alternated between second- and third-person pronouns. "We all went in with full gear and equipment." "They" wanted to see if they could beat the system, meaning the motion-detector lights around the temple. "We made it through the sensor; the light never came on. It was just going to be a joke and it just went downhill."

Sinsabaugh had changed from badgering inquisitor to appreciative listener. "Go ahead. Just keep telling us."

Doody sounded proud of the planning. "Everything was done in clockwork, everything was on clock. We had it down to second. . . . They entered the temple and there was basically . . . no way for the monks to get out."

"We" moved the monks out of their rooms and counted them. "We had eight." Then there was a noise in the kitchen, and a monk told "Mrs. Nun" to come out.

"They" searched the bedrooms for weapons. Then one of the guys slipped up, calling another one by name. The slip was a turning point. "There were debating about what to do. And, ah, get out and leave no witnesses."

Doody also said someone wrote "blood" on the wall with a knife. This was much closer to what had happened at the temple than Mike McGraw's talk of "logos" and "something like blood on the floor or wall."

Still debating, "they" sent Doody outside to see if the building was soundproof. While he was out there, "One shot was fired. The place wasn't quite soundproof . . . you could still hear the bullet." He didn't have time to tell the guys; they started firing before he went in. "There were two weapons used," Doody said: "Rollie's semi-automatic .22" and a shotgun. He walked in just as the shotgun fired three times. After that the .22 "went off constantly."

Next, as Doody told it, "they grabbed their stuff and ran out," and "we" got into a car and took off.

Doody mentioned only one car, his Mustang, but the detectives wanted to hear about two. Pressed to identify a second one, he came up with, "And somebody else's car."

Sinsabaugh asked what kind of car three times before Doody said, "A Monte Carlo SS." This answer matched his earlier claim that George, who drove a Monte Carlo, might have borrowed Caratachea's rifle. But it clashed with Captain White's view of the crime—that is, McGraw's version—in which the killers traveled in a Blazer and a Bronco.

Later Sinsabaugh asked, "Did anybody threaten you guys?"

Doody took the hint. After the murders, he said, they went to "Camelback Road and Agua Fria River." There, on the dry riverbed, an unnamed "he" told Doody that if he talked, "They would eliminate me and somebody I love."

Sinsabaugh asked, "Gangs involved in this? Is that why you're afraid to say? . . . Are you afraid of those guys in Tucson?"

"They had nothing to do with it," Doody insisted. "They weren't from Tucson at all."

"I know you were with Alex," Sinsabaugh said. "Right? Say yes or no."

"Yes." As for who else was there, Doody said only, "The other people."

He said there were five in all. Sinsabaugh indicated that this was the wrong number.

At one point Sinsabaugh appealed to Doody's interest in the military. "You're a soldier, you got to be brave and you got to trust us. It's just like when you go into combat, man, you got to trust somebody. . . . You're not telling us everything."

Doody obliged. "There are more than five people." Asked who they were, he replied, "They came from Avondale."

Riley got Doody to confirm that George and a friend of his had been at the temple. "You, Alex, and George," he counted. "There's two more."

"I don't know who the other guy was."

"Well, obviously if Rollie's gun is there—was Rollie there? Come on, Johnathan, was Rollie there?"

"Yes."

Later Sinsabaugh asked, "How long before, did you guys plan this?"

Again the note of pride sounded in Doody's reply. "They presented the plan to me and . . . asked me, would the plan work."

"Did you feel it could work?"

"No, it wouldn't." The plan didn't have "any principle in it."

"So what did you do?"

"I made it work."

Doody said he knew Alex, Rollie, and George, but not the other guy. Sinsabaugh asked, "Was the other guy a black guy?"

"They were all white. He was white."

That didn't go over well. "You're not telling the truth."

The accusation got a rise out of Doody. "There was no black guy involved. When you caught those people in Tucson, they were laughing at you, 'cause they had nothing to do with it."

Pushed to say who had come up with the flawed plan, Doody finally named George. The goal was to see if they could beat the system. Asked what George meant by beating the system, he retorted, "They wanted to see how good you guys were."

"I don't buy that one bit," Sinsabaugh said. "You didn't murder, they didn't murder nine monks to see how good we were."

That turned Doody's thoughts to why they *did* kill the monks. Somebody yelled George's name, he explained, and a monk "looked up and gave him a funny look. George knew him."

He had more to say about the plan. "We were just gonna leave, that was the whole plan. . . . Our plan was to check, just go in there, get through the light sensor and the dog, basically touch the door." When they got as far as the kitchen door—they could see monks inside watching TV—Boy was coming out to feed the dog. He turned on the outside light, and "we took off, jump over the wall, and went back to the car . . . we went back and they said let's do it again, this time go inside and see what we can get." Before going back, they "synchronized the watch" and waited until the outside light went off.

Doody probably did not mean that they synchronized one watch. In Thai, his first language, a singular noun has the same form as its plural. His interrogation makes clear many times that he had not yet mastered this difference between Thai and English.

By dawn on Saturday, October 26, Doody had been sitting in room 424 for more than seven hours. His confession was on tape, and now the search warrant had yielded hard evidence connecting him and Garcia to the crime—something the task force had not found for the Tucson defendants. But Captain White remained determined to link the guys from Tucson to the boys from Avondale. In pursuit of that goal he would prolong Doody's interrogation for almost six more hours.

When Kimball called Detective Sands out of Garcia's interrogation to talk about "big developments," he meant the results of the search warrant at the Garcia house. While Troutt and Sands had driven Alex to headquarters, their colleagues had stayed at the house to execute the warrant and interview Alex's father.

Juan Garcia said he owned several weapons, including a 20-gauge shotgun that Alex often used. The shotgun was found in Mr. Garcia's closet. The closet in Alex and Johnathan's room yielded two cameras, a dual cassette player, plus a "camouflage hat, an Army green face mask and scarf, and black tank goggles." A second search the next day would turn up other relevant items: "Cold Weather military boots," gloves, duffle bags, books on combat and survival, and a "musical powerhorn."

Alex surely knew the house was being searched, since he had been there when the search team arrived. Perhaps partly for that reason, Garcia soon invoked his *Miranda* rights and stopped talking. Tape 2 of his interrogation ended at 5:15 a.m., but according to Kimball, he invoked his rights about fifteen minutes after that. What Garcia, Sands, and Troutt said in that last quarter of an hour was apparently not recorded.

The gap between tapes lasted more than three hours: tape 3 would not begin until 8:36 a.m. Information about that period can be pieced together from Kimball and Garcia's conversation on tape 3 and other sources, including Riley's summary of the case and testimony Kimball later gave in court.

According to Riley, Garcia invoked after investigators informed him "that the rifle he and Johnathan had borrowed from Rollie was the weapon used in the temple murders." Garcia did exactly what he should have done: he insisted that they stop talking to him and requested an attorney. Sands and Troutt did what they had to do: they terminated the interview. Garcia also asked them to call his father. At 6:25 that Saturday morning, Sgt. Mullavey called Juan Garcia and told him his son was fine and wanted to see him. Mullavey dispatched a car to transport the senior Garcia to headquarters.

According to Kimball, at around 7:30 a.m., with the interrogation at an impasse, Kimball set up a "passby" to show Caratachea that "investigators were testing the veracity of his statements through other individuals." He sent Garcia to be fingerprinted and photographed and arranged for Caratachea to be photographed at the same time. "It is assumed they saw each other," he reported, "but Caratachea had no noticeable reaction."

During Garcia's fingerprinting, Kimball got his first glimpse of the six-foot, three-inch suspect. Surprised to see the "very large young man" alone in a room with the fingerprint technician, Kimball walked in and spoke to Garcia. Garcia asked what would happen to him if he "told the complete story without any lies." He said he didn't like Troutt and Sands;

he wanted to talk to different detectives. Kimball told him that before making any decisions, he should talk to his dad.

According to Riley, when Juan Garcia arrived at headquarters, he was greeted by the top brass: Sheriff Agnos and Chief Deputy John Coppock joined Mullavey in the lobby to meet with him. They told him Alex was being interviewed about the temple murders and had "chosen not to speak with investigators any longer." They added that the decision of whether or not to make a statement was up to Alex.

According to both Garcias, Riley omitted part of the story. They testified in court that the brass had offered Juan Garcia a deal to pass on to his son: if Alex cooperated, he would get only seven to nine or seven to eleven years in prison.

Father and son were left alone together in Alex's interview room, and their conversation was not taped. Afterward Juan Garcia came out and said Alex was willing to talk.

He would do his talking in a new room, with new interrogators, and with a dramatic change in tone.

While Garcia was invoking his rights, Captain White was launching an all-out effort to get Doody to confirm McGraw's story. White said Doody had no reason to be afraid; the "big tough guys" were in jail. And telling about them wouldn't be snitching—they had already confessed. Moving toward the door, White asked, "Do you believe me?"

"Yeah," Doody said.

Munley kicked off the next stage. "Tell us about the guys from Tucson." But that "yeah" was Doody's last word for several minutes.

Sinsabaugh harangued him. "You're not listening to anything I'm telling you, you're not listening to nothing I'm telling you, look at me, you're not listening to anything I'm telling you." This section of the transcript reads like a series of chants. "Go ahead Jon, tell us. Jon tell us. Tell the truth Jon, go ahead. Okay, Jon, we're on the right step now, let's clear it up, let's get it out and get it over. Talk to us, Jon, you tell us."

Doody did not talk.

As another forty-five-minute tape began to roll, White popped in again. He said he knew Doody's neighborhood well; he had gone to Agua Fria High School. Back in 1963 he had won the school's award as an outstanding athlete. Then he read an excerpt from "a confession of one of the people from Tucson." Doody had mentioned a rendezvous with the other guys at Camelback Road and the Agua Fria River; White said the Tucson guy was describing the same location.

Mike McGraw was the only Tucson suspect who had said anything about Camelback. Reading aloud from McGraw's transcript, White made an interesting change. In the transcript McGraw says they went "up to Camelback," and Riley asks if he's talking about "the mountain, Camelback mountain?" McGraw replies, "Yeah, we ride ATCs and stuff like that." White's version of Riley's question omits the word "mountain," asking only, "When you say Camelback, you talkin' about Camelback?" The omission allowed White to conflate McGraw's mention of Camelback (the mountain) with Garcia and Doody's references to Camelback Road—and to believe he had found a link between Tucson and Avondale.

After Sinsabaugh stopped questioning Caratachea, the recorder in room 467 was off for nearly three and a half hours. Caratachea would later say he fell asleep "right here on the floor, which wasn't too comfortable."

By the time taping resumed, Doody had told Riley that Rollie had been at the temple, and Riley and Sinsabaugh had traded places. Riley was Caratachea's new interrogator.

When Riley said he knew Rollie had been at the temple, Caratachea snapped, "I do believe that in the United States it is innocent until proven guilty."

"Well, you're right, yeah."

"Okay, then I'm innocent for one, and you're proving me guilty here yourself."

"I'm just asking you—"

"No, you weren't asking me, you were telling me."

"Only because I was told by other people." Riley asked why someone would hate him enough to call him a killer.

Caratachea thought of Doody. "The murder rap's coming down on him, he's gonna blame it on the person that he likes least." But, he told Riley, "For all I know you're lying to me."

Riley protested that he didn't make a habit of lying to people, and besides, "What do I expect to gain from you if I lie to you?"

"Trying to get me to admit to something I didn't do."

"Well, no," Riley said. "People don't admit to things that they didn't do." That belief, which the brass shared with Riley, would come back to haunt Sheriff Agnos and the entire MCSO.

Riley didn't see Doody as the ringleader. Calling the leader "very methodical, very precise and very well organized," he pointed out that Caratachea had described himself as somebody just like that.

"J. D. is smart," Caratachea responded. "He isn't a dumb person. . . . Personally I think he is capable of masterminding some event like this." As if that was more praise than Doody deserved, he undercut it. "But he's dumb enough to follow through with it. You see, I'm smart, I'm also smart enough not to go through with something like this."

He said Doody was a planner. When they talked about breaking into cars, he "would plan it out in detail and go over it and over it and over it till he thought it was perfect." He described Doody's plan to "mug somebody and take their car and take their money." "Like on a road that's hardly traveled, someone waiting at the stop sign, like in the bushes, and another car pull up behind them, bump the car, most likely the person sitting at the stop sign would get out. . . . When the one in the car got out, the one in the bush would run around, jump in the car and take off. And you both take off and leave the guy standing there."

As for who would work with Doody, Caratachea could think of only one person. "Him and Alex hang around each other all the time, they tell each other everything, and it seems sensible that if he was going to plan something he would plan it with Alex."

After reading to Doody about Camelback, Captain White didn't make his usual quick exit but took over the interrogation himself. When he asked, "There were other people out there, right?" Doody capitulated, changing his claim of five participants to "no more than ten."

White's questions made it obvious that he expected to hear that some of the other guys were black, some "Mexican." As Doody gradually came up with answers, White interpreted them to fit his expectations.

For example, when Doody conceded that one guy "had a dark-colored skin," White said, "Dark-colored skin, is he black?"

"His skin is fairly dark."

"Dark, dark, probably black? Okay, dark, probably black."

Eventually Doody told White there were two or maybe three black guys, but he didn't know if anyone was Mexican. In the darkness, even "Rollie looked like he was black." White gave up on that topic, but only temporarily.

Going through his confession a second time, Doody told the same story as before but with expanded roles for "the other guys," especially Caratachea. Now Rollie was the mastermind. He was talking to Alex, and "they came up with this idea." About three days before "we went in," they showed Doody the plan and asked him to make it work.

In the revised version, Doody and Garcia didn't borrow Caratachea's rifle and didn't carry guns at all; their only weapons were knives. Rollie had his own gun plus "one of George's," a shotgun.

White knew how to ask a leading question. He wanted to know who had the shotgun. "Was it George or George's friend or one of the guys from Tucson?" Doody said he couldn't tell.

This time there were about ten guys. They all met at the river bottom. He didn't know if the others were speaking Spanish; it "just sounded like a whole bunch of mumbling." Finally Rollie, "or George or one of them," said, "We're going."

Doody and Garcia, in Doody's Mustang, led the way to the temple. He thought the other guys were all in one car.

"Remember," White said, "we're talking about eight people. Is there a possibility there was more than one car?"

Doody guessed it was possible. Sinsabaugh asked what kind of car.

"Um," Doody said.

"Pickup, station wagon, passenger car?"

Multiple choice helped. "It looked like a pickup but it also looked like it had a top on."

"Suburban," Sinsabaugh suggested.

White amplified the hint. "Suburban or a Bronco or a Blazer or station wagon?"

"I don't know," Doody replied.

At the temple, Doody said, Caratachea gave the orders. He told Garcia and Doody to scout the area and start the countdown; in five minutes, the others would be in position at another door, and they would all go in. But the countdown didn't work. A few seconds early, Doody heard someone say, "Freeze, get your hands up." When he ran in, the other guys already "had them all covered."

At the part when "somebody took a knife and wrote something on the wall," White probed, "Black guy? Or Mexican guy or white guy?"

"Yeah, I think so," Doody said.

Urged several times to "tell us what race he was," Doody replied, "He looked, he kinda like black, I think. But then again, I mean . . ." His voice trailed off.

His account of the shooting was the same as before: one shot from "a small gun," like a .22, while he was outside; three shotgun blasts as he ran back in; then "constant .22." When he got back, "they were pointing a gun aiming at their heads." He didn't know *who* was aiming the rifle. "I didn't see that at all." A bit later he said he thought Rollie was using his .22, "but I could have been wrong."

Back at the "rendezvous point" after the shooting, Garcia and Doody found Rollie and one other guy.

"What does he look like?" White asked.

"I don't know, he was dark, dark-colored skin."

"So, black, black man?"

Doody hedged. "Yeah, kind of like, well, it wasn't, it was like you could hardly see it, but it look like a mustache, you know."

The only conversation he remembered was a threat. "If I speak they will be coming after me, they will coming after my girlfriend and my family. And they let me suffer and then they will kill me."

Pressed to say who had threatened him, Doody said, "I really wasn't paying attention at all." Later he was less vague: "All I know is he was a colored guy."

White said, "He was a black guy, you called him a colored, but that means black?"

"Kind of," Doody agreed, "but then again, I mean, it was dark enough where *I* even look black."

The next time Doody mentioned the rendezvous at the river bottom, he placed more than four people there. "Everybody was all upset at that point and some of them were happy." The happy ones were "hyper."

"How would you know that they were happy?" Sinsabaugh asked. "Were they saying, 'Way to go,' or—"

"They were saying . . . 'Did you hear the blood coming out from him?' stuff like that."

Garcia's interrogation resumed at 8:36 a.m. in room 471, with Kimball and Mullavey as the questioners. His first interview room had been next to Doody's; now he was near Caratachea. Kimball told him they were being recorded, then went back over their between-tapes conversation to get it on the record.

Guided by questions, Garcia confirmed what Kimball had told him during the break. He might go to jail for "quite some time" or he might "walk out." Telling the truth was always best. If he decided to talk to them, it had to be completely his own choice, and before deciding anything, he should talk with his father. Garcia also confirmed that Kimball had not made him any promises.

Then Kimball asked formally, "Do you right now feel like you want to talk to Mark and I?"

"Yes," Garcia answered, "I do."

The next step was to repeat the juvenile *Miranda* warnings. Mullavey went out to get Garcia a Coke and order "Breakfast Jacks or McMuffins" while Kimball read him his rights.

Kimball stressed that they didn't want to hear any lies. "Only you know the truth, but we're gonna be a judge of that truth."

Asked how he got involved in the temple murders, Garcia began, "It was just an idea that me and Johnathan—should I mention names?"

"Absolutely," Kimball and Mullavey chorused.

From there the story poured out in a smooth narrative. Doody came up with the idea, "basically for money" to buy a car. From the unsuspecting David Doody, they learned there were no alarms, as well as "when they lock the doors, how many people were there, who was gone at what time." They collected information until "it came to a point . . . that it was a go."

At first the plan was just to get money, but later Doody "started, you know, that we can't have no witnesses, just go and shoot everybody."

They needed guns for protection. Garcia smuggled his father's 20-gauge pump shotgun out of his house, with four shells, and asked Caratachea if they could borrow his rifle. They talked about who would use which weapon: according to Garcia, Doody chose the rifle because it held more rounds.

They wore camouflage battle dress uniforms (BDUs), gloves to avoid leaving fingerprints, and "snow boots, which might sound weird, but the tracking on the snow boots was bigger than my foot or smaller than my foot." Garcia wound a green scarf around his face; Doody wore a hat, a scarf, and "tank driver goggles." The gear came from the family store at Luke Air Force Base.

They made a silencer for Rollie's gun and tested it in the White Tank Mountains. It muffled the sound of the first shot, but each subsequent shot got louder. So they dropped the silencer idea but "decided to go for it that night anyway."

They drove to the temple in Doody's Mustang. Doody was supposed to go in first, but he thought someone was about to spot them, so they took off and came back in half an hour.

Garcia's story was interrupted by shouting from outside the room: "I did not do this, man. I wasn't there." Garcia recognized Caratachea's voice. When the yelling stopped, Garcia went on with his confession.

At the temple a second time, Doody went in first. "I followed him and I covered where the people were sitting and watching TV." Doody got the rest of the people out of their rooms, and "we had everybody look straight up with their hands up." Garcia covered them while Doody went through the rooms getting "cameras, stereos, piggy banks, money rolls." Doody walked Boy to his room to look for money, then brought him back. They tried to open the safe, but the head monk said the lady who knew the combination wasn't there. Doody guarded the people while Garcia rechecked the rooms and put everything in two military bags.

Then "Johnathan said it was time to go, and then he wanted, his intentions were to kill everybody for witnesses." Garcia assured Kimball and Mullavey that he was being "completely honest, okay? I will sign anything, I will lie detectors, whatever. I told Johnathan that I didn't want to kill 'em. . . . I told him that if we do, that it was going to be tried as murder, and that if we didn't, we could get armed robbery, which I would say armed robbery is a little bit less than murder."

Ignoring this warning, "Johnathan started shooting the people. . . . And then I just shot my four shots and that was it. I don't know where I aimed. . . . I know I aimed at down, which we had everybody lay down with their hands behind their head." Johnathan shot the people "in the back of the head with a .22 caliber a couple of times to make sure that they were completely dead."

Garcia went on, "I don't think that the shots that I fired would have, was enough to kill somebody. . . . But Johnathan was the one."

He insisted that the two of them had done it alone. "The four people in Tucson had nothing to do with it. . . . Rolando, the one that was heard screaming, had nothing to do with it. We just used his rifle. Michael Myers? Nothing to do with it. It was just completely me and Johnathan."

From the temple they drove to a river bottom at "Indian School or Camelback," he wasn't sure which, to count the money. It came to $2,650 in bills and about $140 in change. According to Garcia, Doody spent the money on the car, but "I helped my parents with bills." (As would come out in court, Garcia bought a handgun for himself and a "promise ring" for his girlfriend, and he put several hundred dollars in his credit union account.)

Garcia and Doody had felt relieved when someone else was accused of the crime. After that, they had stopped thinking about it. "It just escaped my mind. Like Johnathan, it just escaped his mind."

Less than an hour into Garcia's renewed interrogation, his confession was on tape. He blamed Doody for the actual killings but otherwise cast himself as an equal participant in the crime, and he specified that they committed it on their own, without help from anyone else. But that story did not satisfy Captain White's task force. Garcia's interrogation would continue for eight more hours, and it would end with frustration on both sides.

By 9:00 in the morning, Doody and Garcia had both confessed, and Captain White was determined to end Caratachea's denials. He and Chief Deputy George Leese entered room 467, where Sheila Caratachea had rejoined her son.

"Johnathan's telling us everything," White said. "Everyone's telling us everything. Right now you're the only one that's standing by yourself." He summarized Doody's account of the events at the temple, with Rollie as the shooter.

"No, man," Caratachea said. "I wasn't there."

"We didn't sit here and make all this up," White told him. "We didn't put that gun in your hand. We didn't take your gun and go out and kill nine monks with it."

"I didn't take my gun out and go kill someone."

"You're not listening," White chided. "You're running your mouth and you're not listening, and when I'm telling you something for your own good. I am trying to help you help yourself."

He brandished a bound folder. "That's a confession from one of the people down at Tucson. We have four of these . . . from the people down at Tucson that told us what happened. Now we have confessions from the people up here."

"Show me where my name comes up," Caratachea said.

White couldn't do that: no one from Tucson had named any of the Avondale boys. But his theory covered the problem. "You all used phony names . . . the people down there don't know what your first name is, but they can sure identify you. The people up here do know your names and they can identify you."

Caratachea didn't budge. "I'll take it to my death bed saying that I didn't do it, because I didn't."

As she had the night before, Sheila Caratachea asked her son, "Who knew the people from Tucson?"

He said he didn't know them.

"Rollie, Sheila," White said, "I, you know, I have absolutely no reason to lie."

Caratachea could think of a reason. "You wanna solve this case and you're gonna really go with any story."

"The case is solved," White insisted. "The case is solved."

Leese was an echo. "The case is solved, Rollie."

Rollie's mother said she had good rapport with her kids, and if Rollie had done something, he would tell her. "He would come to tears and tell me the truth."

"Sheila," White assured her, "we have got all these people that have absolutely no reason to lie, we have got physical evidence that his gun was the one that was there, now isn't that a real odd coincidence that all of these people—"

Caratachea cut him off. "Because they borrowed it."

White didn't like being interrupted. "I wanna tell you something, you're gonna sit there and you're not gonna do that again . . . do you understand that?"

"He borrowed the gun."

"You saying that black is white does not make it white, you saying that night is day does not make it day, and you can sit there and you can deny your involvement from now until forever, and it doesn't make it so." He added, "I'm not saying you were the shooter, but you were there."

"I was not there," Caratachea said again and again. And, "I lent the gun."

Sheila Caratachea broke in to ask White, "So you want him to say that he's guilty, and then he says he's guilty, and then what?"

"That's up to a judge and a jury."

She said her son hadn't been raised to do such a thing, and she believed with all her heart that he hadn't done it.

"I don't blame you for saying that, Sheila, really I don't."

The condescending answer made her mad, but not at White. "I wanna get those little suckers out myself and talk to them."

Like mother, like son. Caratachea lost his temper and shouted so loud that his voice was picked up by the recorder in Garcia's interview room. "I wanna get the little mother-fuckers and beat the shit out of them and get the fuckin' truth out . . . I did not do this, man, can't you get that through your head, I didn't do this. I wasn't there."

White appealed to Mrs. Caratachea. "Tell him to quiet down."

"Sssh," she said, and her son quieted down.

Soon Sinsabaugh reappeared, taking over Caratachea's questioning with his earlier friendly manner. They knew Rollie had been at the temple, he said; the only question was who had pulled the trigger. Sinsabaugh was on Rollie's side; Rollie had to come clean. "I don't want you goin' down as a killer."

Sheila Caratachea seemed to take the amiable interrogator's words to heart. When Sinsabaugh told Caratachea that the people who had threatened him wouldn't be allowed to fuck with his family, she interrupted. "Rollie . . . if you are afraid of your daddy, don't even think about Daddy getting upset."

"I wasn't there," her son said.

"And if you're afraid of me being upset, you just tell the truth, period. If you were there it doesn't matter."

"I wasn't there, I was not there, I wasn't there."

Sinsabaugh said he couldn't protect Rollie's family unless he got the truth. That may have worried Rollie's mother. She left to check on her younger son.

In the long argument that followed, Caratachea repeated "I wasn't there" like a mantra. Finally he asked, "What's gonna happen to me?"

"You're gonna go to jail."

"Well, then take me to jail, because I'm gonna keep saying I didn't do it, because I did not do it." Angry again, he demanded to talk to Doody and Garcia. "Give me a chance, see if they change the story."

"I can't do that, that's not fair to them."

"Yeah, it is, because it'll pull the truth out of them. Cuff me to something so I don't get up or anything."

Sinsabaugh told him to sit down, mellow out, "relax, think about what I told you." Then he left Caratachea's interview room for the last time.

Kimball and Mullavey guided Garcia through his confession again from beginning to end, gathering more details.

The planning, Garcia said, began soon after Doody got his driver's license. Doody had his mom's van, and they sat in a mall parking lot and made plans. The boys seemed to get their ideas from crime shows or spy thrillers. They talked about "communication . . . like, one person would go through one door and then the other person would go through the other door, you know, from different sides, that we would get like headphones, you know, to talk to each other to make sure there was no one around."

Sitting in the van, Garcia decided to make a sketch, "like a blueprint"— "where everything was, motion detectors, doors, lights, where the grass, where the rocks, trees, walls, rooms." Doody had given two versions of the plan's origin, neither of which matched Garcia's. In the first, Doody drew the plan himself; in the second, George drew it and asked Doody to correct it. Both boys claimed credit for the operational planning.

After that first talk, the topic came up weekly, then almost every day. It "just kept building up—'When are we going to do it, when are we going to do it.'" They had to wait until David Doody left the temple because "Johnathan didn't want to shoot his own brother."

The day came. They had borrowed the rifle the night before. In the morning they took it out to White Tanks to test their silencer, a metal pipe filled with bottle caps. On the first shot it worked, the second shot was louder, and the third one "got really loud." "I guess the silencer was only a one-shot deal," Garcia quipped. They went ahead with the rest of their plan.

That night they sat around at Amanda's until about 8:30, then drove to a dirt road between Indian School and Camelback, where they put on their camouflage gear. Garcia wasn't sure what time they arrived at the temple; he didn't have a watch, and he implied that Doody didn't have one either. The clock in Doody's car was twenty minutes fast; whenever they wanted to know the time, "we would base it on that." So Doody's statement that they "synchronized the watch" may have been merely part of their fantasy of a precise military operation.

They knew the monks had to be in before twelve, so they waited until then. They didn't want anyone coming back, seeing them inside, and calling the cops.

In the parking lot they made a big turn to avoid the motion detectors. They squatted down to sneak past the windows. Outside the kitchen, Garcia crouched behind a freezer while Doody went over to the doors. "Johnathan started telling me, 'Go in, go in.' I said, 'You go in.'" Then Doody looked in a window and saw someone coming, so they ran back to the car and drove away.

About ten minutes later they came back and started over. This time they did go in. The plan called for them to enter the temple simultaneously through different doors, but they decided it was less risky to go in together.

Doody herded the people into the living room, where Garcia covered them with the shotgun. He seemed to enjoy recalling the scene. "We told them that we were the police, that really got them going. We told them that there was, like, escaped prisoners from Perryville, the prison right over there." Garcia got the people to kneel, then had a guy who spoke English tell them to "put their hands in the air and look straight at the ceiling." He cut the phone line and held both guns while Doody ransacked the bedrooms.

"The grandma" showed up. She was wearing white, her hair was gray, and she walked with "a hobble . . . like a limp." She sat down near the others.

All nine temple residents were now in the same room, eight of them kneeling with their hands in the air. The English speaker said they were getting tired. Garcia had him tell them to lie down and keep their hands where he could see them. Nobody gave him any trouble; nobody tried to get away; nobody started to cry.

Next Garcia checked the rooms. Doody had turned over all the beds, pulled drawers out of dressers, and put anything valuable in the doorways. Garcia didn't find anything else to take. He did find a fire extinguisher, though. The memory made him laugh. "I wanted to see what it was like," he said, "and I just sprayed it." He gathered up the valuables and put them in military bags.

In the living room, Doody tried to open the safe. It required a key but also had a combination lock. The head monk said the lady who knew the combination was out of town, in California or somewhere. They never did get it open.

Doody carried the loot to the car, the two bags plus a portable stereo. After he came back, the shooting started.

In Garcia's account, Doody told the one who spoke English to get everybody face down on the floor. Then he got up on a couch and fired his first shot from there. "I'm at the doorway, he's on the couch, and then he looks at me . . . like the look that's saying, ya know, 'Go ahead, start.'" But Garcia called Doody over and whispered to him. "I told him, ya know, that I didn't want to shoot them."

"At that point," Garcia told Kimball and Mullavey, "Johnathan says, 'No witnesses,' that's his exact words, 'no witnesses.'"

Kimball wanted to know how Garcia felt when Doody gave him that look.

"That feeling that I, I, I wasn't gonna start shooting."

"That's not a feeling," Kimball said. "Were you happy, scared, frightened, nervous, worried, upset?" Mullavey added another choice. "Excited?"

"Uh, combination of all of it," Garcia decided. "I didn't know what I was feeling. Like my body was numb, ya know."

Doody got back up on the couch, fired one or two shots, then climbed down and circled the group, firing into the back of each head. Afterwards he methodically shot each one again, "like making sure they're dead."

At Doody's first shots, Garcia said, "I just panicked then just pulled up and I just started shooting." He fired his four rounds quickly.

When Doody stopped firing, Garcia "turned around and ran." Doody followed him. They drove to the Agua Fria river bottom, to a place where people rode ATCs.

Asked what made him think ATCs used the area, Garcia said people rode ATCs "throughout the entire Agua Fria river bottom."

At the riverbed they divided the cash and property. One boom box each, cameras. They split the bills evenly, $1,325 apiece, and Garcia kept the change because Doody owed him money.

At 12:52 p.m. by Kimball's watch, Garcia reached the end of his second confession. Asked how he felt, he said he was glad it was over. "And I'm sad a little bit because if, I do get, you know, charged for murder and all this other stuff I blew my life away." He had a girlfriend, and he could

"tell that she was going to be the one . . . and I was going to start school-
ing all over and get out of trouble. And then, ah, Mr. Kojak comes knock-
ing on my door."

Kimball had another kind of feeling in mind. "Do you understand
that devastation, and the pain that the family and loved ones of those
nine individuals have experienced since the murders?"

"Oh yeah."

"Does that hurt you?"

"In a way it has." Summing up, Garcia said, "At this point I regret even
doing it. I regret even thinking about it."

Those words made a fitting ending to a confession, and Garcia must
have thought his interrogation was nearly over. He had no way to know
that, to the task force, no confession was complete without the guys from
Tucson.

While Sinsabaugh talked to Caratachea, Doody rested on the floor of
room 424. It was after 9:00 a.m., and he had been sitting in the padded
chair all night long. In the daylight hours, activity in the halls and conference rooms accelerated. The rest of Doody's interrogation would be
interrupted by many knocks at the door and short breaks.

Sinsabaugh returned to Doody with one issue on his mind: the difference between Doody's statement and Caratachea's. "Was Rollie there?"

Doody wavered. "I guess he was there."

"I know you don't like the guy," Sinsabaugh said, "but if he wasn't
there, I mean, let me know . . . just like these pictures, if you're unsure, I
don't want you picking out anybody." He said he knew Doody and Garcia
hadn't killed anyone. He also knew Caratachea wasn't the killer. Then he
began to explain the legal reality of Doody's situation. "Putting the gun
in Rollie's hand, is not lessening the blame to you."

Captain White cut off that topic by calling Sinsabaugh out of the
room.

Later Sinsabaugh announced that Caratachea "said he wasn't there.
He said he lent the gun to you guys. Is he lying?"

"No."

The answer caught Sinsabaugh by surprise. "Huh?"

"I don't know."

"What do you mean you don't know? . . . Is he lying?"

"Uh, it depends on how you want to look at it."

"You told me that Rolando helped plan this with you. Did he go inside the temple?"

"Uh, yeah," Doody said, then added, "Like who you gonna believe?"

"Well," Sinsabaugh said, "I just hope you're telling the truth." With that admonition he again left the room.

He returned to find Doody in tears. "What's wrong?" he asked. "Tell me, man. What's wrong? Huh? Tell me."

Doody was crying too hard to answer. Finally he managed to say, "I don't think all this stuff was worth it."

Sinsabaugh thought "this stuff" was the killings, but Doody meant something else. "I told you what I knew. You came out and make it sound like you don't believe."

Doody was right. His interrogators were not prepared to believe any account of the temple murders that absolved the guys from Tucson.

The sobs continued as Sinsabaugh offered water and soothing words. "No, I believed ya, mo, I believed ya." It probably didn't help when he qualified the reassurance. "I believe you, my man, the only thing is, Johnathan, I want to make sure you're helping me." He asked, "Do you have any more to tell me?"

"No."

Doody had been answering questions for more than twelve hours, after a full day of school and ROTC duty at the football game. During that period he had been given cans of soda but had eaten nothing. Now he was distraught, but Sinsabaugh kept asking questions.

In the final minutes of the interrogation, Doody named Caratachea as the person he was afraid of. Rollie had classes with Vickie; Rollie knew his parents; Rollie had threatened him and Alex about "getting some guys after us." He wasn't afraid for himself. "I don't care if they have me killed 'cause I just want to be, I'm already dead."

Bringing things to a close, Sinsabaugh said, "You understand you're not going home today, right?"

In response, Doody made his last statement of the interrogation. "Never meant to get involved at all. I've never meant to get involved."

Then Sinsabaugh went out to get him his first meal since early the previous evening, "a candy bar and a pop." The tape recorded no more words from Doody—just minute after minute of harsh, racking sobs.

Later that day, Johnathan Doody was booked into the Maricopa County Juvenile Detention Center. A court order required him to let investigators take his fingerprints, photographs, and samples of his blood, saliva, and hair.

When Sinsabaugh left the angry Rollie Caratachea, his departure marked the end of any substantive questioning. His replacement was DPS detective Geoff Himmelstein, whose mission seemed to be to help the suspect "mellow out."

Himmelstein assured Sheila Caratachea that they would "sort things out."

She was dubious. "They're not sortin' no more, it seems like they've already made up their mind."

"Yeah, guilty," her son said. "I have to prove myself innocent."

"Well," Himmelstein replied, "despite what you think, the real approach is to prove a person innocent first . . . we have to eliminate people, and by eliminating the innocent people then you narrow down and you hone in on the guilty ones."

"I wish I was one of the ones that was eliminated first."

"We're working on it, Roland."

Himmelstein brought up the guys from Tucson. He had a theory about their initial denials and later confessions. "In a real traumatic situation your mind just flat blanks it out, even though a person could've been there, these people from Tucson, just flat it took hours and hours and hours before their minds would accept what they did."

"I think twenty hours is enough," Caratachea snapped. "I wasn't there." He asked what Himmelstein was "in here to do."

Himmelstein said they had a court order to take his hairs and fingerprints. They'd do that at the county hospital. Then they'd let him "relax for a while, you know, settle down a bit emotionally." The boss would decide what happened next.

Sheila Caratachea went off to find cigarettes, and Himmelstein said, "Kind of worried about you, ain't she?"

"I almost hit one of the guys in here, talking to my mom, she started crying."

They discussed Caratachea's upbringing and his anger problem. Caratachea pointed out the marks where he had kicked "that wall there" and "punched the one over here." Hitting something, he said, "relieves all the anger at once." Himmelstein recommended relaxation exercises instead of wall punching: "Just breathing . . . real slow deep breaths." But Caratachea had more to say about his anger. "Whenever I blow up my adrenaline starts pumping and I have twice the strength that I normally would have. And I can fight and if they're six foot four I can take them down."

Just then Detective Sands entered the room, and Caratachea's seventeen-hour interrogation came to an end. After Himmelstein handcuffed the suspect, Sands escorted him to a police car to be driven to the juvenile detention center.

With Garcia's confession recorded not once but twice, Kimball told him, "I think you've probably been pretty honest with us up to this point." Then came the "but." "But I also think there may be an area you stayed away from." He asked if Garcia was afraid of anything.

"Not being able to, I don't know, go to school anymore. Like still have a relationship, not being able to go into the service."

Wrong answers. Kimball asked if he was afraid of any person or group of people. Garcia said no.

Mullavey tried another tack, asking if anyone had written anything in the temple.

"I did," Garcia said. "Blood, bloods, something like that."

"Why?"

"I don't know . . . just, you know that saying, throw a wrench in the works." That part of Garcia's plan had already succeeded, consuming many task force man-hours and depriving the temple of one of its walls, which would later appear as evidence in a courtroom.

Mullavey asked if Garcia could look them in the eye and say he'd been absolutely honest about who was "involved in this."

"Yes, I can," Garcia said. He offered to take a lie detector test. "I heard the shit Johnathan was telling. . . . He's involving new people, you know, like racisms and stuff." As he listened, something "just clicked inside, 'Damn, why don't I just tell the truth.'" That way, he explained, no one could come back to him and say his story wasn't true. Garcia would soon lose that illusion.

Asked how many people in the world knew what happened at the temple that night, he was unequivocal. "Me and Johnathan."

Kimball told him other people admitted being there. "Better than that," Mullavey said. "Little things, Alex. We have someone who tells us that from the temple they went out to where ATCs were in the river bottom. . . . We cannot manufacture somebody telling us something that you're now saying is true."

The investigators were relying on "little things" indeed. McGraw had mentioned going to Camelback Mountain, where "we ride ATCs." Garcia had said ATC riders used the entire Agua Fria river bottom. Camelback Mountain and the usually waterless Agua Fria riverbed are in different parts of the Phoenix area, although Camelback *Road* does pass the mountain and cross the riverbed. In their determination to link the Avondale boys with the guys from Tucson, Captain White's interrogators treated all references to Camelback as equivalent and the mention of ATCs as a major clue.

Kimball and Mullavey believed Garcia must be terrified of the guys from Tucson—otherwise he would have named them by now. But Garcia insisted, "As much as I would want there to be other people, there isn't anybody else."

If the suspect wouldn't name his accomplices, the interrogators would do it for him. Mullavey listed the Tucson Four one by one, starting with "Have you ever heard the name Mark Nunez?" Garcia said he'd never heard of any of them.

Having made it clear who they wanted him to implicate, Kimball and Mullavey left Garcia alone to think. They came back with two books of newspaper coverage of the temple case.

"You still got it in your mind that there was someone else," Garcia said.

Mullavey asked, "Does this sound familiar?" He read aloud, "We won't kill you right away."

"No," Garcia said. "No one ever came after me. No one gave me a call to tell me I was going to die slowly, no one." The only thing he was scared of was that he wouldn't "have a life anymore because of this . . . that I'm going to be put in jail for the rest of my life."

Kimball had one card left to play—an enhanced version of the family card. He and Captain White would enlist Garcia's own father to beg his son to talk about the guys from Tucson.

Garcia was positive his dad would confirm his story. "I told him exactly what I told you. That it was me and Johnathan." Kimball and Mullavey's sneering disbelief made him frantic. "God damn, can't trust, can't trust the, the system anymore."

Mullavey shot back, "System's the only thing you can trust right now."

"Not at this point I can't. . . . I'm telling you the truth, the complete truth. No one has threatened me. I don't know where these other people get this story. . . . I know for a fact they were not there."

Mullavey didn't buy it. "Alex, if you're going to . . . try to convince us that there were only two people at the temple that night, when these people got murdered, you and Johnathan, you're lying."

"What do you want me to tell you? Do you want me to, like, start lying and all this other stuff? 'Cause from this point on, that's what, all you're gonna get."

In retrospect, Kimball's reply has an ironic ring. "You can't make up lies about it, because we have the other four stories. So we would know instantly, if you began to lie."

The four other people, Kimball said, were "giving up themselves, and others." "And you know what's so amazing," he went on, "is the numbers of people that they give up are very close, if not identical. Seating positions in vehicles are very close, if not identical; vehicle descriptions are very close, if not identical; locations stopped at are very close, if not identical. Things inside the temple are amazingly close. And amazingly close to what you told us tonight."

"It's gonna be a long night," Garcia said. "We're gonna be here until hell freezes over, because I have no idea what you guys are talking about."

Kimball turned off the tape recorder, and father and son conferred in private for about an hour. When the tape started running again, Juan Garcia's theme quickly became clear. The son might not feel threatened, but the father did. "If there's somebody else behind this situation," he told Kimball and Mullavey, "they may retaliate by making, showing him an example, hurting my oldest son, burning my house down . . . blowing up my car, maybe hurting my wife."

In the monitoring room, Captain White had listened to much of Garcia's second confession, but he refused to believe that the boys from

Avondale had acted alone. The Tucson suspects must have been with them. Now he decided to question Garcia himself.

White arrived with some reading material. He showed Garcia four black binders, the confessions of Bruce, Nunez, Parker, and McGraw. Holding up Bruce's binder, he said, "This is one of the men from Tucson, who told us how he did the shooting, with the .22." He picked up Parker's binder and said it belonged to "one of the black guys, . . . probably the most fearsome looking of the bunch." He held up McGraw's binder and said this guy had told them about the meeting at Camelback and the river bottom where people rode ATCs.

After a lengthy monologue, White asked if Garcia was ready to "go ahead and put it all together so that all of these people are where they should be."

Garcia wondered if he could talk with White alone.

"You betcha," White said. Mullavey and Kimball left the room. Alex, crying now, walked over and embraced his father.

Juan Garcia had some parting words for White. "I would like to protect the family as much as I can. I ain't afraid. Yes I am. I'm, god, afraid." And for his son, a dramatic plea to give White what he wanted. "I don't know how your mama—okay. She will be heartbroken." But Alex shouldn't worry about the family: friends would help protect them, and "I've dodged rockets and shit, I can definitely take care of four punks. . . . You tell these people what they need to know. Okay. It's time, mijo."

"I love you, Dad."

"I love you too. . . . And for you to get involved in this bullshit, that broke my heart. Now you want to put my heart at ease and your mama's heart at ease, tell them what has to be told."

"Okay, Dad."

Alone with Garcia, White got started. "How many people were there that night, Alex?"

"I don't know what I can tell you."

"You still don't want to come out and tell the truth? Your dad wants you—"

"I don't have to tell you."

"Let me go through and tell you what I know."

White listed the names Doody had provided—George, Rolando, and George's friend—plus "two or three blacks, and the guys that came up from Tucson." He gave a long speech that ended, "You think you can go ahead now and get into it and tell what happened?"

If White would "recall the scene" for him, Garcia suggested, he would remember it better.

White said he didn't want to "lay everything out for you." He began taking Garcia through the day of the murders step by step, beginning when Doody picked him up in the Mustang. As the questioning continued, Garcia fell back on the same excuse for vague answers used by Leo Bruce and other Tucson suspects. "Maybe I passed out or something. I don't know what I missed."

Garcia wanted to talk to Doody alone. White said they couldn't do that. What if they left big strong Alex alone with Johnathan, fragile like a toothpick, and "all of a sudden we hear a rumpus in the room and we come in here and poor old Johnathan is laying over there in a heap?" He gave Garcia no chance to reply.

As a substitute for producing Doody in person, Mullavey came in with a tape of part of Doody's confession and played short segments for Garcia. The transcript does not note what this other tape said, but at the end of the playback, White asked, "So do you agree that I did talk to Johnathan, he told me what happened?"

Garcia said, "I would prefer rather not talking."

Soon a knock on the door heralded the return of Juan Garcia. He told Alex he would trust White with his life, his family's lives. "This man would not lie to you. And I don't think he would lie to me."

Then he joined his son's interrogators. "Mijo, something is not coming out. You are afraid. You may think you're not. I don't know what these boys . . . said, how they intimidated you. . . . Is it worth your life and your future to protect these people?"

"I just thought of something," White said. "Maybe the threat's not from people down in Tucson, but from people out on the west side area that you know. That's what it is, because I just saw your face change. . . . You're not afraid of the guys down in Tucson, you're afraid of the guys that are still out that are in the west side area, that are close to home. Right?"

Garcia's response was noncommittal: the typist rendered it as "Mm huh." But the family card was working: he began to tell a new story. Someone he didn't know had approached him in the neighborhood and told him, "I shouldn't talk about it, if my life was that important to me."

White was gracious. "I ask for your forgiveness and I apologize because I set here like a dummy and talked to you all this time, and didn't realize what the problem was, until it hit me that you weren't afraid of the people from Tucson, that it was closer to home."

If Alex hoped his new story would please his father, he was disappointed. Now Juan Garcia was utterly terrified. "For sure, they know Mama's car. For sure, they know my truck. They've probably followed my ass to work, they probably know where I park my truck every morning . . . they've probably followed Mama or Ricky, in the car, to school or after school. . . . If they need to do something, they going to pick the time and place and we won't be able to see it coming."

He said much more, imagining horrible events and begging his son to "tell them what has to be told."

The son was clear about one point: "It's not the guys from Tucson. I'm not worried about that." He said he didn't know who had threatened him. They'd been in "a bluish car." The man he'd seen was black, medium size, in his thirties, but he'd had his face covered.

As White went over the names Doody had given, Garcia never actually said, "George was there," but he did say the name "George" several times. Each time White filled in the blanks, saying, "George was there with you."

When pressed for more names, Garcia said he was scared. His father pleaded, "Say it for me. Say it, Mijo, please."

White asked, "Was Rolando there?"

As with George, Garcia avoided an outright accusation. "I believe so," he said.

Then he volunteered, "There was a black man there." White asked where the black man was from. "I believe Tucson."

"What makes you think he came from Tucson?"

"I think it was mentioned or something. . . . It seemed like they were saying it at the river bottom."

Like Doody, he was vague about how many black men. "It was really pretty much dark, everybody seemed dark." After further pressing, he said there were two or three.

"There were other men there, though, right?"

"I believe so."

White asked if he had heard anyone speaking Spanish.

"Perhaps. I think so."

"So you think maybe there was some Hispanic people there?"

"Maybe."

"Were there any Anglos there?"

This time Garcia named Rollie; he added that George's friend was white.

The captain approved. "I think we have pretty well established the cast of characters." Next he proposed to "start from day one and go through this thing and get your version of who did what."

Instead, Garcia requested a break. He turned down an offer of soda pop, and when asked if he needed anything else, answered wryly, "A car."

Garcia didn't want to go through it again. White said, "We're gonna make it easy, all right?" If Alex couldn't answer something, "We'll work through it."

One more time they traced Garcia's activities on August 9. When they reached the part where he and Doody were leaving Amanda's house that night, Garcia said, "Dad, you can leave."

White wanted to know what vehicles were at the river bottom besides the Mustang. "I remember a truck," Garcia said. "I remember a car."

Probing for details, White asked if the truck had any chrome on it. "Yeah, it probably had chrome on it. It shined once in a while, you know, like if the light would hit it. . . . It could have had chrome on it."

This answer may have sounded too acquiescent; White threw in a test question. "Was there an ATC up in the back?" In McGraw's story there had been no ATC.

Garcia didn't pass the test. "I believe so, I don't know."

Moving on, White asked, "Who did you see?"

"I think I saw Parker. Yeah . . . someone said 'Parker' and I don't know, there was a black man." But right after giving White this gift, Garcia snatched it away. "Or some park . . . like, I don't know, make a left at the park, or I don't know, I remember 'park.'"

As for how many people, he said, "Um, maybe three, four. No, maybe four or five, whatever."

"How many white people?"

"White? Um, I know I saw a black."

"So how many blacks?"

"I said three or four, two or three."

"How many Hispanics did you see?"

"Um, ah, I think they might have been sleeping then."

White repeated the question.

"One."

"Just one Hispanic?"

"One or two."

"One or two Hispanics?"

"Something like that."

White kept the questions coming, and Garcia kept the answers vague. At one point, trying to come up with another name, Garcia seemed to be inspired by the recent hit movie *Die Hard 2*. He remembered "something like George or, you know, I don't know. George Willis."

"Was Willis there?"

"Or Bruce, ah, maybe Bruce. I don't know."

White had had enough. He walked out, ending Garcia's interrogation. As Riley explained it, when questioned about his mention of Parker, Garcia "became very evasive and reluctant to provide details. Because of this growing adversarial relationship developing between Alessandro and Captain White, the interview was not pursued any further."

As Garcia's final tape, tape 12, ran to its end, he asked an unnamed officer what would happen next. "Am I going to be like tried as an adult or, or what's going to happen like tomorrow?"

"I think to juvenile," the officer said.

"Is everybody going to be going to the juvenile detention?"

"Only the juveniles."

"You mean everybody under eighteen?"

"Yeah."

"Which would probably be everybody."

Riley reveals what did happen next. At approximately 7:52 p.m., Garcia "was booked into the Maricopa County Juvenile Detention Facility on nine counts of murder and other related charges."

The interrogations of Caratachea, Doody, and Garcia fill forty-seven tapes and more than a thousand pages of transcript. Eventually a jury would hear the actual words of two of the boys—Doody and Garcia. Caratachea, like Victor Zarate, was not charged with any involvement in the temple murders. Those two suspects did not confess, and without the "queen of proofs," the county attorneys did not have enough evidence to make a case against them.

Doody was seventeen years old; Garcia was sixteen. These teenagers—with their "full gear and equipment," their BDUs and misleading boot prints, their countdowns and rendezvous points and synchronized watch—apparently imagined themselves as trained secret agents or commandos (or perhaps master criminals). The contrast is stark between that fantasy and the characteristics the FBI profiler predicted the temple murderers would have: "youth and stupidity."

POLITICAL WRANGLING

By the end of October, with Doody and Garcia in juvenile detention, public and political pressure to drop the case against the Tucson Four was mounting. It seemed clear that the Tucson defendants had no connection to the case, despite their confessions. That is, it seemed clear to everyone but the MCSO command staff. Scores of lawyers, judges, reporters, and members of other law enforcement agencies had read part or all of the two sets of confessions and come to the same conclusion: the Tucson confessions were obviously coerced and disingenuous; the Avondale confessions seemed plausible and verifiable—at least up to the point where Doody and Garcia were questioned about the guys from Tucson.

Even before Caratachea's rifle linked the Avondale boys to the murders, the MCSO's treatment of the Tucson suspects drew outraged criticism—and not only from the suspects' friends and neighbors. In early October the *New York Times* quoted Louis Rhodes, executive director of the American Civil Liberties Union of Arizona: "It's kind of 'The Keystone Kops enter the Twilight Zone.' It's the kind of thing that almost becomes a classic of everything you don't do in an investigation."

The controversy intensified after Doody and Garcia were indicted. On October 31 the *Arizona Republic* ran a front-page article calling the case a "hodgepodge of conflicting witness stories and mystery suspects." Reporter Charles Kelly noted that the Tucson men had recanted their confessions, and that those confessions disagreed on many points. Even so, investigators believed that each of them knew too many details about the crime to be innocent. But defense lawyers argued that the interrogators had fed the suspects those details.

The task force itself was divided over whether the two sets of suspects were connected. An anonymous official told the *Republic*, "There is incredible pressure coming from the sheriff for a link." Some of the unnamed sources who leaked information about the task force were just trying to do their jobs without making the mess any worse. They saw themselves as realists, and they saw no connection between Tucson and Avondale. Captain White and others who continued to search for a link were widely discredited.

Sheriff Agnos stood behind his command staff. He held a question-and-answer session on Phoenix's west side in attempt to placate public opinion. But he sidestepped certain questions. Asked why the sheriff's office was so controversial, Agnos said, "What do you mean, controversial? Give me some specifics of what we've done that has been controversial." When the questioner mentioned the temple case, Agnos countered with the only position he could take: that a judge and a grand jury had felt there was enough evidence to charge the Tucson Four with first-degree murder.

On November 19 a *Los Angeles Times* story called the case a "career-threatening minefield" for the sheriff and the county attorney. Jane Fritsch reported that authorities were struggling to sort out a "muddled criminal case" with two sets of apparently unrelated suspects. She cited an opinion poll showing that the reputations of both Agnos and County Attorney Richard Romley had been damaged by their handling of the case.

Articles like these discussed the difficulties facing the investigators, but they did not spell out the differences between the police power of the county sheriff and the prosecutorial power of the county attorney. Because the decision to charge anyone with a crime belongs exclusively to the prosecutor, not the sheriff, the internal politics of the case simmered and seethed.

County Attorney Romley gave Sheriff Agnos a deadline. If the task force did not find stronger evidence against the Tucson Four by November 23, he would ask a court to release them. Investigators claimed they were still processing evidence and following leads. According to an unnamed "source close to Romley" quoted in the *Arizona Republic*, "Agnos doesn't have the evidence right now, but he thinks if Romley decides to cut the four loose, he'll be leaving Agnos hanging out to dry. Romley's upset because he thinks this is just as much of a moral issue as it is a legal issue. If the evidence isn't there, Rick wants to let them go."

Sheriff Agnos and Captain White had kept their team busy scouring the state for evidence linking the Tucson Four with the Avondale boys; now the deadline intensified those efforts. The *Republic* reported on November 20 that Agnos had "spent thousands of dollars trying to establish a connection between the two sets of suspects. He sent two detectives to Tucson about a month ago, and they reportedly have been working night and day, with no success."

White did some of the scouring himself. For example, after learning of the deadline, he decided to talk to Alex Garcia's father, who had been so helpful during his son's interrogation. On November 9 he visited Juan and Gloria Garcia and informed them of Romley's plan. "Mr. Garcia," White noted, "became visibly upset and said the link was the subject who was with George Gonzales that night and Alex would not name him." White advised the Garcias to have Alex's defense attorney contact the county attorneys "to see if the link information could be provided."

With Romley poised to dismiss the charges and release McGraw, Nunez, Bruce, and Parker, Agnos tried to turn police power into political power. In an effort to put pressure on Romley, he appointed a Blue Ribbon Committee to review the situation. Its members were six well-known legal and law enforcement figures: former Phoenix police chief Ruben Ortega, Phoenix lawyer Jeremy Toles, former U.S. attorneys A. Melvin McDonald and Michael Hawkins, former FBI agent Bud Gaskill, and former Tucson police chief Bernard Garmire. They examined the sheriff's evidence and all the confessions. Agnos asked them to persuade Governor J. Fife Symington III to intervene and "order" Romley to continue the case.

In a "seventy-five-minute closed-door meeting" with the governor, committee members outlined the case against the Tucson suspects and presented Symington with three options: appoint a special prosecutor, transfer the case to the state attorney general's office, or ask Romley to delay the dismissal for sixty days. But the governor refused to intervene. Romley told the *Republic* that the ultimate decision was his to make and that he would not be swayed by political pressure.

Romley did offer Agnos a way to save face. He suggested that Agnos write a letter asking him to dismiss the charges *without prejudice,* meaning that new charges could be filed against the Tucson Four in the future if more evidence turned up. On Friday, November 22, the charges were in fact dismissed without prejudice.

Thus Romley's decision did not clear the names of the Tucson suspects or free them from investigation: Leese and White would spend the next year and a half trying to link them with Garcia and Doody. In February 1993, with the possibility of renewed charges still hanging over them, Nunez, Bruce, and McGraw filed motions asking a judge to dismiss the charges permanently. Superior Court judge Frank Galati said that he could not do so without a request from the county attorney. In his ruling, the judge scolded Romley, writing that if he believed the defendants were innocent, it was "his ethical duty to file a motion to dismiss with prejudice."

The key disagreement between the sheriff and the county attorney was over the strength of the Tucson confessions as evidence. Agnos, and at least some of his deputies, thought the confessions were sufficient to make a case against the men in court. Romley knew better. He knew very well how hard it would be to convince a judge and jury to believe those confessions. If he did not dismiss the charges, he would have to defend obvious misconduct by the deputies who had extracted the confessions. He knew he would never be able to justify holding the suspects in the Sheraton Hotel for three days to keep them away from magistrates, lawyers, and family members.

Romley, a conscientious lawyer, reviewed the files on the Tucson Four before dismissing the charges. "I read all those confessions," he said, "and I have to question how they were obtained. I told Agnos that I thought he should take the time to read each of the confessions and I thought he would come up with the same conclusion. I don't think he's bothered reading them word-by-word." He said he had also read Doody's and Garcia's confessions and "had problems with the way deputies tried for hours to get them to admit that they were connected with the Tucson men."

Agnos had never read the transcripts because he had been recuperating from open-heart surgery. He'd relied on White to brief him on the authenticity and credibility of the confessions. Had he been able to read them himself, he might well have agreed with Romley's decision to dismiss the Tucson charges and focus on the real killers.

Citing an unnamed member of the task force, the *Arizona Republic* reported that investigators claimed Romley had *not* read the transcripts. The source maintained that Romley did not become dissatisfied with the evidence against the Tucson Four until after the Avondale boys were taken into custody. Before that, he "vigorously pressed the case," even going public in Parker's preliminary hearing, portraying Parker as "the mastermind of the crime." But when Doody and Garcia were arrested, "all hell broke loose."

Task force members disagreed among themselves about whether the two sets of suspects were connected. But their commander, Captain White, insisted they still had leads to follow up—enough to justify holding the Tucson men.

The weakness of the sheriff's position and the strength of the county attorney's was illustrated by the meeting between Governor Symington and the Blue Ribbon Committee. The governor's aides pointedly asked whether committee members were sure the Tucson suspects had been involved in the massacre. According to the committee's spokesman, Mel McDonald, members responded that "the courtroom is the place for that to be determined." Symington and his staff recognized the lack of certainty in that answer and knew a political quagmire when they saw one. Aides told the committee, "It would be political suicide for the governor to take a position on this."

By this time the sheriff's task force had devoted hundreds of man-hours to unsuccessful attempts to establish a connection between the two sets of suspects. Romley was not Agnos's only problem. Several of his most experienced detectives were privately critical of White's handling of the investigation. They felt Agnos and Leese had made a mistake in choosing the task force commander: they had "bypassed veteran officers who had investigated numerous homicides" in favor of White, whose experience was in drug enforcement.

The *Arizona Republic* continued to chronicle the public dispute. On November 21 reporters quoted Agnos's pledge to continue to investigate the Tucson Four. "I feel it is my duty and my obligation to do everything I can to pursue this. . . . There is no doubt in my mind we are going to make this case."

The article also quoted Romley. "Tom says he 'hopes' they will uncover evidence; I've been hearing this 'I hope' for months. But that's not how our system of government works. We just can't hold people like that." Romley warned that Agnos's appointment of the Blue Ribbon Committee and his determination to keep pursuing Tucson leads might undermine the case against Doody and Garcia. Committee members might be called as defense witnesses, Romley said, "maybe against me." "We could lose the whole ball of wax, including the case against the juveniles." The reporters gave Romley the last word: "To say you have to stay with the same tactics is not good law enforcement. You've got to adapt to changes."

Talk radio loved the story. Most callers seemed to support Agnos and disagree with Romley's decision to drop the charges. Agnos told Phoenix radio station KFYI, during one of its call-in shows, "The four should have been held on the value of their confessions. Why would four street-wise individuals, two of them ex-convicts, make statements about their participation in a crime of this magnitude? It just doesn't make any sense that they would do that, under any conditions."

The sheriff's attitude was a natural one: although a considerable and growing body of evidence demonstrates that false confessions are not rare, most people probably believe they themselves would not confess to a crime they did not commit. But Agnos, as a senior law enforcement officer, had a responsibility not shared by the public at large. He should have been willing to consider the possibility that a confession was not absolute evidence of guilt.

As a result of Romley's decision, McGraw, Bruce, and Nunez were released. Dante Parker was remanded to the custody of California authorities for his parole violation. Victor Zarate, freed weeks earlier, was among the crowd of friends and relatives waiting to greet Bruce and Nunez when they walked out the door of the Maricopa County Jail. McGraw found no welcoming friends outside the jail; instead, a reporter picked him up for a trip to Wat Promkunaram, the setting of the dramatic tale he had spun for his interrogators. The reporter, Philip Martin of the Phoenix newspaper *New Times*, wrote that McGraw "swears it'll be his first visit." But, he added, McGraw "always has a story to tell."

Although the search continued, White's team never did manage to link the Tucson men to Doody and Garcia. As commander of the MCSO's criminal investigations unit, White had to turn his attention to other cases as well. One of the homicides handled by his unit would come back to haunt him in early 1993: a murder committed in October 1991, a few days before the marathon interrogations of the boys from Avondale.

The temple murder investigation, too, would come back to haunt its commanders. In the 1992 election, Agnos would be ousted from office by a new sheriff. And in 1993, when the temple case finally went to trial, the dissent within the task force, which had led some disgruntled members to leak their opinions to the press, would become public knowledge.

As Agnos and White's task force disintegrated over the coerced— and false—Tucson confessions, a retired DEA agent named Joe Arpaio watched the spectacle and saw an opportunity. Although at the time

Arpaio was virtually unknown in local political and criminal justice circles, he ran against Agnos in the September 1992 Republican primary,
beat him soundly, and became the new sheriff. Many regarded the election as a referendum on the handling of the temple case; Arpaio called
the investigation "bizarre" and said it "rated an F for being mishandled."

Soon after taking office, Arpaio issued an apology to the Tucson
Four and demoted Jerry White and other MCSO commanders he held
responsible for botching the case. In an early press conference he said, "I
don't like confessions. . . . Make sure you've got corroborating evidence
before you arrest somebody." That was a philosophy never before applied
in Maricopa County law enforcement.

Sheriff Arpaio did more than just talk to the press and demote task
force commanders; he also ordered an "investigation into the investigation" by the MCSO's internal affairs unit—its "infernal secret police," as
Kimball later called them. Arpaio assigned Lt. Terry Chapman to find
out why the temple investigation had gone so badly wrong. Handwritten
notes from this probe, which became known as the Chapman Audit,
would later come to light, embarrassing both the MCSO and the county
attorney's office.

Chapman began his investigation in February 1993. One officer he
interviewed was Detective Dan Faulk. Back in October 1991, White had
selected Faulk to prepare the "investigative file for discovery"—the file
that would be turned over to the defense attorneys—and had given him
only six days to create order out of chaos. Talking with Chapman, Faulk
called task force headquarters "a zoo, with everybody running around
helter-skelter." He recalled being given large unorganized stacks of documents. Culling out papers that did not belong in the discovery file,
Faulk organized the rest by date and subject. They filled eleven large
three-ring binders.

White instructed Faulk that no material should leave the sheriff's
office without being read and approved by Kimball. But when presented
with the eleven volumes, Kimball paged hurriedly through portions of
them and then told Faulk, "Skip it."

Chapman also interviewed Detective Pat Riley, who admitted, "We
didn't do anything in this case like we would normally do it." Riley complained that pulling detectives out of interviews broke up continuity, and
that when one interrogator took over from another, "It was impossible
for one detective to know what the other detective had talked about."
Riley, who had interrogated Parker, Nunez, and Zarate, said he had been

surprised that they later confessed. (In fact Zarate had not confessed; a year after the fast-paced, overlapping interrogations, Riley apparently had trouble telling the Tucson suspects apart.) When Riley and Detective Scoville left Parker's interview, both thought he "was telling the truth when he said he wasn't involved." And yet the next team to tackle Parker, Officer Troutt and Detective Sinsabaugh, extracted a confession.

Riley was sharply critical of his bosses. "None of the command staff," he said, "wanted to hear that there was a division of opinion about the involvement or non-involvement of the Tucson suspects." He was clearly no fan of the task force commander: "White expressed the opinion that the reports we were writing were too conservative. We began to fear that an alteration of the facts in our reports might occur. Kimball advised us to make sure we kept a set of our reports back when we submitted anything in finalized form." In contrast to the top brass, "most of the detectives had changed their minds about the Tucson suspects but were fearful and discouraged about expressing their true opinions."

Other detectives interviewed by Chapman confirmed Riley's statement. Sergeant Kimball said, "Mark Mullavey knew early on that we focused on the wrong suspects." In November 1991, after reading Leo Bruce's transcript, Mullavey shared his misgivings with a chief deputy, John Coppock. Soon after that conversation, White told Mullavey "his negative attitude could poison other investigators" and "discussed removing him from the case." Kimball and Mullavey, who had been partners on many homicide cases, told Sheriff Agnos directly that they didn't think the Tucson suspects were involved. "Apparently he didn't believe us," Kimball said, "because he is still out there calling these guys criminals."

Detective Rick Sinsabaugh had a similar story. "I told [Agnos] what I thought. He said 'Maybe you need some time off.'" Coppock called Sinsabaugh a good investigator, but added, "You don't have the killer instinct" and told him to "stay focused on the objective." Agnos's other chief deputy, George Leese, told Sinsabaugh "not to worry about a little doubt." Sinsabaugh added a comment of his own: "Jerry White cannot face the facts. He is still convinced the Tucson Four are involved. I like Jerry but he is wrong. It is a problem when you can't listen to those around you."

Kimball told Chapman that the problems with the investigation had begun long before the interrogations started. "We couldn't control the crime scene. . . . With the sheriff and so many higher-ranking command personnel present, I could not maintain control of the scene." The chaos

Kimball described is the antithesis of good professional law enforcement. "The crime scene looked like Viet Nam, helicopters were landing and taking off. Asians were milling and running about in the prop wash of the choppers. The news media people were clamoring for admittance and seeking interviews with anyone willing to talk to them."

"The thing that sidetracked the train from the beginning," Kimball continued, "was the reported demands from the top to get results now! There was constant pressure to provide an answer immediately no matter how unreasonable the request. It was constant, work, work, work. . . . I was putting in over a hundred hours a week. Other detectives were doing the same. It affected all our work. You would get so tired you couldn't think straight."

Sinsabaugh was more colorful. "We were going off in all directions at ninety miles per hour with our head up our ass. I was as guilty as anyone else."

Riley, Kimball, and Sinsabaugh gave examples of specific instances of unproductive and foolish orders from the command staff. They complained that the top-down investigation left the real detectives out of the real work. They felt the interrogations were too long and violated too many court rulings. Kimball spoke for all the "real detectives" when he said, "We were made to look time and time again like fucking fools because of this type of unreasonable orders and demands."

Internal affairs inquiries and reports usually remain just that: internal. These sensitive investigations of colleagues by colleagues are kept within the department, away from public scrutiny. The formal audit Chapman produced did remain under wraps. But when the temple murder case finally went to trial, his handwritten notes, with their revelations of internal dissent and slapdash command decisions, would make their way into the public record.

What did not make sense to Sheriff Agnos in 1991—that innocent people, under interrogation, might confess to murder—makes a great deal of sense to most people in the criminal justice system today. Police interrogators *do* induce innocent suspects to confess to crimes. The sociologist Richard J. Ofshe, who has spent many years studying this phenomenon, calls the problem of police-induced false confessions "significant, recurrent, and deeply troubling." Furthermore, Mike McGraw is surely not the only person who has *volunteered* a false confession for psychological reasons.

In a long article in the *Arizona Republic* in October 2004, Dennis Wagner cited findings by the Death Penalty Information Center that nearly a quarter of all murder suspects later exonerated by genetic tests had falsely confessed, and that "juries convict defendants who make those admissions 73 percent of the time—even when incriminating statements are withdrawn and rebutted by evidence."

Wagner focused on the case of the Tucson Four along with that of Robert Armstrong, a suspect questioned by the MCSO in 2003 for another multiple homicide. MCSO interrogators got Armstrong to say he must have committed the murders during an alcoholic blackout, but belated investigation of his alibi proved he had not been in Arizona at the time of the killings. (The Armstrong case will come up again later in this book.)

With these two cases as examples, Wagner quoted Ofshe's finding that false confessions are almost always caused by "police misconduct, where someone is made to believe that if they continue denying responsibility they will receive the worst possible punishment." Wagner continued, "Because the law allows detectives to lie during interrogations, Ofshe says, they claim proof and witnesses that don't exist. Some suspects, especially the mentally disabled, become so confused they believe they are guilty. Others are convinced that they will be put to death or jailed for life unless they 'cooperate.'"

The problem of false confessions is particularly disturbing when defendants are charged with capital crimes. The death penalty has long been controversial in the United States. Some Americans are opposed to it for moral or ethical reasons; others consider it essential as a punishment for heinous crimes and a deterrent to potential criminals; still others believe it has a place in the judicial system but worry that it is applied unfairly and that, worst of all, innocent people may be put to death.

In the 1990s, as in the twenty-first century, Americans were struggling with the way the death penalty was administered. At the heart of the debate was the sense that innocent people were being sent to death row. Professor Welsh White, in an acclaimed article published in 2003, described strong empirical evidence that in the past century, "a substantial number of capital defendants were wrongfully convicted and, in some cases, sentenced to death."

White pointed out that U.S. Supreme Court justice Sandra Day O'Connor, although she often voted to affirm death sentences, had spoken of "serious questions" about whether the death penalty was fairly administered. He quoted Justice O'Connor: "If statistics are any indication, the system may well be allowing some innocent defendants to be executed." White noted empirical evidence showing that miscarriages of justice in capital cases are unexpectedly frequent, and that "a significant number of them have resulted from police-induced false confessions." Acknowledging the opinions of people like Agnos, White noted that until recently, such confessions had been viewed as "extremely unlikely to produce a wrongful conviction in any case, much less one in which a defendant's life is at stake."

White cited Hugo Adam Bedau and Michael L. Radelet's comprehensive compilation of such wrongful convictions, published in 1987. That was four years before the temple murder case prompted Sheriff Agnos to proclaim that "no one would plead guilty to a murder that he didn't commit." Bedau and Radelet identified 350 wrongful convictions in potentially capital cases in the United States from 1900 to 1985 and traced the causes of 336 of them. White reported their conclusion that "a police-induced false confession was the primary or contributing cause of the wrongful conviction in forty-nine, or 14.3 percent, of the cases."

Richard Ofshe and Welsh White came to their conclusions about police-induced false confessions through extended study; Bedau and Radelet by analyzing empirical information. Mark Nunez, Leo Bruce, and Dante Parker acquired similar knowledge more quickly and far more traumatically. And, as the ordeals of two more innocent men, Robert Armstrong and George Peterson, would demonstrate, the Tucson Four were not the last suspects to whom the MCSO would administer that same terrible lesson.

A MURDERER TEN TIMES OVER   *8*

After the arrest of Doody and Garcia and the release of the Tucson Four, the temple murder case progressed with fewer headlines and less public drama. Doody and Garcia faced charges in juvenile court and remained incarcerated in the juvenile detention center.

Doody's court-appointed defense attorney was Peter Balkan; Garcia's was Luis Calvo. Both were highly regarded Phoenix lawyers with experience in death-penalty cases. Balkan was known for taking on big cases in which juvenile offenders appeared likely to be transferred to adult court.

As part of the pretrial proceedings, Balkan and Calvo moved to suppress their clients' confessions. In ruling on their motions, Judge Gregory Martin defined the issue regarding Doody's confession as "whether the defendant's will to resist confessing was overborne" by his interrogators. In Garcia's case, the issue was "whether the defendant's *Miranda* right to counsel was violated" when Garcia invoked that right "and then later confessed after further interrogation without counsel present." In November 1992 Judge Martin denied both motions: prosecutors would be allowed to use Doody's and Garcia's taped confessions as evidence against them.

Garcia's girlfriend did not desert him. Michelle Hoover wrote to him at the detention center, enlisting her friend Liz Rhinehart to send the letters when her parents forbade her to communicate with him. Garcia's parents provided emotional support. His mother, who described her son as "shy, quiet, sensitive, helpful, supportive, and loving," visited him "as often as allowed by the system." Doody, whose family lived in Colorado, had a lonelier life behind bars. In his parents' absence, two other adults received permission to visit him: a family friend and the faculty sponsor of his beloved ROTC program. Like Garcia, Doody got letters from girls at Agua Fria High School, including Hoover's friend Liz.

Both Doody's and Garcia's cases were transferred from juvenile court to adult court. The transfer was not unexpected: no judge was likely to allow sixteen- and seventeen-year-olds charged with mass murder to be tried as juveniles. Their trials were scheduled for the summer of 1993. Because they were charged with capital offenses, no one pressed for earlier trial dates.

Captain White, although he still managed to look for links between the Tucson suspects and the temple, was busy as commander of the MCSO's criminal investigations unit. In October 1991, just days before White's task force identified the temple murder weapon and picked up Doody and Garcia, his unit had investigated another local homicide, that of a woman named Alice Marie Cameron. MCSO deputies quickly apprehended a suspect, who confessed and was jailed to await trial on first-degree murder charges.

In the temple case, prosecutors decided to offer a plea bargain to Garcia but not to Doody. Their reasons were strictly pragmatic: the State had a stronger case against Garcia than it did against Doody. A footprint matching Garcia's boots had been found at the crime scene, and property stolen from the temple had been recovered from his bedroom. Moreover, Garcia was ready to testify against Doody, but Doody had shown no willingness to implicate Garcia. And Garcia had clearly admitted his role in the shootings, while Doody had only admitted having been present at the temple when the killings occurred.

Under Arizona law, prosecutors are the sole decision makers regarding whether a defendant should be subject to capital punishment. If the prosecutors notify the court that they will seek the death penalty if a defendant is found guilty, the court must allow them to do so; if they do not seek the death penalty, the court may not impose it. Garcia's plea bargain stipulated that if he pleaded guilty and met certain other conditions, he would not be sentenced to death.

Calvo explained the offer to Garcia, including the requirement that he disclose any crimes he had committed after the temple murders. The penalty for not admitting his other crimes would be the loss of the plea bargain. The defense attorney was shocked by his client's response.

On January 4, 1993, Calvo asked for an urgent meeting with Deputy County Attorney Paul Ahler and Assistant County Attorney K. C. Scull. At the meeting Calvo dropped a bombshell: Alex Garcia had participated in another murder shortly before his arrest for the temple killings.

At the time, Calvo did not give Ahler and Scull any specifics. He merely said there *was* another murder and he wanted it included in Garcia's plea bargain. If it was not included, he would withdraw the guilty plea and the State would have to prosecute both Doody and Garcia in separate capital trials.

The prosecutors needed Garcia's testimony. After conferring with their boss, Rick Romley, Ahler and Scull met with Calvo again. Without knowing the victim's name or any details about the crime, they agreed to include it in the temple plea bargain if Garcia met three conditions. He had to plead guilty to this new murder, give sworn testimony about it immediately, and testify in court against anyone else who had been involved. In exchange, Garcia would spend his life in prison but would not get the death penalty for any of the ten murders.

The next day, Scull, Ahler, Calvo, and Sgt. Kimball gathered in Scull's office to hear what Garcia had to say. The court reporter swore him in, and Garcia described the crime under oath. Back in October 1991, he said, he and his girlfriend, Michelle Hoover, had shot a woman at a campground north of Phoenix. The woman's name was Alice Marie Cameron.

Garcia's revelation was disturbing in itself, a tale of two teenagers calmly killing a friendly stranger. It was even more disturbing to the prosecutors and the MCSO because they had long considered the Cameron case closed. MCSO interrogators had extracted a confession from a mentally disabled Vietnam veteran named George Peterson. Peterson had already spent fourteen months in jail, awaiting a trial that might well have brought him the State of Arizona's harshest punishment: death by lethal injection.

Garcia's January 5 deposition was the first step in the legal process of freeing Peterson and arresting Hoover. Notably, it also inked another favorable deal for Garcia. Under oath, he spun another story in which he was involved in a homicide—his tenth—but never really killed anyone.

At the start of the deposition, Calvo confirmed the plea agreement. Garcia would "give a complete and truthful statement" about Cameron's killing, which would be admissible against him. In return, the State would not seek the death penalty for him in either murder case.

Responding to questions from Scull, Garcia went through the details. Michelle Hoover had become his girlfriend in late September 1991, when she was fourteen and he was sixteen. They dated for about a month, until his arrest in late October.

In October they went shooting in the desert. Garcia borrowed a .22-caliber rifle; Hoover took along a .22 Magnum rifle plus a 9mm handgun. Garcia also carried ammunition from his stash of "personal ammo"—the same stash that had supplied the shells for the temple murders. Neither teenager had a driver's license, but they took Hoover's parents' company truck.

In the desert after dark, Garcia drove into a sandy area, and the truck got stuck. They could have called for help on the car phone, but Hoover's father wasn't "the understanding type," and they were afraid of his reaction. All night they sat in the cab and talked. In daylight they managed to free the truck. Garcia claimed that Hoover then called home and hung up when her dad answered, but inquiries would reveal that no calls had been made from the car phone.

With Hoover afraid to go home, they decided to run away. At Garcia's house, where no one was home, he grabbed some clothes plus military-style boots, web gear, and duffle bags. He took fifteen dollars from his mother. After buying gas and food, the runaways were left with no more than five dollars.

At a campground northeast of Phoenix, they spent another night in the truck. The next day, in need of money, they drove around looking for "potential, I should say, victims to rob." Scull asked about Hoover's role. "She was for it," Garcia said. But she hadn't made any suggestions, just agreed with what he decided. They cruised the camping area to find people who were alone or in small groups. They saw Alice Cameron.

To be sure Cameron was alone, they walked over to her campsite and chatted with her, exchanging names, asking if she was by herself, borrowing a book of matches. Then they walked back to their own site, where they agreed that she would be their "target." The plan was to "hold her at gunpoint and rob her and then shoot her"—kill her so they wouldn't "get fingered for it."

Asked who was going to do what, Garcia reprised the role he had perfected in the temple case: nonlethal participant turned helpful witness. As he told it, he asked Hoover if she wanted him to do the armed robbery, and she said she'd do it herself.

Scull moved on. "How did you proceed to carry out the plan? What happened next, in other words?" Whatever "other words" Scull expected to hear, he surely did not anticipate Garcia's cold, matter-of-fact account of the murder of a woman who had been friendly to two young strangers.

Before going back to Cameron's camp, Michelle put on "some web gear with a 9mm holster and gun on the side." Much later, Garcia would say that the web harness he strapped on Hoover was the same gear he and Doody had worn when they'd invaded the Buddhist temple. Hoover had her dad's handgun in the holster, while Garcia carried a rifle. Both weapons were loaded.

Scull asked about their approach to Cameron's camp. "Did you sneak up, or did you just walk boldly up, or how did you go up there?"

Garcia conferred with Calvo, then said they walked up the trail and hid behind bushes so Cameron wouldn't see them. He stayed hidden while Hoover went to Cameron's truck. He couldn't see her, but after two or three minutes, he heard gunshots. Two shots. He heard nothing else: no shouting, no sounds from Hoover or Cameron.

He ran out and saw Michelle holding the gun and Cameron in the bed of the truck. When he went closer, Cameron said, "She shot me, she shot me." He told Michelle to go get their own truck. When Hoover drove up a few minutes later, "I guess Mrs. Cameron thought it was someone else, and then she started, she said 'help, help,' or something like that."

Scull asked, "Was this in a loud voice or a small voice?"

"In a medium voice. She wasn't screaming it, and she wasn't, you know, 'Help! Help!' It was more like a medium."

"So what did you do?"

"I went up and I grabbed her." At Scull's request, he elaborated. "I grabbed her by her mouth. . . . I wouldn't say threw her down. I just grabbed her down to keep her from screaming."

Cameron resisted, trying to pull his hand away from her mouth. Michelle came over and grabbed her legs. Garcia described Cameron saying, "we didn't have to do this, as in, like, keep her from screaming. She wasn't going to scream." She asked why they were doing this. "And I told her, I really don't know."

That may have been as close to the truth as Alex Garcia was capable of getting. This was his tenth murder of a helpless victim in ten weeks. He seemed to give little thought either to the lives of others or to his own motives and emotions.

Garcia and Hoover let go of Cameron, who first sat upright and later lay down in the bed of her pickup. They stayed at her campsite for an hour or so. In his famous song "Folsom Prison Blues," Johnny Cash sings about shooting a man "just to watch him die." Garcia and Hoover lived that song.

Scull asked what the two of them were doing "during this hour that you are sitting there."

"Basically just waiting till she died."

"Did she ask for help?"

"Yes. I believe twice. No, I would say about three times." Garcia wasn't sure if she was still conscious when they left, but he knew she was alive. "She wasn't talking, but she was moving." At one point he touched the back of her head, and she was cold. She was still breathing, though.

While they waited, Hoover grabbed Cameron's purse from the back of the truck. They had shot her to get money, but they found only about a dollar. They took that and a bank debit card, plus Cameron's keys and "a bag of stones that you would buy off television, you know, the good luck stones." Later, on their way out of the campground, Garcia tossed the stones out the window. The next day he had Hoover throw the rest of Cameron's things in a portable toilet at a gas station.

They tried several times to get cash at ATMs, but without Cameron's PIN, her card wouldn't work. So they drove around looking for the address on her driver's license, hoping to find something worth stealing in her house. They also filled up the truck with gas and tried to pay for it with the debit card. It didn't work, but the gas station attendant let them drive away with a full tank after they agreed to leave the card with him and promised to come back with cash. They never did go back.

While they were still waiting for Cameron to die, a car came toward them. Garcia stopped it and told the driver that this section of the campground was full. During that hour Garcia and Hoover didn't talk much, "just on and off. Just she would ask me, you know, 'How long is this going to take?' . . . as in how long is it going to take her to die." He told Hoover he had no idea.

Scull wondered about Hoover's "attitude or demeanor." "Was she mad? Was she happy? Was she sad? Was she impatient?"

"I'd say impatient," Garcia replied, "probably say worried." Both were worried about getting caught.

"Did she seem upset that someone was laying here in the back of a truck dying in front of your eyes? . . . Or was she happy, or was she neutral, or was she—"

"Impatient. Like I said before."

"Impatient to do what?"

"To get out of there."

"So why didn't you just get out of there?"

"I have no idea."

As for Garcia's feelings, "I did say to Michelle that it was a shame someone that nice had to die. . . . I shouldn't say had to die, but died or was shot, you know, robbed." But he "didn't really feel anything except nervous." "It's really hard to explain how I was feeling, but I would say the shooting wasn't . . . uncommon. I'm not sure how to say it. . . . It was something that I've already, you know—"

Scull helped him along. "Experienced?"

"Yes, experienced."

"You experienced it at the temple?"

"Yes."

"Would you call yourself a stone-cold killer?"

"No."

"Would you call Michelle a stone-cold killer?"

"No."

Scull summarized the reaction Garcia was describing. "You know, 'I wish she'd hurry up and die so that we can get out of here and get down to Dairy Queen or something.' I mean, a pretty casual, cold approach to a human being [whose] . . . life's blood is sort of seeping out of her as you are standing there wondering why in the heck she doesn't hurry up and die for us so we can get out of here. Is that a fair representation as to how you felt?"

The deposition transcript does not reveal Garcia's "attitude or demeanor" at this moment—whether his eyes flared, or his shoulders tensed, or whether he seemed even mildly irritated at the suggestion that he was casual about murder. The transcript simply records his one-word answer: "Yes."

Garcia had shielded himself in the temple case by insisting that Doody was the killer. Now he shielded himself in the Cameron case by insisting that Hoover was the killer. The prosecutors chose to accept his story both times. Many people both inside and outside law enforcement believed he was lying both times.

In short order, Rick Romley made three decisions. He ordered the immediate release of George Peterson. He ordered an investigation into how the MCSO had obtained Peterson's false confession. And he confirmed that Garcia would be spared the death penalty in exchange for testimony against Hoover and continued cooperation in the temple case. In essence, he folded Garcia's tenth murder into the plea agreement for the first nine.

The botched investigation of the temple murders had devastating consequences. Peterson, an innocent man, spent fourteen months in the shadow of the death penalty, while Garcia, a murderer of ten people, never faced that ultimate punishment. Peterson's ordeal, like those of Nunez, Bruce, and Parker, was a direct result of the MCSO's investigative methods and tunnel vision. But at least Peterson and the Tucson Four survived their encounters with Maricopa County authorities and lived to sue for compensation. Alice Marie Cameron suffered most from the mistakes in the temple case. More competent and more timely investigation of Garcia's first nine murders would have prevented her death.

Although she did not die until mid-October, September 10 was a fateful—a fatal—day for Alice Cameron. On that day, Detective Sinsabaugh confiscated Caratachea's rifle, and his interviews with Doody and Garcia revealed connections between the boys and the Buddhist temple. Also on that day, Mike McGraw began the tale spinning that would lead to the police-induced confessions of the other three members of the Tucson Four. With those confessions in hand, the task force stopped looking for suspects, so Sinsabaugh's early Avondale interviews were not followed up; meanwhile, the MCSO neglected to have the rifle examined by the state crime lab. Had the gun been tested promptly, the task force would have learned it was the murder weapon and easily traced it to Garcia and Doody, who surely would have been arrested in mid-September. Instead, thirty-eight days *after* the sheriff's office obtained the rifle, Garcia killed again.

Cameron's death gave the MCSO another opportunity to solve a murder. Unfortunately, the brass and the deputies rushed forward with the same techniques and the same mindset that shaped the temple investigation. They quickly settled on a suspect and extracted a false confession. This time the suspect was George Peterson, whose mistake was to choose a campsite near the one where Garcia and Hoover would soon kill Cameron.

Peterson was a man of simple tastes. He lived alone, kept to himself, and made his troubled way in the world with as little fuss as possible. The *Arizona Republic* characterized him as "a transient with a history of mental problems." That description hints at both why he was so quickly suspected and why he was so easily swayed by his interrogators.

Captain White's first impression of Peterson was as "a bearded Grizzly Adams." (This comparison was more accurate than White probably realized: the movie and TV character Grizzly Adams was an innocent man accused of murder.) The *Republic*'s photo of Peterson shows a bespectacled man with a graying beard and shaggy hair long enough to cover his ears. His oversized black plastic glasses give his eyes a larger-than-life look. Easily startled under the best of circumstances, Peterson gazes at the camera like the proverbial deer in the headlights. Unfortunately for him, sheriff's deputies caught him in their headlights at the Mesquite Flats Campground on October 18, 1991, seventy-five yards from the campsite where they found Alice Cameron's body.

Since his service as a Marine during the Vietnam War, Peterson had been hospitalized many times for mental problems. Chief among them, according to his VA records, was PTSD: posttraumatic stress disorder. Stationed on Okinawa, Peterson had not seen combat, but his job as a mechanic, cleaning and repairing bloody vehicles from Vietnam, had left him with nightmarish memories and flashbacks. He also had physical problems. Because of a back injury, he walked with a cane and suffered chronic pain, but he tried not to take pain medication unless he badly needed it. Use of his left hand, his dominant hand, was hampered by carpal tunnel syndrome.

Peterson had spent the last few years traveling back and forth between his own property south of Sanders, Arizona, and the VA hospital in Phoenix. If the deputies had thought to ask, the VA psychiatrists and counselors could have given them a very different look at the man they so easily induced to give a false confession. His medical records chronicle a life of looking back to times when he was not always confused and not so likely to misunderstand the motives of people who seemed to befriend him. The VA could also have confirmed that Peterson was not a transient but a property owner, that he was not indigent but received full disability benefits, and that he was a compliant patient who followed his psychiatrist's advice and took his medication as directed.

His family, too, could have made it clear that Peterson was not a drifter or a ne'er-do-well looking for someone to kill. He lived alone by choice on a remote, unimproved high-desert acre. While saving up to buy a house trailer, he was content to camp on his own land, hauling water from a neighbor's well and getting supplies from town. He made the monthly payments on his mortgage and his Chevy Blazer faithfully, set aside money for food and supplies, and traveled as he pleased, staying at campgrounds all over northern and central Arizona. His sister, Debra Peterson, described him as a man who "often made self-sacrifices in order to help others" and who was "probably more concerned over how his family is coping with the news of his arrest than he is for himself."

Peterson was not much of a planner but managed to organize his life around what he'd done in the past. He had routines that kept him safe, places where he felt comfortable. But once he caught the attention of the MCSO, he would feel neither safe nor comfortable for many months to come.

Peterson arrived at the Mesquite Flats Campground on Tuesday, October 15. On Friday he changed campsites to avoid the weekenders who flocked to his favorite area. Finding a site just south of the Verde River, he set up camp in the same ordered way he went about taking his VA-prescribed antidepressant and antianxiety medication.

While his dinner, a military "meal ready to eat," was heating, he started a letter to his mother, recently widowed by his stepfather's death. With dinner he took his doxepin, as he did every night.

As usual, Peterson fell asleep shortly after the sun went down. Soon something woke him. He heard a shot, then a second one. Between them he thought he heard a "rebel yell." In hindsight, he told his lawyer Evan Haglund in 1993, he thought the sound was "Michelle Hoover shrieking, or possibly a yell of 'sick joy' by Alex Garcia."

A week earlier, near Lake Roosevelt, Peterson had thought someone was shooting at him and had reported the incident to the local sheriff's office. Now the shots in the night alarmed him. He took out his .44 Magnum revolver but stayed in his tent, alert and listening. Later he heard two or more vehicles, male and female voices, and a cat meowing. He also heard a thud like something being loaded into a pickup truck.

He spent the next day around his campsite, reading, taking a walk. In the afternoon he noticed a commotion, people standing around talking, vehicles coming and going. On his way to the camp's porta-johns, he saw crime scene tape around a campsite and got worried. As Haglund noted, "he associated the crime scene tape with death."

An officer asked the onlookers to fill out witness statements. While Peterson was writing his statement, one of the other men, who was "very under the influence," told him, "I wouldn't want to be in your shoes." Peterson had no idea what the man meant, but the words sounded ominous.

Alice Marie Cameron's body was discovered at approximately 4:00 p.m. on Saturday, October 19, by two campers, Charles Lee Blaylock and David Bittinger. Blaylock drove off to notify Chuck Corrigan, the Salt River Project dam keeper at nearby Horseshoe Dam, leaving Bittinger to guard the crime scene. While waiting, Bittinger drank three Bud Lights, dropped the cans on the ground, and spread the news to other campers; by the time Corrigan arrived, at least five people had joined Bittinger at Cameron's campsite. Several of them had "contaminated the scene for possible suspect(s) shoe prints."

Corrigan radioed his dispatcher, who passed the word to the MCSO at 4:57 p.m. Detectives arrived to find the victim lying face up, partially covered by a "dirty white sheepskin blanket." She had been shot twice in the back.

Over the next two hours, deputies took statements from eight campers, including Peterson. One camper, Dena Raymond, said that when she and her boyfriend had arrived at the campground the night before, a "Mexican male" had stepped in front of their truck, signaled them to stop, and said, "My dad told me to say don't come down here, we're camping down here." They turned around and drove to another campsite.

Peterson overheard Raymond saying something about a Mexican. He also heard someone say there was blood on Cameron's chest, which he took to mean she had been shot in the back, since, as he told Haglund, "exit wounds are bloodier than entry wounds." This deduction would do him great harm later on, when investigators would take his apparent knowledge that she had been shot in the back as evidence of guilt.

Peterson's handwritten statement consists of twelve lines of printing.

At approximately 10 PM judging from moon in sky light of my tent, I was woke up by loud noise probably a gunshot, bit of rebel like yelling and comotion of some conversation and another shot. Definatly a gunshot very near. Being a little skiddish remained awake about two hours. Heard two vihicals in that time. Also cat meowing during that time. In the morning a white Cheve van was parked near where I'd heard one vehical stop. My skiddishness came from walking into line of fire of shooter at Lake Rossevelt 10th or 11th this month. Slept with 44 under pillow rest of night.

Later in the evening detectives Douglas Beatty and Charlie Norton interviewed Peterson. Beatty reported that Peterson asked if the victim was a woman he had met at the campground in the past. He described her as white, about thirty, with sandy brown hair, and said she drove a blue pickup. He also said she liked to read books.

At some point Peterson mentioned having a gun. At his campsite, Beatty sniffed the gun and concluded that it had not been fired. He photographed it and asked if he and Norton could take it with them. Peterson refused, but he let them search his tent and his vehicle and take samples of his hair. He also showed Beatty his medication and told him it was for anxiety and depression.

Asked about hearing the gunshots, Peterson said they "did not sound like a hunter's weapon, more like a 9mm or a .38 caliber handgun." Beatty noted that he based this judgment on "his Marine Corp training and previous shooting experience." Peterson later recalled telling the detectives that "a .22 sounds like firecrackers, but a 9mm or .38 sounds more like a car backfiring."

As darkness fell over the campground, the detectives left, posting uniformed deputies to keep watch overnight. After they were gone, some of the campers yelled at Peterson, making him anxious. He took his pills and went to bed without any dinner.

The next morning the detectives returned to search the scene. A license plate check had identified the victim as Alice Marie Cameron. The purse found near her body contained no wallet or driver's license. Two spent 9mm shell casings were lying on the ground, and one 9mm bullet was lodged in the side panel of the bed of the pickup.

Talking with Peterson again, Beatty asked about the woman who liked to read. Peterson said he had last seen her about five weeks earlier. His memory of her was vivid. "She was sitting in a lounge-type lawn chair, with her feet propped up on the tailgate of her pickup truck, reading a little paperback book. She was wearing a one-piece powder-blue bathing suit with a diagonal stripe running from her left shoulder to her right hip, thick light-colored shower shoes and a straw-colored floppy hat. The hat led him to believe she was an artist, because it was the type an artist would wear, made of cloth, with a round brim, straight sides and a flat top."

During the morning, Peterson finished the letter to his mother, telling her about the murder at the campground.

I'd gotten woke up by a couple of gun shots, very nearby and some Ya Ha! yelling. I've been skiddish since the Lake Rosevelt thing. So stayed awake a while. Then more or less said the hell with it, go to sleep about 2 hours later. About 5 or 6 the next evening I found out a murder had occured about the area I'd suspected the shots had come from. Been racking my brain to recall anything to help the Police and Sheriff's Department. It's about 12:00 now the following day. They are still checking the area. I'll stick around as long as they desire to do whatever I can to seek justice for the person. But I'm telling you now. This is sure putting pressure on me to check in on the VA Hospital. Keep my head on straight, and keep authority informed at least on my where abouts. Its also tearing at my confidence in myself for the com- ing hard years, I forsee as well as you've foreseen.

Far in the back of my thoughts is this. Are they going to think I did it. It didn't help but last night a fella very under the influence was saying now and then, 'I wouldn't want to be in your shoes!" I felt like telling him, "If your feet hurt as much as mine when I walk, then I'd know its the shoes that are the problem." Instead asked him to leave me be to get clearer facts straight for the Officers.

The letter, which became part of the MCSO file on the Cameron case, is unsigned and appears unfinished. The file does not indicate whether Peterson ever got his letter back, or whether it was ever mailed to his mother.

Of the eight campers interviewed at the crime scene, Peterson was the only one who looked disheveled, appeared to be a transient, and had "mental problems." And he was the only one asked to appear at the sheriff's office for a formal interview. The detectives were skeptical of Peterson's claim that he could distinguish the sound of a 9mm gun- shot and suspicious because he would not let them take his .44 Magnum Ruger handgun. They had no probable cause to confiscate his gun. But they focused on him because he had mentioned a 9mm: the casings col- lected at the scene indicated that the murder weapon was a 9mm pistol.

As requested, Peterson presented himself at the sheriff's office on Tuesday, October 22, while in Phoenix for a visit to the VA hospital. Detective Donald Walsh began questioning him at 9:10 a.m., with Norton looking on through a two-way mirror. Except for a few ten-minute breaks, the interrogation continued until nearly 1:00 a.m. on Wednesday—more than fifteen hours. It included a trip to the Mesquite Flats Campground to have Peterson reenact the events of the night of October 18. Most of the interrogation was not taped, so the detectives' reports are the only records of what was said. Somehow, during the untaped period, Walsh induced Peterson to confess to murder.

Walsh did not get around to reading Peterson the *Miranda* warnings for nearly five hours, until 1:52 p.m. When asked if he understood his rights, Peterson replied, "Yes, sir."

At 11:35 p.m. the detectives turned on the tape recorder. In a move reminiscent of Leo Bruce's Enhanced interview, they waited until the suspect had already confessed, then had him repeat the confession on tape. Guided by Norton, Peterson told a rambling, inconsistent story starring himself as Cameron's killer. At times he sounded bewildered: "I have difficulty with this one point, that it seems I had another weapon. It seems like it's a 9mm." And later: "I don't have no visualization of what this thing looked like."

At 1:00 a.m., Walsh advised Peterson that he was "under arrest for first-degree murder for the homicide of Alice Cameron." Later that day Peterson was booked into the Maricopa County Jail, where he would stay for fourteen months.

The interrogations of the Tucson Four, six weeks earlier, had been both manipulative and brazenly confrontational. Those of the boys from Avondale, three days after Peterson's, would be less combative but just as manipulative. With Peterson, the interrogators had an easier time eliciting a confession. His insecurity and mental fragility enabled them to implant false memories of the night Alice Cameron died.

All three sets of interrogations were conducted by the same agency in a short span of time; both crimes were committed by the same young man; and the commander in both investigations was the same officer, Captain Jerry White. White's name appeared on all departmental reports in both cases, and he observed or listened in on many of the interrogations. He also listened to some of the tapes, gave sworn testimony, and was later sued in both cases for civil rights violations, including false arrest and false imprisonment.

On October 25, the day before Garcia was taken into custody for the temple murders, Walsh wrote a summary of the investigation leading to Peterson's arrest, including the interrogation. The story he reported eliciting from Peterson is implausible, but Walsh and his colleagues considered it credible enough to support a charge of first-degree murder.

In this account, Peterson was awakened by voices at around 10:00 p.m. It was too hot to get back to sleep, so he went for a walk, taking along "his 9mm semi-auto handgun." The walk took him near Cameron's campsite, and he saw her truck. Hearing an "unknown movement," which he took to be a "threat to himself, not to the victim," Peterson drew his 9mm and fired two rounds toward the campsite. Just as he fired, Cameron stood up in the bed of her truck "and was struck in the back by both bullets."

According to Walsh, Peterson "said that he attempted CPR but later recanted this statement. He went on to say that . . . he laid over her and kissed her on the forehead. He stated he did not know if he engaged in sexual contact and/or intercourse with the victim." When he realized she was dead, he tried to remove her pants, intending to "redress her into her blue bathing suit because 'he wanted her to look her finest.'" Unable to get the pants down over her buttocks, he gave up. "He further stated that the victim was not wearing any panties." Walsh added that Peterson "believed that he threw his 9mm pistol into the river."

Peterson spent almost a year in jail before his court-appointed lawyer, Kimberly O'Connor, got around to taking a deposition from his chief interrogator. This delay is indicative of the treatment Peterson got from Maricopa County. He was coerced and manipulated by the Maricopa County Sheriff's Office, indicted by the Maricopa county attorney, and represented by a Maricopa County public defender. To put it mildly, he was shortchanged by all three agencies.

O'Connor took Detective Walsh's deposition in September 1992, while preparing for Peterson's trial. Jean Frimodig attended for the county attorney's office. At the outset, Walsh explained that White had not assigned him to the Cameron case until three days after the murder; thus he had not investigated the crime scene.

Walsh said Peterson had showed up at the sheriff's office "on his own, voluntarily."

"Did you tell him that he could leave if he wanted to," O'Connor asked, "that he didn't have to stay and talk with you?"

Walsh said no. "At that point he was just an investigative lead and I was just interviewing him."

Paging through Walsh's report on the interrogation, O'Connor noted that Peterson had told Walsh he was taking medication and had recently been hospitalized for anxiety. She wanted to know if Walsh had asked him about the medication: whether he was taking it and what it was for. Walsh said he had read the label on the bottle.

When O'Connor mentioned the crowd at the crime scene, Walsh needed a memory boost. "Was that at night time, that occurred, or during the day?"

His query is typical of the way the deposition went. Because Walsh had not worked the case from the first day—and because O'Connor had waited more than a year to take his deposition—his knowledge of the case had large gaps. During the interrogation he had been ill equipped to evaluate Peterson's ramblings. At the deposition he was able to avoid serious cross-examination by emphasizing how little he knew.

O'Connor reminded him that Peterson recalled hearing "shots that he felt were a 9mm or smaller. . . . Did you think all of that was strange, that he would be able to identify—"

"Extremely."

"Why?"

"I carry a 9mm, and if I was asleep and heard a gunshot, I certainly wouldn't be able to tell you whether it was a 9mm or a .38 or even a .357. I could probably tell you maybe whether it was rifle, you know, like a thirty-aught six, or if it was a shotgun. Now that also depends on how much I was asleep. He'd been asleep."

"He said 9mm or smaller."

"Yes."

"That's too limited, is what you're saying? Too specific, for him to say 9mm or smaller?"

"Yes. Especially with the victim being shot with a 9mm, which that was not disclosed to him." Later Walsh said, "When he used the word 9mm, that to me was basically a red flag."

At one point Walsh had described Peterson as emotionally upset. O'Connor asked what had happened.

"He started crying," Walsh replied. "He stiffened up and his eyes were watering, and he just kind of changed just like that. . . . I don't know why."

By that time Peterson had been interrogated for several hours, and his mental state had steadily deteriorated. He began to "pause and mumble to himself." Instead of recognizing his fragility, Walsh took these psychological signs as indicators of guilt. Whenever Peterson paused before answering a question, Walsh assumed he was "thinking what he's going to say next."

Untrained in dealing with mentally or emotionally impaired people, Walsh misread these responses. Peterson was not struggling to think of what to say next—he was struggling to figure out what Walsh *wanted* him to say.

After a short break, Walsh reported, Peterson "did not appear to be upset and again seemed calm." He would soon have a new reason to be upset.

Walsh read the *Miranda* warnings, then shifted from questions to accusations. He told Peterson that Cameron's shooting might have been accidental and that he believed Peterson "was responsible for the shooting." To O'Connor he said he had been "setting a theme." The theme was, "Okay, you shot her but it was an accident."

Those words do much to explain Peterson's responses for the rest of the interrogation. The longer Walsh accused him, and the more Walsh emphasized the theme of accidental shooting, the closer Peterson came to believing Walsh rather than trusting his own memory. His Marine Corps training, coupled with his mental disability, made him highly vulnerable to suggestions from authority figures.

As Walsh talked about "discrepancies" in his story, Peterson "appeared to become confused and paused many times." Between pauses he sketched two scenarios that placed him at the scene when Cameron was murdered—though not as her killer. Walsh's report presented Peterson's responses as a narrative, omitting Walsh's own questions and comments, so there is no way to tell how much the detective "helped" Peterson "remember."

In the first scenario, Peterson was walking along the river when he heard a commotion and saw "a young Mexican male wrestling with the lady behind her truck." He went to help her, but she "thought he was a second assailant and jumped on his back." The Mexican aimed a gun at them; Peterson held Cameron by the waist and "lunged into the rear of the truck for protection," landing face down with Cameron on top of him. "She was shot twice in the back by the Mexican male," who then disappeared.

The second scenario matched the first except that now Peterson was carrying "his 9mm weapon." When he went to help Cameron, "the Mexican male overpowered" him and took the gun, shot Cameron, then ran off.

O'Connor pointed out a passage in Walsh's report that read, "I then asked Mr. Peterson when did he know that she was not alive. He stated, 'She is dead, her eyes are open.' He then became extremely emotional. . . . His left hand was clenched and in his right hand he was clenching a pencil. . . . I felt he may become violent. At this time I got up and removed the pencil from his right hand and also a Swiss Army type knife from a case that was on the right side of his belt."

The interview room was small, Walsh told O'Connor, and "I've got George Peterson, who's what, is he 6'10"? He's gotten a little nervous here and he's got this pencil . . . and, just like he was getting violent."

Norton, who watched through the two-way mirror as Walsh took the pencil and the knife, noted Peterson's height as "six feet zero inches" and his weight as 245 pounds. Other records indicate that Peterson walked with a cane and that his left hand was weakened by carpal tunnel syndrome. These details seem to have escaped Walsh.

After this scene, Walsh wrote, Peterson "continued trembling, just staring at the wall in front of him."

O'Connor asked for clarification. "Like in his mind he was elsewhere . . . he wasn't reacting to you?"

"No," Walsh said. "I think what he might have been doing is reacting to the fact that he was responsible for her death."

O'Connor asked why they had booked Peterson for first-degree murder rather than second-degree murder or negligent homicide. After all, they didn't have a "straightup confession to first-degree murder, 'She's standing there and I'm going to kill the bitch' . . . something like that."

Walsh said evidence from the bullets contradicted Peterson's claim that Cameron was standing in the bed of the truck when he accidentally shot her. That inconsistency led to the first-degree murder charge.

"You never did end up with any fiber or any blood or a weapon," O'Connor said, "or anything that connected him to that except [his] statements."

"That is correct."

"There's nothing on him. . . . He handed everything over to you guys and you didn't get any blood off of him, any blood on the clothes you found, didn't get any footprints that match, I mean your scene was pretty trashed. You never found the gun. . . . There's nothing except the 9mm bullets and the statements."

"Yeah," Walsh retorted, "his statement that she's shot three, twice in the back. He particularly described where she was shot with a 9mm and where he was standing."

O'Connor was dubious. "I think, personally, Detective Norton was kind of helping him along on that. . . . You have a tape, we know what it says."

Walsh conceded that the tape showed Norton "reminding" Peterson of certain things. But, he claimed, "I don't interview people that way." He asked, "Did you find myself leading George Peterson?"

"No." Since only Norton's exchanges with Peterson had been taped, O'Connor had no idea whether Walsh had led the suspect or not. She was flattering Walsh, implying that she trusted him more than Norton. "I did not find you doing that, which is why I next wanted to ask you about the sex stuff that came out in the car. . . . Where did the sex come in? Did you bring that up or did he bring that up?"

Walsh changed the subject, saying Peterson "smokes like a fiend." "He smoked my cigarettes and I think the county owes me a pack." When O'Connor nudged him back toward the sex stuff, he tried another diversion, this one about Peterson looking for Cameron's car keys. O'Connor had to tug him back to the point. "What I really want to know about, what I hope you're leading up to, is sex. Where did that come up?"

Finally Walsh said Peterson had brought it up, talking about trying to put Cameron's blue swimsuit on her. "I asked, 'Did you take her pants off?' And he says, 'Yes, I believe I did but I couldn't get the suit on.'" Asked if he had had sexual intercourse with her, Peterson "said, 'I don't think I did. If I did I'll kill myself.'"

Moving on, O'Connor mentioned the Hispanic male seen at the campsite. Walsh told her there was a whole section in the case file about attempting to identify the Hispanic male. She said she'd check on it.

Jean Frimodig spoke up, saying there was a composite drawing of the Hispanic male. This was news to O'Connor, but the drawing had been released to the media by Duane Brady, the MCSO's public information officer, and been publicized on television and in newspapers. It had appeared in the *Arizona Republic* on October 24, the same day the ballistics report on Caratachea's rifle turned Caratachea, Doody, and Garcia into suspects in the temple murders. Like many such sketches, it had a generic look, and it did not lead the investigators to Garcia.

Finished with Walsh's report, O'Connor turned to a transcript of the taped portion of Peterson's interrogation. She found the page where

Norton asked if Peterson remembered "your *Miranda* warnings? Your rights?"

"Something about the rights," Peterson replied.

"Do you remember the right to remain silent?"

"Something, yeah, something, something to remain silent, something about representation?"

"A lawyer?" Norton hinted.

"I wish I could afford one."

O'Connor said, "Nobody told him that he could have a lawyer for free at that point. When he says 'Wish I could afford one' and nobody says, 'Well, you have the right to a lawyer and if you can't afford one, one will be appointed for you.'"

Walsh protested that Peterson had already been "admonished his *Miranda* warnings."

"Two o'clock in the afternoon, this is at midnight."

"It's still a continuation."

"But a comment 'I wish I could afford one' was sort of an indication that maybe I'd like a lawyer, and to me it would seem a good point to say, 'Well, you know, if you can't afford one we'll get one for you.' And since that's not in here, I can assume it was never said."

"That's correct," Walsh admitted.

Convinced that Peterson was Cameron's killer, Walsh and Norton failed to consider the possibility that he might be a bona fide eyewitness. His statement about seeing a "young Mexican male wrestling with the lady" might well have referred to Alex Garcia, who, in Garcia's own words, "grabbed her down to keep her from screaming."

According to Peterson's later, calmer recollection, he never left his tent that night. But other witnesses saw a Hispanic male near the campsite. And if the Mexican male's assault on Cameron was merely a figment of Peterson's agitated imagination, created from what he had overheard at the campground and the pressure of interrogation, it was impressively close to what Garcia described.

In the temple case, the MCSO fixed on one set of suspects, badgered them into confessing, and neglected to follow other leads. In the Cameron case, the MCSO fixed on Peterson, easily induced him to confess, and again neglected other leads: failing to launch a full-scale search for the young Hispanic male; failing to check on whether anyone had attempted to use Cameron's missing bank card. In both cases, Garcia benefited from the MCSO's tunnel vision while innocent men were blamed for his crimes.

By the end of his interrogation, Peterson believed he had somehow been involved in "the accident." The interrogators' suggestions and his emotional vulnerability led to his confused confession. The very confusion of that confession, plus the investigators' conviction that, contrary to what they told the suspect, Cameron's death had *not* been an accident, led to his indictment for first-degree murder.

Sgt. Kimball, the lead investigator in the temple case and also involved in the Cameron case, wrote an article subtitled "Deadly Teen Lovers in the Mesquite Flats Campground." He used a pseudonym to conceal the innocent suspect's identity, but his article provides a look at the MCSO investigators' view of Peterson.

As Kimball told it, Deputy Beatty, who had interviewed Peterson at the campground, saw him as "an oddly pathetic character and got immediately suspicious of him."

Kimball painted Peterson as a "portrait of torment, a transient," living on the "lunatic fringes of society, his gray hair a trap of snarled knots, his clothes clotted with soil. His piercing blue eyes orbited in their own private galaxy of mental illness. He suffered from psychiatric disorders that caused profound depression, extreme anxiety, emotional turmoil, fear, and confusion."

If Kimball's colleagues shared his view of Peterson as sick and vulnerable, why did they so readily accept his confession, and why did Walsh and Norton confront, vex, and confound a man who had stopped by their office on the way to see his VA psychiatrist? As the Tucson Four learned the hard way, custodial interrogations can cause intense stress and false memories even in people who are of "sound mind."

The fact is that the MCSO had no procedures for interrogating suspects with mental disabilities. To Walsh and Norton, the meandering and contradictions in Peterson's story, and his reactions such as shaking and mumbling, were signs of guilt rather than of what his doctors might have called "decomp": decompensation, defined by one medical dictionary as "the deterioration of existing defenses, leading to an exacerbation of pathologic behavior; see *Nervous breakdown*." They also never considered Peterson's deeply engrained training to give authority figures what they asked for. The MCSO investigators recognized that Peterson was mentally unbalanced, but to their minds his condition simply made him more likely to kill.

Kimball praised Norton and Walsh for using "finesse and patience to get Peterson to come clean." Actually, unlike the Tucson suspects, Peterson began to "confess" early in his interrogation. Any finesse and patience displayed by his questioners went into making his ramblings fit the crime.

Writing after Garcia and Hoover pleaded guilty to murdering Cameron, Kimball had to admit that "something was fishy" in the case against Peterson. "Try as they might, detectives couldn't unearth witnesses or physical evidence to corroborate [Peterson's] account of the slaying. For one thing, they couldn't find the murder weapon. . . . Nothing showed up during several searches of [his] property that could even remotely be associated with Alice Cameron or her murder."

When Peterson was being interrogated, the MCSO was only three days away from arresting one of Cameron's real killers, Alex Garcia. And yet Peterson would spend fourteen long months behind bars. Like his fellow psychiatric patient Mike McGraw, Peterson gave a wildly implausible story riddled with inconsistencies. And once again, the MCSO stopped searching for the real killers and concentrated on building a case against an innocent, emotionally disturbed man.

Alex Garcia's opinion that Michelle Hoover was not a "stone-cold killer" would have rung true with people in her hometown of Litchfield Park, an upscale bedroom community near Luke Air Force Base. Before meeting Garcia, Hoover had never been in trouble with friends, family, school, or the police. Was she a reluctant participant in Alice Cameron's killing, enthralled or intimidated by her older boyfriend, or did she share his disregard for human life? Hoover's friends and relatives believed they knew the answer to that question. But MCSO investigators, attorneys, mental health practitioners, and judges would wrestle with it from the day Garcia named her as Cameron's killer until her sentencing six months later.

Mike Sager, who would write about the case for *GQ* magazine, interviewed Michelle's parents, Ted and Kathy Hoover. To them, Michelle was "an only child, a tomboy, an honor student, daddy's pet." Ted Hoover had never raised his voice to her. Father and daughter were inseparable. The Hoovers saw their family as loving and happy. Both parents worked for a construction firm, Ted in a managerial position. They owned five acres in Litchfield Park, had four Dobermans, and attended the Church of the Beatitudes, where Michelle helped with vacation Bible school. Michelle "was known by all to be responsible, artistic, sweet, 'one of those few people who's a saint.'" She took ballet and tumbling and liked Troll dolls and the New Kids on the Block.

At Scott Libby Elementary School, Hoover had earned average to above-average grades, had many friends, and made a good impression on teachers and staff. She turned fourteen in February 1991, graduated from eighth grade that May, entered Agua Fria High School in August, and met Garcia in September. He was in ROTC; soon Hoover began going to ROTC drills just to see him. He broke up with his girlfriend—the one whose "promise ring" he had bought with money stolen from murdered Buddhists—and began dating Hoover.

Garcia was Hoover's first boyfriend. She was pretty but not petite, new at the school, and young for her age; he was tall and handsome, two years older. In love for the first time, Hoover underwent what her teachers called a sea change. She lost interest in school, friends—everything but Garcia.

Garcia's arrest for the temple murders did not end their relationship. Her parents discouraged her from having anything more to do with him, but with help from friends, she kept in touch with her incarcerated love.

As Garcia's girlfriend, Hoover had come to the MCSO's attention when he was arrested for the temple murders. Her first two interviews took place on October 27, 1991, nine days after she and Garcia killed Alice Cameron. But her interviewer, Detective Don Griffiths, was interested only in the temple case. He was not involved in the Cameron investigation—and besides, with Peterson locked up, the MCSO considered the Cameron case solved.

In front of the Hoovers' house that afternoon, Michelle sat in the front passenger seat of Griffiths's patrol car, her mother in the back. Hoover said she had met Garcia two months earlier. They dated once a week or so, usually going to a movie. Her mother would pick Alex up, drop them off at the movies, and later drive Alex home. On other dates they rode ATCs in the desert near her house and went out shooting together.

She described Alex as a funny person who liked to joke around. He wanted to join the army or the air force. He was interested in cars, including her father's race car, but the only one she had ever seen him in, besides her mother's, was Johnathan Doody's Mustang.

Hoover said Alex had called her the day before and said he was with his dad. Griffiths knew Garcia had told his girlfriend the truth, if not the whole truth. Father and son had indeed been together the day before— in interview rooms at task force headquarters. Hoover and her mother weren't telling Griffiths the whole truth either. They didn't mention that Michelle and Alex had recently run away together.

That evening Griffiths returned with more questions. This time both parents were home, and he interviewed Michelle in their living room, all three Hoovers sitting on a couch facing him. By this time he knew about the runaway episode, and he got Michelle to talk about it. Her story matched the one Garcia would tell in 1993, except that in her version the fugitives drove directly to a cabin owned by her family. She said nothing about stopping at a campground along the way, let alone committing murder.

Griffiths announced that Garcia had been arrested for the temple murders and warned that if Michelle didn't tell him what she knew, her silence might hurt Alex. "Michelle agreed with this and tears started to swell in her eyes." Her parents then got up and went to the kitchen, leaving Griffiths alone with their daughter.

On October 16, Hoover said, she took her mom's truck and went shooting with Alex. Out in the desert, Alex started "like playing Twenty Questions." The first clue he gave her was "by Cotton Lane," then "monks," then "nine people." When she asked if he was talking about the temple, he said yes. "They went in to rob them, and some of his friends started shooting." He told her about getting a camera and some gold, and about a safe they couldn't open.

The next day Griffiths talked to Hoover a third time, at task force headquarters with a court reporter present. She was sworn in as a witness, and he took her through the story again. She said she hadn't wanted to believe Alex's story about the temple; she couldn't imagine him "being a participant or even witnessing it." Ten days before Hoover made this innocent-sounding statement under oath, she and Garcia had shot Alice Cameron and watched impatiently as her life drained away.

On January 11, 1993, after Garcia's plea bargain reopened the Cameron case, Kimball and Detective Riley interviewed Hoover's parents. Both Ted and Kathy Hoover said Michelle had never talked to them about the murder, so their interviews focused on her "runaway incident" in 1991.

Michelle's mother had discovered her absence on Thursday, October 17, when she'd gone to wake her up. She called Michelle's friends, who claimed not to know where she was. She also called Agua Fria High School and learned that Garcia was absent that day. Ted Hoover drove to the Garcias' house, where the only person he found was Johnathan Doody. Doody claimed he didn't know where Alex and Michelle were, but Ted thought he was lying.

Ted's company truck was gone. The truck had a phone, but the service carrier, U.S. West, determined that no calls had been made in the relevant period. Nothing else seemed to be missing. Ted had a large collection of guns, but it didn't occur to him to check those. Over the weekend he noticed that a .22-caliber rifle was gone, plus four hundred rounds of ammunition. Even then, he didn't realize Michelle had also taken his Helwan 9mm semiautomatic handgun and two dozen rounds of 9mm ammunition.

Kathy Hoover had a feeling Michelle might have gone to a family cabin, owned by Kathy's nephew. It was in Payson, ninety miles north of Phoenix. She called her sister, who called the nephew, who called a neighbor in Payson. The neighbor reported that someone was using the cabin and that the missing truck was parked at the Double D Bar. At 8:44 p.m. on October 22, Kathy called the Gila County Sheriff's Office.

Gila County deputy David Vaughn got a key from the neighbor, but he had trouble opening the cabin door, which was jammed with a chair. The ground floor was a mess: "heavy quilts pinned over all windows, lamps unplugged, numerous dirty dishes in the sink, miscellaneous clothing . . . soiled towels in bathroom, Nintendo video game with accessories lying on floor." Upstairs was more of the same—plus a locked room. Knowing the runaways were armed, Vaughn "withdrew to the lower level and requested supervisory assistance."

Minutes later, Sgt. Dan Alexander arrived. By phone, the cabin's owner granted permission to force the locked door if necessary. Alexander and Vaughn approached with guns drawn, identified themselves, and called Alex Garcia's name. A barely audible male voice replied. Alexander ordered Garcia to turn on the light and open the door slowly, "with his hands exposed." Alex complied, and both teenagers were taken into custody. The deputies got the truck's keys from Garcia and left them "secured at the Double D Bar."

Since Hoover and Garcia were thought to be merely runaway juveniles, the authorities questioned them minimally and soon released them to their parents, who drove to Payson to pick them up.

On the way home, the Hoovers stopped at the Double D Bar's parking lot to retrieve Michelle's belongings from the truck. In the cab they found two rifles and Ted's "Egyptian-made automatic 9mm handgun with Egyptian writing engraved on the weapon." Ted also saw a military duffle bag and "Vietnam-style combat boots." A second duffle bag was later found at the cabin, containing a camouflage jacket, other clothing, and "two handfuls of .22 ammunition."

Ted Hoover told Kimball and Riley he had taken Michelle out shooting only once. They had fired a .357 Magnum revolver, a .22 revolver, and a shotgun; as far as he knew Michelle had never fired his automatic handguns. At the time of Cameron's murder, he had kept his weapons and ammunition in unlocked cases.

At the police station, according to her mother, Michelle cried and said she was "real happy they had found her." Kathy and Ted didn't ask much about her five days with Garcia; their few questions focused on "why Michelle ran away and whether she had sex with Alex." Michelle assured them she had not had sex. As punishment for running away, her parents grounded her for thirty days.

In 1991 the Hoovers informed no one in law enforcement about the guns, the military boots, or the duffle bags. They gave the boots, the bags, and the rifle to the Garcias and put Ted's .22 and 9mm back in his gun case. The investigators' reports do not indicate whether he still kept the case unlocked.

To their parents and the Gila County deputies, Garcia and Hoover claimed they had been at the cabin since the day they ran away, October 17. Alice Cameron's body was found on the nineteenth, but no one connected the underage runaways with her murder. On October 24, a day after the teenagers went home, the composite sketch of the young Hispanic male seen near Cameron's campsite appeared in the media, but again no one made the connection. Two days after that, Garcia was taken into custody for the temple murders, but by that time George Peterson had confessed to shooting Cameron. No suspicion of involvement in Cameron's death would fall on Alex Garcia or Michelle Hoover until Garcia himself revealed their secret.

Michelle Hoover's first inkling that the past was catching up with her came on Tuesday, January 5, 1993, when the media reported Garcia's surprise confession to a tenth murder. On January 6 she told her parents she was sick and stayed home from school.

That morning Kimball and other MCSO deputies arrived at the Hoovers' address with a search warrant. Finding Michelle alone, Kimball spoke with her parents on the phone and agreed not to question her until they got home. He told them he was investigating "a serious incident in which Michelle and Alex involved themselves as runaways in October 1991."

Michelle overheard the phone call and "became visibly nervous. She looked worried, paced, and fidgeted with her hair." She invited Kimball and Detective Norton to wait for her parents in the living room. Asked if she knew why they were there, "She sighed, looked down at the floor, and replied resignedly, 'Yeah, I do.'" She also said, "'Seeing Alex on television yesterday really flipped me out.'" Asked if she still loved him, she again said, "'Yeah, I do.'" The rest of the conversation touched on "the family's collection of video tapes, their satellite dish, dogs, and her favorite actor, Chevy Chase."

When her parents arrived, Kimball gave them the search warrant and informed them of "our belief that Garcia and Michelle had committed a murder when they ran away." Ted Hoover said he would encourage Michelle to cooperate, but he wanted her to have an attorney. After a family conference in the kitchen, Michelle, "sobbing quietly, came into the living room and sat on a couch." Kimball assured her that "everyone makes mistakes in their lives." "Yeah," Michelle responded, "but this was a big one!"

Ted and Kathy Hoover advised Michelle not to say anything without an attorney. Kimball "politely" pointed out that "the right to remain silent was Michelle's choice, not theirs." When he read Michelle her rights from the juvenile *Miranda* form, she declined to talk more without a lawyer.

The search of the house yielded a Helwan 9mm semiautomatic pistol. Ballistics tests at the state crime lab were conclusive: Ted Hoover's Helwan pistol had killed Alice Marie Cameron.

A week later, on January 14, Michelle Hoover, her parents, and her attorney, Tom Martinez, presented themselves at the sheriff's office, where Hoover formally surrendered and was arrested for the murder of Alice Cameron. Hoover was booked into the juvenile detention center.

Martinez had arranged the one-week delay because Michelle was pregnant. She gave her parents this news on January 7, after hearing that one of her friends had already told the police. The father was "a twenty-one-year-old boy from Avondale." With both the elder Hoovers in poor health and unable to care for a grandchild, the family decided to abort the pregnancy. When Hoover surrendered, Martinez said she had had an abortion on January 13 and would need to take medication while in custody. Riley photocopied the prescriptions and the instructions for her postsurgical care.

Hoover would soon plead guilty to second-degree murder. Her version of the murder at the Mesquite Flats Campground largely matched Garcia's, though she claimed to be unable to remember many details and did not give a statement to investigators. She did soften Garcia's portrait of her. In his version, Michelle volunteered to kill Cameron and was impatient that she took so long to die. In Hoover's version, Alex told her to shoot Cameron, saying, "If you love me you'll do it." Afterward, "weeping, realizing what she had done," she apologized to the dying woman, who forgave her.

Hoover's walk through the court system was relatively short. After her arrest she spent two months at the juvenile detention center before her case was transferred to adult court. In March she pleaded guilty, posted $100,000 bail, and was released to wait for sentencing. Judge Ronald S. Reinstein conducted her initial sentencing hearing on May 14, four months after her arrest.

During this period, Mike Sager interviewed both Garcia and Hoover. Both had fond memories of their relationship. "There was an instant flame," Garcia said in his jailhouse interview. "She was outgoing, she was funny, she was bursting with energy." Hoover recalled, "I was drawn to him. On a scale of one to ten, it was a ten, you know, I cared so much about him." Sager got Garcia to show a reflective side. "With some girls," Garcia mused, "it's only sexual. But I liked who she was. I mean, here you've got a guy who does what he wants when he wants, and he's got to live for himself. But then you get a girl that you really need, that you really like—it's weird how that shit works." When they ran away, they talked about having sex, but Michelle said she wasn't ready, and he didn't press her.

Releasing a confessed killer on bail drew some negative attention. After entering her guilty plea, Hoover told a reporter that before going to prison, she hoped to play miniature golf, go to the racetrack with her dad, and "indulge her fondness for spicy food." She also said she was sorry about Cameron's death: "If I could have one wish, it would be to take it back." But both her comments were printed under the headline "Girl Admits Slaying, Now Wants Some Fun." Writing about reactions to that article, *Arizona Republic* columnist E. J. Montini quoted an irate reader: "How could we let this murderer out for a month's vacation?" Montini explained that Hoover got the "vacation" because her parents could afford to post bail. And he quoted Ted Hoover, who said he and his wife were not trying to "reward" Michelle; they just wanted some quality time with their daughter. "Because of my health, this could be the last time I get to do anything with her."

Not all public opinion was against Hoover. One Avondale reader wrote to the *Republic* that Hoover had been "goaded and pushed into doing Garcia's dirty work." Another believed that in being transferred to adult court, Hoover had been "victimized not only by Alex Garcia but also by the politics surrounding the Temple Murder Case."

Under the plea bargain that Tom Martinez struck with Paul Ahler of the county attorney's office, Hoover would plead guilty to second-degree murder. The "presumptive" sentence for such a plea was fifteen years, but Ahler and Martinez negotiated a "stipulated" ten-year sentence. If the deal went through, Hoover would be released from prison in her midtwenties.

But the plea bargain would not be valid unless accepted by Judge Reinstein, who would consider information from many sources before making his decision. Three psychologists examined Hoover, and probation officer Gregory Miller conducted a presentence investigation. Miller reviewed the psychologists' assessments, interviewed Hoover several times, and spoke with her family, friends, teachers, and school officials. Then he prepared a report for Judge Reinstein.

Dr. Phillip Esplin, the psychologist selected by the defense, found Hoover immature and "clearly taken with, and influenced by, Alex Garcia." In Esplin's view, although her offense was heinous, Hoover demonstrated "empathy and compassion" rather than "a callous disregard for others." He did not see her as a risk to reoffend, regarded her as treatable, and concluded that "nothing would be gained by long-term incarceration."

Dr. Michael Bayless, the psychologist chosen by the State, found it inconsistent that Hoover supposedly "could say no to Alex Garcia about

sexual intercourse, but could not say no to shooting the victim." In talking to Hoover, Bayless did not detect any remorse, even though she had
"walked up to the victim, . . . shot her, and waited for [her] to die."

Dr. Stan Cabanski, a psychologist at the county's Juvenile Court
Center, also cited Hoover's "absence of guilt, remorse, and depression."
He agreed with Esplin that she was treatable and not dangerous to the
community, but he made the point that for fifteen months after the crime,
Hoover had not admitted the offense. For many, her silence itself was an
offense, given that an innocent man was in jail awaiting trial—and possibly execution—for her crime.

The principal of Scott Libby Elementary School remembered Hoover
as "never disruptive or a problem child"—except for her "association with
older boys." A school secretary recalled her as a "delightful young lady,"
but now had mixed feelings about her. Hoover's social studies teacher
expressed the general opinion: Michelle "was always very nice and polite
and seemed to be a good kid."

Miller collected similar testimonials at Agua Fria High School. The
school psychologist told him Hoover had participated in group counsel-
ing "for self-esteem." She called Hoover "positive and upbeat," "a genu-
inely nice girl who made a tremendous mistake." But she also noted that
after Garcia's arrest, Michelle showed no remorse, only sorrow that her
boyfriend was in jail. A guidance counselor reported that Hoover had
begun to fail her courses because of nonattendance and eventually had
withdrawn from school for the rest of her freshman year.

Miller's job was to make a sentencing recommendation to the court.
He listed Hoover's youth, her lack of a record, and the apparent influence of Garcia as factors that might warrant a reduced sentence. But in
his opinion, other, more important factors suggested the plea agreement
was too lenient: the violence of the crime, the motive of monetary gain,
Hoover's stalking of and failure to help Cameron, her attempts to use
Cameron's bank card—plus her fifteen-month silence. If Garcia had not
confessed, Hoover might never have been held responsible for Cameron's
murder. Implicit in Miller's paragraph was the point that Hoover's silence
had allowed an innocent man to be blamed.

To Miller, Hoover's refusal to have sex with Garcia proved she could
make her own decisions. And yet she "did not refuse to stalk the victim or walk into Cameron's camp, or refuse to pull the trigger. Instead,
she shot the victim twice in the back." He concluded that Hoover had
demonstrated "a complete disregard for the value of human life, thereby

posing a risk to the community." Accordingly, he recommended a "term of incarceration greater than the presumptive." He did not say how much longer than fifteen years he thought Hoover's sentence should be; that decision was entirely up to the judge.

Judge Reinstein had played a significant role in the temple murder case. He had conducted Dante Parker's preliminary hearings, ruled on search warrant applications, and accepted the county attorney's recommendation to dismiss the charges against the Tucson Four. He had a clear understanding of the cases against Doody and Garcia, which at this time were working their way toward trial. Now Reinstein took a careful look at Hoover, and at her relationship with Garcia, before ruling on her plea bargain.

Along with Miller's report, Reinstein considered a letter from Martinez, Hoover's defense attorney, urging him to accept the plea agreement. Martinez summarized the defense view: "Michelle Hoover is a child who made a grave error." He argued that ten years was enough punishment.

Hoover's family and friends agreed. With his letter Martinez enclosed nineteen other letters asking the judge to be lenient. The writers portrayed Hoover as still a child, a girl who had been "eager to please, kind, thoughtful, artistic, talented, and fun to be with" until Garcia entered her life. An aunt analyzed Michelle's devotion to Alex. "Society puts such pressure on what the ideal female should look like. And when you are far from being a size six you can easily be robbed of your self-esteem. Along came a big, strapping guy, named Alex Garcia, that convinced Michelle that her size didn't matter. It didn't take long for Michelle's self-worth to be dependent upon Alex."

The writers were disturbed by Hoover's transfer to adult court, especially because if sent to prison she would have to live in isolation until she turned eighteen. Under Arizona law, prisons could not mix juvenile offenders with adults. As the state's only female juvenile in an adult prison, she would lead a lonely existence until her eighteenth birthday. As one writer put it, "That amounts to solitary confinement for two years."

Hoover's supporters put the full blame for Cameron's death on Garcia, "a murderer ten times over." As Hoover's aunt put it, Alice Cameron "had her life ended solely due to Alex Garcia's evil, twisted behavior of mind-controlling a sweet fourteen-year-old." Hoover's grandmother agreed:

"She met a mass-murderer named Alex Garcia, who controlled and manipulated her to do this crime for him."

Their view of Garcia led the letter writers to question Johnathan Doody's guilt as well as Hoover's. Garcia, one woman pointed out, "was present at the temple murders and the campgrounds but says he did not harm anyone." She queried why people accepted the claim "that a young man of great size and outgoing personality would just stand back as several people are being murdered," and yet no one considered Garcia's "influence and control" over Hoover and Doody.

The letter writers considered Hoover a victim, not only of Garcia but of the prosecutors' eagerness to close the temple murder case. One cited the "lack of the 'presumption of innocence' since the day the county attorney's office announced that their star witness in the Doody trial was not the trigger man." Ted Hoover noted that Judge Martin had asked the prosecutors "the appropriate question": "Are you certain Alex Garcia is the defendant with which the county wants to make a deal?"

Another set of letters reveals a side of Michelle Hoover that her relatives did not see. For eight months after Garcia went to jail, Hoover wrote to him. The enormity of the crime they had committed had not dimmed her infatuation. As she gradually moved on with a busy life, full of friends and even new boyfriends, she continued to express her love for Alex.

Garcia's replies are not in the MCSO's files. Hoover's letters to him became public because his revised plea bargain required him to give the MCSO all correspondence received during his incarceration. In January 1993 he turned over more than fifty pages of handwritten letters, most of them from Hoover and Liz Rhinehart.

The investigators were looking for more than high-school gossip. They examined each missive for incriminating statements about the Cameron murder. They found nothing. Hoover never referred to either the temple murders or the terrible secret she shared with Garcia.

In some ways the letters confirm her family's view that Hoover was still a child. But if this child had ever been "upbeat" about school, her letters reveal no evidence of it. Every word about her courses is scathingly negative. "Another stupid day in the hell hole. We are learning about graphs." "We just took a vocabulary test. I hate having to know words I aint gonna use when I'm older." The only bright moments of her day involve talking to friends and mocking teachers.

The letters do hint at Hoover's emotional and academic troubles. "The test I took yesterday probably failed it but that's normal for me. My stomach hurts I think I have a ulser." "I started smoking again I know its bad real bad!!" "Im eating but not sleeping that's something I got to work on." "I keep crying and crying its hard not seeing you, I dream about you everynight & how we were together."

Besides school, the main theme in the early letters is her love for Alex. "I found a button off of your shirt when I was going through my school bag. I taped it to the back of your picture." "I love you forever and ever and ever and ever and ever → → → and on and on and on until there aint no more evers in the world."

In mid-November, less than a month after Cameron's death, Hoover wrote, "Guess what, 8 more days and we will be going out for 2 months. Cool huh!" "I still want to marry you too, your my bestfriend always and forever." "I wish I could come and see you. I'll have my mom talk to your lawyer and see if and when I could see you."

At that stage Hoover was allowed to write to Garcia openly and talk with him on the phone at least once, but her parents may have been discouraging the relationship covertly. After the telephone call, Hoover wrote, "I did change my phone number. My mom will give it to your lawyer." Several later letters mentioned that her mom had tried to call his lawyer, and on November 22 she said, "My mom still aint got ahold of your lawyer he hasn't returned any of her calls." By mid-December she apparently recognized her mother's stalling tactics and called the lawyer herself but was told she could not visit Garcia. Later that month she was mailing her letters from Liz's house and planning to talk to Garcia in secret. "You call Liz's house & she'll call me 3 way cuz my mom wont let me give you the phone # yet."

By December 19 Hoover seemed to need to reassure Garcia—or perhaps herself—about their love. "Alex, this letter will state every way I feel about you and always will feel for you. My feelings toward you havent changed and never will change. . . . Baby I love you, I want to marry you." But in the same letter, she let Alex know she was getting attention from other boys. She said a guy at school "wouldn't leave me alone. I told him I have a boyfriend and he goes so, you'll never see him. And I said thats not the point. Its the feelings I have in my heart, feelings I'll never have for you!" From that time her letters became rarer, shorter, and less emotional.

Apparently she wrote to Garcia only once between New Year's Eve 1991 and late April 1992; Garcia's letters from Rhinehart indicate that Hoover's parents forbade her to write, but also that Hoover "broke up" with him during this period. Hoover's one February letter was chatty rather than intimate, full of gossip about her friends.

Liz occasionally talked to Alex on the phone, and Michelle was one of their topics. On April 23 Michelle broke her four-month silence, writing, "I know Liz told you that I was going out with someone! My reason is because I thought I would never get to see or be with you again. But believe me my feelings for you are stronger than they will ever be for someone else."

On April 29 Liz began corresponding with Garcia. Her first letter began, "Alex, I know you didn't do it, you couldn't!" Garcia, from his jail cell, had come between Hoover and her friend. Now Liz wrote that they had made up. "All that crap about Michelle and I is over with. . . . I was not 'mad,' only jealous. Because, well, I liked you. But I knew you wouldn't go for me anyways." Then Liz confided, "You will never guess what I did!!!! Well actually what Brian & me did!! Yep, yep, you got it! I lost it Friday the 13th." She had been going out with Brian for three weeks at the time. "Aint it cool?"

Michelle evidently followed Liz's social example, and Liz made sure Alex heard about it. On May 24 she wrote, "Michelle and Willie have done it. Just don't say anything OK?! I shouldn't have told you! I guess I gave her a lot of pressure, talking about how great it is and how she should go for it with him. I know she wishes she could have saved it for you two. But your there, she's here, and well!!" She added, "But, uh, Alex, she is truly 'in love' with you! She told me how you two *almost* did it. But she is always thinking of you!"

Three days later Michelle wrote a matter-of-fact letter, ending with "P.S. I love you and always will. P.S.S. Write back soon please!" In mid-June she sent another note, the last one from her in the file. There may have been more letters than the MCSO collected: on June 26 Liz mentioned that Alex and Michelle were writing to each other again, adding, "I hope you will still write to me even though you and her speak now." She included a news bulletin: "Michelle and Willie broke up." And she got serious: she had read that "you and Doody are being tried as adults and you both may suffer the death penalty. That scares me because Michelle still has major feelings for you. She loves you so much."

It seems unlikely that Liz, whose correspondence with Garcia picked up as Hoover's waned, would have abruptly stopped writing to him after her June 26 letter. But that letter was the last one Garcia turned over to investigators.

The high school girls revealed in these letters did not let multiple murder come between them and an attractive older guy. Liz may have hoped Garcia was innocent despite his confession. But Hoover had heard the truth about his first nine murders from Garcia himself, and she alone knew there had been a tenth. Just as she kept the secret of Cameron's killing from her parents, her friends, and the authorities, she wrote nothing about it to her partner in crime.

If the letters had been made public when Garcia turned them over, Hoover's supporters would surely have seen them as evidence of her immaturity and Garcia's continued power over her. Others, including Alice Cameron's family, would have noticed that Hoover expressed no hint of regret. The letters would not have ended the debate over whether Michelle Hoover was "a child who made a mistake" or a "stone-cold killer."

At Hoover's initial sentencing hearing, on May 14, her friends and family packed one side of Judge Reinstein's courtroom. Alice Marie Cameron's relatives and friends sat on the opposite side. They were fewer in number but as passionate about the victim as the Hoovers were about their only child.

Helen Fletcher, Cameron's sister, was a thoughtful and persuasive witness. Fletcher had traveled from St. Louis to Phoenix to make the judge understand the "unceasing agony" Hoover had caused when she "cold-bloodedly, with much forethought and a total lack of compassion for a human life," killed Cameron.

Fletcher dismissed the view of Hoover as a helpless child controlled by a psychotic boyfriend. Michelle, she said, "ran away willingly with Alex. She was not coerced into doing so nor was she kidnapped." Instead, she "made clear and deliberate choices: to steal her mother's car, her father's guns, to stay out overnight . . . to stalk Alice in her camp early in the day to make sure she was alone and defenseless."

Knowing the prosecutor would not recount the details of the murder because of Hoover's plea bargain, Fletcher did it for him. "How cold blooded and merciless was it to plan that afternoon to wait until dark, strap on a holster and gun, walk over to Alice's campsite, point a gun at her and fire two shots into the back of this 'nicest lady.' . . . After the shooting, she and Alex restrained Alice while waiting over an hour and a half for her to die."

"We are told by Michelle," Fletcher went on, "that ten years is forever." Then she spoke directly to the defendant. "No Michelle, ten years is not forever—it is 3,650 days in which you can receive letters, gifts, visits and phone calls. *Death* is forever, and death is what you gave my sister."

From the other side of the courtroom, the judge heard that Hoover herself was a victim: a victim of Alex Garcia. From Fletcher, he heard that justice would not be done as long as Michelle was "allowed to live." Regretting that a death sentence was not an option, Fletcher proposed an alternative. "Alice had at least twenty-five to forty more years to live. I would like to see Michelle Leslie Hoover serve the forty years she denied Alice. If an eye for an eye is not a possibility, perhaps a year for a year would be fair."

After hearing the evidence and testimony, Judge Reinstein rejected Hoover's plea bargain. He cited the need to "balance the scales of justice" and said he found a ten-year sentence too lenient for Cameron's "cold, calculating, chilling" killer. As required by law, he gave Hoover three options: she could accept the fifteen-year sentence he deemed appropriate; she could find another judge to consider the case; or she could withdraw her guilty plea and go to trial for first-degree murder, risking a life sentence. Hoover and her lawyer chose the second option, and Judge Reinstein transferred the case to Judge David Roberts.

At Hoover's second sentencing hearing, on July 15, her supporters urged the court to restore her ten-year deal. Martinez insisted that "she was not the Bonnie to Garcia's Clyde." Friends said she had been in "a trance-like state" and following Garcia's orders when she shot Cameron. Martinez made the point that both Hoover's parents were in poor health—her father with heart trouble, her mother with multiple sclerosis—and might be dead before she got out of prison. Ted Hoover called his daughter a victim and implored Judge Roberts to remember that Alex Garcia, not Michelle, was the "cold blooded murderer."

Hoover also spoke on her own behalf. The *Arizona Republic* noted that she was in tears when she said, "I am sorry for the Cameron family. I have great remorse. I wish to God I could bring her back." The paper also quoted Cameron's stepdaughter, Lynda Johnson, who pointed out that Hoover "showed no remorse until she was caught."

Prosecutor Paul Ahler had the next-to-last word at the hearing. He reminded Judge Roberts that Hoover's long silence about Cameron's murder had kept George Peterson in jail for fourteen months after he confessed. Given that Peterson's confession was false and coerced by MCSO deputies, Ahler's use of it against Hoover was heavy with irony. He said, "It's likely George Peterson would have been convicted and possibly sentenced to death."

The judge, as is always the case in court, had the final word. Hoover's crime, Judge Roberts said, was "completely out of character, a bizarre aberration, but it was also murder." He sentenced Hoover to fifteen years in prison, minus the sixty days she had spent in juvenile detention. The revised plea bargain specified that she would not be released until she had served the entire sentence: she would remain in prison until May 2008.

Michelle Leslie Hoover was the youngest woman ever sentenced to an Arizona prison. Many lawyers believed that if she had turned herself in soon after the crime, when she was fourteen, she would not have been transferred to adult court. If she had been sentenced as a juvenile, she could not have been kept in detention beyond her eighteenth birthday. But, as the *Republic* put it, "that's not the turn her life took."

Because the law prohibited mingling juvenile prisoners with adults, Hoover could not be placed in the general prison population. According to a Department of Corrections spokesman, the State spent $6,700 to build her a special room at the women's prison. She would live in it until she turned eighteen, then join the dubious company of adult offenders.

Hoover served her sentence without incident. On May 12, 2008, the Arizona Department of Corrections noted her "commitment status" as "complete and verified" and marked her file "inactive." At the age of thirty-one, Michelle Hoover became a free woman.

JOHNATHAN DOODY ON TRIAL

Nine people died at Wat Promkunaram. Eight suspects were arrested for the murders: five from South Tucson and three from Phoenix's west side. Six of them confessed. With the charges against the Tucson suspects dismissed, two defendants remained. But only one, Johnathan Doody, was put on trial and faced a possible death sentence.

Judge Gregory Martin presided over Doody's trial. He directed the drama and managed the evidentiary flow in the first mass murder case in Arizona history. Hundreds of photos and tens of thousands of pages of transcript were admitted in evidence for the jury, along with audiotapes, videotapes, and other exhibits ranging from medical and investigative reports to lab tests.

With Doody's confession on record, the two-month trial was a highly charged exchange of views about a single issue: whether he had been the instigator of the crime and the actual killer, or whether he was somewhat less culpable. The jury spent those two months listening to witnesses and examining exhibits, then deliberated for only two days before reaching a verdict.

There were many factual disputes in the case, but the major issue was a legal one: the statutory distinction between felony murder and premeditated murder. In American jurisdictions, all those who participate in a felony during which someone dies are guilty of murder, whether or not they directly cause the death. The charge of felony murder is widely used by prosecutors because it does not require proof of intent to kill. In fact, it does not require proof that the defendant intended to cause harm of any kind.

The United Kingdom abolished felony murder in 1957, and several other countries followed suit. By 2007 the *New York Times* was calling it a "distinctively American legal doctrine." That doctrine was alive and well in Arizona in 1991. In Arizona felony murder qualifies as a capital crime, although there are limitations on the imposition of the death penalty for defendants convicted *only* of felony murder.

The justification for a charge of felony murder stems from the legal notion of "transferred intent." Defense lawyers commonly argue that transferred intent is a legal fiction—that prosecutors pretend a person who intended to commit one wrongful act also intended all the consequences of that act, however unforeseen. Prosecutors counter that a person who commits a crime should be held responsible for all its consequences. Those were the positions taken in Doody's trial by Peter Balkan for the defense and K. C. Scull and Paul Ahler for the prosecution.

The prosecutors charged Doody with both felony murder and premeditated murder. Premeditated murder involves a conscious intention to kill someone. Contrary to popular belief, premeditation does not have to be a carefully considered decision; it can happen in seconds.

In the temple killings, the time between the decision to kill and the act of killing was certainly longer than a few seconds. At the crime scene, the four spent shotgun shells were found close together, indicating that whoever fired them stood in one place while pulling the trigger four times. In contrast, the seventeen .22-caliber rifle casings were scattered around the bodies. All nine victims were shot in the back of the head, most more than once. Tests for nitrates around the wounds indicated that three of them had been shot at close range. Taken together, this evidence showed that the killer must have circled the victims, firing from many locations around the room. All this took time.

Thus if the jurors decided Doody had fired the fatal shots, they would probably find him guilty of premeditated murder. A verdict of felony murder would mean either that they were not sure who had fired the rifle or that they believed it had not been Doody.

For the prosecutors, the ideal outcome would be for the jury to convict Doody of premeditated murder and the judge to sentence him to death. The crime was mass murder—and even worse, mass murder of peaceful, devout people in their place of worship. It cried out for the ultimate punishment. Anything less would be a personal disappointment for Scull and Ahler and a political failure for their boss, County Attorney Romley, whose continued job tenure depended on the approval of Maricopa County's voters.

For Balkan, the hoped-for outcome was anything less than a death sentence. Doody's own words might get him convicted of felony murder: he admitted being at the temple during the crime. But he claimed he had not killed anyone, and Balkan would work hard to raise enough doubts in the jurors' minds to avoid a verdict of premeditated murder.

Before the trial could begin, there were vital pretrial issues to be resolved. In November 1992 Judge Martin denied Balkan's motion to suppress Doody's confession. In May 1993 the judge conducted a hearing about other pretrial motions. Every case twists and turns as new evidence surfaces. As Balkan put it, "things pop up that we never heard of." One twist in the Doody case involved the internal affairs inquiry into the temple murder investigation ordered by Sheriff Arpaio. Specifically, it involved the handwritten notes taken by Lt. Terry Chapman, the officer Arpaio had assigned to carry out the probe.

The notes popped up when Balkan urged the judge to admit the Tucson confessions as evidence in Doody's defense. To be admissible, evidence has to be both relevant to the case and reliable enough that a reasonable person could believe it. In Balkan's opinion, Chapman's notes illuminated the issue of reliability. The notes quoted MCSO officers saying that they no longer considered the Tucson confessions valid—and yet those same officers had believed the confessions in the beginning. Balkan wanted to reinterview Kimball, Riley, and Sinsabaugh about this. He asked the court for more time to conduct those interviews.

Balkan viewed the notes as potential exculpatory evidence: information that might establish the defendant's innocence or cast doubt on his guilt. Chapman's notes portrayed Agnos and White's task force—the same force that had interrogated Doody—in harsh, if not comical, terms. Balkan argued that they alleged "significant improprieties in the manner in which the entire case was conducted." In filing his motion to admit the Tucson confessions, he attached copies of the notes, thus making them part of the public record.

Judge Martin did not consider the Chapman notes sufficiently relevant to delay Doody's trial. He said Balkan was free to reinterview the detectives, but he would not be granted more time to do so.

Most of the hearing concerned whether to admit the confessions of the Tucson Four. Again, the criteria for admissibility were relevance and reliability. In 1991 the prosecutors had used those confessions to secure murder indictments, claiming they were reliable. In 1993 it was Balkan who claimed that they were reliable, while the prosecutors tried to keep them out of Doody's trial by arguing the opposite.

Balkan had no interest in convicting the Tucson Four, but he hoped the petit jury in his case would be as receptive to Mike McGraw's version of the temple murders as the grand jury had been when it had indicted the Tucson suspects. His argument to admit their confessions centered on the idea that if the jurors believed them, they might find his client not guilty. But he also hoped the jurors would connect the coercive techniques used on Bruce, Nunez, and Parker with the anguished confession extracted from Doody.

The prosecutors' case relied on getting the jury to accept Doody's confession and to believe the testimony of Garcia, their star witness. They feared that if the jurors heard the Tucson confessions, they would ignore Doody's confession and base their verdict entirely on their opinion of Garcia's credibility. Worse yet, they might wonder why the State had put Doody on trial rather than Garcia. They might group Doody with the innocent men from Tucson—as victims of the same coercive tactics—and decide that only Garcia was guilty, even though only Doody was on trial. This was high-stakes poker for the prosecutors, who had dismissed the charges against the Tucson Four and then given Garcia a favorable plea bargain. Many trial lawyers who followed the case agreed with that first decision but doubted the wisdom of the second.

Balkan had gathered some allies to buttress his argument that the confessions should be admitted. He told Judge Martin he had four witnesses who would be happy to testify. The four helpful citizens were former sheriff Tom Agnos, his chief deputies George Leese and John Coppock, and Captain Jerry White. They were waiting outside the courtroom, ready to testify that the Tucson confessions were "absolutely reliable."

The State's position was that no reasonable person could believe the confessions. Ahler noted that the entire case against the Tucson suspects came from McGraw, who had been committed to psychiatric institutions up to a dozen times before becoming the task force's prize informant. He emphasized that no evidence had been found linking McGraw, Nunez, Bruce, or Parker to the killings. Furthermore, Ahler pointed out, all four men had recanted their confessions.

Balkan quipped that if recantation proved a confession was false, the judge might as well dismiss Doody's confession, too. "I'll have him recant right here and we can all go home."

"That is foolish," Judge Martin admonished him.

After debunking the confessions, Ahler called the case against the Tucson Four "very dim." "We knew from the very beginning that there were problems with the case."

Judge Martin nailed him, asking how, "on that kind of evidence, any prosecutor could make a decision to charge people." Ahler must have realized he was on thin legal ice. "Judge, we weren't the only people that believed it. I mean three grand juries and a superior court judge felt at that time that there was enough evidence for probable cause."

In the end, Judge Martin admitted the Tucson confessions. His ruling must have sent shivers down Ahler's spine. Addressing the prosecution's assertion that the confessions were irrelevant to Doody's defense, the judge asked, "What could be more relevant than somebody else having confessed to the crime that the defendant is accused of committing?"

The judge pinpointed the fundamental problem that coerced confessions create for prosecutors. The State's task, he wrote, would be to prove "the defendant's guilt beyond a reasonable doubt with its evidence which includes a confession by the defendant elicited by law enforcement which it argues is voluntary and the defendant argues is involuntary, while at the same time having to confront the confessions of four other individuals elicited by the same law enforcement personnel which it now contends are totally unreliable." "Certainly," he added, "there is a question about whether any of the statements were given voluntarily. And that issue will have to be resolved by the jury. That is one of the reasons why the case may be prolonged."

Before the hearing ended, Balkan raised one more issue. Mr. and Mrs. Doody and their son David were coming from Colorado for the trial. Both sides had listed them as possible witnesses, so they would routinely be banned from the courtroom except when testifying. But they hoped to sit behind Johnathan to give him support. Balkan asked the judge to grant them an exception to the rule excluding witnesses from the courtroom. "It would be a comfort for them," he said. "It would be a comfort for my client to have them present." Judge Martin denied the request.

Murder trials fascinate the public, and many people see a confession to murder as the ideal civic solution. The perpetrator takes responsibility, and the public sleeps soundly. But murder trials rarely examine how the confession came into being: whether it is a product of the suspect's guilty mind or of the interrogators' will and perseverance.

Under the Arizona Constitution, every defendant charged with a "serious offense" has a right to trial by jury. Johnathan Andrew Doody was charged with murdering nine people, a serious offense indeed. His trial began on May 17, 1993.

The first two days were devoted to jury selection. In the process known as *voir dire*, the lawyers questioned potential jurors and attempted to pick the best jury for their clients. They selected fifteen jurors, of whom three would serve as alternates. By the time the jury was empaneled, its members knew the basic elements of the case: both Doody and Garcia admitted being at the temple at the time of the murders, but Garcia accused Doody of doing the actual killing. With Garcia's plea bargain a done deal, the stakes were high for Doody: if found guilty, he might be sentenced to death.

The lawyers gave their opening statements on May 19 and 20. The press sometimes writes about "opening arguments," but arguments are precisely what these presentations are not supposed to be. Procedural rules define an opening statement as a "plain, simple statement of the facts and evidence in the case." It is not an attempt to persuade jurors to agree with either side's position. Nevertheless, in high-profile cases, especially death-penalty cases, the temptation to slip into persuasive language is strong, and the niceties of trial practice are often relaxed. As Judge Martin put it, "You have got to give counsel a little leeway in histrionics and things like that."

In criminal trials the prosecution speaks first because it has the burden of proving its case beyond a reasonable doubt, while defendants do not have to prove their innocence. As K. C. Scull rose to begin, Doody sat quietly at the defense table, not reacting in any visible way. Describing the crime, Scull told the jury, "You probably know that it's the biggest homicide in the history of the State of Arizona."

Balkan stood up. "Objection."

"Sustained," said Judge Martin.

A seasoned trial lawyer, Scull took the ruling in stride and moved on. His pattern at the start of a major trial was to establish his central themes, then let them carry him to a crescendo of "no reasonable doubt." A major theme in this case was "no witnesses."

"Folks, two of the most bizarre and chilling words in the English language would have to be 'no witnesses.' This bizarre idea to rob the Buddhist temple and leave no witnesses was hatched in the brain of one man, Johnathan Doody." With those two sentences, Scull gave the jurors the theme and asserted that only Doody was responsible. He went on to elaborate on the motive, the plan, and the result: "[Doody's] evil idea to execute in cold blood nine human beings."

Then he informed the jury that there actually *was* a witness: Doody's "cohort in crime, Alex Garcia." The prosecutors had to hope the jurors would find Garcia more believable than detestable. In pretrial appearances, his words and his manner had made many people in the courtroom shudder. He talked about killing people the way some teenagers talk about cars or girls. Scull hoped that because Garcia had already pleaded guilty to this grisly crime, the jurors would think he had nothing to gain by lying about it now.

The prosecution's evidence would come mostly from Garcia's testimony and the audiotapes of Doody's interrogation. Scull would skillfully play his live witness against a defendant who sat mute at the defense table while his recorded voice filled the courtroom. Since both Garcia and Doody admitted being present during the murders, and thus admitted being guilty of felony murder, the jurors may have wondered what the trial was about. In time, the answer would become clear. This trial was not about guilt; it was about punishment.

Building sympathy for the victims was crucial to Scull's success. Buddhism, he said, "taught self-discipline and peace, with a strong emphasis on love, and a disregard for the personal accumulation of material goods and wealth. Buddhists are not cultists. They are not Hare Krishnas or Branch Davidians of the David Koresh type, extremists. It is an ancient religion, hundreds of years older than Christianity." In their temple, a "serene and, for these folks, holy place, these nine peaceful people of God met their violent and premeditated deaths." He told the jury, "The person that is responsible for this atrocity is Johnathan Doody."

Scull had more to say about the victims. "The commingling of these people's blood, in the pool of blood in the center by their heads, now unites them in death, as they were united in life." Balkan objected to this dramatic turn of phrase, but the judge overruled him.

Gesturing at a forty-eight-inch diagram of the prostrate bodies, Scull described the victims and their wounds, pronouncing each name carefully. He began with the seventy-five-year-old nun, Foy Sripanprasert, the only woman and the only victim dressed in white. She was shot twice in the back of the head and hit by shotgun pellets. Like all the victims, she was face down on the floor.

Lying with his head near Foy's was Somsak Sopha, a forty-six-year-old monk skilled in "the English language, typing, and accounting."

Before coming to Arizona, Somsak had been a teacher, an abbot, and a missionary. He suffered two rifle shots to the head and "vicious but non-fatal" shotgun wounds.

The next three bodies lay together in a row. Siang Ginggaeo, thirty-four, a teacher of Buddhist studies, was grazed by shotgun pellets and shot twice by the rifle, in the back of his head and below his right ear. Unlike the others, Siang had his arms flung up as if he had been moving when the bullets cut him down.

To Siang's right was Surichai Anuttaro, the temple's best handyman, who could "drive the tractor or cook the meals." Surichai also had two .22 shots to the head: one to the rear center of the skull, the other to the right cheek.

Chirasak Chirapong, known as Boy, twenty-one years old, had come from Thailand to visit his cousin, the temple's abbot. Boy wore his hair at collar length, while the others had closely shaved heads. His blue T-shirt and tan shorts contrasted with the monks' saffron and orange robes. He was killed by one .22 bullet to the back of the head. Here again Scull risked some emotional language, describing Boy's hands as "clasped in a prayerful, begging, or beseeching position at the top of his head." This time Balkan did not object.

The next three victims lay even closer together, their bodies touching. Nearest to Boy was his cousin Pairuch Kanthong, the head monk, or abbot. Pairuch, who had been at the temple since 1983, was "a very tactful leader and everyone loved him." He was shot twice on the left side of his head.

Sixteen-year-old Matthew Miller was next to the abbot. Scull told the jury that Miller, the nun's grandson, had been staying at the temple "to pray, to meditate, to cleanse [himself], spiritually and physically and, hopefully, to find peace." In all other ways, he was a typical teenager and high-school student. He was shot twice in the back of the head.

On Miller's right, with his arm across the boy's head and shoulder as if in protection, was Chalerm Chantapim, thirty-three, a missionary and teacher. He had been "uncharacteristically shot *three* times with the .22, all to the back of the head."

The last victim Scull mentioned, Boonchuay Chaiyarach, lay between Chalerm and Foy, completing the rough circle of death. Boonchuay, thirty-seven, had served as a missionary in Asia and Europe; in Arizona he taught Sunday school, Buddhist studies, and meditation. "His personal motto," Scull said, "was work and serve." He was severely wounded by shotgun pellets and killed by one .22 shot to the back of the head.

After introducing the victims, Scull summarized the findings of their autopsies. The medical examiners had reached the same conclusions about all nine: "Cause of death: gunshot or gunshot wounds to the head. Manner of death: homicide."

Mindful that Judge Martin had overruled the State's objections to allowing the jury to hear the Tucson Four's confessions, Scull talked about those confessions as if they were part of the prosecution's case. One of the hundreds of leads, he said, came from a man who phoned from the Tucson Psychiatric Institute. Scull walked the jury through the mine-field that Mike McGraw had created for the prosecution. McGraw "spun quite a long and involved tale [about] coming to Phoenix with several other people from Tucson, and he confessed they committed all of these crimes." By this time everyone who followed the temple case—every-one, that is, except the former MCSO command officers—had ceased to believe McGraw's story. Now Scull wanted the jurors, too, to disbelieve McGraw and all the Tucson confessions.

Describing the confessions as vague, inconsistent, and quickly recanted, Scull asked, "Why did the Tucson suspects admit their involve-ment to these crimes? We may never know, folks. Perhaps it was their fear. Perhaps it was . . . exhaustion or coercion, or desire to please their interviewers. I don't know the answer. But we do not have a single piece of evidence to corroborate their initial statements where they admitted they were involved." He warned the jury, "Don't be distracted by red her-rings. Johnathan Doody is the man that's on trial here today."

Half an hour into his opening statement, Scull finally moved to his case-in-chief, giving chapter and verse of the case against Doody, alert-ing the jurors to what to listen for when they later heard the tapes of his interrogation.

Doody's brother David had lived in the temple in the summer of 1991. "Perhaps that's where the seed was germinated to start this entire, awful ball of wax forming." Despite the awkwardly mixed metaphor, Scull gave the jurors something to speculate about: Doody's personal connection to the temple. They might wonder: Did the monks mistreat David? Did David have some role in the awful ball of wax?

Scull anticipated the defense argument that Doody's confession had been coerced. When he admits borrowing the rifle, Scull said, Doody "is not exhausted. He is not falling over. He is not being pressured. He is already starting to tell us significant facts about this investigation, facts significant enough that the officers' ears perk up. . . . 'Oh really? You borrowed this gun? And this is the murder weapon.'"

He moved methodically through all seventeen tapes. "Now on tape ten Doody is starting to tell us the story as to his involvement in this horrible crime." With the first-person pronoun ("tell *us*"), Scull linked himself, and the jurors, with the interrogators who had extracted Doody's confession.

Doody claimed the killing was not planned, but Scull called that claim "another lie," thus communicating his low opinion of the defendant's credibility. Lawyers are not permitted to give juries such personal opinions, but Balkan didn't object, and Scull kept it up. Doody, he said, had called the temple invasion a joke that went downhill. "I don't know how you can go to this temple with guns and call it a joke, but he does." As he previewed the tapes, Scull made sure the jurors knew the State's position on which of Doody's statements were lies and which were truths.

On tape 15, Scull said, "there was a conference where it was decided to kill everyone." To underline the clear implication of premeditation, he said it again. "A conference where it was decided to kill everyone."

When Judge Martin interrupted to say it was almost time for the mid-afternoon break, Scull quickly gave the jurors a gory detail to think about. Doody claimed he had heard someone ask, "Did you hear the blood coming out from him?" But a witness, Scull said, would testify that Doody himself used that phrase in conversation.

After the break, Scull resumed his chat with the "folks" in the jury box. This time his topic was the State's prime witness. He recounted Garcia's version of the crime, emphasizing details that pointed to Doody as the mastermind and the killer. "Doody wanted to use the .22 because it held more rounds" than the shotgun. "They made the silencer because Doody intended to kill everyone."

Scull assured the jury that when Garcia told his story, "he had absolutely no deal from any authorities." That assertion was both literally accurate and misleading. The jurors had no way of knowing what the deputies had told Juan Garcia that they would recommend for Alex if he confessed. And Scull did not mention Garcia's maneuvers to secure a deal to save his own life, which put Doody at risk for the death penalty.

Scull listed other witnesses he intended to call. Angel Rowlett would testify that Doody had said he and Garcia shot the monks and that Doody "started shooting first . . . because he didn't want anyone to recognize him." Marvin Cook would say Doody had owed him two thousand dollars for his Mustang and had paid a thousand five days after the murders. Vickie Jones would recall Doody talking about shooting people in the head for money. Ben Leininger would report Doody's boast that he and Garcia "had been used by the OSI as snipers, that the monks were invading national security and OSI had to eliminate them." Leininger was also the one Doody had told about hearing "the blood rush from their heads." Brandon Burner would testify that he and Doody had not seen a movie the night of the murders, and that Doody had said he and Garcia were going on "an invasion alert" near the temple.

Near the end of the day, Scull reached his most difficult task: convincing the jury that Garcia was telling the truth about the shootings and that Doody was lying. It is a truism in criminal justice that every killer will cop out at some point to avoid the death penalty. But not everyone on a jury knows that. Scull's challenge was to paint Garcia in truthful colors in order to win a guilty verdict against Doody. He said Garcia's plea agreement required him to testify truthfully at Doody's trial and "tell us about any other crimes that he might have been involved in." In return, "the State agreed that it would not seek the death penalty against Alex Garcia."

As for Garcia's disclosure that he had indeed been involved in another crime, Scull implied that by confessing to a tenth murder, Garcia had done a good deed. If he had not come forward, "An innocent man may have been convicted for that crime, and a killer might have escaped justice."

Scull described Garcia as "a strapping youth, to say the least . . . a real big fellow. But even though he was sixteen years old, he didn't want to work. He'd rather rob and kill people." In Scull's account, he was a lazy and rather passive boy who simply went along with Doody's plan to invade the temple. "I'm not praising Alex Garcia," Scull added, "and I am certainly not in bed with Alex Garcia. I am just telling you that his testimony . . . is straightforward. It is frank. It is honest. And we can corroborate fact after fact after fact that Alex Garcia tells us."

Scull ended his opening statement with a peroration against the defendant. Doody, he said, "is the one that started this, got the information, had the motivation, pursued the plan, carried it out, was the leader,

profited most by it. And he is the one that's on trial here. And we are
going to ask you to come back with a guilty verdict on all counts."

At 9:30 the next morning, Thursday, May 20, Judge Martin's bailiff gaveled him back into the courtroom. As he would for the next eight weeks,
the judge said, "Let the record show the presence of the jury, the lawyers, and Mr. Doody." Then he invited Peter Balkan to begin his opening statement.

Balkan walked to the jury rail and paused while he gathered the jurors'
attention. The second lawyer to make an opening statement is always at
a disadvantage: jurors, like everyone else on the planet, can rarely resist
the temptation to make quick judgments. Balkan would do his best to
overcome that disadvantage.

The State's exhibits in the trial, Balkan said, would "probably range
from big to huge," but "the truth in this case might not come to you in
huge packages. The truth might not be shouted from newspaper headlines or TV headlines or from the mouths of prosecutors. The truth may
come in this case in very small packages or might be whispered to you in
the sound of undeniable doubt."

That last phrase may have perplexed the jurors. They knew that the
legal term for what Balkan needed for his client was "reasonable" doubt.
In asking them to listen for a whisper of undeniable doubt, he seemed to
make his own job harder.

Balkan said the investigation of the temple murders had involved "one
of the largest police forces ever assembled in Arizona." And yet, "with all
of that, ladies and gentlemen, you are going to find that there is no direct,
physical evidence of guilt for Johnathan Doody." The jurors would see
"rooms of exhibits," and would hear from the "finest of experts" about
fingerprints, footprints, handwriting, firearms. But none of the evidence
could be "linked directly to Johnathan Doody, without accepting the
words of somebody else." Not only that, but "one of the things you are
going to hear people say is, 'I did it.' You are going to hear about four
people from Tucson who said they did it. And you are going to have to
decide what that means . . . to a case in which everything depends on
what people say."

The gist of Doody's confession could be expressed in one sentence. "Johnathan told police officers that he was there at the temple [but] never, ever said that he shot anybody or was responsible for this crime." With this admission, Balkan acknowledged his client's complicity in a felony murder case while distancing him from premeditated murder. It was the difference between life in prison and death by lethal injection.

Knowing the case would come down to whether or not the jury believed Garcia, Balkan turned to a standard argument, the bought witness. "What the State did was to make their exhibits larger, brighter, to buy more experts to say the very same thing over and over again . . . [but] they still didn't have a case; so they bought themselves a witness. They bought themselves Alessandro Garcia."

At first, Balkan noted, Garcia claimed that only he and Doody went to the temple. After learning from his father that he would get a deal, he said the Tucson people and Caratachea were there. "At one point it almost sounds like Mr. Garcia says Bruce Willis was there." Then, when he was offered the deal and told he could save his life with his testimony, he went back to his earlier story: "'I did it with Johnathan Doody.'"

Listing Scull's other witnesses, Balkan tried to debunk their future testimony in advance. Cook's story of when Doody had paid for the Mustang varied from a few days after the murders to a few days before. Rowlett would say, in effect, "I guess he told me he did it, but I didn't report it." Leininger was a person who "tells a lot stories and, because he is so gullible, has a lot of stories told to him." According to Balkan, just before Leininger told the police about Doody's supposed boast of being an OSI sniper, he and Doody had been fighting over a girl.

Balkan laid the foundation for an alternative theory of the crime: that Rolando Caratachea had been at the temple and had used his own gun. The crime scene, he said, had been "virtually chaos," contaminated by people walking through to gawk and stare. He let the jury know that every officer with brass on his collar had shown up at the temple. Nevertheless, he asserted, there was hard evidence that "more than two people were at the scene when the monks died."

He was careful not to accuse Caratachea of murder in his opening statement. The strength, if any, of the alternate-shooter defense would have to come from the witness stand, not the lawyers' podium. Instead Balkan asked a series of "what if" questions, such as "What if I told you that another person was found in possession of the murder weapon just days after the temple killings?" His questions added up to this: Caratachea owned the gun, hated to lend it to anyone, had some of the loot from the temple, "changed his alibi two or three times," and was Garcia's choice for a third person to help with the invasion. In sum, "Rolando Caratachea attracts temple evidence like a magnet."

Eventually Balkan turned to the Tucson Four. In reality, the false confessions of McGraw, Bruce, Nunez, and Parker had no probative impact on either Garcia or Doody. But because the judge had ruled their interrogations admissible, both lawyers felt compelled to present mind-numbing recitations about true and false confessions. And both made the same point—that the MCSO command staff decided in advance that the defendants were guilty, then ignored evidence that contradicted that opinion. The lawyers were correct, but it did not serve justice to have so much of Doody's trial focused on police-induced confessions extracted from innocent men.

Balkan told the jury, "All the people in this case were interrogated over an incredibly lengthy period of time, the Tucson suspects, as well as Johnathan Doody, as well as Alex Garcia, because time gets you the confession." The tactic was "to fool these tired suspects into thinking . . . that the way to end the ordeal of interrogation is to simply say whatever they want to hear, and don't worry about it, it won't hurt you." Balkan hoped the jurors would see Doody's confession as a bad apple from the same rotten tree that had produced the Tucson confessions.

He also encouraged the jurors to wonder why the Tucson Four had confessed if they were innocent. He asked them to keep that question in mind during their deliberations, and to remember that "even a single reasonable doubt" required them to find Doody not guilty. "Mr. Scull himself told you he does not know why these people would make those statements, if they were untrue. Mr. Scull, by not knowing, has indicated doubt."

At the end of his opening statement, Balkan repeated the mysterious phrase he had used at the beginning. "Ladies and gentlemen . . . the truth in this case might come to you in small packages. And in whispers of undeniable doubt."

As soon as Balkan sat down, the judge told Scull to call his first witness. Scull began with Chawee Borders, who had found the bodies on that August morning in 1991. Many other witnesses followed. Borders's friend Premchit Hash testified, and Joe Ledwidge, the neighbor who had helped them. Deputy Don Wipprecht told the court the scene had been so upsetting that he'd had trouble counting the victims. Riley and Kimball testified about examining the crime scene, Sinsabaugh about confiscating Caratachea's rifle; all three officers talked about the interrogations. The medical examiners explained the autopsy results. Bill Morris from the state crime lab specified that Caratachea's gun was the murder weapon. Other technical witnesses pieced together the evidence against Doody. Each prosecution witness was first questioned by Scull, then cross-examined by Balkan. By the time Scull was ready to call his star witness, the trial was at the end of its third week.

Alex Garcia took the stand on Friday, June 4. The jurors knew he was shielded by his plea bargain, but they also knew that the way they dealt with Doody would depend on what this overfed young man, Scull's "strapping youth," had to say.

The one person in the courtroom who probably dreaded Garcia's appearance was Johnathan Doody. This would be the first time the former best friends had seen each other since their last day of freedom, October 25, 1991. In the intervening months they had heard about each other from lawyers and visitors and through the jail grapevine, but this was the day of reckoning for both. They could exchange glares across the courtroom, but neither could change the deal that guaranteed life to one and risked death for the other.

Until then Doody had not responded to anything that had happened at the trial. He ignored the lawyers and never looked directly at the jury, although he seemed deferential to the judge. Often he doodled on a yellow pad. When Garcia walked in, according to Mike Sager, "The change was remarkable. He narrowed his eyes, glowered at his former best friend, diddling a ballpoint pen so fast between the first two fingers of his right hand that it blurred." Doody looked at Garcia as the doomed Julius Caesar must have looked at Brutus. That betrayed look showed the jury that Doody too was, in some way, a victim.

Scull guided Garcia through a tightly scripted story. It may or may not have been true, but no one doubted its high drama and its low moral base. In preparing for the trial, the prosecutors had created an "in court" voice and persona for Garcia. Although his demeanor and tone might not match his rehearsed words, the idea was to portray him as, in most respects, a normal adolescent suffering from teenage angst. The forensic evidence against Doody was weak: physical evidence from the crime scene could be linked to Garcia, but not to Doody. To make the case against Doody, Scull needed a powerful appeal from this witness.

In his questions, Scull stuck close to the story Garcia had told his interrogators. The plan to invade the temple was Doody's idea, a way to get money. They borrowed Caratachea's .22 rifle, and Garcia took a 20-gauge shotgun from his dad's closet. As Garcia told it, Doody discussed mass murder as if it were a business matter between teenage entrepreneurs. Garcia tried to talk Doody out of killing the victims by arguing that armed robbery was a lesser charge than murder. But Doody was determined to leave no witnesses. Garcia fired the shotgun four times without aiming at anyone; Doody shot each victim in the head and then went around the circle shooting them again. The two of them committed the crime without help from anyone else; other local boys and the Tucson Four had nothing to do with it.

Scull painstakingly asked about the events at the temple—the minute details that matched forensic evidence the jury had already heard. Like any seasoned prosecutor, he wanted to match the person to the scene and the scene to the charge. In addition, he wanted the jury to see Garcia as follower, Doody as leader.

Reporters in the courtroom took notes and tried to guess what the jurors were thinking. They listened to Garcia's emotionless description of the way he and his friend ended the lives of nine defenseless people. Despite the "in court" voice Garcia had been coached to use on the witness stand, some of the reporters saw him not as an angst-ridden boy but as a malevolent young man.

Sager painted word pictures of the defendant and the witness. Doody was "more mature now, beefy and thick-necked with bad skin, a close-cropped haircut." As for Garcia, "From a three-quarter view he seemed handsome, with high cheekbones and almond-shaped eyes. The jaw, thick and square, his father's, lent a sort of haughty, rakish air to the face of a teenage boy. From dead on, though, the impression was altered. You saw the stick-out ears, the chipped front teeth, and the meaty expanse of forehead; he appeared vaguely feral."

Johnathan Andrew Doody was *on* trial, *at* trial, and *in* trial, but he did not appear on the witness stand to speak on his own behalf. Defendants have a right to testify under the Sixth Amendment and a right *not* to testify under the Fifth Amendment. Balkan had informed the court that his client would probably not take the stand.

Keeping Doody off the witness stand deprived the State of a chance to cross-examine him. He did not have the language skills or the cognitive anticipatory judgment to avoid prosecutorial traps. He had not confessed to shooting anyone, but if he testified, Scull might be able, in the back-and-forth of cross-examination, to put the murder weapon in his hands. For Doody, the risk of cross-examination was the risk of death versus life. So Balkan wisely did not call the defendant as a witness.

And yet, because Judge Martin had denied the motion to exclude his taped interrogation, the jury heard Doody speak. Live testimony can be supplanted by recorded testimony. There is no oath to tell the truth, but that may not make a difference to jurors. Admitting Doody's taped confession allowed the prosecution to put his voice, his veracity, and his credibility before the jury. At the time, that central legal decision seemed to be a blow to the defense. But it may have boomeranged and worked against the prosecution.

Judge Martin did not make the decision lightly. His hearing on the issue lasted ten days. His formal ruling, that Doody had confessed voluntarily, knowingly, and intelligently, led to the legal conclusion that in the interrogation, Doody had waived his constitutional right to counsel. The practical consequence of the decision was that the jury would hear Doody's voice and get to know him in a way that cross-examination could not undo.

The prosecutors played the tapes in court, all seventeen of them. Doody's words—along with many *more* words from his interrogators—filled the courtroom for more than two days. He had an official position: not guilty. That was his plea. It was up to the jury to decide whether his words supported that position.

Since speaking those words, Doody had spent nineteen months in jail, awaiting trial. During that time he had turned eighteen, and his official government status had changed from "juvenile detainee" to "adult prisoner." He was heavier now—beefy, as Sager put it—but in other respects, he seemed the same impassive but polite, present but distant teenager whom Riley, Munley, and Sinsabaugh, with help from Captain White, had grilled for more than twelve hours.

Doody's younger voice reached the jury through state-of-the-art audio equipment. Each juror had a headset, complete with volume control and a flexible cord to allow a little mobility in the jury box. The defendant also had a headset. The jurors watched him across the room as they listened. He did not look back at them.

Doody retained his stoic demeanor throughout the playing of the tapes. He did not argue, frown, make a fuss, or insert himself into the proceedings in any way. He participated only on the tapes, sounding scratchy and far away. His manner implied that even if he had given live testimony, it would have sounded scratchy and far away.

Judge Martin's pivotal decision to admit the taped interrogations—both Doody's and Garcia's—did more than just allow the jury to hear Doody's confession. It forced Garcia to his official position: guilty by admission. Simply put, Garcia pled out. His plea agreement was a wild card in this case. Would the jury believe Doody, after hearing him on tape, or would they believe Garcia, who would testify in person, and who would put the rifle in Doody's hands to save his own life?

Out of all the words—almost a hundred thousand of them—on the seventeen tapes, Doody's "confession" can be summarized in one paragraph:

He was at the temple on the night of the murders. Garcia was with him; later he added Caratachea, George Gonzales, and George's friend. "They" planned to approach the temple without setting off the motion-detector lights. He thought the goal was just to "get past the light sensor and the dog, basically touch the door." After a scare on their first try, the others decided to "go inside and see what we can get," and he went with them. He helped gather the victims into one room, then "they" ransacked the living quarters. When a monk recognized George, "they" sent Doody outside to confirm that the walls were soundproof. By the time he got back inside, the shooting had started; he didn't know who had fired the shots.

Summary alone is as silent as justice is blind. Doody's actual responses to his interrogators are immune to summary. From the first tape, which revealed the MCSO's meandering, dismissive approach to the *Miranda* warnings, to the seventeenth, with Sinsabaugh trying to calm a distraught suspect with offers of candy bars, the jurors listened to every word, groan, and sob. In the end, it may have been the sobs that were probative and the groans that guided the jury's decision.

Doody's interrogation was chronicled in chapter 6; readers who wish to endure it a second time, as Doody was forced to do in the courtroom, may reread that chapter. Here a few comments will suffice.

The early tapes gave the jury a sense of Doody's gullibility and his difficulty with English. He had lived in Thailand until the age of seven, then in Germany, not moving to the United States until he was nine. Thus English was his second or perhaps third language, and in his late teens, he still had trouble with it.

One turning point came about two hours into the interrogation, when Riley was pressing for information about Caratachea's rifle. After Riley promised that whatever Doody told them "is gonna stay right here," Doody made his first admission: "Me and Alex borrowed the gun for two days." Just as the belated testing of the rifle had changed the course of the investigation, this short utterance probably changed the jurors' view of Doody. Jurors pledge to reserve their decisions until they are deliberating in the jury room, but Doody's admission may well have changed his position, in their minds, from "not guilty" to "probably guilty."

As the tapes droned on, the reporters and others in the back of the courtroom alternated between shock and boredom. Four hours passed between Doody's first small admission and his second. Riley, Munley, and Sinsabaugh alternated between pleading and demanding, but most of the time Doody sat in silence. They shouted. He sat. They pleaded. He withdrew. The jurors may have wondered whether Doody was dozing off, or even sinking into a catatonic state. After all, it was the middle of the night, and he had been under interrogation for six hours.

Near the end of tape 9, the detectives' harangues at last paid off. The question that broke through Doody's denial was "Were you involved?" Sinsabaugh hammered him with those three words over and over, chipping away at his silence. Doody must have thought the blows would never end. After nine repetitions, he caved in. "Yes," he said.

The detectives got nothing else from Doody until Captain White paid a visit at four in the morning. White's announcement that the killers were already in jail, with its clear implication that Doody was not one of the killers, changed Doody's attitude dramatically. Listening in the courtroom, the jurors heard his entire confession in the next few minutes.

If that brief dramatic outpouring focused the jurors' attention, they may have had to struggle to stay awake for the remaining tapes—five more hours of interminable questions and laconic, evasive answers. During most of that time, Sinsabaugh, Riley, and White tried to get Doody to connect the Tucson Four to the murders.

On the seventeenth tape, after more than twelve hours of questioning, the jurors heard a new sound in their headsets. Johnathan Doody began to cry. Again drone gave way to drama, as the courtroom echoed with racking sobs. The jurors heard Doody say, "I didn't know this was suppose to happen." They heard him accuse Caratachea of threatening him. And they heard his final cry that he "never meant to get involved at all." For several minutes more he continued to wail, mutter, and sob. Sinsabaugh came and went, offering candy, soda, trips to the bathroom, but got no response. Finally he told the inconsolable Doody, "Go ahead, sleep," and apparently left him, collapsed and incoherent, on the floor.

Everyone in the courtroom sat in silence during tape 17. The jurors, whose gaze usually roamed from Doody to the prosecutors to the judge, now started to look back and forth among themselves. It is surprising that the prosecutors allowed that last tape to keep running. If they were playing the tapes to provide evidence of Doody's guilt, why play a section that seemed to prove that his emotions were genuine, and perhaps that he spoke the truth?

The jurors probably assumed that the remainder of the trial would focus closely on Doody's guilt or innocence, and mostly on his innocence: it was now Balkan's turn to present his defense. If so, they were mistaken. For the next several days, Balkan would attempt to create "undeniable doubt" by guiding the jury down several paths, all of them leading *away* from Doody.

The first path led to Rollie Caratachea, Doody and Garcia's classmate. All three boys had been interrogated at approximately the same time, on the same floor, by the same detectives. But Caratachea had not confessed, and he had not been charged with any involvement in the murders. Now Balkan worked hard to link Garcia's favorable plea bargain to Caratachea's favorable walkaway. He noted that under interrogation, both Garcia and Doody had implicated Caratachea—but that Garcia, after negotiating his plea bargain, no longer recalled Caratachea's role in the crime. Balkan also argued that Caratachea had benefited from the politics of the temple case: after the debacle over the Tucson Four, his refusal to confess made the prosecutors reluctant to charge him.

When Balkan took Caratachea's pretrial deposition, Caratachea had refused to answer questions, invoking his Fifth Amendment right not to incriminate himself. Nevertheless, Balkan subpoenaed him to appear at the trial. To find out whether he was willing to testify, Balkan first questioned him without the jury present.

Caratachea walked into the courtroom with his lawyer, Gary Rohlwing. Balkan got right to the point, and the exchange quickly became monotonous. "Mr. Caratachea, were you involved in any way in the shooting of nine individuals at the Buddhist temple on August 9, 1991?"

"On advice of counsel, I will plead the Fifth."

"Do you have any information concerning that particular incident?"

"On advice of counsel, I'll plead the Fifth."

"Would it be your intention to invoke your privilege against self-incrimination on each and any question that I ask . . . concerning that incident?"

"On advice of counsel, I plead the Fifth."

Balkan addressed the judge. "I think he can answer that yes or no, whether he is going to invoke or not."

Rohlwing agreed, and Caratachea said, "I'll answer it yes."

Again addressing the judge, Balkan argued that because, in his plea agreement, Garcia had sworn that Caratachea was not involved in the temple crimes, the State could not prosecute Caratachea for those crimes without abandoning its agreement with Garcia. Thus, he concluded, Caratachea was not in danger of prosecution and should not be allowed to invoke his Fifth Amendment right against self-incrimination.

Rohlwing pointed out that his client had not been offered immunity from prosecution. "Who knows what's going to happen in the future? You know, there has been a lot of people, the Tucson Four and many other people have been talked about and implicated in this case."

Judge Martin ruled that Caratachea did have the right to take the Fifth. If he did so on the witness stand, Balkan could use parts of the testimony he had given earlier in juvenile court, having excerpts read to the jury. The judge asked, "Why are you offering him as a witness at all? What are you going to get out of this on behalf of your client?"

Balkan had a ready answer. "He's the person I say did it."

As it turned out, Balkan did have sections of Caratachea's juvenile court testimony read to the jury. In juvenile court Caratachea had not been asked whether he had participated in the temple murders. In adult court he was asked but took the Fifth. Whether his silence on that crucial point had any effect on the verdict in Doody's trial is unknown—locked, as it should be, in the jury room.

Balkan's next path to doubt about Doody's guilt took an unlikely turn. He called witnesses who, almost everyone agreed by then, had nothing at all to do with the crime. Mark Nunez and Leo Bruce took the stand; Balkan also played the tapes of Dante Parker's confession.

He focused most closely on Bruce, who had falsely confessed to killing all nine victims. Ostensibly Balkan hoped the jury would conclude that Bruce might have killed the monks. But he also hoped the jury would see Bruce as a victim of coercion and his ordeal as evidence that Doody's confession, too, might be false.

Leo Bruce would have preferred not to testify. He was, as he had been in September 1991, bewildered and frightened by the attention. Back then he had been yelled at, lied to, tricked, and threatened. And after giving the interrogators what they wanted, he had been jailed, indicted, and humiliated before finally being released. Now, more than a year later, he was back in Phoenix, subjected to more questions and a courtroom full of unfamiliar faces. Those Phoenix people were doing it to him all over again.

Balkan asked Bruce to describe his interrogation in his own words, but Bruce was not a man of words. Balkan had to coax the story out of him.

Naming Bruce's first interrogators, Munley and Casey, Balkan asked if they were the people he talked to. Bruce made a gentle correction. "They were talking to me."

After walking Bruce through the steadfast denials of his first three hours of questioning, Balkan asked, "Were you calm or were you nervous or crying or what?"

"I was very scared, very, very tired."

Balkan asked if Munley and Casey had threatened him in any way.

"They mentioned the gas chamber."

Asked why the threat made him more likely to admit involvement in the murders, Bruce replied, "I just wanted the interview to stop, so I just agreed to it."

A series of Balkan's questions began with "Isn't it true." "Isn't it true that you didn't answer them for about thirty seconds, that you just sort of sat there?" "that you were sort of resting your chin on your chest?" "that you had tears in your eyes?" To each question, Bruce answered, "I don't recall." But Balkan did not need Bruce to remember such details. He relied on the wording of the questions themselves to reveal Bruce's vulnerability to coercive techniques.

Balkan never thought Bruce was guilty. His plan was to create a link in the jurors' minds, a chain of common experience, between Doody and Bruce. Bruce was confused by the interrogators' lies; so was Doody. Bruce was scared by threats; so was Doody. Bruce broke down and cried; so did Doody.

This kind of witness inquiry is quite rare in death-penalty litigation. In most capital cases, defendants do not testify because they might not withstand cross-examination. In this case, the jurors knew Doody had been at the scene of the crime. They had heard his anguished, inconsistent confession on tape, but they would not hear from him live in the courtroom. So Balkan put Bruce on the stand as a proxy for Doody. While questioning Bruce, Balkan hoped the jurors were looking not at the witness but at his client.

When Balkan asked why he had never told his questioners, "Let's just stop," Bruce said he was exhausted and couldn't think straight. Again, his precise answer was irrelevant. Balkan simply hoped the jury would remember that Doody, too, had allowed himself to be subjected to questioning for nearly thirteen hours—and that, in spite of the interrogators' casual recitation of the *Miranda* warnings, neither Bruce nor Doody had understood that he had a right to stop the interrogation.

Balkan later recalled Bruce as one of the nicest guys he'd ever met and one of the most compliant witnesses he'd ever put on the stand. "I was afraid he was going to confess again, right there in the courtroom." A confession was the last thing Balkan was looking for. He wanted the jury to believe the truth about Leo Bruce—that he was guilty only of false confession.

"Isn't it true," Balkan asked, that the officers said "they thought you were, in fact, the shooter?"

"They were saying I was the trigger man."

"Then they asked who you shot at the temple and you replied, 'All of them.'"

"Yes."

"After you made these admissions . . . did you act relieved? Did you act more relaxed?"

"Yes."

"Why were you relieved and relaxed to have confessed to nine murders that you say you didn't do?"

"It took pressure off me, and since I was scared I wasn't thinking straight."

Balkan asked a crucial question: "At any time . . . did you start to actually believe that you did it?"

"No."

"At every second that you were making these admissions, were you always thinking, 'These are lies'?"

"Yes."

In fact, Bruce had confessed at least twice: during the gap between tapes and again in the "enhanced" interview. Balkan asked, "How were you able to make the story the second time close to or identical to the story the first time?"

"Just remembering everything of whatever was in the prop room and stuff."

Balkan was trying to show the jury what psychologists call the power of the situation. The interrogation process alone can make some innocent people confess to a crime. "Coerced-compliant" confessions are made to escape the duress, mental pain, and confusion created by coercive interrogation techniques. "Coerced-internalized" confessions come about when defendants actually begin to believe they were responsible for a crime although they have no memory of it. According to Bruce's testimony, his confession had been coerced compliant.

Balkan asked why Bruce had confessed to "the worst mass murder in the history of Arizona" if he had nothing to do with it.

"I was real scared. I wasn't thinking straight, and I was real exhausted. I just wanted to cooperate with them. If I told them what they wanted to hear, then it would end."

"Didn't it at any point occur to you that rather than ending this thing that you were going to ensure that you would be eventually charged and prosecuted and possibly convicted?"

Balkan spoke in his best lawyerlike, incredulous tone. He did not mean to sound condescending, but he wanted the jury to know something important about the power of the situation. Some people are more vulnerable to that power than others; they don't consider the consequences of what they say when they say it. He hoped the jurors would hear Bruce's answer as though it were Doody's.

He could not have gotten a better reply if the defendant himself had been on the stand. "At that time," Bruce said, "no, it didn't."

Back in 1991 Bruce had faced tag teams of interrogators; now he had to face one lawyer after another. As soon as Balkan sat down, Paul Ahler stood up to cross-examine.

Ahler's first question got the jurors' attention. "Mr. Bruce, have you ever killed anyone in your life?"

"What's that?" Bruce sounded startled.

"Have you ever killed anyone in your life?"

"No, never."

"Have you ever been to Wat Promkunaram Buddhist temple?"

"No, I wasn't."

"Do you know an individual by the name of Alex Garcia?"

"No, I don't."

"Do you know the defendant in this case, Johnathan Doody?"

"No, I don't."

"Do you know an individual by the name of Rolando Caratachea?"

"No, I don't."

The rapid-fire questions laid the groundwork for showing the jury how unreliable the State now considered Bruce's confession to be. The trick was to make the jury forget that the State had originally thought the confession was reliable enough to indict Bruce for first-degree murder.

Ahler informed the witness—and the jury—that Bruce's gun had been "positively excluded" as the weapon fired at the temple. Then he asked, "Your gun was not involved at the temple, was it?"

"It was not."

"And you know that for a fact because you weren't there?"

"That is correct. I was not there."

The jurors may have wondered where this was going. The defense had spent several hours making two points: Bruce was not at the temple, and his confession was false. Now the prosecution seemed to be making exactly the same points.

Asking about Bruce's relationships with McGraw, Nunez, and Zarate, Ahler confirmed that Bruce was close to Zarate and Nunez, and that all of them distrusted McGraw.

"Does Mike McGraw have a nickname?"

"Yes."

"What's his nickname?"

"Crazy Mike."

"Do you know how he got that name?"

"He just would go out and do crazy things."

In asking if Bruce had ever read the transcripts of his interrogation, Ahler inadvertently gave the jury another primer on the power of the situation. Bruce said he didn't want to read them. "Every time I think of this case, it hurts me. I get scared, I just freak out."

Ahler got Bruce to confirm that the deputies had made him sit in the prop room and look at pictures of the bodies, diagrams of the crime scene, and a chart with his name on it. He asked if Bruce had looked at the chart closely.

"I just was mainly concentrating on my name." Seeing the name, Bruce said, "made me feel real scared because they had the wrong person."

When Ahler brought up the twelve untaped hours of Bruce's interrogation, during which Griffiths and Bates had induced him to confess, Bruce recalled a coercive technique that no tape or transcript could reveal. Ahler asked if he could "distinguish in your mind one of the detectives from the other."

"One was a big guy, tall, and the other one was shorter with bad breath."

"Why does that stick in your mind?"

"'Cause he was real close to me, and I was just trying to get away from him, because I don't—his breath was just getting to me."

To some of Ahler's questions, Bruce replied that he didn't recall.

"There appear to be some things that you can recall and others that you can't recall. Mr. Bruce, is there a reason for that?"

"It's just probably 'cause I'm real—I feel pressure on me right now . . . when I'm under pressure and stuff, I cannot think right. My mind is not here with me."

That answer tied Bruce and Doody together. Here was another young man who, like Doody, had succumbed to pressure and admitted participating in nine murders. Yet everyone now agreed that Bruce was innocent. If a lawyer could make Bruce feel pressured in open court in such a short time, what might determined interrogators have done to Doody's mind during thirteen hours in a small, closed room? Thoughts like these were not what Ahler hoped to inspire in the jurors.

Ahler ended his cross-examination by asking if Bruce felt bad about what he had done. Bruce said yes.

"In what way?"

"To lie to them, and lie to myself, that I was there."

Ahler sat down. His questions had reinforced the point that Leo Bruce was not involved in the temple murders—that his confession should not raise any doubt about Doody's guilt. But his questions may also. have encouraged the jurors to compare Doody to the innocent Bruce rather than to the guilty Garcia.

Lawyers always argue. In criminal trials, their final speeches to the jury are known as closing arguments. Usually only one side "wins" the argument. In Doody's trial, it was possible that both might win. The jury might end up finding Doody guilty of felony murder (a win for Scull) but not of premeditated murder (a win for Balkan).

Scull and Balkan gave their closing arguments on July 8, 1993. They knew there were only thirteen important people in the courtroom that day, and that just one really mattered: Judge Martin. In Arizona capital cases in 1993, juries decided guilt or innocence, but sentencing, including the decision of whether to impose the death penalty, was reserved to the trial judge. There was little doubt of Doody's guilt; the jurors' real deliberations would concern whether to find him guilty of premeditated murder or merely of felony murder. The outcome would depend on whether they saw Doody as the cold-blooded killer Garcia claimed he was, or saw Garcia as a liar *and* a killer.

Balkan and Scull understood the power of the podium. Closing arguments can move a juror from one side of the case to the other. In a death-penalty case, which requires a unanimous verdict, moving just one juror may save the defendant's life.

This jury was charged with deciding the fate of only one young man, Johnathan Andrew Doody. Alessandro Garcia was untouchable, shielded by his plea bargain. The Tucson Four, about whom the jurors had heard so much, had been released from the MCSO's clutches. Nonetheless, the jurors had all of them in mind. They had listened as Scull and Ahler built their case on Garcia's credibility, and as Balkan linked Doody's interrogation to the coerced Tucson confessions.

In the closing arguments, as in the opening statements, the prosecutor spoke first; here he would also speak last. The burden of proof beyond a reasonable doubt is a heavy one. The defense, bearing no such burden, can concentrate on picking apart the prosecution's case. So after the defense attorney's closing argument, the prosecutor gets one more chance to talk to the jury: a rebuttal argument.

Scull rose and walked to the pit of the courtroom, surely savoring the thrill that envelops a trial lawyer at such moments. He faced the jury. "Folks, let's get right to it." Then he said, "The bottom line in this case is that Johnathan Andrew Doody is a cold-blooded killer." Gesturing toward the defendant, Scull said, "the seed was hatched in that brain sitting right there. . . . It led to nine people being executed, massacred, and he started it all."

In Scull's scenario, Garcia played a secondary role. "Unfortunately for the Buddhist people, Johnathan found a very willing participant, Alex Garcia." Doody's fate depended on whether the jury bought Scull's characterization of Garcia as merely a "participant." Knowing this, Scull called Garcia "every bit as bad as Johnathan Doody. I'll just say that up front. Whatever names that Mr. Balkan wants to call Alex Garcia, I'll second them. He is no star. He is no jewel. But he didn't pull the trigger that killed these people."

Scull's comparison of his star witness with the defendant was a risky move. If Garcia was as bad as Doody—or if he was even worse, as Balkan would later argue—why was Doody the only one facing a death sentence? And who actually *did* "pull the trigger that killed these people"? What if it was Garcia, or what if, as Balkan had argued, a third person did the shooting? Scull had to sell Garcia's credibility and undermine Balkan's efforts to instill reasonable doubt.

Accordingly, Scull painted Doody with a black brush and Garcia with a gray one. "No witnesses," he said. "That's chilling. That's cold. Johnathan Andrew Doody, folks, is a stone-cold killer. . . . He came up with this phrase, 'no witnesses,' because he wanted to kill everyone in that temple." In contrast, Scull portrayed Garcia as thinking the plan was a joke at first and only later agreeing to "go along."

Despite his efforts to separate them into leader and follower, Scull talked of Garcia and Doody as a team. "They went in there with a plan to rob and murder nine people." "They get their camouflage gear together, and they get their scarves and their tank-driver goggles." He again tied Garcia to Doody in recounting the entrance of the nun. "Johnathan calls her Mrs. Nun. Sort of a cute phrase to refer to a seventy-five-year-old lady that you are about to put a bullet in her head. . . . [Alex Garcia] calls her a grandma, which is another . . . sentimental, nice term for an older lady that he is about to help murder. Cold-blooded killers, folks."

Scull reviewed Garcia's account of Doody's conduct during the killings. "He starts to fire. And this isn't a nervous, excited, panic sort of firing. . . . Those shots go right into each of those heads, center shots. He is aiming that gun, folks. He is not wildly spraying the room. He is cold-blooded." Furthermore, Scull said, the shootings were premeditated. Doody "had plenty of time to think about it. Each time he pulled the trigger, he had to think about it. And he did that seventeen times."

Turning to Balkan's attacks on the evidence, Scull admitted that the crime scene had not been well preserved. He also admitted that intense media attention to the case had caused problems. He called the organization of the task force a "big mistake." "But," he asked, "did any of that have anything whatsoever to do with Johnathan Doody's guilt? Well, I haven't heard it yet."

Scull needed to downplay the MCSO's extraction of false confessions from four innocent men, while at the same time justifying Doody's "true" confession. Spinning the matter of the Tucson defendants as well as he could, he referred to McGraw as "Crazy Mike," minimized his phoned-in tip as one of thousands of leads, and called the investigation of his question about "blood on the wall" "one of the biggest wild goose chases in Arizona history." He criticized the interrogators for feeding the suspects information, but he was careful not to accuse them of coercion.

This was a high-wire act, and Scull kept his balance. "Was the investigation flawed? . . . Yes, it was. But does that change Johnathan Doody's guilt? Not in the least. Because the system worked. Because at the very time that we were picking up the Tucson people and bringing them to Phoenix . . . the wheels were set in motion to resolve this case once and for all. And that was the .22 Marlin semi-automatic weapon that belonged to Rolando Caratachea."

Getting back to bolstering Garcia's credibility, Scull prepared the jurors for what they would soon hear from Balkan. The defense wanted them to believe some parts of Garcia's testimony: he cut the phone cord, he carved "Bloods" on the wall, he "did this, he did that." As for other parts, the defense would tell them, "Oh, but he is lying when he says that Johnathan did shoot them, or he's lying when says Rollie wasn't there." Scull encouraged the jurors to accept Garcia's entire statement. "It's factual. It's concrete. It was challenged for hours by strong, strong cross-examination, and it held up."

If the defense wanted the jurors to believe only parts of Garcia's testimony, the prosecution wanted them to believe only parts of his confession. Scull blamed Captain White, with his fixation on the Tucson Four, for prompting Garcia to lie. After Garcia confessed, White came in and said, "'But what about Tucson? We know they were there.'" As Scull told it, White "gets right in his face, and he is wanting to know about Tucson, Tucson. And Alex just sorts of laughs at them." Eventually, "You can almost see the light bulb go off in Alex Garcia's head. . . . 'Wait a minute. These guys don't know near as much as they think they know. Maybe there is a way out for me.'" So Garcia started saying, "'Well, yeah. There were other people there.'" Scull commented, "There is nothing after the point when Captain White comes in there that is worth anything."

Scull acknowledged that Garcia had said "he would do anything to get a plea agreement. That's true. But he understood that once he entered the plea agreement, that he agreed to be truthful in everything that he testified to about this case. . . . In exchange for his truthful testimony at all times, what we agreed was, is, that he would not receive the death penalty."

Scull did not address the question of why Garcia got the deal while Doody faced a possible death sentence. The harsh reality was that the prosecutors had strong forensic evidence against Garcia but none against Doody—and no hope of convicting him without Garcia's testimony. Scull also did not mention Garcia's tenth victim, Alice Marie Cameron, or the fact that her murder was folded into Garcia's plea bargain with no added penalty.

In closing, Scull again warned the jurors not to be distracted by red herrings. In England during fox hunts, "they would actually go out on the trails with red herrings to throw the dogs off, to give the fox a little extra advantage. But it's a fake. It's a false lead." He listed the red herrings in this case: "Tucson did it, Rollie Caratachea did it, George Gonzales did it, it was some sort of drug rip-off. . . . Maybe even gangs were involved." Instead of following those false leads, Scull urged, the jury should focus on the "direct evidence that Johnathan Doody was not only involved but that he had the motivation; he did the planning; he recruited Alex Garcia; he carried it out."

Judge Martin gave the jurors a ten-minute break, then invited Balkan to give his closing argument.

Balkan quoted Scull: "'Why did the Tucson suspects admit their involvement in these crimes? We may never know, folks.'" Then he turned Scull's own words against him. "How do we, as people, express our reasonable doubts? . . . How does Mr. Scull express his doubts? 'We don't know.' That's an extraordinary statement in a case. As Mr. Scull stands before you today, he doesn't know. And when we talk about reasonable doubt . . . we talk about not only those doubts that are in your mind now, not only those doubts which may come into your mind during your deliberations, but what about those doubts that will come to you in whispers in the months and years to come?"

Balkan knew he couldn't win this case in the traditional sense—his client's guilt was a given—but he also knew that in the political sense, Doody was not the only one on trial. The State's conduct of the investigation was also being judged. "What would you do," Balkan asked, "if you had assembled the largest police team in the history of this state and it still failed to give you a credible case? What would you do? Why, you'd buy one. It would cost you, but you'd buy one. And I ask you to think about what would this case be like without Alex Garcia. The witness that they bought."

The prosecutors, Balkan said, had changed their theory in the middle of the case. First they charged the Tucson defendants with multiple murder; then they dismissed those charges and arrested Caratachea, but when he didn't confess, they changed theories again and left him out. They charged Doody and Garcia, then changed one more time and put only Doody on trial.

Balkan poured on the sarcasm. "What do you do when you have to settle for the purchased testimony of a mass murderer, a serial killer, and a person who says, finally, that he would even say that the president of the United States did it if he could get the deal? What do you do then, if you are these prosecutors? You have to get the jury to trust you. You have to get the jury to join your team. Remember Detective Sinsabaugh's words? 'Trust me. Trust me. . . . Be on our team.'" He asked the jurors, "Are you going to trust, though?"

Knowing when to fire up the jury and when to let it smolder, he retreated to the topic of forensic evidence, mentioning a witness, "the man who did the fingerprint and footprint work." The prosecution, Balkan said, had brought him in to impress the jurors with technical terms so they wouldn't wonder "why there aren't any fingerprints of Johnathan Doody, why there aren't those glove prints, why there aren't the fabric prints, why there aren't footprints . . . linking anything to Johnathan Doody." Furthermore, "Why did you have to see that many autopsy photographs, that many gory, bloody pictures? . . . If you see the pictures enough, maybe you won't notice that there isn't a whole lot of evidence against Johnathan Doody. Maybe you'll start to trust the State . . . maybe you'll join their team."

The jury had smoldered long enough; Balkan stoked the blaze again by discussing Doody's interrogation. "You had to listen to these tapes for three days. You didn't have to live through it, like Johnathan did. You didn't have to sit there in one sitting without a break, without any sleep, without any meals, alone, scared." As for the dramatic final tape, "Did you hear how the sobbing continues, ladies and gentlemen, after Sinsabaugh left the room? . . . He was broken. He was exhausted. He had completely lost the ability to resist, to deceive, or anything. All he could do was sob."

Implicitly, Balkan linked Doody's interrogation to those of the Tucson Four. "Do it at nighttime . . . always at nighttime. People are tired. People are vulnerable. People are going to give you what you want sooner. Make sure the room is bugged secretly; whether it's legal or not doesn't mean a thing. Promise them confidentiality . . . 'What you say won't leave this room. It doesn't count, so tell us what we want to hear. You will if you like us. You will if you trust us. You will if you want to be on our team.'"

"Speaking of teams," Balkan said, "let's bring out the teams. The first team, led by Sergeant Riley, slow, methodical, low-key pressure applied firmly, constantly. And at a certain point bring out the next team, Sinsabaugh, the aggressive, confrontive, raising voice, constantly probing . . . And then bring out the next team, Jerry White, Captain White . . . And he says, 'Trust me. Join the team. I'm with you on this one.'"

One of Balkan's core premises was that Doody had gone to the temple to play an innocent war game, not to commit a crime. For ROTC cadets like Brandon Burner and Doody, he said, war games were like "military hide and seek." Doody had told his girlfriend and Burner about the planned game near the temple. To him the temple was a "great pretend target with its walls and motion detectors, with its proximity to Luke Air Force Base."

Balkan asked the jurors to consider the way the temple invaders were dressed. On a hot August night, why would would-be murderers wear "military winter combat battle fatigues"? To reduce the risk of arousing suspicion, "Wouldn't the urban camouflage be to dress up like a couple of ordinary teenagers?" Also, Balkan pointed out, if the killings had been planned in advance, there would have been no need for disguises. In Balkan's theory of the crime, Garcia, and probably Caratachea, had donned BDUs to make Doody think the plan was merely a war game.

Turning to the murder weapon, Balkan ridiculed the idea that Garcia and Doody had waited until the day of the crime to borrow Caratachea's rifle. He hoped the jurors would conclude that they hadn't borrowed it at all—that Caratachea himself had carried it to the temple.

Balkan recited a list of what he called "I dids." "Who got the guns? Alex Garcia says, 'I did.'" Who made the maps and drawings? Who ended up with the loot? Who loaded the guns? Who left footprints at the temple? Who sprayed the fire extinguisher? Who cut the phone cord? Who wrote "Bloods" on the wall? After each question, Balkan repeated, "Alex Garcia says, 'I did.'" The litany ended with a hint about Caratachea. "If we didn't know better, somebody might think that there was, indeed, another person that was doing some of these things that Alex Garcia claims. He didn't say Johnathan did it, so I guess he has to say *he* did it all, except, of course, murder."

To get his plea agreement, Balkan said, Garcia had "betrayed his friends, strangers alike. Tucson people. Johnathan Doody. You heard on his tape when he was talking about that special girl, the one who meant so much to him . . . And now we know that's the girl that he has agreed to testify against in a murder case in his deal. Do you trust him? Do you really want to be on his team?"

For the killing of Alice Cameron, Garcia's deal "gave him a free murder." In his original deal for the temple murders, the minimum sentence had been set at 25 years and the maximum at 240. After Garcia confessed to the Cameron killing, the minimum was still 25 years, but the maximum was raised to 271. Balkan let his disgust show. "Ladies and gentlemen, I take my hat off to the State. They are tough. Because if Mr. Alex Garcia ever lives to be 250 years old, he's going to be in big trouble." Balkan declared, "Here is what we can give Alex Garcia. Here's what he deserves. We can give him a fair trial."

This measured challenge to the State was the high point of Balkan's closing argument. The State had tried Doody for seven weeks. Fairness is always elusive, and this trial was no exception. The State's case relied almost entirely on Garcia's testimony, and Garcia's testimony was only as good as his plea bargain. Had he not been given a deal, Garcia would have been on trial himself instead of on the witness stand testifying against Doody. Without that deal, the only probative evidence against Doody would have been his own confession, which Balkan believed would not have carried the day.

As part of his effort to convince the jurors that Doody did not deserve a harsher penalty than the one Garcia received, Balkan reminded the jury of a witness he had called earlier—a jailhouse snitch named Leroy Hughes, who had met Garcia and Caratachea in the juvenile detention center. According to Hughes, Garcia bragged that he had gone to the temple with Doody, Caratachea, George Gonzales, and others. Hughes reported the boast to Caratachea, who denied being involved. Hughes went back to Garcia, who got mad and told him, "He was there. It was his gun. Who do you think did it? Who do you think shot 'em?"

But eleven days later, Hughes changed his story. He claimed his earlier statement was bullshit, and he spoke what Balkan called "the best words of the trial"—"'Here is the new and improved shit.'" Then he told the exact story that Garcia would tell on the witness stand. By that time, Balkan suggested, Garcia had "had a chance to get his act together . . . Maybe he has had a chance to get in touch with Rollie . . . And the story changes under those conditions." In his original interrogation, "Alex did say that Rollie did it."

Balkan explained why he had spent so much time on the Tucson Four, calling Bruce and Nunez as witnesses and playing Parker's tapes. "I'm not here to convict people, ladies and gentlemen. I am here to establish and demonstrate reasonable doubt in your minds. And you deserve to hear . . . the people who confessed and said they did it." Again quoting Scull's remark about why they had confessed if they were innocent—"We may never know, folks"—he said emphatically, "'We may never know' is not enough. That is doubt."

Balkan's best hope for instilling reasonable doubt was his third-man theory. "Let's see what we have in this case about Rolando Caratachea. Mr. Scull wants facts. Here are the facts that came out at trial." Balkan had a long list. Caratachea owned the gun. He wouldn't lend it out. He had it soon after the murders. He kept changing the date when Garcia and Doody borrowed the gun. Under interrogation, both Doody and Garcia placed him at the temple, and Caratachea said that if he *had* been there, he would have carried his own gun.

Balkan recalled cross-examining Garcia about Caratachea. "He said, 'Yeah, we wanted him there.' . . . And I said, 'Why would you think

Rolando would help you?' . . . And he said, 'Rolando is that kind of guy.'"
Summing up the third-man scenario, Balkan wondered how Caratachea
could "have so many distinct and material contacts with the temple case
and still maintain that he has nothing at all to do with it? How is that
possible? I said this guy attracts temple evidence like a magnet. And you
heard the evidence. The case is over. It's for you to decide."

Balkan closed with a point that lawyers have been making for centuries in cases where doubt may be nothing more than a whisper. "Ladies
and gentlemen, this may be the most important decision in your life.
It is final. It is one that you have to be sure of beyond any reasonable
doubt, not only today and tomorrow but for the rest of your life. . . . I
have watched you. I saw how serious and conscientious you are. You
will do the right thing. You will do it for yourselves. You will do it for
justice. You will do it for Johnathan Doody. He has no choice but to
trust you."

As Balkan joined his client at the defense table, Scull stood up and
launched his rebuttal argument. "Two main points, folks," he began.

The points were about degrees of guilt. Doody had admitted going
into the temple "to see what he could get." "They went in there with
force, and that's armed robbery, and that's a conviction of felony murder." But felony murder, Scull asserted, was the least of what Doody was
guilty of. Garcia had testified that the killing was premeditated: they
talked about it for weeks beforehand; they tried to make a silencer; they
"were going to kill them all." And Doody "shot every single one of them
in the head."

Scull noted that Balkan wanted the jurors to believe everything
Garcia said—except the part about Doody being the killer. "Well," he
commented, "Alex Garcia has a heck of a motive to tell the truth in this
case, and he told you what it was. 'I wanted to save my life.'" That was "a
motive so strong, he gave up his best pal, Johnathan Doody; a motive
so strong, he gave up the love of his life, Michelle Hoover; a motive so
strong, I submit to you, folks, that he would give up Rolando Caratachea
in a heartbeat." He did not implicate Caratachea, Scull argued, because
Caratachea was not involved. "This is another attempt at misdirection
. . . . Let's keep our eye on the ball. The ball is Johnathan Doody."

"We are here," Scull said, "because nine people were slaughtered."
He began to name the victims one last time. "Foy Sripanprasert was
seventy-five years old, a nun. She was killed in cold blood. When I say

stone-cold killer, I mean it. This is a stone-cold killing if you can do that to a seventy-five-year-old lady and kill her grandson at the same time, sixteen-year-old Matt Miller. And Somsak Sopha, and Siang Ginggaeo, Suti—"

Suddenly Scull stopped, seeming too choked up to continue. For a moment he faced the jury in silence. Then he spoke. "Well, that's it. Sorry." And he sat down.

Judge Martin gave the jurors final instructions on the law and sent them home for the night. When they had left the courtroom, and when Doody had been escorted out, Balkan asked the judge to declare a mistrial. Scull's last-minute emotional display in front of the jury, he argued, might "have a devastating impact on this case." Judge Martin denied the motion. Doody's fate was now in the jury's hands.

The jury deliberated all day on Friday, July 9, took the weekend off, and resumed deliberations on Monday morning, July 12. Shortly before 3:00 p.m., court staff alerted the lawyers, the sheriff's office, and the media: the jury had reached a verdict.

K. C. Scull and Paul Ahler were alone at the prosecution table, which was no longer cluttered with papers, sheaves of files, exhibit tags. At the defense table, also cleared of the tools of trial, sat Peter Balkan and his ever-impassive client, Johnathan Doody.

Judge Martin warned the spectators against engaging in outbursts or commotion when the verdicts were read. Many of them had a large stake in the jury's decision—and not just the defendant and his family and friends. The State had a huge investment in Garcia's credibility. The Maricopa County Sheriff's Office, trying to restore its reputation, hoped the jury would ignore its flawed interrogation procedures. Relatives of the victims, as well as representatives of the Buddhist faith and the Thai government, sought atonement and closure.

The jurors filed in. The lawyers studied each somber face as the twelve men and women took their seats in the jury box. The foreman, Robert Bass, carried a sheaf of verdict forms.

Judge Martin asked, "Have you reached a verdict?"

Bass stood up and replied, "We have, your Honor." He gave the verdict forms to the bailiff, who delivered them to the judge. Judge Martin looked them over and handed them down to his courtroom clerk at her desk beside the bench. He asked the defendant to rise, and Doody and Balkan stood up in unison. Then the clerk read the verdicts. The jury found Doody guilty of nine counts of felony murder, nine counts of armed robbery, one count of burglary, and one count of conspiracy to commit armed robbery.

The papers Bass gave the bailiff included a separate verdict form for each victim, indicating how many jurors had voted for premeditated murder and how many for felony murder. The form for Foy Sripanprasert, whom Doody had called "Mrs. Nun," showed a twelve-to-zero rejection of premeditation and a unanimous finding of felony murder. The forms for the other victims were unanimous on felony murder, but eleven-to-one in rejecting premeditation. Since a unanimous finding is required for guilt, the fact that one juror considered Doody guilty of eight premeditated murders was legally irrelevant.

The verdicts announced by the clerk sounded like a victory for the State and a loss for the defense. But a glance at the defense and prosecution tables revealed a different truth. Balkan did not smile, but his relief showed as he put an arm around his client—the client he had probably saved from the death penalty. Judge Martin was unlikely to send a juvenile to death row for felony murder. Scull and Ahler's faces were glum. Their only real reason to put Doody on trial had been to get a conviction of premeditation and a sentence of death. They could have saved the effort and expense of a trial by making a deal and putting him in prison for life for felony murder. So the trial was a total loss for the prosecution.

By refusing to convict Doody of premeditated murder, the jury sent a message to officialdom. Like all complex messages, it was subject to some speculation. The jurors might believe Doody was the killer but feel the State had not proved its case beyond reasonable doubt. And yet, given Scull's impassioned portrait of the shooter taking his time, methodically aiming seventeen bullets into the heads of the nine victims, it seemed highly likely that if the jurors had seen Doody in that role, the verdict would have been premeditated murder. Another possibility was that the jury considered Garcia the mastermind and the killer. Still another was that the jury believed Balkan's "third man" had fired the fatal shots.

Speculation aside, the jury's findings were a rejection of Garcia's version of the case and an acceptance of Doody's anguished confession. In legal effect, Doody stood guilty only of the burglary and armed robbery counts. Because nine deaths occurred during the commission of those crimes, he also stood convicted of felony murder. That verdict might save his life, but he was not yet entirely out of the woods. Judge Martin still had to consider whether the death penalty was a legal option in his case, and if so, whether to sentence him to death for felony murder.

MITIGATION, AGGRAVATION, AND SENTENCING 10

The verdict was in, but Judge Martin could not yet sentence Johnathan Doody. Next came the mitigation and aggravation stage of the case, when prosecution and defense presented evaluations of the defendants that might influence the sentencing decision. Legal maneuvering at this stage took several months.

In September 1993, the State filed its sentencing memorandum, arguing that Doody deserved the death penalty. Balkan countered with motions to exclude that penalty and to strike the sentencing memorandum from the record on the grounds that it was "contrary to the verdict of the jury." Specifically, he moved to strike all portions that suggested premeditation on Doody's part.

Balkan pointed out that the State was ignoring a plain fact: that the jury had rejected Garcia's version of the temple crimes. He quoted from the State's memorandum. "It is apparent that once the shooting started, and Johnathan Doody shot two or three rounds, killing perhaps two or three people, Alex Garcia then shot the shotgun." In his motion Balkan retorted, "It was certainly not apparent to the jury that Johnathan Andrew Doody shot two or three rounds, or any rounds, for that matter."

Again Balkan quoted the State: "coolly, calmly aiming and shooting into the center of the heads of each of Doody's victims." And again he made a scathing response. "Such an argument presupposes that Doody actually was the shooter; a fact that has been proved only in the minds of the prosecutors and not in the verdict of the jury."

The State's memorandum culminated in a dramatic appeal to the judge. "What kind of a depraved mind could cold-bloodedly take the lives of nine peaceful innocent people of God? . . . To slaughter a sixteen-year-old boy, his eighty-two-year-old grandmother, a friend and six Buddhist monks is totally inexcusable, and the fact that Johnathan Doody perpetrated these crimes means that he must be sentenced to death for each and every single one of these horrible homicides."

Ignoring the State's use of poetic license in exaggerating the nun's age and her grandson's youth, Balkan protested this "emotional and personal harangue." He wrote, "To now begin the solemn and terrible process of determining a capital penalty under these conditions and with this type of argument is both improper and unfair."

In November, Judge Martin postponed his decision on whether the death penalty was legally available in Doody's case. He would wait and consider arguments on that issue in the context of mitigating and aggravating circumstances. Giving the lawyers two months to marshal their evidence and their expert witnesses, he scheduled Doody's mitigation hearing for January 14, 1994.

Under Arizona law at the time, the judge alone decided what penalty to impose in capital cases. (That would change in 2002, when the U.S. Supreme Court ruled that such decisions must be made by a jury.) In the mitigation phase of a trial, defense lawyers try to get the judge (now the jury) to see their clients as human beings, beyond the cold language of the charges and the harsh characterization by the prosecution. Prosecutors, meanwhile, want the judge (now the jury) to focus on what defendants did, not who they are. These hearings are all about description. Balkan would present witnesses who would describe Doody's background and personality in a way that softened what he had done. Scull's witnesses would portray Doody in a way that aggravated his situation— as a cold-blooded killer.

Before the mitigation hearing, the world had seen Johnathan Doody only as a dour image on television or in newspapers. Media reports about him were lifeless abstractions. In court, the judge and the jury saw a mysterious young man who seemed either uninterested in or oddly unaware of what was happening to him.

Doody had neatly formed seashell ears and a broad nose. His lips were generously full but slightly everted, giving him a pensive or pouting look; some saw it as sullen. His dark eyes were sunk behind heavy epicanthic folds and horizontal, slightly puffy lower lids. His skin was waxen or parchment colored, depending on whether you saw him in natural light or in the fluorescent glare of a courtroom. He had changed in the two years since the murders at Wat Promkunaram. The jailhouse diet had added pounds, filling out his cheeks and making his rounded jaw line even rounder. At times, he seemed to be about to smile, or perhaps to smirk, at the exact moment you glanced his way. Then, as if caught on camera, he invariably looked down. No one could hold his gaze.

Judge Martin had seldom seen Doody move, and he had heard him talk only on those seventeen anguished tapes. Whenever the judge was gaveled into court, Doody was already seated at the defense table, motionless and mute. From twenty-five feet away, it was difficult to tell whether he was half-asleep, sulking, or petrified. At the mitigation hearing Scull and Balkan would introduce the judge to their two very different views of this young man.

It was as though Doody had been wrapped in gauze all through the trial, making his true self invisible. But now that the jury had found him guilty, it was time to remove the wrapping and let the judge see him as a person, not just a defendant. Scull's aim was to rip off the gauze to show the hardened killer underneath; Balkan wanted to peel it back tenderly to reveal the wounds and scars of his client's unusual life.

During the next two months, both defense and prosecution put finishing touches on evaluations of Doody's background and personality. The evaluating had begun back in 1991, soon after his arrest, when the question was whether to charge him as a juvenile or as an adult. Half a dozen experts pored over records and interviewed Doody and his family, teachers, and friends. They tested and examined him for social, intellectual, educational, and cultural characteristics. Their findings would guide Judge Martin's sentencing decision.

In November 1993, Balkan filed memoranda arguing that Doody's age was a reason to avoid the death penalty. In December, he filed his full mitigation memorandum, listing thirty-two separate mitigating circumstances—ranging from Doody's lack of a criminal record, to his polite and respectful demeanor in court, to his "new-founded religious belief"—as reasons to send his client to prison for the rest of his natural life rather than sentence him to execution as demanded by the State.

Judge Martin would consider all thirty-two of the mitigating circumstances cited by Balkan, but he would say years later that age was a major factor in his decision. Doody had been only seventeen at the time of the temple murders. Balkan submitted an affidavit by Dr. Victor Streib, an expert on the application of the death penalty to juveniles. Streib noted that in 125 years of juvenile cases, Arizona had used the death penalty only twice—and those cases had been long ago, in 1880 and 1934. In more recent times, two juvenile offenders had been sentenced to death in the state, but their sentences had been reversed on appeal. Furthermore, as Balkan summed up Streib's findings, no Arizona court had *ever* sentenced to death a juvenile who had been "convicted on the sole theory of felony murder."

At the time, Balkan was unable to argue that the U.S. Constitution prohibited the execution of juveniles. That would take another eleven years. In 2005 the U.S. Supreme Court would resolve the debate, at least for the time being, holding in a contentious five-to-four decision that the Eighth and Fourteenth Amendments forbid the execution of offenders who were under eighteen when they committed their crimes. Justice Anthony Kennedy wrote in the majority opinion, "When a juvenile commits a heinous crime, the State can exact forfeiture of some of the most basic liberties, but the State cannot extinguish his life and his potential to attain a mature understanding of his own humanity."

Balkan hoped that Doody's age would be enough to keep him off death row. But with his client's life at stake, he could not take the chance that Judge Martin might do what no other Arizona judge had ever done. Accordingly, he devoted much of his mitigation memo to revealing who Johnathan Doody was, beyond the withdrawn, silent figure sitting in the courtroom. Citing experts, he presented a sympathetic view of his client's "difficult early years" and his "cultural disorientation."

The court had appointed Mary Durand to examine Doody. Durand, an investigator of infinite patience and impressive skill, was Arizona's preeminent specialist in the mitigation phase of capital cases. Her report summarized Doody's social history.

Johnathan Andrew Doody's birth name was Verpol Khankaew. He was born to Kamol and Lliad Khankaew on May 9, 1974, in a village called Nakon Nayok in the Korat province of Thailand. His boyhood nickname was Noy, meaning "junior" or "shorty." He lived his first six years in a single large room with sixteen other members of his extended family. The room, on fifteen-foot-high stilts, was perched over a rice paddy, his family's sole source of income.

When the boy was six years old, his father died, and his devastated mother became too depressed to care for her two young sons. Leaving them in Thailand with an aunt, she fled to the other side of the world, to a sister who lived in Germany. There Lliad met and married Brian Doody, a noncommissioned officer in the U.S. Air Force. Lliad spoke only Thai, Brian only English: they "had to employ a dictionary during the wedding ceremony for translation." When Verpol, whose name would soon become Johnathan, was eight and his brother was six, their mother and her new husband "suddenly appeared" in Thailand and took the boys to Germany, wrenching them away from their relatives and everything familiar.

The renamed Johnathan had to face not only a world of strangers but also a mother he had not seen for two years and an unknown, foreign stepfather. He also had to adjust to a total change of climate, culture, and food—he told a psychiatrist he had been "terrified of spaghetti." And he was surrounded by not one but two new languages: English and German. Verpol had reportedly been doing well in Thailand's school system, but when Johnathan was thrust into a second-grade classroom on the American air force base, the dislocation and the language barrier disrupted his education. In addition, he "suffered from severe racial prejudice as his race and inability to speak English became the subject of numerous taunts and jeers."

Durand's picture of the family's life in Germany was troubling. Until Johnathan and David learned English, they had no way to communicate with their stepfather. Brian Doody was an alcoholic, and his drinking and frustration boiled over into verbal and physical abuse of his new family. Johnathan was too young to defend himself, let alone his mother and brother. Durand had learned about the abuse from Brian Doody himself, not from his stepson: Johnathan's "loyalty to his family prevented him from talking about this period or these incidents except to say that he received deserved 'spankings,' sometimes with a belt."

During Johnathan's first year in Germany, the family changed yet again with the birth of his half-sister, Crystal. And just when he was beginning to adjust, Brian Doody was transferred to the States, and the family abruptly moved to Valdosta, Georgia. Johnathan attended third, fourth, and fifth grades in Valdosta, and his half-brother, Michael, was born there. Brian Doody was next transferred to Guam, where Johnathan attended sixth, seventh, and eighth grades; and then to Arizona. With each move, Johnathan suffered "the trauma of the transition, and the racial insults of his peers."

As he grew up, Johnathan became less and less able to communicate with his mother. She never became fluent in English, and his ability to speak Thai did not progress after he left Thailand. Thus he could not "converse with his mother about complex or emotional issues at a level beyond that of approximately an eight-year-old child." The language barrier also came between him and his stepfather, preventing "the formation of any close relationship based upon mutual trust."

Balkan summarized Durand's impression of the family relationships at the time of Doody's trial. "With all of their difficulties, the Doody family, both direct and extended, has managed to form a cohesive and loyal unit, dedicated to Johnathan, and to one another. This Court should . . . consider the love and devotion that the family feels toward Johnathan and the hurt and disruption that this home will suffer if the death penalty is imposed."

Doody's level of intelligence, and the way the schools had dealt with him, were prominent on Balkan's list of mitigating factors. Testing by Roger Martig, a court-appointed psychologist, had revealed that Doody had a very low verbal IQ of 92 but a performance IQ of 134; his full-scale IQ was 109. The spread between verbal and performance scores was unusually wide. Doody, Balkan wrote, was "a child who is incredibly polite and respectful, but who, through a variety of communication handicaps, lacks the fundamental skills to receive complex information, and to express himself in complex terms." Durand found his information-processing ability "at the same level as one of very low intelligence or even somewhat marginally mentally handicapped."

Balkan argued that these learning disabilities refuted Detective Riley's "grossly inaccurate" opinion that Doody was the "probable ringleader in this case because Alessandro Garcia is too stupid to provide such leadership." In fact, although Balkan did not mention it, Doody and Garcia's patterns of IQ scores were remarkably similar.

Durand noted that Doody's "high innate intelligence" had allowed him to disguise his language problems. He had "mastered the skill of nodding his head at appropriate times during explanations." Drawing on this finding, Balkan painted a vivid picture of Doody as extraordinarily intelligent but "trapped in a virtual prison in which his intellectual potential is held captive by his inability to communicate."

At school, Doody's intelligence and good manners would actually have worked against him. He would have seemed to understand his teachers even when he was confused. Ingrained obedience would have made him fade into the background while less cooperative classmates got the teacher's attention. In spite of his profound linguistic problems, Doody had never been offered classes in English as a second language or any other special assistance. His case, Balkan declared, "represents the failure of the American education system to respond to even the most reasonable needs of its deserving students."

Judge Martin knew that the court system was incapable of altering educational environments or mandating sophisticated tests. But, he later recalled, learning that even basic IQ testing would have revealed Doody's problems gave him pause. He could not go back in time and change Doody's educational environment, but he could save his life.

Doody's character was another of Balkan's mitigating factors. Except for the crimes at the temple, he had never been accused of any misbehavior or violent or criminal tendencies. He had worked his way up through the ROTC ranks to become the leader of the honor guard. Even his interrogators had commented on the "respect and obedient good behavior which Johnathan exhibited during the ordeal of his interrogation and which he maintained until he finally broke down."

The State had a very different opinion of Doody's character. Its theory of the crime required viewing him as a criminal mastermind obsessed with the military. In his *Phoenix Magazine* article, Sgt. Kimball expressed the way his colleagues saw Doody: "a quiet, intense boy, dedicated to the exacting drills and elaborate costuming, of Junior ROTC and Civil Air Patrol. A military brat, he is consumed with military hardware, and jargon." Dr. Hadley Osran, the psychiatrist who evaluated Doody for the prosecution, also noted his "obsessive fascination with the military."

Balkan, citing Durand's investigation, refuted that point. In Durand's view, Doody had become interested in flying to win his stepfather's approval, and was interested only in military aviation, not in weapons or violence.

Contending that his client was not a ringleader but a follower, Balkan cited Martig's battery of psychological tests, which indicated that Doody was "emotionally quite timid and unsure of himself." Balkan also contrasted Doody's "peaceful and cooperative demeanor" under interrogation with Caratachea's "violent and belligerent verbal and physical behavior" and Garcia's "testy arrogance." In Balkan's view, a comparison of the three interrogations "should forever end any question of who was leader and follower among this trio."

Another facet of character on Balkan's list was his client's "new-founded religious belief." This, he suggested, showed that Doody could be rehabilitated. He cited a prominent spokesman for U.S. Buddhists, Mettanando Bhikkhu, who would testify at the mitigation hearing. The Oxford-educated monk, who was studying at Harvard Divinity School, had taken an interest in the case. Traveling to Phoenix in September

1993, he had visited Doody in jail and taught him traditional Buddhist meditation. Mettanando had also met with prosecutors to convey his fellow Buddhists' feelings about the death penalty. In Buddhism the sanctity of life was a central concept, and someone Doody's age was "a yet unformed person, who is still in the process of becoming the person that will emerge." Thus the thought of sentencing someone so young to death was anathema. Balkan noted Mettanando's opinion that "if Johnathan is willing to embrace his ancestral religion, he can eventually find the peace and identity which will rehabilitate him and allow him to eventually accept a lifetime of incarceration."

Because the crimes at the temple "were an attack upon the religion of Buddhism as much as upon the individual victims," Balkan argued that all Buddhists were victims in the case. He urged the judge to consider their combined feelings and their beliefs, "so as not to desecrate those beliefs with actions that defile their moral tenets."

Judge Martin had a solid understanding of the law of sentencing, which can be bewilderingly complex. After careful consideration of the hearing's two days of testimony and all the reports and evaluations, he made his decision. The jury had not convicted Doody of premeditated murder, and neither would he. On February 11, 1994, the judge pronounced Doody's sentence: not death, but "a term of imprisonment." The sentence began with nine life terms, one for each murder victim, to be served consecutively. After that, Doody was to serve twenty-one years for armed robbery—nine concurrent twenty-one-year terms—then twenty-one years for burglary, then fourteen for conspiracy to commit armed robbery. Together, his terms of imprisonment added up to nine lifetimes plus fifty-six years.

In addition, Judge Martin ordered Doody to pay restitution for his crimes: $65,636.11 to the Wat Promkunaram temple and $4,361.36 to its insurance company. He was to make regular monthly payments of $50.00 starting on January 1, 1995. At that rate, the full restitution would be paid in 117 years.

Once Doody began serving his sentence, the State's star witness against him could be sentenced as well. By testifying against both his girlfriend and his best friend, Alex Garcia had fulfilled his agreement with the prosecutors. His guilty plea was officially accepted on February 25, 1994. But Garcia did not face Judge Martin for the last time until July 15, at his mitigation and sentencing hearing.

Despite the plea bargain, which spared Garcia any possibility of the death penalty, Judge Martin had a certain amount of discretion in sentencing. He would decide whether Garcia's ten life sentences were to be served all at once or one after another. The State's sentencing memorandum focused on aggravating factors and urged the judge to give Garcia the maximum allowable prison terms to be served consecutively. In the defense sentencing memorandum, Luis Calvo cited mitigating factors and asked for concurrent sentences so Garcia could "prove his rehabilitation and be released from prison in his lifetime."

In most criminal cases, the State and the defendant file sharply opposing sentencing memoranda, but in Garcia's case, the dividing line between the two sides was somewhat blurred. Both defense and prosecution had an interest in portraying Doody as the ringleader in the temple murders. Scull had smoothed Garcia's path through the criminal justice system from the beginning. His case against Doody had depended on Garcia. Now he praised his witness: "It is amazing how consistent and unassailable his testimony was." He asserted that Garcia had "solved the temple case" and in doing so had absolved the innocent Tucson suspects.

Scull omitted the contrary fact that the jury, in acquitting Doody of premeditated murder, had rejected much of Garcia's testimony, including his statement that Doody had fired the fatal shots. The jury's verdict and the judge's decision to spare Doody's life had not changed the State's version of the temple killings. Scull still maintained that Doody "opened fire on the prostrate victims, shooting them point blank in their heads as some of them prayed." Meanwhile, Garcia fired the shotgun. "Garcia says he tried to aim so as not to hit anyone. The fact is that he did hit several of the Buddhists and he caused serious wounds; however, none of them were fatal injuries."

As for the murder of Alice Cameron, Scull noted Garcia's and Hoover's conflicting stories. "The defendant claims his role was an equal partner with Michelle and that they discussed the need to leave 'no witnesses' adopting Doody's phrase as his own. Michelle readily volunteered to commit the crime. Michelle . . . claims she was persuaded by Garcia to shoot Alice Marie Cameron to prove her love for Garcia." Hoover "did not say 'we did it because Garcia bullied me into it.'" Scull gave Garcia credit for breaking the case. "By the defendant's coming forward, an innocent man was freed, the truth of Ms. Cameron's death was learned, a culprit (Hoover) was brought to justice." If Garcia had not confessed, "it is safe to say we would never have solved this crime and Hoover would have escaped uncharged and unpunished."

But what else was safe to say about the Cameron case? Certainly the MCSO had *thought* the crime was solved with George Peterson's arrest. Was it safe to say that if investigators had checked the security videotapes at ATMs in Scottsdale after the murder, they would have seen Garcia and Hoover trying to use Cameron's bank card? Surely it was safe to say that if the task force had tested Caratachea's rifle in September 1991, Alice Marie Cameron would not have been murdered. Scull did not mention these troubling aspects of the case, but Judge Martin was well aware of them.

After praising Garcia for helping the MCSO solve two cases, Scull turned to aggravating factors, describing Garcia's conduct in both crimes as, in the legal phrase, "cruel, heinous, or depraved." Even then he put the heaviest blame on Doody. "These murders are noteworthy because of the dispassionate, senseless evil, the calculated, cold-blooded taking of human lives without reason or pity. It boggles the mind to think of Doody executing nine people without so much as a second thought. Yet the defendant Garcia was there and although he claims second thoughts, he not only didn't do much to dissuade Doody but inexplicably he fired into the victims wounding some severely."

At the end of the memorandum, Scull addressed the differences in the State's treatment of the two defendants. "The State recommends that no death penalty be given to Garcia. The State strongly recommended the death penalty be imposed on Doody, but the court disagreed and based on a disparity of sentences argument (primarily) refused to give death to Doody."

In reality, the court rejected the death penalty for Doody because the jury decided Doody was not guilty of premeditated murder; the jury apparently believed Doody and did not believe Garcia. Scull overstated the importance of the "disparity of sentences" argument to lead up to his own plea to the judge. "The other side of the coin is before us. If we can't give Doody death when the evidence was that he was the shooter, how can we, in good conscience, argue that Garcia shouldn't receive life also?"

The State did not ask for any additional leniency. Garcia's full "reward for coming forward and testifying" was "no death penalty." In closing, Scull declared that no amount of cooperation by his star witness could "offset in any way the merciless cold-blooded slaughter of ten innocent people; none of whom would have died but for the participation of Alessandro Garcia."

Luis Calvo defended Garcia with considerable skill, managing to avoid both a trial and the death penalty. In his sentencing memorandum, Calvo focused on Garcia as "a troubled sixteen-year-old youth." Alex was "despondent over being perceived as fat and dumb." He lived in a "hostile, bleak home environment," with a father who was often drunk. Like Scull, Calvo tried to deflect attention away from Garcia, saying, "Unfortunately, this environment fostered his relationship with Johnathan Doody."

Also like Scull, Calvo credited Garcia with the release of five innocent men. He did not mince words. "It would have been extremely easy, and less embarrassing for the State, to tie the Tucson men into the temple case. Likewise, George Peterson had confessed to killing Alice Cameron. Alex's silence would not have disturbed the prosecutorial machine."

But Calvo's argument centered on a description of Garcia himself, intended to show Judge Martin what had shaped him into a teenager who could participate in multiple murders. Garcia, like Doody, had been subjected to a series of psychological tests since his arrest. Detailed reports by two psychologists and a juvenile probation officer had been filed earlier in the case. For the mitigation phase, Calvo selected a clinical and forensic psychologist, Dr. Richard Lanyon, to evaluate his client. Lanyon interviewed Garcia at length, administered more tests, talked to Garcia's parents and brother, studied his school records, and reviewed the other experts' reports.

Garcia told Lanyon the atmosphere at home was "always hostile. His brother was treated better, and Alex always got beaten up by his brother." School records indicated that by September 1991, soon after the temple murders, Garcia's father had moved out of the house, leaving his wife and sons. To Lanyon, this suggested "much more serious conflict in the home than admitted to me by either the parents or Alex's brother."

Garcia was placed in learning disability classes in elementary school and repeated fourth grade. As a sixth grader, he was two years older than his classmates and weighed 232 pounds. Then, for reasons not made clear in the records, he skipped seventh grade. In eighth he did poorly, but "nevertheless he was promoted to ninth grade, where he did even worse." By the end of that year, he "had dropped two academic subjects and received F's in three of the remaining four." That summer, he and Doody invaded the Buddhist temple.

Dr. Kathryn Menendez, who examined Garcia before his transfer to adult court, attributed his "extremely high scores in anxiety and thought disturbance" to distress over being arrested and jailed. Lanyon disagreed. In his view, a more likely cause was "the highly conflictful home environment and the school system," which kept promoting him even though he was "hopelessly out of his depth."

In Menendez's tests, Garcia registered a superior performance IQ of 129 and a below-average verbal IQ of 84, for a full-scale IQ of 103. Such a large discrepancy between verbal and performance scores, Lanyon noted, often indicates "significant brain impairment or malingering." Suspecting the latter, he retested Garcia's verbal IQ. This time Garcia scored 96, twelve points higher than before, raising his full-scale IQ to 111, "in the high average range."

Menendez found Garcia able to organize his thoughts and respond appropriately, although he "limited the elaboration of his responses and minimized information." To illustrate his tendency to simplify, she quoted his comments about Caratachea: "At first [I] thought he was pretty cool, then he started being dumb, thinking that he was better than other people." And about Doody: "I can get along with him, even though he's weird. He knows the military and we have that in common."

Summing up her impressions, Menendez wrote, "Alex behaves purposefully rather than impulsively, although not always rationally. He is capable of drawing up plans and executing them quickly and efficiently. Although he is learning disabled, he is clearly not retarded. Thus, Alex is appropriate for transfer to the Adult Division."

Dr. Roger Martig, the other psychologist who evaluated Garcia before his transfer to adult court, detected signs of "antisocial personality characteristics, in which he would like to be able to be smart enough to avoid prosecution."

Lanyon's own report on Garcia provided one of Calvo's central themes: "Alex is very much a follower." ("Even as a follower," Calvo added, "Alex could not bring himself to kill.") Lanyon saw Garcia's relationship with Doody as "motivated by the opportunity to have a friend (especially one with superior status in his interest, military matters), one of the few positive things in a life of failure and confusion."

Lanyon asked Garcia if, back in 1990, he could have foreseen that he would commit these crimes. Garcia replied, "Killing no; robbing yes."

In sixth grade he and his friends had done some "little things," such as shoplifting and breaking car windows. When he got older, "One of his friends had a car, and they were now becoming more interested in planning more complex activities." That friend was Rollie Caratachea.

Garcia told Lanyon he knew almost nothing about his ten victims. But he "readily agreed that what he did was a very bad thing indeed. I inquired as to his thoughts about why he did it, and he said he simply didn't know."

In conclusion, Lanyon noted that Garcia "has no brain damage, minimal character disorder, no mental retardation, and no major mental disorder. He has a history (in elementary school) of trying hard in the presence of serious difficulties. He has superior skills in the spatial/mechanical area. With these characteristics, he is potentially treatable through psychotherapy."

The sentencing hearing was the first time Judge Martin was able to look at Garcia through the eyes of his victims. This young man was directly responsible for ten murders. No one appeared in court to speak on behalf of the victims at the temple, but Helen Fletcher again made the trip from St. Louis to Phoenix to speak for her sister, Alice Marie Cameron.

Making her way to the witness stand, Fletcher clutched a copy of a letter she had written to Judge Martin four months earlier. After the preliminaries, she read the letter aloud. "I cannot believe there should be a question in anyone's mind that someone who has confessed to being involved in the deaths of ten people should himself not die. However, since I understand fully that a plea bargain has been put forth; I would ask you put him away for the remainder of his life so that he can never again walk among innocent people."

Fletcher called Garcia a "manipulative instigator of murder ten times over." "I feel it is not fair that Alessandro Garcia will be provided three meals a day, exercise, recreation, medical, and dental care in a climate controlled environment all the days of his life, while my sister, Alice, and nine other very decent people lie still in their dark graves." At the end of her testimony, Fletcher drove her point home. "I ask for Alice as well as the other nine people that Alex Garcia killed or participated in killing that he be kept away from society for the remainder of his life."

Gloria Garcia, Alex's mother, did not speak at the hearing, but she wrote to Judge Martin about her son. She described him as "shy, quiet, sensitive, helpful, supportive, and loving," a boy who had often helped neighborhood children fix their bicycles and volunteered to mow neighbors' lawns. At home, he "was always assisting me with the housework and preparation of meals as well as shopping." Alex "got along with his teachers and peers" and had never had problems with "discipline or schoolwork." She mentioned his affection for ROTC and civil air patrol. As a member of the freshman football team, "When Alex would tackle an opponent too hard, he would apologize." She said he had expressed regret for "the pain he has created." Her mother's plea was for a son who "wishes he could change time and [do] things differently."

It was fortunate for Garcia that his jailhouse interview with Mike Sager was not part of the evidence Judge Martin considered in choosing his sentence. On the scale balancing mitigating and aggravating factors, its weight would have fallen entirely on the "aggravation" side. The interview revealed a very different Alex Garcia from the helpful son recalled by his mother or the polite, cooperative suspect and witness seen by the police, the lawyers, and the court.

In the courtroom, Scull had covered Garcia's background in short, factual questions, and Garcia's answers, in his rehearsed "in court" voice, had been intended to give jurors the impression that he was just another west-side teen with a family not unlike their own. That voice was nowhere to be found in Sager's article. Instead, Garcia described his family this way: "A bullshit lazy faggot for a father, a mother that works all the time, and a dick for a brother. I was the younger one. You know? The younger one gets beat? Well, I got beat a lot of times. To me, it was like, fuck you, life's too short. I didn't want to be told what to do. I'd go where I wanted, I'd wear what I wanted, I'd say what I wanted. It was like, fuck it, you know?"

The Garcia the jury saw in Doody's trial was a boy dutifully doing his job—fulfilling his plea bargain. The one Sager saw in the jail was a freer Garcia, one who loved being in the spotlight. Maybe neither persona was real. The jurors heard Garcia tell his story on tape and from the witness stand. But they did not hear the brutally candid account of the temple killings he gave Sager. In recalling that scene, he did not sound like a reluctant accomplice who had tried to talk his friend out of mass murder. On the contrary, he seemed to relish the details of death. "You gotta imagine. You got nine people, all laying face down with their hands clasped behind their heads. Every time a bullet hit, you know, every time the sound went off, you could just see them jerk. Like their body jerking. And then I remember the gurgling, the gurgling of blood in their throats. I wish I was a good enough artist to draw it. It's hard to put into words."

When interviewed by the court-appointed psychologists, Garcia claimed to have no feelings about his crimes and no idea why he had committed them. He also minimized his interest in robbery, blaming the temple invasion on Doody's need for money, not his own. Talking with Sager, he revealed far more about his motivations.

About the money stolen from the temple, he said, "We had a big grudge about it. We got I think $2,650. Jonathan owed $2,000 on the Mustang, and it was like he wanted to take that much and give me $650. Shit. I wasn't gonna play that. You're getting a fucking car and I'm getting a couple shirts and a pair of shoes? Fuck that. We split even."

As for regrets, his focused on getting caught rather than on harming other people. "You know, it's funny. You can pull a caper and when you're there, you can say, 'Yeah, that looks right.' And then afterward you're like, 'Why in the fuck did we do *this*?' That was the only thing: If we could have gotten rid of the .22, we could have, hell we could have had robes, we could have jars of blood in our closet, we could have had anything from the temple. As long as they didn't have the murder weapon. That's what caught us. We could have dumped it in the river, filed off the serial numbers, just thrown it on the street. We were stupid."

What Garcia said next must have made Sager's readers agree with Helen Fletcher that he should "never again walk among innocent people." He told Sager, "Right now, after my case and everything, I could write a guidebook about how not to get caught. You could follow my handwriting and do all the crimes you wanted. To tell you the truth, if me and Jonathan couldn't have been caught, I think there would have been more crime. I know for a fact there would have been. A lot more crime. A lot more murders."

Before the July 15 hearing, Judge Martin read and listened to the arguments of counsel, considered the letters of Gloria Garcia and Helen Fletcher, and studied the psychological reports. At the hearing, he listened to Fletcher and offered the defendant a chance to speak, which Garcia declined. Then the judge pronounced sentence.

As specified in the plea agreement, he found Garcia guilty of all ten murders. He sentenced him to life in prison for each of the murders at the Buddhist temple and a tenth life term for the murder of Alice

Cameron—to be served consecutively—plus an additional twenty-one years for burglary. Calvo's hope that Garcia might be released in his lifetime would not be realized. Also following the plea agreement, Judge Martin dismissed the counts of armed robbery. In the temple case, he ordered Garcia to pay the same restitution as Doody: $65,636.11 to the Wat Promkunaram temple and $4,361.36 to its insurance company. The payments were to be 30 percent of his earnings while incarcerated, not less than $40 per month.

At the end of the hearing, Garcia's thumbprint was affixed to the sentencing order, and—just as his erstwhile best friend had been six months before—he was taken away in chains.

SUING MARICOPA COUNTY   *11*

Soon after their ordeal at the hands of the MCSO and its task force, three of the original Tucson suspects were reunited in a joint effort—suing Maricopa County. The false-arrest lawsuits were both predictable and inevitable. Predictable because the county attorney did his job, dismissing all charges against the Tucson defendants. Inevitable because the sheriff insisted his men had done nothing wrong and continued to search for a link between the Tucson Four and the Avondale boys.

Leo Bruce was the first to file suit, on November 27, 1991—five days after his release from jail. Bruce's $10 million civil claim alleged that the sheriff's deputies had violated his civil rights and defamed him. Ten days later Mark Nunez filed the second claim, asking for $15 million; his mother-slash-sister, Romelia Duarte, sought an additional $1 million. Duarte told the press, "What Sheriff Agnos and his men did to my son was a planned execution, to try and convict him without a trial." Marky, she said, "doesn't leave home anymore. He's confused often and scared." Before his arrest he had attended Pima Community College, but he had dropped his premedical studies after being shown "gruesome pictures of the temple victims."

At the end of December, Victor Zarate, who had been released from jail after six days because he had refused to confess, topped both his friends, suing for $20 million to make county officials pay for "the hell they put me through." "People shouldn't have to go through what I had to go through," he declared. "They should have evidence before they take people in." Zarate's claim asserted that his interrogators had denied two requests for a lawyer, kept him awake for forty-four hours, and forced him to urinate into empty soda cans. The claim acknowledged that money could not buy back his self-esteem, reputation, or peace of mind but stated, "money is the only thing the law allows him to recover."

By 1993, the Bruce, Nunez, Duarte, and Zarate complaints were combined in a lawsuit known, for short, as *Bruce et al. v. Agnos et al.* The list of defendants named in the suit began with "Tom Agnos, both individually and in his official capacity as Maricopa County Sheriff, and Jane Doe Agnos, husband and wife." It continued with fifteen of Agnos's deputies (and their wives), Maricopa County itself, County Attorney Rick Romley, and four of Romley's deputy county attorneys (and spouses). The defendants, according to the complaint, had entered into a conspiracy to violate the plaintiffs' rights. Specific offenses included illegal searches, physical assaults, emotional distress, illegal arrest and detention, and "oppressive, coercive, suggestive and forced interrogation."

Dante Parker, preoccupied with his California legal problems after the dismissal of Maricopa County's charges against him, later filed a separate false-arrest suit. By the time the county was ready to settle, Parker's suit was being considered along with *Bruce et al.*

The one member of the Tucson Four who did not sue for wrongful arrest was Mike McGraw. That made sense, given that McGraw had practically begged to be arrested, and that long after the civil suits were filed, he was still elaborating on his confession. In July 1992, Sheriff Agnos and detectives Riley and Lewis—still trying to link Tucson with Avondale— flew to Colorado Springs to reinterview McGraw. He told the sheriff that on the day of the murders, Victor Zarate had photographed him standing in front of the temple with Bruce, Parker, and Nunez. He claimed he had held up a newspaper (to show the date) while the others held their guns. Later, he said, they buried the picture on a mountain in Tucson, along with some ammunition and a bag of rice. He provided detailed instructions about where to dig to find this stash.

But the day of his release from jail, McGraw fantasized to a reporter that he'd get $15 million as a settlement. "Hell," he added, "I'd take $10 million. I don't need that much. But I could spend $1 million so fast, I could spend it in my dreams." "First thing," he went on, "I'd buy a really fine car and tint all the windows. You know what my license plate is going to say? T-H-X-T-A." Then he gave the puzzled reporter the punch line: "Thank you, Tom Agnos." Apparently McGraw tried to turn that fantasy into reality but could not find an attorney willing to represent him.

Public opinion on the lawsuits was divided. Many people defended the sheriff as a good man trying to do his job in the glare of national and international publicity. No one who knew Tom Agnos seriously doubted his good faith—but almost everyone doubted the competence of his senior command staff. Knowledgeable observers defended Rick Romley's release of the Tucson Four because their confessions were riddled with coercion. For legal and law enforcement insiders, there was little doubt that the Tucson plaintiffs would win their civil cases.

The only question was how much Maricopa County, and its insurers, would be willing to pay to avoid having its disgraceful treatment of Bruce, Nunez, Parker, and Zarate rehashed in a public trial. A trial would have aired the MCSO's dirty laundry on the front page of every newspaper in the state. Since the Tucson suspects were patently innocent, the internal pressure for a quick out-of-court settlement was strong.

Although the plaintiffs had separate counsel, their civil claims asserted common legal theories. Examining the arguments in Leo Bruce's case makes clear the legal positions of all four. Bruce was represented by Michael J. Vaughn and M. E. "Buddy" Rake Jr. Vaughn was the criminal defense specialist; Rake stepped in to lead the effort on the civil suits. Rake reorganized the weak criminal case against Bruce into a strong civil case against the county, shaping the facts, legal theories, and damage claims in a way that got the attention of the county's insurers, not to mention responsible law enforcement leaders all over the state. In his role as lead counsel for all the civil cases, Rake, a skilled trial lawyer, put Bruce, Nunez, and Zarate in the catbird seat.

Rake knew he could count on favorable testimony from Chief Deputy John Coppock and Sgt. Russ Kimball, as well as members of the interrogation teams who had come to regret their roles in extracting the Tucson confessions—but probably not from Sheriff Agnos, Chief Deputy George Leese, or Captain Jerry White. And he felt confident that Romley would testify truthfully and fully. Romley's views about the coercion of the Tucson defendants were widely known. Rake also retained the country's leading expert on false confessions, Dr. Richard Ofshe, as his expert witness and trial consultant.

Rake filed the suit in state court and, as expected, framed his case under the federal civil rights law, which makes it illegal for those "acting under color of law" to deprive any person of "those rights, privileges, or immunities secured or protected by the Constitution." In a memorandum filed with the court, he stated the issues succinctly: "Leo Bruce was stripped of his freedom, liberty and constitutional rights, while at the same time subjected to public humiliation and ridicule, all as a result of Defendants' malicious and willful abuse of police and political power."

Bruce was taken into custody without probable cause, then coerced into making a false confession. His arrest received massive publicity, with his picture, his name, and his supposed guilt featured in newspaper and television reports around the world. Although the confession was the only evidence against him, Bruce spent seventy-one days in jail while officials "consciously failed to pursue evidence in their possession which would exculpate him from any involvement in the murders." Even after being released for lack of evidence, Bruce was victimized by a fourteen-month "witch-hunt" as the sheriff's men tried to link him to the crime "by any means possible, illegal or otherwise."

Rake pointed out one of the egregious legal flaws in the handling of the temple case: the way the original Tucson search warrants were obtained. A search warrant authorizes investigators to look for specific objects, at a specific location, at a specified time. To get a warrant, investigators must swear an oath and convince a judge they have probable cause to believe evidence of a crime may exist at the specified location. Detective Pat Riley wrote, and swore to the accuracy of, the affidavit applying for the initial Tucson warrants.

The "probable cause" underlying Riley's sworn affidavit rested entirely on the statements of Mike McGraw. Rake argued that McGraw's story was riddled with "lies, guesswork, and inconsistencies" and was uncorroborated by evidence; thus the search warrants were based on faulty information.

Rake also argued that the warrants themselves were defective. They listed multiple locations but did not specify what was to be found where. They stated that the items were "believed to be possessed or concealed in the City of Phoenix," and yet they called for searches in Tucson. As Rake put it, K. C. Scull of the county attorney's office had approved the warrants despite these defects because the county was determined "to get the Tucson defendants at any cost."

Riley's affidavit was no more reliable than McGraw's ramblings. Riley had spent six days investigating the crime scene and knew its details inside out. He had also participated in all six taped segments of McGraw's interrogation. He used his knowledge to "clean up" McGraw's account, making it closer to the facts than it actually was.

A consultant on Rake's legal team compared the interrogation transcript with Riley's crime scene report and highlighted more than a dozen significant inconsistencies between the two. McGraw described the shotgun shells used in the crime as "red and bigger green ones" and the shotgun as a 12 or 16 gauge. But Riley knew the shotgun shells were yellow 20 gauge. McGraw said there was no furniture where the victims were killed. But Riley knew the bodies were surrounded by sofas, chairs, and tables. McGraw said he saw three women in the temple, but Riley knew there had been only one. The list went on.

Such discrepancies should have made Riley doubt McGraw's story, or at least made him cautious about the search warrants. Instead, Riley edited McGraw's tale to fit the evidence found at the temple. For example, McGraw described the motive for the temple invasion as robbing the people there; as his helpful interrogator Larry Troutt put it, "The more people, the more money." But Riley knew the killers had robbed the temple itself, not the people in it. Several victims still had money when their bodies were found, and the amounts were not trivial: the pocket of Chalerm Chantapim's robe held $263. In writing his affidavit, Riley used the real motive, not the one given by McGraw: he said the men had heard that the temple held money and other valuables.

Also, McGraw said the people in the temple had "straight long black" hair and wore "mixed colors, like Hawaiian dress," then changed his mind and described the clothing as "more like a gown, white gown or red." But Riley knew the monks wore orange robes, the nun wore white, and all the victims but one—the visitor called Boy—had shaved heads. In his affidavit Riley ignored the inconsistency about hair and claimed McGraw had seen a woman dressed in white and men dressed in orange robes. He was writing fiction, which—under oath—he would present to a judge as fact.

Another discrepancy between the affidavit and the interrogation was Riley's assertion that during McGraw's initial interview at the Tucson Psychiatric Institute, "it was established" that he and others had driven to Phoenix and committed the crime. It was not established at the hospital interview; indeed, it was never established at all. The investigators wanted to believe it. McGraw may have wanted to believe it, and he seemed to enjoy the notoriety it brought him. But he never established anything.

Rake argued that Leo Bruce's arrest was illegal and a violation of his constitutional rights. Bruce was picked up at his apartment complex in Tucson, in Pima County; under the Arizona Rules of Criminal Procedure, he should have been taken to the nearest magistrate in Pima County. Instead, the deputies took him to Phoenix, without telling him where he was going or why.

According to Rake, when Bruce's interrogation began at 2:30 a.m. on September 12, he had been awake since 5:30 a.m. the previous day. The deputies knew he had not slept in more than twenty hours, and yet they interrogated him for twenty-two hours more. Parts of the interrogation were tape recorded, but, "suspiciously," the portion in which his questioners "completely broke his will and made him 'confess'" was not on the tapes.

Earlier on September 11, while Bruce was at work, Detective Brian Sands and others searched his apartment, executing one of Riley's search warrants. Although the apartment was unoccupied, the Tucson Police Department SWAT team made the entry, using an explosive diversionary device. Sands found nothing to seize except a gun-cleaning kit plus "various documents" from the kitchen counter, a bedroom drawer, and the headboard of Bruce's bed. On September 12, after Bruce's Enhanced confession, a team searched his mother's house and found what they thought must be the murder weapon, his .22-caliber Marlin rifle. They also confiscated a Dallas Cowboys jacket but looked in vain for the "Dallas Cowboy socks" McGraw said Bruce had worn on his hands at the temple.

None of this material was ever connected in any way to the temple murders. Ballistics tests showed that Bruce's rifle had not fired the fatal shots. But to the task force brass, Bruce's confession outweighed everything else. According to Kimball, even after the belated testing of Caratachea's rifle proved it to be the murder weapon, the "question of the hour was how in the hell did Caratachea and Leo Bruce—how did Leo get Caratachea's gun."

Rake accused the MCSO of "using any means available to persecute and unjustly punish" his client. Exhaustion was one tactic. Another was fear. Deputies handcuffed Bruce and drove off into the night without explaining what they wanted or where they were taking him. In the interrogation room, they threatened him with the gas chamber and intentionally lied, saying his friends had fingered him as the killer. A third tactic was what Rake called the "setup." Detectives gave Bruce a newspaper and took him to the prop room, showing or telling him the details he later regurgitated in his false confession. By the time he made that confession, Bruce knew a great deal about the crime, and, in Rake's words, he "just wanted the torture and nightmare to end." He could see no way to end it but to tell the inquisitors what they wanted to hear. Citing Ofshe, Rake pointed out that "the consequences of confessing were made to seem insignificant compared to the relief a confession would bring."

What happened after Bruce confessed brought out Rake's sarcastic side. The next section of his memorandum opened with a mock quotation from the task force commanders: "He's a confessed mass murderer—what do we do with him? Take him to the Sheraton, of course!" Rake wrote that there were only two possible reasons for checking Bruce into the hotel, where he might encounter innocent members of the public, instead of booking him into the jail. One: they didn't really believe he was the murderer, so they did not consider him a threat to anyone. Two: they wanted to "perpetuate the facade that Mr. Bruce was not under arrest," so they could keep questioning him without providing him with a lawyer.

Although Bruce recanted his confession the next day, and despite the complete lack of evidence against him, he was charged with nine counts of murder, indicted, and jailed. Publicity about the case made him infamous, not only locally but nationally and around the world, as a mass murderer. Even after the real killers were caught and denied that anyone from Tucson had been involved in the crime, the task force brass insisted, to their own officers and to the public, that Bruce and his friends were guilty. And even after the charges against the Tucson Four were finally dismissed, the brass pursued a "witch-hunt" against them and continued to persecute them in the media.

Rake discussed the lasting effects of Bruce's ordeal. Bruce had worked hard to build a secure future. He had a steady job—two, in fact. He avoided the alcohol, drugs, gangs, and crime that were rife in his neighborhood. And except for one minor traffic violation, he had never been in trouble with the law. But when the officers "seized" him, Bruce's orderly routine was replaced by a terror that would "haunt him for the rest of his life."

During his seventy-one days in the Maricopa County Jail, Bruce was not only terrified but also "overcome with desperation and loneliness." He believed the detectives' threats about the gas chamber. If they could "seize him in the middle of the night, take him away from his family and friends, and torture him to such an extent that he confessed to the murder of nine people, Leo had no doubt they could send him to the gas chamber. It is a thought he can never forget."

The humiliation he faced after being released was just as damaging. Many people would never believe the truth about him—there was no good way to explain to strangers that even though he had confessed to nine murders, he was innocent. Long after his release, the MCSO brass continued to "publicly link him to the crime," and people on the street still whispered and stared. As Rake put it, Bruce remained imprisoned by the MCSO's "malicious and unjustified acts."

The ordeal had caused "permanent psychological damage," and Bruce sought therapy to help him cope. His psychologist, Dr. Hector Fernandez-Barisillas, treated him for fifteen months and predicted that he would need medication, including antidepressants, as long as he lived.

Rake closed the memorandum in a tone reminiscent of a trial lawyer's address to a jury. "The damages sustained by Leo Bruce in this matter are irreparable. The two and one half months in which he was deprived of his freedom are permanently lost. This twenty-nine-year-old man has had severe pain, suffering, and ridicule inflicted upon him that will last a lifetime. He must be compensated for that lifetime."

George Peterson also sued Maricopa County for false arrest and detention. His suit, filed in federal court under the 1983 Civil Rights Act, named Captain Jerry White and six other members of the MCSO, plus County Attorney Rick Romley. The $7 million complaint, filed on April 30, 1993, was a joint venture prosecuted by Phoenix attorney Larry Hammond and four other top-flight lawyers: Howard Ross Cabot, John W. Rogers, Evan Haglund, and Michael A. Berch.

Their legal position was clear: Peterson had spent fourteen months in jail for a crime he had not committed, charged with first-degree murder solely on the basis of a confession extracted from him by MCSO interrogators. Hammond and Haglund listed his "primary claims for relief": coercion of an involuntary and unreliable confession; refusal to respond to a request for counsel; arrest without probable cause; continued prosecution despite a "plethora of exculpatory evidence"; plus state law claims including "false arrest, malicious prosecution, grossly negligent investigation and supervision, and negligent and intentional infliction of emotional distress."

Most civil lawsuits arise out of disputes about facts, but no one disputed the facts in the Peterson case. The lawyers on both sides agreed: Peterson's confession was false, and no physical or other corroborating evidence connected him to the case. In that sense, there was nothing to contest.

But there was a mighty contest on the law of the case. MCSO deputies had mismanaged the investigation and manipulated an innocent man into confessing to murder; Hammond's team accused the MCSO of failing to provide those deputies with adequate training and supervision. The defendants' lawyers did not deny Peterson's innocence in the death of Alice Cameron, nor did they deny that his confession was the sole reason he had been charged. Belatedly, they also agreed that his statement under interrogation was a classic police-induced false confession. But they argued that the investigators' treatment of Peterson was a fluke, not a result of poor training and supervision.

The defendants asserted that they had not realized Peterson's confession was untrue until Alex Garcia confessed to Cameron's murder, and that soon after Garcia's surprise revelation, Peterson had been released. Garcia's specific, fact-filled account of the killing did make it obvious that Peterson's confession was false—but Hammond pointed out that, all along, the prosecution had known about other evidence that "should have led reasonable law enforcement personnel to conclude that Mr. Peterson's confession was unreliable." The MCSO claimed Peterson had raped Cameron after shooting her, but no physical evidence was ever found. Samples of Peterson's hair, skin, clothing, saliva, and blood did not match any evidence found at the crime scene; neither did Peterson's fingerprints or footprints. The State, Hammond wrote, must have known the confession had resulted from "law enforcement overwhelming an emotionally troubled and vulnerable innocent bystander."

When Peterson got out of jail, he immediately checked himself into the VA Hospital. Tracked down by reporters, he explained that he was there because "my anxieties are so high. At my age, do I have it in me to pick up the pieces again?" County Attorney Romley told the press he was "outraged" that a false confession had kept a man in jail for more than a year. Romley noted disturbing similarities between Peterson's confession and those of the Tucson suspects in the temple murders. Sheriff Joe Arpaio, who owed his election to his predecessor's mishandling of the temple case, expressed similar concerns and promised to "review both murder investigations to see whether his officers needed additional training."

In fact, Arpaio had already reviewed the temple investigation by commissioning the Chapman Audit. But he refused to release Chapman's report to Hammond's legal team until U.S. District Court judge Paul Rosenblatt ordered him to do so. The Chapman Audit was highly critical of Captain White and other MCSO commanders for their department's methods of extracting confessions. Its contents sank the MCSO's defense in the Peterson case and helped both Peterson and the Tucson suspects win settlements.

Because Peterson's lawsuit focused on the MCSO's training and supervision, Hammond paid considerable attention to Captain Jerry White, who had headed the criminal investigation unit at the time of both murder investigations. White was listed as "approval officer" on all investigative reports in the Cameron case, and as commander, he was responsible for training and supervising the officers in the unit and vouching for their techniques. Hammond deposed White in August 1993 and again in November. Like the Chapman Audit, White's daylong testimony proved damaging to the MCSO and helped break the logjam in the settlement negotiations. Once the command staff and the county's insurers read White's deposition, they acted swiftly to arrange a settlement with Peterson.

Peterson's lawyers knew the MCSO had heard about Garcia's involvement in Cameron's death as early as November 1991. Back then, Leroy Hughes, the jailhouse snitch who reported Garcia's conversation about the temple murders, also reported Garcia's boast that he and his girlfriend had killed a woman who was camping at a lake. Detective Gary Eggert, who interviewed Hughes, checked to see if there had been such a murder in the county, then wrote a report on the interview and gave it to his superiors, but they failed to follow up on the tip about Cameron.

White, who had been Eggert's commander in 1991, claimed he had not heard about Garcia's involvement in Cameron's death until January 1993. Hammond believed White had a selective memory. He had attended briefings about Hughes's statements, but he said Cameron's name had never been mentioned at the briefings, so he hadn't made the connection. He also said he didn't know whether or not Hughes's information had been passed to the team investigating her murder. If it had been, he told Hammond, the person who received it would have "had a responsibility to match this information with what we had." In fact that responsibility was White's. His name appeared on every report, and he should have connected the dots. But his preoccupation with finding a nonexistent link between the Tucson Four and the temple murders no doubt distracted him from his duties as head of the MCSO's criminal investigation unit.

Hammond put the issue squarely to White. Assuming that investigators knew in November 1991 that Garcia had admitted being involved in the Cameron murder, was it appropriate to leave Peterson in jail until January 1993? White consulted with his lawyer, David Damron, then refused to answer. Debbie Heller, a paralegal who wrote a summary of the deposition, noted that when White heard this question, his "color changed to beet-red." From a trial lawyer's perspective, when cross-examining a witness, if you can't get an admission, the next best thing is a refusal to admit the obvious.

By the time of his deposition, White no longer commanded the criminal investigation unit. Soon after taking office, Sheriff Joe Arpaio had demoted him and transferred him to the homicide cop's equivalent of Siberia: the transportation division. White told Hammond he had welcomed the reassignment and was only disturbed by the rumor that Romley had pushed Arpaio to transfer him because of his stand on the temple case.

Then, perhaps to prove his stubbornness, White asserted that part of Peterson's confession was probably true and emphatically declared that he had "never had a false confession." Hammond jumped on that, beginning to ask about other confessions, but Damron instructed White not to answer anything concerning the Tucson Four.

White admitted he had "never investigated whether the Peterson confession was accurate." His excuse was that from October 1991, he had worked solely on the temple case, and that in his absence, Detective Richard Teal had been in charge of the criminal investigation unit. He said he *had* investigated four other confessions—but again Damron advised him not to talk about the Tucson Four.

As commander, White was responsible for the training of his detectives. He said this training covered crime scene investigation but not interrogation techniques. Asked about his own training, he couldn't recall whether he had studied interrogation techniques at the academy. He estimated that in his sixteen-year career, he had conducted five to ten interrogations in homicide cases and several dozen in narcotics cases.

Hammond asked many questions about White's role in George Peterson's in-custody interrogation, and White's answers made clear that he had largely ignored it. He recalled watching through the two-way mirror for a few minutes and seeing "a bearded Grizzly Adams" but being unable to hear the conversation. All his recollections of Peterson's ordeal were vague at best.

Presented with the investigative reports in the Cameron case, White confirmed that every one showed his name as reviewing officer. He said the computer automatically put the commander's name on each report, but in fact he had not reviewed any of them. His memory of the case seemed almost nonexistent. He didn't know that evidence from the autopsy had been compromised or that hair retrieved from a sleeping bag was missing. He said he had never heard that Peterson had recanted his confession. He *had* heard a rumor that even if Peterson was not the murderer, he had molested Cameron's body.

Despite the murkiness of his memory, White did help Hammond on several key points in Peterson's civil case. He inadvertently destroyed the only defense the MCSO had—reasonable error. After his deposition, the MCSO's attorneys could hardly argue that its deputies were trained in proper methods of interrogation or monitored by supervisors, or that they conducted meaningful follow-up investigations to corroborate confessions.

White also helped by insisting, in his November deposition, that he had never read the Chapman Audit. Chapman had not interviewed White, the boss in both the temple and Cameron investigations, but his name turned up in every section of the damning audit. According to his officers, White considered investigators' reports "too conservative"; threatened to remove Sgt. Mullavey from the temple case for doubting that the Tucson suspects were involved; rejected reports on Dante Parker's interrogation until inconsistencies with the facts were edited out; and labeled subordinates who disagreed with him "imbeciles." And yet White claimed he had not read the audit and was not aware of Chapman's finding that the MCSO had a "confused organizational structure."

White surprised Hammond by saying he did not know enough about the Cameron case to "even form an opinion" about whether Peterson's rights had been violated. It was a rare event in a civil rights lawsuit: a commanding officer claiming to know almost nothing about a case handled by his department. When asked to rate the homicide unit's performance in 1991, at the time of the temple and Cameron investigations, White replied that it had done "very well." When asked if this assessment included the Peterson case, he said it did. In Hammond's view, White had shown "virtually total indifference to Mr. Peterson's rights."

Peterson's civil case was aided by five expert witnesses, who agreed to work without pay or at reduced rates. They dissected the investigators' reports and examined the elements necessary to establish the breach of Peterson's civil rights. Hammond considered hiring Richard

Ofshe, the expert on false confessions, although Arizona law would not have allowed him to say directly that he believed a confession was false. Expert witnesses are permitted to give opinions about police procedures and techniques used to obtain confessions—that is, about coercion and voluntariness. But the jury is the sole decision maker about the truth or falsity of a confession, so on that crucial issue, the experts are required to be silent.

Everyone involved knew that if Peterson's case went to court, some evidence would spill over from the Tucson suspects' civil suits. Peterson's false confession had been extracted only six weeks after those of the Tucson Four, and by the same unit of the MCSO. The capstone argument was the MCSO's failure to pursue crucial leads in both the temple and Cameron cases. Valuing confessions—however self-contradictory, and however induced—over other types of evidence, investigators had not tracked down the Hispanic male seen near Cameron's campsite. They had also failed to investigate Cameron's missing bank card. A simple phone call to the Valley National Bank would have yielded crucial information; it might even have turned up a security tape of Garcia and Hoover trying to use Cameron's card at an ATM. And the investigators had ignored Hughes's tip about Garcia killing a woman who was camping. Following these leads would have led them to Garcia and spared Peterson those fourteen months in jail. But the deputies had stopped looking for Cameron's killer when they decided Peterson was guilty.

Everyone also knew that Peterson's incarceration and anguish were not the worst consequences of the MCSO's shoddy investigation. If Caratachea's rifle had been sent for ballistics testing when it was confiscated instead of six weeks later, Garcia would have been arrested in September, and he and Hoover could not have killed Alice Cameron in October. That fact, if nothing else, dictated the certainty, if not the size, of an out-of-court settlement for Peterson.

George Peterson's civil suit was settled out of court in January 1994, with Maricopa County agreeing to pay him $1.1 million, of which a third would go to his lawyers. Three months later, the Tucson suspects' suits were settled as well. On April 22, newspapers announced that the civil cases related to the temple case would cost the county $2.8 million.

Leo Bruce and Mark Nunez would each receive $1.1 million, Dante Parker and Victor Zarate $240,000, and Romelia Duarte $120,000. Zarate's lawyer Sean Bruner acknowledged to reporters that his client's share of the settlement amounted to $40,000 for each of his six days in jail. But, Bruner went on, the case was not about money; it was about the abuse of power.

Bruce and Nunez would also receive an additional one dollar each, to make their compensation larger than Peterson's. The extra dollar, according to Buddy Rake, was an acknowledgment that "the constitutional rights of some Hispanics from Tucson are just as valuable as those of someone else."

Judge Lawrence Fleischman of the Pima County Superior Court, who mediated the settlement, called it a "win-win situation": a fair outcome for the plaintiffs and a bargain for taxpayers, saving the State an estimated $2 million in legal fees by avoiding a trial. The judge did not mention that if the case had gone to trial, a jury might have awarded the plaintiffs much larger compensation. David Damron, one of Maricopa County's lawyers, also praised the settlement, but he took a glass-half-empty view. Predicting that some critics would say the county was paying too much, while others would believe the plaintiffs weren't getting enough, he said, "If both sides are unhappy, then it's probably a good settlement."

The MCSO deputies named in the lawsuits did not have to pay the settlement from their own pockets, but they paid for their actions in other ways. Most of them were transferred or replaced by Sheriff Arpaio. Within two years, none of the deputies involved was still employed in the public sector. The out-of-court settlement saved them from the public rebuke they would have received if the case had gone to trial.

Two of the Tucson plaintiffs spoke to the press after their settlement was announced. Reached by telephone, Mark Nunez said he hoped the settlement would clear his name and let him get on with his life. Leo Bruce, flanked by his lawyers, met with reporters in person. "Slap me and wake me up," he said. "To me, this money means that the county is finally admitting they were wrong from the beginning." It was a day for celebrations. But, Bruce added, "the nightmares of being incarcerated and being in jail are still there. It'll be with me till the day I die."

EPILOGUE

By August 1994, Maricopa County officials could hope that both the temple and Cameron murder cases were finally behind them. Johnathan Doody, Alex Garcia, and Michelle Hoover were in prison. Leo Bruce, Mark Nunez, Dante Parker, Victor Zarate, and George Peterson had their settlement money. Mike McGraw was out of Arizona and engaged to be married (but still causing trouble: in 1992 his fiancée pawned her engagement ring to bail him out of a Colorado jail). And with a sheriff who had vowed to learn from past mistakes, the county officials could also hope that the days of police-induced false confessions and botched investigations were over.

Both these hopes would prove unfounded. In 2003 another murder case would parallel elements of both earlier cases: victims shot while camping, unreliable informant, mentally fragile suspect induced to confess, alibi evidence ignored, an innocent man in jail for fourteen months. Then, in 2008, the temple case would be revived by a scathing opinion by a three-judge panel of the Ninth Circuit Court of Appeals holding that Doody's confession had been coerced.

On June 9, 2003, MCSO detectives interrogated a fifty-year-old machinist named Robert Louis Armstrong and extracted a confession to a triple murder that had gone unsolved for five years. As a direct consequence of its embarrassment in the temple and Cameron murder cases, the MCSO had begun to videotape all interrogations. But Sheriff Joe Arpaio's new policy did not put an end to his deputies' extraction of false confessions. Instead of correcting the deputies' interrogation abuses, the policy merely documented them on videotape. Watching Armstrong's three-volume videotape is as excruciating as listening to the audiotapes of George Peterson and the Tucson suspects.

The threads connecting Armstrong's confession to those of the Tucson Four and, particularly, Peterson, are like copper wire running through the interrogation rooms, separated by eleven years, but still carrying the same MCSO message: Confess because we know you did it. None of the suspects in these cases was presumed innocent or capable of telling the truth. All were emotionally vulnerable and terrified. All confessed to gruesome murders they had not committed. The same techniques and shortcomings that were so egregious in the temple and Cameron investigations—coercion, inattention to detail, lazy acceptance of an easy confession—marred the MCSO's treatment of Armstrong.

In the early morning hours of Easter Sunday, April 12, 1998, three young campers, Ronald "Eddie" Hutchison, Dewey Peters, and Crystal Allison, were shot to death in the back of their pickup truck in the Agua Fria river bottom on Phoenix's west side. It was the same dry riverbed where Doody and Garcia had gone to divide the spoils of the Buddhist temple massacre.

The MCSO thought the triple homicide had been committed by robbers. For five years, investigators had no idea who the robbers were. Today, more than a decade after the killings, they still don't know.

In April 2003, a patron in a Phoenix bar overheard someone implicate a man named Dave Majors in the murders. Perhaps motivated by the posted $11,000 reward, the eavesdropper called the Phoenix Silent Witness Program, which alerted the MCSO.

The tip led Arpaio's deputies to Majors's ex-girlfriend Peggy Sue Brown, who was in jail on a probation violation and eager to get out. Brown's record made it clear that she had a long history of severe mental illness and substance abuse. Nevertheless, detectives took her very seriously when she claimed to be an eyewitness to the crime and named Majors and his friend Armstrong as the killers. It was a familiar story in the annals of the MCSO.

Detectives interrogated Majors but could not get him to confess. His DNA sample failed to connect him to the crime scene. They got a search warrant for his house but found no incriminating evidence. So, lacking either a confession or hard evidence, they did not charge him with the murders.

The MCSO had no more evidence against Armstrong than against Majors, but it did get him to confess. In a long interrogation reminiscent of those of George Peterson and the Tucson suspects thirteen years before, its detectives managed to extract yet another false confession. This time the suspect was, like Peterson, mentally impaired, with a need to please authority figures. Armstrong had an IQ of 90 and had suffered a traumatic brain injury when a car had knocked him off his bicycle. He was also, like Mark Nunez, easy to convince that the murders he didn't remember committing must have happened during an alcoholic black-out. And like Peterson, he spent more than a year behind bars, charged with first-degree murder, for a crime he had not committed.

As with the Tucson suspects and Peterson, the MCSO had no foren-sic evidence implicating Armstrong, but using his confession, they per-suaded the county attorney's office to indict him on three counts of first-degree murder. As in the temple case, the MCSO based its presumptions about Armstrong on the accusations of a mentally disturbed informant, and no one checked his alibi until long after he was charged with the crime. Armstrong said from the beginning that on the day of the mur-ders he had been in Oregon, having Easter dinner with his mother.

Skilled interrogators always adjust their tones and other techniques to fit a suspect; in Armstrong's interrogation, the style of persuasion seems to show that the deputies knew their suspect was mentally impaired and used his disability against him. For example, they made a long string of dubious assertions: "if he had courage to confess, his children and grandchildren would consider it 'the proudest moment of your life for them'; jail was a happy place; there was a pot of gold at the end of the rainbow; under the worst scenario he would only do five years in jail; going to jail for a few years was not a big deal; all his basic needs would be taken care of; and [the detectives] personally knew people in prison that would never get out and they had never been happier in their life." And after Armstrong's confused and false confession, his interrogators presented him with a certificate saying he was awarded "a Red Badge of Courage for standing up and coming forward with the truth."

The detectives also gave Armstrong plenty of information to fill the gaps in his nonexistent memory of the crime. They told him that two men and a woman were killed; when, where, and from what distance they were shot; and even details such as "there was a bonfire made of pal-lets of wood" and "one victim died with a beer in his hand."

They also asked Armstrong to take a "truth verification" examina-tion that would measure microtremors in his voice. They explained that "microtremors are only present when a person's not telling the truth, no other times."

Like many law-abiding citizens, Armstrong thought he had nothing to fear from the police. He sighed, then said, "Yeah, I guess so, I ain't got nothing to hide."

He was given a release form to sign; because he didn't have his glasses, a detective read it to him. The form said, among other things, that he submitted to the "truth-verification technique" "voluntarily without duress, coercion, promise, reward or immunity"; that he released the MCSO from "any and all claims arising out of the examination"; and that "to the best of my knowledge at this time I have no physical or mental conditions which would prevent me from taking this examination."

Armstrong asked, "Should I talk to a lawyer before doing any of this?"

The detective administering the test declined to advise him about a lawyer one way or the other, then added, "but if what you're telling the investigator is in fact true, you wouldn't have even been in the state of Arizona when this [crime] occurred. . . . If that is true, this examination will demonstrate that."

"Okay," Armstrong said.

The detective turned on a machine and asked Armstrong a mixture of innocuous questions and queries about the crime and his alibi. Afterwards he claimed that Armstrong had flunked the test, particularly the question of his whereabouts on Easter Sunday 1998.

The detectives also confronted Armstrong with Peggy Sue Brown, who repeated her version of the killings. Armstrong first insisted that she was lying, but eventually admitted doing what she and his interrogators claimed he had done.

The case against Armstrong began to unravel when Marianne Brewer, a social worker with the Maricopa County Legal Advocate's Office, got the Greyhound Bus Company to dig through its records for Armstrong's bus ticket from Oregon to Phoenix. That ticket confirmed his alibi: the bus left Portland on Easter Sunday, 1998, and did not arrive in Phoenix until the next day. The county attorney's office dismissed all charges against Armstrong, and he was released in August 2004, fourteen months after his arrest.

In yet another echo of the earlier cases, Armstrong hired Buddy Rake to sue Maricopa County for wrongful arrest and imprisonment. Rake consulted the same experts as in Leo Bruce's civil case, and he accomplished the same result. Armstrong's lawsuit, filed in federal court in 2005, was settled out of court in May 2006. The parties agreed to keep the size of the settlement confidential.

Rake used two of Sheriff Arpaio's own public statements to buttress Armstrong's claims. When first elected, Arpaio had said about the mismanaged temple investigation, "What happened was a sad day for law enforcement, and we're going to move forward and I hope everyone learns from it. My philosophy is: I don't like confessions. . . . Make sure you've got corroborating evidence before you arrest somebody." Eleven years later, when announcing Armstrong's arrest, he told the *Arizona Republic*, "These killers deserve to be executed for these brutal, violent murders." Arpaio's second statement speaks volumes about the MCSO's attitude toward the presumption of innocence. Taken together, the two are proof of unheeded lessons and lost opportunities.

Seventeen years after the temple murders, when Johnathan Doody had spent exactly half of his life behind bars, his case was in the news again. On November 20, 2008, a three-judge panel of the U.S. Court of Appeals for the Ninth Circuit reversed Doody's conviction and ordered that he be given a new trial.

Once again the MCSO's approach to interrogations was an embarrassment. Reporter Michael Kiefer, writing about the reversal for the *Arizona Republic*, put the panel's ruling in plain language: "Detectives from the Maricopa County Sheriff's office forced a confession from Doody." Kiefer also quoted Alan Dershowitz, Doody's attorney: "They used every trick in the book. They denied him the right to have a parent there. They created all the circumstances for false confession and they got it—a false confession."

And once again the State pressed ahead with the case. Kent Cattani of the Arizona Attorney General's Office told the media that the next step would not be to retry Doody. Instead, the State would ask the Ninth Circuit to reconsider the case *en banc*, that is, with its full panel of judges, and if that effort failed, the State would ask the U.S. Supreme Court to review the case on certiorari.

Back in 1994, when Doody was sentenced to serve nine consecutive life terms, no one was surprised that he appealed his conviction to the Arizona Court of Appeals. What did surprise many was the identity of his new attorney. Doody's case was taken up by Alan Dershowitz, the Harvard Law School professor known for representing famous and infamous clients such as O. J. Simpson, Mike Tyson, and Patty Hearst. Speculation about who had hired the very talented and very expensive Dershowitz focused on a wealthy Buddhist temple in California, Wat Thai of Los Angeles. Mettanando Bhikkhu, the monk who testified at Doody's mitigation hearing, later said the money had actually been raised by four temples in Thailand. Believing Doody had been made a scapegoat in the temple case, Mettanando had appealed to his fellow monks.

Dershowitz argued that Judge Martin should have suppressed Doody's confession prior to trial because it was not made voluntarily, and that without the confession, there was no credible evidence against Doody. In September 1996, the Arizona Court of Appeals rejected Dershowitz's arguments.

Judge Ruth McGregor (who wrote the appellate opinion) and her colleagues found that the length of Doody's overnight interrogation did not, in itself, "establish that the officers overcame Doody's will to resist confessing." Although Dershowitz described the tone of the interrogation as coercive, to the court the audiotapes revealed a "courteous, almost pleading style of questioning." The court also rejected Dershowitz's argument that the deputies had tricked and unfairly pressured Doody, noting that courts "tolerate some police gamesmanship, so long as the games do not overcome a suspect's will and induce a confession not truly voluntary." Thus the court upheld Judge Martin's decision to admit the confession and affirmed Doody's conviction.

In January 1997 the Arizona Supreme Court declined to review the case; in June 1997 the U.S. Supreme Court also declined. Next Dershowitz filed a petition for a writ of habeas corpus in the U.S. District Court for the District of Arizona, which waited until 2006 to decide that the writ lacked merit. He appealed that ruling to the Ninth Circuit Court of Appeals, which took until November 2008 to issue its opinion reversing Doody's conviction.

The November 2008 opinion was vacated on May 12, 2009, when the Ninth Circuit ordered that the case be reheard *en banc*. The case was briefed, and reargued on June 23, 2009. Eleven of the court's twenty-seven active judges heard a second round of oral arguments.

The court, sitting en banc, issued a 106-page opinion on February 25, 2010. By a vote of eight to three, the court reversed and remanded the case to the district court, ordering it to grant Doody's habeas petition "unless the State of Arizona elects to retry Doody within a reasonable time."

The Ninth Circuit decided that the 1996 decision by the Arizona Court of Appeals constituted "an unreasonable determination of the facts and an unreasonable application of the governing law." It went on to say, "The Arizona Court of Appeals unreasonably concluded that the Miranda warnings were clear and understandable, despite the detective's erroneous warnings regarding Doody's right to counsel and the use of qualifying language to downplay the warnings' significance." Accordingly, it held that Doody was entitled to a writ of habeas corpus because the Miranda warnings the police gave him were inadequate, thus rendering his confession inadmissible.

Additionally, it said the Arizona Court of Appeals ruling that Doody's confession had been voluntarily given was "an unreasonable determination of the facts in light of the audiotapes that reflect the relentless, nearly thirteen-hour interrogation of a sleep-deprived juvenile by a tag team of detectives."

Moreover, said the Ninth Circuit, "The Arizona Court of Appeals also unreasonably applied clearly established federal law when it failed to consider the totality of the circumstances to determine if Doody's will was overborne by the interrogation."

The Ninth Circuit was blunt in its criticism of the Maricopa County Sheriff's Office and harsh in reciting the legal failings of the Arizona Court of Appeals. Finally, using an "elephant in the room" metaphor, it tied Doody's October 1991 coerced confession to those given by the Tucson Four in September 1991:

> Let us not forget that this same task force questioned four adult men and, undoubtedly using the same tactics, procured what the State concedes were false confessions from all four. That the will of four adult men was overborne to the extent that they confessed to murders they did not commit further persuades us that the will of this young teen was similarly overborne. And that is the real elephant in the room, an elephant that both the Arizona Court of Appeals and the dissent studiously ignore—the undisputed evidence in the record that this same task force, undoubtedly using the same "courteous, almost pleading style of questioning" extracted false confessions from four adults for the same crime with which Doody was charged. Is there any doubt that the wills of those individuals were overborne?

The U.S. Supreme Court will have the last word if it decides to review the Ninth Circuit's reversal of the Arizona Court of Appeals. If not, the likelihood that the State will retry Doody is slim. Nearly twenty years after the murders at the Buddhist temple, and seventeen years after Doody's original trial, it will have no forensic evidence, no confession, and no finger-pointing by Alex Garcia. As it stands now, six men confessed to the Temple murders. Four were exonerated in 1991. The fifth man, Johnathan

Doody, will probably be released soon. Only Alex Garcia, who made what he thought was a favorable plea bargain, will stay in prison.

The ordeals of Leo Bruce, Mike McGraw, Mark Nunez, Dante Parker, George Peterson, and Robert Armstrong are classic examples of the way some law enforcement agencies manipulate suspects, exploiting their vulnerability or their naiveté while ignoring hard evidence. Americans need to be wary of confessions in general and incensed by the ready acceptance of police-induced confessions by investigators, prosecutors, judges, and juries.

The *Arizona Republic*, which kept its readers informed about all these murder cases as they unfolded, summarized the consequences of over-valuing confessions. False confessions, wrote reporter Dennis Wagner, "undermine America's justice system. They allow real perpetrators to get away with murder, perhaps to kill again. They squander tax dollars. They leave survivors with empty justice."

In each case—the temple massacre, the Cameron murder, and the Easter 1998 shootings—the suspects were told, but did not understand or did not remember, their *Miranda* rights. They represent an unknown number of others who falsely confess every year in small, windowless interrogation rooms, under pressure from interrogators skilled at instill-ing hopelessness. The defining premise in the Warren Court's opinion in the *Miranda* case was to make confession evidence admissible *only* if it was voluntary. But the reality is quite different. Many innocent peo-ple waive their *Miranda* rights and participate in interrogations with-out counsel. Some fail to understand the warnings because of youth, low intelligence, mental illness, or drug or alcohol dependence—or because their interrogators portray the warnings as insignificant. Others waive their rights because they have nothing to hide and trust that telling the truth will convince the authorities of their innocence. Instead, the authorities induce some of those innocent people to confess.

Once a confession is obtained, its veracity tends to be assumed. Prosecutors scratch below the skin of a confession to see if it has real muscle: Is it strong enough to be admitted in evidence during the trial? Judges consider whether confessions meet procedural rules and substan-tive standards handed down by appellate courts. But the vital question of *truth* is the exclusive province of juries. And as every trial lawyer knows, jurors rarely question the truth of a confession. If the defendant said he did it, they believe him. Like most of the public, they cannot fathom why or how anyone could ever confess to a crime he or she didn't commit.

Police-induced confessions have been part of the criminal justice system throughout recorded history. For centuries, since medieval times, they have been regarded as the queen of proofs. If they were accorded lesser value (say about a four of clubs), police would not work so hard to get them, and prosecutors would not accept them in the absence of corroborating evidence. True confessions play a central role in convicting the guilty. The problem arises when interrogators induce innocent suspects to make *false* confessions and then use those confessions to convict the innocent.

There are almost as many proposed solutions to the problem of false confessions as there are denials that the problem exists. Mandatory audio- or videotaping of interrogations, changes in rules covering the admission of confessions in evidence, improved training of interrogators, heightened oversight of police agencies, and better use of forensics at crime scenes have been offered as solutions.

Custodial interrogation of suspects is theoretically conducted to learn the truth. But it is a truth that is too often shaped by the interrogators' preconceived belief in the suspects' guilt. There is no scientific method in the station house. Scientists actively try to *disprove* the hypothesis under consideration; only if it survives all challenges do they accept it. Interrogators accept it if the suspect "breaks" and tells them what they want to hear. Pharmaceutical tests are double-blind. So are wine tastings. But in many cases, confessions are pursued by interrogators who already assume them to be true. It works for them; they can close the case.

Perhaps it is time to consider a bolder, systemic solution. One possibility would be to put a third party in the interrogation room, a person with responsibility not to the police or the suspect but to the pursuit of truth. This third party could serve as "counsel for the interrogation," ensuring that interrogators not be coercive and that suspects be allowed to remain silent, explain, or confess as they see fit.

Louis Brandeis coined the term "counsel for the situation" to describe lawyers who attempt to accommodate their clients' interests to those of other parties, "looking after the interests of everyone." That concept came under fire when Brandeis was nominated to the Supreme Court in 1916, as opponents accused him of unethical conduct for failing to offer his clients the traditional one-sided advocacy. But the Senate rejected those charges and confirmed his nomination, and in the following decades, counsel for the situation gradually gained acceptance as a legitimate role for lawyers under certain circumstances.

Similarly, the "counsel for the interrogation" could mediate custodial interrogation, insisting that the police play fair and that the suspect respond to legitimate inquiries. In the traditional lawyer-client model, having the suspect's attorney in the interrogation room is not likely to balance interests, work toward a fairly acquired confession, or resolve doubts about the client's guilt, participation, or knowledge of the crime. But counsel for the interrogation—not bound by the rules of adversarial justice or obligated to help one side defeat the other—could serve the interest of the authorities in identifying the guilty, while also serving the suspect's interest in fair treatment and society's interest in avoiding the conviction of the innocent.

What if we made counsel for the interrogation a formal part of the criminal justice system? Creating such an office might involve considerable expense and would undoubtedly draw even more criticism from opponents than the concept did in Brandeis's day. Many would call it idealistic and impractical: quixotic. But we need *some* way to attack the many-armed windmill of police-induced false confessions and stop the use of those confessions to convict innocent people. With thought, time, and a commitment to change, we could establish the role of counsel for the interrogation to do just that.

Decreased reliance on coercive custodial interrogation would return the high ground to hard-working police officers in the fight against real crime while allowing prosecutors to focus on real criminals. Judges would no longer have to cringe when hearing coercive confessions read aloud in open court. Insurance companies could reduce premiums for public agencies in their losing battle against false-arrest suits. The Fifth Amendment privilege against self-incrimination would be meaningful in the police station as well as in court.

However, even if all of that were accomplished, it is likely that little would change in the minds of the public. Most of us would continue to assume that only guilty people confess, and to think of ourselves as too smart and too strong to be manipulated into confessing to crimes we did not commit.

Acknowledgments

The Maricopa County Sheriff's Office is a subdivision charged with providing law enforcement in Arizona's most populous county. While the MCSO's employees, constituents, and stakeholders regard it as an entity unto itself, the men and women who patrol the county roads, maintain order, and do their best to investigate crimes are only human. Most of those officers serve admirably and rarely succumb to the tunnel vision that leads to false confessions like the ones chronicled in this book. But the good work of many does not compensate for the psychological root canals administered by a few. By narrowing its focus to only one investigative technique—coercive interrogation—the MCSO task force allowed misplaced belief in guilt by interrogation to drive the rest of its investigation.

Sgt. Russell Kimball was in the thick of it from the instant the temple massacre was discovered until Johnathan Doody was spared the death penalty three years later. Kimball did his best to tell the truth under adverse circumstances, believing as he did that justice for the victims should not vanish in the harsh reality of coercion and mismanagement. He opened his own veins, along with the flabby muscle of the MCSO command staff, in a revealing series of articles in *Phoenix Magazine* in the fall of 1993. He opened his mind, his files, and his conscience to me in 2006, when he shared his insider's view of those frenetic interrogations. For his candor and his courage, I am most appreciative.

Leo Bruce was an intensely honest young man and—from the instant he was ordered to hit the ground, then handcuffed and driven to Phoenix—an intensely bewildered one. His utter lack of guile, his faith that the truth would protect him, and his vulnerability to men in uniform were his undoing. Like Mark Nunez, Dante Parker, George Peterson, and Robert Armstrong, Bruce was innocent until interrogated. Then his interrogators made the mistake of giving him a four-hour sleep break and a chance to talk to his mother. Understandably, he became innocent again. There never was a killer in Bruce, or a liar. That he was branded both, for seventy-two days of his life, is proof of the power of coercion, the danger of custodial interrogation, and the risk every man and woman in America faces when presumed guilt drives an interrogation. In time, Bruce regained his balance, and fifteen years after the fact, he told his story to me.

Bruce was, metaphorically and literally, the innocent man that Sgt. Kimball could not see. These two men gave me word pictures of both sides of the interrogation chamber, where suspect and interrogator faced each other for hours and days on end, until the cop's will overpowered the suspect's innocence. Without their insider views, this book would only be about what happened in the interrogation rooms, not about how or why it happened.

My attempt to expose the evils of organized coercion, the frailties of prosecution, and the frustrations of defending cases like these is a product of a lifelong fascination with the law, its nuances, and its contradictions. A project of this magnitude relied on the goodwill and openness of the people who populate this book—cops, lawyers, judges, and suspects. All told, more than a hundred of them inspired and pushed me to write this book.

Once I got started, many others provided invaluable help. Within the public record about the Tucson suspects, the Avondale boys, the temple victims, and the murder of Alice Marie Cameron, I discovered scores of reporters, witnesses, psychologists, forensic experts, court staff, opinion writers, policy makers, and profoundly distressed family members. All of them, and especially Helen Fletcher, were generous with their time, open about their fears, and explicit in their recollections. I was given access to hundreds of people, thousands of documents, and enough secrets to sink a literary battleship. A few spoke grudgingly, but all spoke truthfully. Through access to records, and by cross-checking those records against Peter Balkan's database, I acquired thousands of files, digital and otherwise, and hundreds of snapshots, yellowed newspapers, crumpled letters, longhand lists, and fragmented notes.

Most of those who helped me did so without any expectation of acknowledgment, and some prefer not to be thanked by name. I could never name them all, so I acknowledge their contributions *in absentia*.

Still, some must be named. My sincere thanks to the following alphabet soup of informed truth tellers: Paul Ahler, Peter Balkan, Judith Becker, Craig Blakey, Luis Calvo, John Coppock, Mary Durand, Helen Fletcher, Bill Friedl, Jordan Green, Larry Hammond, Chris Johns,

Bill Jones, Russell Kimball, Gregory Martin, Tom Martinez, Jamie Matanovich, Melvin McDonald, Charles McNulty, Craig Mehrens, John Michaels, Bill Moore, Mike O'Connor, Buddy Rake, Ron Reinstein, Gary Rohlwing, Rick Romley, Mara Siegel, Stan Slonaker, Gene Stratford, and Jerry Toles.

Although writing is the loneliest profession, many of the words in this book came from the creative minds and incisive critiques of fellow writers. Early drafts of the manuscript disappointed many, including me. Thanks to focused line-by-line edits by Kathleen Gilbert, a top-end review by Craig Blakey and Dave Knop, and an extensive critique by Craig Mehrens, my early errors are now blessedly absent from the book. Thanks to their pointed comments, this book is much better than it was when they thumbed their way through eight hundred draft pages of crime, coercion, and consequence.

How can I properly acknowledge the teaching that comes from reading? This book is better because authors with superior skills wrote other books on demanding subjects and made our world safer and wiser in the process. Without pretending to be their peer, I want to acknowledge that I have been greatly influenced by the works of Anthony Lewis, Irving Stone, David McCullough, Mike Sager, and Joseph Wambaugh. Lewis's *Gideon's Trumpet* blazed a new path for constitutional law. Stone's *Adversary in the House* gave me a structural approach to the presentation of legal drama, in an area where the little guy usually loses. McCullough's *Brave Companions* showed me how to portray ordinary men achieving extraordinary success in the face of great adversity. Sager's *Scary Monsters and Super Freaks* taught me the value of short, pithy language, besides serving as a crucial source of information about a story he knew better than most. And Wambaugh's *Lines and Shadows*, which explores the thin line between lawmen and bandits, helped me sort out suspects from deputies. All these works influenced the way I chose to shape and mold this book.

The prosecutors and defense lawyers involved in the criminal cases arising out of the temple and Cameron murders were generous with their time and their memories. Paul Ahler, Peter Balkan, Luis Calvo, Jordan Green, Bill Moore, Michael Vaughn, Charlie McNulty, Gary Rohlwing, Tom Martinez, and Rick Romley patiently described their roles, their clients, and their legal strategies. While each carefully preserved the attorney-client privilege, they all helped me understand the nuances buried in the legal documentation. Their lawyer-to-lawyer cooperation is greatly appreciated. The civil defense attorneys, including David Damron, Bill Friedl, Bill Jones, John Michaels, Bill Moore, Mike O'Connor, and Georgia Staton, though reluctant to share inside details of their cases, explained the public record in a way that advanced my book. Also, the mitigation expert Mary Durand was a special treat and gave me a view of Doody that few others dug deep enough to see.

Rick Romley deserves great credit for his eventual decision to seek the dismissal of all charges against the Tucson Four. His decision to cut a deal with Garcia while insisting on a death-penalty trial for Doody was as difficult to make as it was to defend. And yet over time, and with a generous helping of second-guessing, it may work to Doody's advantage. The MCSO's coercive interrogation of Doody may ultimately set him free.

Lawyers Buddy Rake and Larry Hammond were extraordinarily helpful, giving me an insider's look into the strategy and the tactics of high-end civil litigation arising out of botched custodial interrogations, wrongful arrest charges, and violations of state and federal civil rights. Their files became mine, and their insights allowed me to connect the dots between the criminal and civil cases. I am much in their debt.

Judges Gregory Martin and Ronald Reinstein did the bulk of the judicial work in the murder cases. Judge Martin presided over the only trial that was conducted and, perhaps most difficult of all, measured the possibility of the death penalty for Doody. The cases aroused intense media scrutiny, which was exacerbated by the hostility between the MCSO and the county attorney. But Judges Martin and Reinstein ignored all external influences; in a word, they were *judicious* at all times. Our conversations gave me rare insight into the complexity of the cases and the difficulty of ensuring that every pretrial defendant was afforded the full measure of due process. These two judges are illustrative of the many others, in both state and federal courts, who made hard decisions on disputed facts in these cases.

I owe very special thanks to Peter Balkan. He took on Doody's defense almost single-handedly and paid dearly for his efforts. But through it all, he maintained a healthy respect for his professional opponents and a resolve to see the case through, even during its darkest days. His careful attention to detail at Doody's voluntariness hearing laid the groundwork for Doody's later success in the Ninth Circuit Court of Appeals. Balkan gave me a searchable database containing thousands of digital files, including the transcripts of all JV hearings, voluntariness hearings, and interrogations; MCSO departmental reports; photos; and many trial documents. These proved invaluable as source materials. And because the database was searchable, I was able to peer, over and over again, into the nuances of Doody's legal defense and the details of how death-penalty litigation is managed from the inside. Balkan's willingness to respond to what he probably saw as an endless series of questions, challenges, and memory-stretching exercises contributed greatly to the book.

As with Russ Kimball and Leo Bruce, without Peter Balkan's help, this would have been merely a what-happened book. His contribution, not to put it too strongly, was his willingness to bare his soul, along with his file. The documents he provided, when compared with the original court files, which Judge Gregory Martin graciously allowed me to copy and use, gave me a graphic picture of what happened and an inside look at why and how false confessions are so easy to extract, so hard to strike, and so dangerous to the legal health of our criminal justice system. My hope is that this book will give the reader, too, an insider's view into the netherworld of secret tapings, the force-feeding of incriminating facts to suspects, the inestimable power of prosecutorial discretion, and the willy-nilly of bargaining for a plea from the wrong defendant.

At the risk of cliché, the following phrases come to mind. "It takes a village." "We are smarter than I am." "I couldn't have done it without you." All these familiar phrases fit the situation, but they trivialize the contributions four remarkable women made to this book.

Kathleen Gilbert, my first editor, suffered through multiple revisions of an original draft containing something on the order of 400,000 words. She clicked her way through it, helped me burn away more than 200,000 expendable words, and gave me the courage to submit the manuscript to the University of Arizona Press.

Christine Szuter, then the director of the UA Press, never wavered in her support. Over the months of academic review, developmental editing, and my frustration with the publishing world's glacial pace, she provided a steady rudder to my soaring enthusiasm and constant nagging.

Camille Smith, my developmental editor, gave new meaning, not to mention editorial brilliance, to the term "makeover." She took my words, sentences, and paragraphs and played with them like chess pieces on a dozen different chessboards. She moved them around in ways that were mysterious to me, right up to the time they became magic dust on a stuffy manuscript. She kept her promise that my themes would survive, that my story would be easier to read, and that my attention to detail would be upgraded by her many suggestions. A greater stickler for detail, accuracy, and comprehensiveness there never was. Most important, she took out the merely clinical and massaged my diction into a profluent story of both the true and the impossible. And she did it using only the chess pieces on my original board. Thanks, Camille, for making my pawns and rooks look like kings and queens, not to mention feeding my knights.

Last but never least, Kathleen Stuart did what she always does: she worked on the author, not the book. She listened attentively to my plot lines, sifted through my irrelevancies, cautioned against backfilling and digging new holes, smiled, and stifled my rants about the unfairness of the literary world. Most of all, she did what good spouses always do for writers who focus on the top of the wave, miss the depths of the trough, and ignore the creaking of the deck. She is my ballast; she keeps me anchored during the storms and sailing when the sea is calm. Thanks be to Kathleen.

Notes

Chapter 1. A Circle of Death

2   "Chawee Borders": Account based on interviews with Borders and Premchit Hash by T. C. Shorts, task force report TF521.612, 08/10/91; and by D. Griffiths, TF174.670, TF175.670, 10/03/91; plus formal interviews by Peter Balkan, 03/03/93, 03/05/93.

5   "first officer at the scene": Crime scene information from the responding officers' reports: P. Ellis, TF516.814; A. D. Hosford, TF518.718; T. Lopez, TF311.925; R. Reyer, TF519.483; G. Sanchez, TF517.885; D. Wipprecht, TF515.722.

6   "agitated by the grisly scene": Prosecutor K. C. Scull, transcript of closing argument in *State of Arizona v. Johnathan Doody*, Maricopa County Superior Court docket no. CR-92-01232.

9   "new abbot, Winai Booncham": Angela Cara Pancrazio, "Time to Remember 1991 Massacre at Thai Buddhist Temple," *Arizona Republic*, 08/09/06.

10 "did indeed return to the temple": T. C. Shorts, interview with Ernie Meeks, report 51112, 11/06/91.

10 "permanent structure in the courtyard": Brent Whiting, "Forgiving, Not Forgetting," *Arizona Republic*, 08/12/01; Erin Zlomek, "Memorial to Honor Monks Killed 15 Years Ago," *Arizona Republic*, 08/11/06.

Chapter 2. The Sheriff's Task Force

14 "media blackout": Kimball quoted in notes from Lt. Terry Chapman's internal investigation of the temple murder investigation (henceforth the Chapman notes). The handwritten notes were attached to a motion filed by defense attorney Peter Balkan, 05/03/93.

14 "4.2 million words": Russ Kimball and Laura Greenburg, "Revelations from the Temple," *Phoenix Magazine*, 10/93.

14 "FBI's Behavioral Science Unit": Gregg McCrary with Katherine Ramsland, *The Unknown Darkness: Profiling the Predators among Us* (William Morrow, 2003; HarperTorch, 2004), ch. 5, "The Buddhist Temple Massacre," quotations from 160–63.

15 "going off in all directions": Det. Rick Sinsabaugh quoted in Chapman notes.
16 "interviewed Chawee Borders": P. J. Riley, case report 50041.679.
18 "stopped twice while driving on the base": R. Sinsabaugh, 51710.714.
18 "to track down the rifle": R. Sinsabaugh, report on interview with Caratachea, 41115.714.
18 "some kind of murders that happened in Phoenix": Transcript of Mike McGraw's initial phone call.

Chapter 3. The Man with Many Names

20 "answered the phone": Quotations in this chapter, unless otherwise noted, are from the official transcripts of McGraw's three phone calls and seven interrogation tapes. In all chapters, wording of quotations is exact except for occasional deletion of repetition and nonwords like "um." Ellipses indicate omitted passages. Words added for clarity appear in brackets.
22 "Lawrence had been at work": R. D. Sinsabaugh, report on visit to McCullough Corp., 09/18/91, TF278.714.
23 "official summary of the case": P. J. Riley, supplemental report 50055.679 (hereafter referred to as "case summary").
23 "Troutt himself gives a different version": L. Troutt, report on interview at Tucson Psychiatric Institute, TF0622.DPS.
25 "provide evidence of his guilt": Charles E. O'Hara, *Fundamentals of Criminal Investigation* (Charles C. Thomas, 1956); many reprintings and new editions, the most recent in 2003.
31 "house on East Culver": Troutt, TF0622.DPS.
32 "lawsuit against the MCSO": Paul Rubin, "Back to the Temple of Doom," *Phoenix New Times*, 07/18/96.
33 "During a five-minute break": Troutt, TF0622.DPS.
38 "Sheraton Hotel": Riley, case summary; R. Minner, TF189.785.
38 "the Tucson tour": Al Tamala, TF325.843.
39 "photo lineups": D. Griffiths, TF10.670, TF12.670, TF13.670, TF14.670; D. Munley, TF841.777.
39 "new clothes"; "advised that he was under arrest": Riley, case summary.

Chapter 4. A Waiting Line for Confessions

57 "first suspect picked up": Information on Sherfield from Riley, case summary, and Troutt, 41104.DPS.
58 "applied to Dante Parker": Riley, case summary.

58 "SWAT team burst in": D. Munley, TF2.777; M. Adams, TF476.686; K. Frakes, TF473.669; V. Hatcher, TF303.637.

59 "prop room was the FBI's idea": Kimball and Greenburg, "Revelations from the Temple."

59 "one to one and a half minutes": Riley, report on Nunez interview, 50057.679.

59 "some formality things": All quotations from Nunez's interrogation are from the official transcripts of his nine tapes.

61 "surveilling Bruce's apartment": M. Mitchell, TF306.663. Other information here from author's interviews with Bruce.

62 "just get something straight": All quotations from the early hours of Bruce's interrogation are from the official transcripts of his first four tapes.

64 "sports, professional football": Information on picking up Parker from Riley, case summary; A. Reilly, TF491.DEA.

64 "not anything to get you all excited": All quotations from Parker's interrogation are from the official transcripts of his twenty-one tapes.

66 "Cooper took his call": P. C. Cooper, 50026.619.

66 "killings of the Buddhist priests": Information on Zarate's meeting with White from Zarate's interrogation transcripts.

66 "a waiting line for confessions": Author's interviews with Kimball.

66 "I think Mr. White told me": All quotations from Zarate's interrogation are from the official transcripts of his fifteen tapes.

68 "became noticeably nervous": Riley, 50057.679.

70 "right to silent part": Author's interviews with Bruce.

76 "queen of proofs": Peter Brooks, *Troubling Confessions: Speaking Guilt in Law and Literature* (University of Chicago Press, 2001), 4.

76 "had in fact been arrested"; Bruce in the prop room: P. Cooper, TF484.619.

80 "definite eye contact": P. Riley, 50032.679.

85 "appeared in a lineup": R. Sinsabaugh, TF255.714; Riley, case summary.

87 "full-scale debriefing": Cooper, 41126.619.

89 "couldn't go on anymore": Kimball and Greenburg, "Revelations from the Temple."

90 "what so thoroughly broke Leo Bruce": D. Griffiths, TF68.670. The quotations from Bruce in this section are probably a mixture of memory and paraphrase by Griffiths.

95 "tour of headquarters": Cooper, 41126.619.

96 "Nunez was incriminating himself": Kimball and Greenburg, "Revelations from the Temple."

99 "no time for phone calls": B. McCleve, TF291.707.

99 "only record of what was said": J. M. Mullavey, TF241.394.

104 "checked Parker into the Sheraton": G. D'Agostino, TF0299.758.

106 "reconsider his denials": Cooper, 41126.619.

110 "advised that he was under arrest": Riley, case summary.

Chapter 5. Recantations and Indictments

113   "Fearing claims of coercion": Kimball and Greenburg, "Revelations from the Temple."
113   "cried several times": McCleve, TF292.707.
113   "lied to you last night": Mullavey, TF208.394.
114   "he would be rich": H. Carpio, report of interview with Romelia Duarte, 10/15/91, TF0616.DPS.
114   "sacrificial lambs": "Two Admit Part in Temple Slayings," *Prescott (AZ) Courier*, 09/17/91.
114   "steps of the state capitol": Seth Mydans, "Investigation Criticized in Thai Monks' Slaying," *New York Times*, 10/10/91.
114   "a real crybaby": Transcript of tape 16206.01, B. Sands. and A. Tamala interview of Javier Cuesta, 9/15/91.
115   "respite at the Sheraton": D. Chrissinger, TF297.753.
115   "corrections in his statement": D. Griffiths, TF0079.670.
116   "confirmed the alibi": T. Bates, interview with Glenn and Peggy Armentrout, 9/22/91, TF24.715; G. Eggert, interview with Diane Collins, 9/20/91, TF196.749.
116   "something I couldn't ever have done": Author's interviews with Leo Bruce.
117   "leave for the Sheraton": G. D'Agostino, TF299.758.
117   "Parker's case was handled separately": "3 More Charged in Monks' Deaths," *New York Times*, 09/24/91.
117   "Rene told a different story": G. Eggert, interview with Trinidad Rene Dan, 9/26/91, TF411.749.
118   "I seen Dante Parker": Mydans, "Investigation Criticized in Thai Monks' Slaying."
118   "no documentation to back this statement": T. C. Shorts, interview with Denise Mills, 9/13/91, TF19.612.
119   "pried upward on the window": C. Lewis, TF365.804.
119   "small dark green Buddha statue": R. Sinsabaugh, TF280.714.
119   "Maria and Victor Zarate": D. Gonzales, TF355.607.
119   "immediately grabbed it": P. J. Riley, TF6.679.
120   "to draw two vials of blood": Riley, TF8.679.
120   "Four days after his arrest": David Schwartz, "Third Claim Is Filed on Temple Arrests," *Arizona Republic*, 12/29/91.
120   "met him at the DPS lot": P. C. Cooper, TF17.619.
120   "souvenir or good luck piece": P. J. Yale, TF343.370.
120   "crude quality and little value": G. Woodling, TF974.FBI.
121   "evidence at the dog track": G. Eggert, TF396.749.
121   "watched it with Kimball and Yale": R. Minner, report 51361, 12/27/91.

121 "spilling out quotes": Philip Martin, "Taken for a Ride: The Confessions of Mike McGraw," *New Times*, 11/27/91.
122 "like a political case": Frederick Bermudez, "We're Like Political Prisoners Now, Tucson Suspect Says," *Arizona Republic*, 11/02/91.
122 "Do this and say this": Martin, "Taken for a Ride."
122 "you're my only brother": ibid.
122 "something big was going to happen": C. Lewis, TF128.804.

Chapter 6. The Forgotten Murder Weapon

126 "By coincidence, David Doody": R. Sinsabaugh, TF1042.714.
126 "from mid-June until late July": Riley, case summary.
126 "room 467": R. Kimball, 50073.656.
126 "something to chew": All quotations from Caratachea's interrogation are from the official transcripts of his eighteen tapes.
128 "Riley drove him to headquarters": P. J. Riley, 41120.679.
128 "started questioning him at 9:25 p.m.": The official transcripts of Doody's seventeen interrogation tapes note beginning and end times. All quotations from the interrogation are from those transcripts. Some details come from Riley, 41120.679.
128 "Doody's lawyer would later complain": Peter S. Balkan, motion to suppress Doody's confession, *State v. Doody*.
138 "went to his parents' house": J. M. Mullavey, transcript of testimony before Judge Ronald Reinstein, 11/10/92.
138 "room 428": Riley, case summary.
138 "at this point": All quotations from Garcia's interrogation are from the official transcripts of his twelve interrogation tapes.
142 "interview Garcia's father"; "shotgun was found": W. Scoville, 41068.710.
143 "second search the next day": C. Lewis, TF954.804.
143 "fifteen minutes after that": Kimball, transcript of testimony at hearing on suppressing Doody's confession, 11/05/92.
143 "information can be pieced together": Kimball testimony, ibid.; Riley, case summary.
143 "no noticeable reaction": Kimball, 50073.656.
144 "offered Juan Garcia a deal": Balkan, transcript of closing argument in *State v. Doody*.
151 "handgun"; "promise ring"; "credit union account": K. C. Scull, transcript of closing argument in *State v. Doody*.
158 "found Doody in tears": Sinsabaugh, 41081.714.
158 "had eaten nothing": MCSO timeline of Doody's interrogation, exhibit 162 at Doody's trial.

163   "arrived with some reading material": J. White, TF1047.235.
163   "embraced his father": Riley, case summary.

Chapter 7. Political Wrangling

169   "Keystone Kops": Mydans, "Investigation Criticized in Thai Monks' Slaying."
169   "hodgepodge of conflicting witnesses": Charles Kelly, "Case Turns Nightmarish for Probers," *Arizona Republic*, 10/31/91.
169   "incredible pressure"; "What do you mean, controversial?": Paul Brinkley-Rogers, Randy Collier, and Charles Kelly, "Probers Divided in Temple Case," *Arizona Republic*, 11/02/91.
170   "career-threatening minefield": Jane Fritsch, "Sudden Surplus of Suspects Marks Case of Slain Monks," *Los Angeles Times*, 11/19/91.
170   "Rick wants to let them go": Randy Collier and Charles Kelly, "Temple Probe Gets Deadline," *Arizona Republic*, 11/11/91.
170   "thousands of dollars": Randy Collier and Paul Brinkley-Rogers, "Dismissal Sought in Monk Case but Panel Asks Governor to Step In," *Arizona Republic*, 11/20/91.
171   "visited Juan and Gloria Garcia": White, 50012.235.
171   "closed-door meeting": Collier and Brinkley-Rogers, "Panel Asks Governor to Step In."
172   "the judge scolded Romley": "Judge Refuses to Dismiss Charges," *Prescott (AZ) Courier*, 02/14/93.
172   "I read all those confessions"; "all hell broke loose": Collier and Brinkley-Rogers, "Panel Asks Governor to Step In."
173   "the courtroom is the place"; "political suicide": ibid.
173   "we are going to make this case"; "adapt to changes": Paul Brinkley-Rogers and Randy Collier, "Sheriff to Keep Probing Tucson Temple Suspects," *Arizona Republic*, 11/21/91.
174   "doesn't make any sense": KFYI Talk Radio, Phoenix.
174   "always has a story to tell": Philip Martin, "The Confessions of Mike McGraw," *New Times*, 11/27/91.
175   "an F for being mishandled"; "I don't like confessions": Arpaio quoted in Dennis Wagner, "How Do False Confessions Occur?" *Arizona Republic*, 10/03/04.
175   "the Chapman Audit": Chapman's interviews with Faulk, Riley, Kimball, Sinsabaugh quoted in the Chapman notes.
177   "significant, recurrent, and deeply troubling": Richard A. Leo and Richard J. Ofshe, "The Consequences of False Confessions," *Journal of Criminal Law and Criminology*, Winter 1998.

178 "73 percent of the time": Wagner, "How Do False Confessions Occur?"
178 "sentenced to death": Welsh White, "Confessions in Capital Cases," 4 *Univ. Ill. L. Rev.* 979 at 980 (2003).

Chapter 8. A Murderer Ten Times Over

180 "will to resist confessing": Order by Judge Gregory H. Martin, 11/19/92.
180 "shy, quiet, sensitive"; "as often as allowed by the system": Andrew Lembo, probation officer, presentence report on Garcia, 05/94.
182 "for any of the ten murders": Statement of Alessandro Garcia, 01/05/93.
185 "to get cash at ATMs": C. Norton, report on interview with Garcia at Madison Street Jail, 01/12/93.
187 "transient with a history of mental problems": Randy Collier, "Temple Murderer Admits Slaying Woman," *Arizona Republic*, 01/08/93.
188 "bearded Grizzly Adams": D. Heller, memo summarizing deposition of J. White, 08/13/93.
188 "bloody vehicles from Vietnam"; "carpal tunnel syndrome": Evan Haglund, memo on part 4 of Peterson interview, 11/23/93.
189 "often made self-sacrifices": Debra Peterson, letter to the MCSO, 11/04/91.
189 "Peterson arrived at the Mesquite Campground": information in this section from Haglund's memo on part 1 of Peterson interview, 11/16/93.
189 "cat meowing": Peterson's witness statement, 10/19/91.
190 "Cameron's body was discovered": D. Walsh, investigative summary of Cameron case, 10/25/91.
191 "liked to read books": D. A. Beatty, report on interview with Peterson, 10/19/91.
191 "Beatty sniffed the gun": Haglund memo, 11/16/93.
191 "lodged in the side panel": Kimball, affidavit for search warrant SW93-00032, 01/93.
191 "memory of her was vivid": Beatty, report on second interview with Peterson, 10/20/91.
193 "Walsh wrote a summary": Walsh, case summary, 10/25/91.
194 "took Walsh's deposition": Kimberly O'Connor, transcript of Walsh deposition, 09/11/92.
196 "again seemed calm": D. Walsh, report on Peterson interrogation, 10/22/91.
197 "watched through the two-way mirror": C. A. Norton, report on Peterson interrogation, 10/22/91.
198 "composite drawing": D. Walsh, report on attempts to locate Hispanic male, 11/17/91.
200 "Deadly Teen Lovers": Russell P. Kimball, "Arizona Shocker: Deadly Teen Lovers in the Mesquite Flats Campground," *Official Detective*, 1995.

201 "daddy's pet": Mike Sager, *Scary Monsters and Super Freaks: Stories of Sex, Drugs, Rock 'n' Roll and Murder* (Thunder Mouth Press, 2003), 314ff.

202 "Her first two interviews": D. Griffiths, reports 41059.670 and 41060.670, 10/27/91.

204 "interviewed Hoover's parents": P. Riley, reports 121670PR.011 and 121670PR.012, 01/11/93.

204 "Deputy David Vaughn": Gila County Sheriff's Office offense report, 10/22/91.

206 "a serious incident": Kimball, report on search warrant and interview with Hoover, Hoover1.656, 01/06/93.

206 "Hoover formally surrendered": Kimball, report, Hoover.Ja1.656, 01/14/93.

207 "Her version of the murder": Gregory Miller, probation officer, presentencing report on Hoover, 05/93.

207 "an instant flame": Sager, *Scary Monsters and Super Freaks*, 314–16.

207 "some negative attention": Brent Whiting, "Girl Admits Slaying, Now Wants Some Fun," *Arizona Republic*, 03/24[?]/93. E. J. Montini, "'Vacation' Fun for Killer Angers Public," ibid., 03/25[?]/93. Lee Johnson, letter to editor, ibid., 04/06/93. Lea Selph, letter to editor, ibid., 05/05/93.

210 "made a grave error": Martinez, letter to Judge Reinstein, 05/12/93. Letters quoted here are from Hoover's aunt Jeanette Abbitt, her grandmother Georgia Hankins, Jane Penska, and Sherryl Nantais.

210 "only female juvenile in an adult prison": Susan Leonard, "Love Turned Girl into Killer," *Arizona Republic*, 07/11/93.

211 "Another set of letters": the letters are attached to two reports by Riley, 121670PR.003, 01/15/93, and 121670PR.013, 01/25/93.

214 "Helen Fletcher": Quotations from Fletcher's typed draft of her address to the court, dated 05/14/93.

215 "balance the scales of justice": J. W. Brown, "Judge Rejects Plea in Killing," *Arizona Republic*, 05/15/93.

215 "second sentencing hearing": Karen Fernau, "Teen Given 15-Year Term," *Arizona Republic*, 07/16[?]/93.

216 "a special room": Susan Leonard, "Teen Gets 15 Years for Killing Camper," *Arizona Republic*, 07/16/93.

216 "complete and verified": Arizona Department of Corrections website.

Chapter 9. Johnathan Doody on Trial

217 "distinctively American legal doctrine": Adam Liptak, "Serving Life for Providing Car to Killers," *New York Times*, 12/04/07.

219 "things pop up": Most quotations in this section are from the transcript of Judge Martin's hearing on pretrial motions, 05/07/93.

219 "significant improprieties": Peter S. Balkan, motion for reinterview of wit-
     nesses, 05/03/93.
222 "leeway in histrionics": Transcript of trial proceedings, *State v. Doody*.
231 "change was remarkable": Sager, *Scary Monsters and Super Freaks*, 319.
232 "beefy and thick-necked"; "vaguely feral": ibid., 319, 308.
235 "borrowed the gun for two days": Quotations here are from the transcripts
     of Doody's seventeen interrogation tapes.
238 "preferred not to testify": Information from author's interviews with Bruce
     and transcript of trial proceedings.

Chapter 10. Mitigation, Aggravation, and Sentencing

255 "contrary to the verdict of the jury": Balkan, motion to strike State's sen-
     tencing memorandum, 10/93.
257 "those cases had been long ago": Victor L. Streib, affidavit, 11/16/93.
258 "on the sole theory of felony murder": Balkan, motion in support of the
     mitigating circumstance of age, 11/93.
258 "difficult early years": Balkan, memorandum re mitigating circumstances,
     12/93.
258 "Doody's social history": Durand's report is summarized in ibid. and in
     Hadley C. Osran, M.D., evaluation of Doody, 11/16/93.
258 "junior" or "shorty": Michael Moerman, professor of anthropology emeri-
     tus, UCLA, evaluation of Doody, 01/18/94.
259 "terrified of spaghetti": Osran, evaluation of Doody.
259 "taunts and jeers": Balkan, memorandum re mitigating circumstances.
260 "level of intelligence": IQ scores from Roger M. Martig, Ph.D., evaluation of
     Doody, 01/14/94.
261 "consumed with military hardware": Kimball and Greenburg, "Revelations
     from the Temple."
261 "obsessive fascination with the military": Osran, evaluation of Doody.
262 "nine lifetimes plus fifty-six years": *State v. Doody*, sentence of imprison-
     ment, 02/11/94.
263 "to be served consecutively": K. C. Scull, sentencing memorandum in *State
     v. Garcia*, 03/21/94.
263 "released from prison in his lifetime": Luis Calvo, sentencing memorandum
     in *State v. Garcia*, 07/14/94.
265 "clinical and forensic psychologist": Richard I. Lanyon, Ph.D., evaluation of
     Garcia, 07/14/94.
266 "anxiety and thought disturbance": Kathryn A. Menendez, Ph.D., evalua-
     tion of Garcia, 11/91.

266 "smart enough to avoid prosecution": Roger M. Martig, Ph.D., evaluation of Garcia, 01/18/93.
267 "read the letter aloud": Helen Fletcher, letter to Judge Martin dated 03/14/94.
268 "helpful, supportive, and loving": Gloria Garcia, letter to Judge Martin, 03/19/94.
268 "bullshit lazy faggot": Quotations here from Sager, *Scary Monsters and Super Freaks*, 310, 313.
269 "guilty of all ten murders": *State v. Garcia*, sentence of imprisonment, 07/15/94.

Chapter 11. Suing Maricopa County

271 "a planned execution": Abraham Kwok, "Ex-Temple Suspect Seeks Restitution," *Arizona Republic*, 12/07/91.
271 "the hell they put me through": David Schwartz, "Third Claim Filed on Temple Arrests," *Arizona Republic*, 12/29/91.
272 "forced interrogation": *Bruce et al. v. Agnos et al.*, third amended complaint, 09/10/93.
272 "still elaborating on his confession": P. J. Riley, 50072.679, report on interview with McGraw in Colorado Springs, 07/23/92.
272 "spend it in my dreams": Philip Martin, "Taken for a Ride: The Confessions of Mike McGraw," *New Times*, 11/27/91.
273 "stripped of his freedom" and later quotations in this section: M. E. "Buddy" Rake Jr., Plaintiff Bruce's settlement conference memorandum, 03/94.
276 "explosive diversionary device": ibid.
276 "various documents": B. Sands, report of search of Bruce's apartment, TF434.708.
276 "question of the hour": transcript, Kimball interviewed by Doody and Garcia's defense attorneys, 10/22/92.
278 "primary claims for relief": Hammond and Haglund memo to Contingency Fee Committee, "George Peterson: case recommendation," 04/26/93.
279 "Peterson's confession was unreliable": Larry Hammond, Howard Ross Cabot, John Rogers, Evan Haglund, and Michael Berch, statement to the press about the Peterson suit, 02/93.
279 "my anxieties are so high": Quotations in this paragraph from "Prosecutor 'Outraged' over Man's Jailing in Killing Later Claimed by Temple Teen," *Arizona Daily Star*, 01/09/93.
280 "Hammond deposed White": D. Heller memo, "Summary of White deposition," 08/12/93; Hammond memo, "Questions for the Chapman deposition arising from the White deposition of November 9, 1993," 11/12/93.

280 "he and his girlfriend had killed a woman": Leroy Hughes interview, 11/12/92. Kimball, interview by Peter Balkan for Doody's defense, 03/15/93; G. Eggert, interview by David Brewer for Doody's defense and Paul Ahler for the State, 04/07/93.

282 "never read the Chapman Audit": Hammond, "Questions for the Chapman deposition."

282 "According to his officers": Chapman notes.

282 "total indifference to Mr. Peterson's rights": Hammond, "Questions for the Chapman deposition."

282 "considered hiring Richard Ofshe": Hammond, memo re meeting with Ofshe, 09/08/93.

283 "cost the county $2.8 million"; "constitutional rights of some Hispanics": Brent Whiting and David Schwartz, "Arizona County to Pay $2.8 million for Bungled Temple Case," Knight-Ridder/Tribune News Service, 04/22/94.

Epilogue

285 "pawned her engagement ring": P. J. Riley, report 50070.679, interview with Angela Charoon, Colorado Springs, 08/04/92.

287 "if he had courage to confess": M. E. "Buddy" Rake Jr., confidential mediation position statement in *Armstrong v. Maricopa County*, 05/01/06.

287 "there was a bonfire": Ibid.

287 "microtremors are only present": Quotations here are from the official transcripts of Armstrong's twelve interrogation tapes.

289 "I don't like confessions": Dennis Wagner, "How Do False Confessions Occur?" *Arizona Republic*, 10/03/04.

289 "deserve to be executed": In his mediation position statement, Rake cites the *Arizona republic*, 04/16/04.

289 "reversed Doody's conviction": Doody v. Schriro, 06-17161, 548 F.3d 847 (9th Cir. 2008).

289 "forced a confession from Doody": Michael Kiefer, "Appeals Court: Buddhist Temple Confession Coerced," *Arizona Republic*, 11/20/08.

290 "four temples in Thailand": Wassayos Ngamkham, "Former Monk Stands by Convicted Temple Killer," *Bangkok Post*, 12/08/08.

290 "Judge Ruth McGregor": McGregor served as a law clerk to Justice Sandra Day O'Connor on the U.S. Supreme Court in 1982. She was appointed to the Arizona Court of Appeals in 1989 and served as chief judge until 1999, when she was appointed to the Arizona Supreme Court. She was elected chief justice in 2006 and retired in 2009.

290 "reversing Doody's conviction": *Doody v. Schriro*, 548 F. 3d 847 (2008). A three-judge panel held that the state court's ruling that the Miranda

warnings were adequate was not an unreasonable application of clearly established law but that the warnings were delivered so as to minimize their effectiveness in protecting against an involuntary confession. The court said it "had no difficulty in concluding that the erroneous admission of Doody's confession had a substantial and injurious effect on the jury's verdict." Accordingly, it affirmed in part, reversed in part, and remanded the case to the U.S. District Court for the District of Arizona with directions to grant Doody's petition for habeas corpus.

290 "Eleven . . . judges": Chief Judge Alex Kozinski, and Circuit Judges Mary M. Schroeder, Betty B. Fletcher, Harry Pregerson, Stephen Reinhardt, Pamela Ann Rymer, Andrew J. Kleinfeld, Sidney R. Thomas, Kim McLane Wardlaw, Richard C. Tallman, and Johnnie B. Rawlinson.

290 "vote of eight to three": *Doody v. Schriro*, 2010 U.S. App. LEXIS 3937. Opinion by Judge Rawlinson. Separate opinion by Judge Kozinski, concurring in the result. Dissent by Judge Tallman, with whom Judges Rymer and Kleinfeld joined.

292 "undermine America's justice system": Wagner, "How Do False Confessions Occur?"

293 "looking after the interests of everyone": *Nomination of Louis D. Brandeis: Reports from the Subcommittee to the Committee on the Judiciary, United States Senate, 64th Congress, 1st session on the nomination of Louis D. Brandeis to be an associate of the Supreme Court of the United States* (U.S. Government Printing Office, 1916).

Sources

PRIMARY SOURCES

MCSO Crime Scene Reports, Buddhist Temple Murder Case, DR 91-16695*

Bates, T.: Chawee Borders interview, TF986.715, 09/18/91
Ellis, P.: Crime scene, TF516.814, 08/10/91
Griffiths, D.: Ford Bronco seen at temple, TF584.670, 08/11/91; Chawee Borders and Premchit Hash interviews: TF174.670 and TF175.670, 10/03/91
Hosford, A. D.: Crime scene, TF518.718, 10/10/91
Lopez, T.: Crime scene, TF311.925, 10/10/91
Riley, P. J.: Investigative summary, 50055.679, 09/91; Re ballistics report, 50080.679, 10/07/92; Chawee Borders interview, 50041.679, 10/23/91
Ryer, R.: Crime scene, TF519.483, 10/10/91
Sanchez, G.: Crime scene, TF517.885, 10/10/91
Serpa, J.: Detailed examination of scene, 50085.0ID, 10/10/91
Shorts, T.: Chawee Borders interview, TF521.612, 10/10/91
Wipprecht, D.: Crime scene, TF515.722, 10/10/91

MCSO Crime Scene Reports, Alice Marie Cameron Murder Case, DR 91-21670

Beatty, D. A.: George Peterson interviews, 10/19/91, 10/20/91
Champion, T. L.: Interviews with campers, 10/19/91
Glennie, S.: Crime scene, 10/19/91
Walsh, D.: Investigative summary, 10/25/91

MCSO Reports and Other Documents by Suspect

Bruce, Leo
Arrest: M. Adams, TF0293.686; M. Mitchell, TF0306.663
Interrogation: T. Bates, TF0086.715; P. Cooper, TF0484.619; D. Griffiths, TF79.670, TF68.670; D. Munley, TF869.777
Hotel: D. Chrissinger, TF297.753
Search warrants: B. Sands, TF434.708; T. Shorts, TF141.612
Alibi: T. Bates, TF24.715; G. Eggert, TF196.749
Recanting confession: Griffiths, TF0079.670

---

* In the temple case, investigative reports were assigned file numbers, which vary in format. Many begin with "TF" for "task force." The final three digits of each file number, following the period, indicate the reporting officer's badge number. Reports in the Cameron case do not have file numbers.

Caratachea, Rolando
Luke AFB traffic stop: R. Sinsabaugh, 51710.714
Interrogation: Sinsabaugh, 41115.714; R. Kimball, 50073.656
Later interview: Sinsabaugh, TF398.714

Doody, Johnathan
Luke AFB traffic stop: R. Sinsabaugh, 51710.714
Original interview: Sinsabaugh, 51966.714, 09/10/91
Visit to temple after the murders: T. Shorts, 51112.612
Arrest: P. Riley, 41120.679
Interrogation: Sinsabaugh, 41081.714; J. White, 41069.235
Family interview: Sinsabaugh, TF1042.714

Garcia, Alessandro
Interrogation: R. Kimball, TF950.656, 50073.656; J. White, 41070.235,
    TF1047.235
Juan Garcia interview: White, 50012.235, 11/09/91
Michelle Hoover interview: D. Griffiths, TF41059.670, 10/27/91
Re confession to Cameron murder: P. Riley, 60189.679, 60192.679
Search warrants: C. Lewis, TF954.804; W. Scoville, 41068.710
Garcia's sworn statements re plea bargain, 01/05/93, 01/06/93, 02/03/93

Hoover, Michelle
Runaway report: D. Vaughn, Gila County offense report, case 911000179,
    10/22/91
Charging summary: R. Kimball, Cameron.sum.656
Interviews: D. Griffiths, 41509.670 and 41060.670, 10/27/91; 41508.670 and
    41111.670, 10/28/91; 51713.670, 02/27/92; Kimball, Hoover1.656, 01/06/93;
    L. Troutt, 51336, 12/17/91
Parent interviews: P. Riley, 121670PR.011 and 121670PR.012
Friend interview: Riley, 121670PR.001
Arrest: Kimball, Hoover.Ja1.656
Search warrant affidavit: Kimball, SW93-00032
Letters to Garcia: attached to Riley, 121670PR.003 and 121670PR.013

McGraw, Michael
Photo lineups: D. Griffiths, TF10–TF16.670; D. Munley, TF841.777
Reinterviews: J. M. Mullavey, TF60164.394, 11/20/92; P. Riley, 50072.679,
    07/23/92
Interrogation: L. Troutt, TF622.DPS

Trips to point out houses: J. R. Eccles, TF150.739; R. Minner, TF162.785;
   A. Tamala, TF325.843
Criminal record check: C. Lewis, TF128.804
Work record check: R. Sinsabaugh, TF278.714
Hotel: Minner, TF189.785

Nunez, Marcus

Arrest: M. Adams, TF476.686; K. Frakes, TF473.669; V. Hatcher, TF303.637;
   D. Munley, TF2.777
Hotel: B. McCleve, TF291.707, TF292.707
Interrogation: J. M. Mullavey, TF911.394, TF241.394; P. Riley, 50057.679
Mother and friend interviews: H. Carpio, interview with Romelia Duarte,
   TF616.DPS; B. Sands and A. Tamala, interview with Javier Cuesta, transcript
   of tape 16206.01
Recantation: Mullavey, TF208.394
Photo lineups: Munley, TF840.777

Parker, Dante

Arrest: A. Reilly, TF491.DEA
Interrogation: R. Sinsabaugh, TF255.714
Hotel: G. D'Agostino, TF299.758
Alibi: G. Eggert, TF411.749
Sherfield interview: L. Troutt, 41104.DPS

Peterson, George

DR 91-21670, investigative file
Peterson's witness statement, 10/19/91
Letter to mother from campground, 10/18/91–10/20/91
Interrogation: C. A. Norton, 10/22/91; D. Walsh, 10/22/91; J. Barber, 10/22/91
Crime reenactment: Walsh, 10/22/91
Criminal record check: Walsh, 10/30/91
Attempts to locate Hispanic male: Walsh, 11/17/91

Sherfield, Patrick

Arrest: R. Minner, TF161.785
Interviews: L. Troutt, 41104.DPS, 41116.DPS

Zarate, Victor

Original phone calls: P. Cooper, 50026.619
Arrest: G. Eggert, TF96.749
Interrogation: Cooper, 41126.619; D. Gonzales, TF352.607; P. Riley, 50032.679;
   J. White, TF1048.235

Search warrants: C. Lewis, TF365.804; B. Sands, TF416.708; R. Sinsabaugh, TF280.714

Dog track videotape: G. Eggert, TF396.749; R. Minner, TF51361.785; Sinsabaugh, TF280.714

"Buddha" figurine: Riley, TF6.679; G. Woodling, TF974.FBI; P. J. Yale, TF343.370

Family interviews: H. Carpio, 52073.DPS; D. Gonzales, TF355.607; B. Sands, TF435.708; T. Shorts, TF19.612

Release of vehicle: Cooper, TF17.619

Motions; Mitigation and Aggravation Pleadings
Doody, Johnathan
JV transfer report, 01/16/92
Presentence reports by Victor L. Streib, Andrew Lembo, Hadley Osran, Roger Martig, Michael Moerman
Defense motions and memoranda: Motion re age as mitigating circumstance; memo on international law re death penalty for juveniles; memo of points and authorities re mitigation

Garcia, Alessandro
JV transfer report update, 02/11/92
Letter from mother, 03/19/94
Presentence reports by Roger Martig, Kathryn Menendez, Richard Lanyon, Andrew Lembo, Gregory Miller
State sentencing memo, 03/21/94
Defense sentencing memo, 07/14/94

Hoover, Michelle
Presentence reports by Gregory Miller
Letters supporting Hoover: attached to T. Martinez, letter to Judge Reinstein, 05/12/93

MCSO Interrogation Transcripts
Armstrong, Robert: *State of Arizona v. Robert Louis Armstrong*, CR-2003-015792, 12 tapes, 06/09/03
Bruce, Leo: DR 91-16695, digital files 16037–40, 16060–63, 11 tapes, 09/12–09/13/91
Caratachea, Rolando: DR 91-16695, digital files 16243–61, 19 tapes, 10/25/91; deposition in *State v. Doody* CR-1992-01232, 04/15/93
Doody, Johnathan: DR 91-16695, digital files 16284–99, 17 tapes, 10/25–10/26/91
Garcia, Alessandro: DR 91-16695, digital files 16263–75, 12 tapes, 10/26/91

McGraw, Michael: Phone calls, 09/10/91: digital file 16396.01T, case 9109108018,
    4 calls; DR 91-16695, digital file 16396.01T, 6 tapes, 09/10–09/12/91
Nunez, Marcus: DR 91-16695, digital file 50075.656, 9 tapes, 09/11–09/12/91
Parker, Dante: *State of Arizona v. Dante Parker*, CR-91-07832, digital file 11447-
    91.1, 21 tapes, 09/12–09/13/91
Peterson, George: DR 91-21670, 2 tapes, 10/22–10/23/91
Zarate, Victor: DR 91-16695, 15 tapes, 09/12–09/13/91

Interviews by Peter Balkan in *State v. Doody*
Bates, Todd, MCSO
Bayless, Michael, Ph.D.
Borders, Chawee
Caratachea, Rolando
Caratachea, Rolando, Sr., deposition
Casey, Robert, FBI
Choosin, Bhandhusavee
Cruz, Moise
Doody, David
Doody, Lliad
Dorn, Tim, MCSO
Eccles, Jeff, MCSO
Eggert, Gary, MCSO
Garcia, Alessandro
Garcia, Juan
Grier, Donna
Griffiths, Donald, MCSO
Haag, Luke, DPS State Crime Lab
Hash, Premchit
Hepburn, Pen
Herron, James
Issertell, Sandy
Kimball, Russell
Labenz, Gary, MCSO
Leininger, Benjamin
Martig, Roger, Ph.D.
Minner, Ron, MCSO
Mullavey, Mike, MCSO
Munley, Dave, MCSO
Riley, Patrick, MCSO
Sands, Brian, MCSO
Shorts, Thomas, MCSO
Sinsabaugh, Richard, MCSO

Sonsim, Amporn, M.D.
Soucy, Pam
Stokes, Norris, MCSO
Tamala, Al, MCSO
Troutt, Larry, DPS
Vilalay, Bongbong
Wattikra, Parapuk
Woodling, Gary, FBI

Interviews by Lt. Terry Chapman, MCSO Internal Affairs Audit
Faulk, Dan
Josephson, Gary
Kimball, Russell
Riley, Patrick
Sinsabaugh, Richard

Maricopa County Superior Court Transcripts
Voluntariness hearings
CR-92-01232, *State v. Doody*, and CR-92-02096, *State v. Garcia*: Judge Gregory
    Martin presiding; testimony by P. Riley, 10/27/92; G. Woodling, 10/27/92;
    R. Kimball, 11/05/92

Juvenile Division transfer hearings
JV-125982, *State v. Doody*. Judge James McDougall presiding, vols. I–VI, 01/27–
    01/29/92, 02/04–02/06/92. Witnesses: P. Riley, R. Sinsabaugh, R. Kimball,
    J. Eccles, J. Serpa, Bernadette Jones, Vickie Jones, Benjamin Leininger,
    Melanie Sprouse, Marvin Cook, Moise Cruz, Joseph Bruner, Angel Rowlett,
    Michael Myers, Mark Arciniega, Rolando Caratachea, Dr. Roger Martig
JV-125983, *State v. Garcia*. Judge Mark Armstrong presiding, vols. I–V, 02/26–
    02/28/92, 03/03–03/04/92. Witnesses: R. Kimball, Melanie Sprouse, Michelle
    Hoover, Amanda Hoelzen, Jason Kubica, Michael Myers, Sheila Caratachea,
    Rolando Caratachea, P. Riley, Richard Morris, J. Eccles, J. Serpa, Sherrill
    Meisner, B. Sands

Jury trial
State v. Doody, CR-92-01232. Judge Gregory H. Martin presiding; prosecutors
    K. C. Scull, Paul Ahler; defense lawyer Peter Balkan
Jury selection, pretrial motions, 05/07–05/10/93
Opening statements, 05/19–05/20/93
Witnesses:
05/20: Chawee Borders, Premchit Hash, Joseph Ledwidge, D. Wipprecht,
    P. Riley

05/24: P. Riley, Steve Miller, Choosin Bhaldhusa

05/25: Dr. Heinz Karnitsching, Dr. Larry Shaw

05/26: R. Kimball, Joseph Turitto, R. Sinsabaugh, William Morris

05/27: William Morris, P. Riley

06/01: P. Riley, R. Sinsabaugh

06/02: Lawrence Roberts

06/04: Alex Garcia, R. Sinsabaugh

06/07: Alex Garcia

06/09: R. Kimball, Alex Garcia

06/14: Alex Garcia, Eugene Spitzer, Mark Yatsko, Randy Oden, Stephanie Lesher

06/15: Wendell Lesher, Brett Ruff, G. Eggert, Michael Myers, Tim Davern, Bongbong Vilalay, Richard Henderson, Cynthia Torres

06/16: Amanda Torres, Lennie Van Tassell, Avelino Tamala, Stanley Slonaker, Sherrill Miesner, J. Serpa

06/17: Angel Rowlett, Victoria Jones, Benjamin Leininger, Marvin Cook, Luke Haag

06/21: Mark Nunez, P. Riley, R. Kimball, Mike McGraw, Leo Bruce

06/22: Leo Bruce

06/23: P. Riley, R. Sinsabaugh, Tom Agnos

06/24: George Leese

06/25: R. Sinsabaugh, P. Riley

06/28: P. Riley, D. Griffiths, Ira Every, Maurice Payne, J. White

06/29: Howard Birbaum, James Hale, William Heath, D. Munley, Jeff Asher, Kirk Meisner, Leroy Hughes

06/30: John Coppock, Leroy Hughes, Brandon Burner, Jason Kubica, Amanda Hoelzen, Douglas Hoelzen, Gary Eggert

07/01: A. Tamala, D. Gonzales, Rolando Caratachea

07/06: Michelle Hoover, Rolando Caratachea Sr., Juan Garcia

Closing arguments, 07/08–07/09

Jury verdict, 07/12

Sentencing, 02/11/94

Trial and Appellate Court Files
Armstrong, Robert Louis
Maricopa County Superior Court, Docket CR-2003-015792-001 DT, *State v. Armstrong* (primary criminal case)

Maricopa County Superior Court, Docket CV-2005-007357, *Armstrong v. Maricopa County et al.* (civil case: false arrest, malicious prosecution)

U.S. District Court for the District of Arizona, Docket CV-05-1563-PHX-DKD, *Armstrong v. Maricopa County et al.* (civil rights case)

Brown, Peggy Sue
Maricopa County Superior Court, Docket CR-2001-009560, *State v. Brown* (primary criminal case)

Bruce, Leo Valdez
Maricopa County Superior Court, Docket CR-91-17811, *State v. Bruce* (primary criminal case and grand jury indictment, 137GJ85)

Bruce, Leo, Marcus Nunez, Victor Zarate, Romelia Duarte
Maricopa County Superior Court, Docket CV-1992-017739, *Bruce et al. v. Maricopa County et al.* (civil case: wrongful arrest, malicious prosecution)

Doody, Johnathan Andrew
Maricopa County Superior Court, Juvenile Division, Docket JV 125982, *In Re Johnathan Doody*, a minor (initial filing: transferred to adult court)
Maricopa County Superior Court, Docket CR-92-01232, *State v. Doody* (primary criminal case)
Arizona Court of Appeals, *Doody v. State of Arizona*, CA-CR-94-0120, 187 Ariz. 363, 930 P.2d 440 (1996); cert denied, U.S.
Supreme Court, 520 U.S. 1275 (1997) (primary appeal of criminal conviction)
U.S. District Court for the District of Arizona, Docket 98-0528-PHX-EHC (LOA), *Doody v. Megan Savage, Warden, Arizona State Prison, et al.*, petition for writ of habeas corpus; filed 03/23/98, denied 09/09/06
Petitioner appealed to the U.S. Ninth Circuit Court of Appeals, 10/20/06
U.S. Court of Appeals for the Ninth Circuit, *Doody v. Dora B. Schriro, Megan Savage, Attorney General of the State of Arizona*, Docket 06-17161: argued and submitted, 12/03/07; opinion filed, 11/20/08: petition for habeas corpus granted, Arizona State Court of Appeals reversed, case remanded to Arizona for new trial; three-judge panel opinion withdrawn; en banc panel reviewed case.
U.S. Court of Appeals for the Ninth Circuit, Johnathan Andrew *Doody v. Dora B. Schriro et al.*, 2010 U.S. App. LEXIS 3937. Petition for habeas corpus granted. Arizona State Court of Appeals reversed, case remanded to Arizona for new trial.

Garcia, Alessandro
Maricopa County Superior Court, Docket CR-92-02096, *State v. Garcia* (primary criminal case, Buddhist temple murders)
Maricopa County Superior Court, Docket CR-93-00536, *State v. Garcia* (primary criminal case, Alice Marie Cameron murder)
Maricopa County Superior Court, Juvenile Division, Docket JV 125983, *In Re Alessandro Garcia*, a minor (court initial filing; transferred to adult court)

Hoover, Michelle Leslie
Maricopa County Superior Court, Docket CR-93-00536, *State v. Hoover and Garcia* (primary criminal case)
Maricopa County Superior Court, Docket 93-02079, *State v. Hoover*, Judge Ronald S. Reinstein presiding (primary criminal case)
Maricopa County Superior Court, Docket 93-91352, *State v. Hoover*, Judge David L. Roberts presiding (primary criminal case)

McGraw, Michael Lawrence
Maricopa County Superior Court, Docket CR-91-00769, *State v. McGraw* (primary criminal case)

Nunez, Marcus Felix
Maricopa County Superior Court, Docket CR-91-07834, *State v. Nunez* (primary criminal case)

Painter, Victoria
Maricopa County Superior Court, Docket CV-1992-16077, *Victoria Painter v. Maricopa County* (civil case: civil rights, false arrest)

Parker, Dante
Maricopa County Superior Court, Docket CR-91-07832, *State v. Parker* (primary criminal case)
Maricopa County Superior Court, Docket CV-93-21633, *Parker v. Tom Agnos et al.* (civil case: false arrest)

Peterson, George Edwin
U.S. District Court for the District of Arizona, Docket CV-1993-00838-PHX-PGR, *Peterson v. Maricopa County* (civil rights case)

Sherfield, Patrick
U.S. District Court for the District of Arizona, Docket CIV-1993-242-TUC-JMR, *Sherfield v. Maricopa County* (civil rights case)

Author's Interviews and Consultants
Ahler, Paul, chief deputy Maricopa county attorney: interview, correspondence, shared records
Balkan, Peter, Doody's defense counsel: consultant; interviews, correspondence, shared records, including digital database of MCSO and county attorney's office investigative reports, crime scene documents, and defense preparation materials

Becker, Judith, professor of psychology and psychiatry: interview, correspondence re psychology of coerced confessions

Blakey, Craig, Arizona Superior Court judge: consultant on criminal procedure issues; interviews, manuscript writing and development

Bruce, Leo: interviews, correspondence, review of evidentiary materials, recollections re interrogations, codefendants, and MCSO personnel

Calvo, Luis, Garcia's defense counsel: interview, correspondence, shared records

Coppock, John, Maricopa County chief deputy sheriff: interview, correspondence, recollections re MCSO command and personnel issues

Durand, Mary, mitigation specialist: interview, correspondence, shared records, recollections re death-penalty phase in *State v. Doody* and mitigation phase in *State v. Hoover*

Fletcher, Helen, Alice Marie Cameron's sister: interview, correspondence, shared records

Friedl, William, Nunez's lawyer: interview, correspondence, shared records

Hammond, Larry, Peterson's lead lawyer in civil rights litigation: interviews, correspondence, shared records; consultant re manuscript scope, Fifth Amendment issues, suppression cases, coerced confessions

Kimball, Russell, MCSO lead detective on temple case: interviews, correspondence, and shared records, including photos, tapes, public records, notes, research documents, and articles; recollections re interrogations, MCSO command and staff issues, and case development

Knop, David, writer: interviews, consultant re manuscript review, content, and scope

Martin, Gregory H., Arizona Superior Court judge: interview, correspondence, document review

Mehrens, Craig, lawyer: manuscript review, advice re criminal law, procedure, and confession issues

Moore, William, Nunez's civil lawyer: interview, correspondence, shared records

Ofshe, Richard, professor of sociology, expert on false confessions: interview, correspondence, shared multimedia materials

Rake, M. E. "Buddy," lead counsel in Tucson suspects' civil cases: interview, correspondence, shared records, logistical assistance re suspects, civil cases, and MCSO investigation

Reinstein, Ronald, Arizona Superior Court judge: interview, correspondence, recollections re arraignments, hearings, and trial management in all cases and re Hoover mitigation and sentencing

Rohlwing, Gary, Caratachea's defense counsel: interview, correspondence, shared records

Romley, Richard, Maricopa county attorney: interview, correspondence, shared records

Sager, Mike, journalist: interviews, correspondence, shared work re temple and Cameron cases and re Doody, Garcia, and Hoover

Expert Witnesses

Bayless, Michael, Ph.D., psychologist: State expert in *State v. Doody*

Durand, Mary, death-penalty mitigation specialist: Defense expert in *State v. Doody* and *State v. Hoover*

Esplin, Phillip, Ed.D., psychologist: Defense expert in *State v. Doody*

Green, Jordan, criminal lawyer: Defense expert re plea bargains and prosecutorial discretion in *State v. Doody*

Hale, John, handwriting analyst: Defense expert in *State v. Doody*

Jayne, Richard, consultant, John E. Reid and Associates: Defense consultant in *State v. Doody*

Lanyon, Richard I., Ph.D., psychologist: Defense expert in *State v. Garcia*

Martig, Roger, Ph.D., psychologist: State expert in *State v. Doody*; evaluated both Garcia and Doody

Menendez, Kathryn, Ph.D., psychologist: Psychological profile of Garcia in *State v. Garcia*

Moerman, Michael, Ph.D., anthropologist: Defense expert in *State v. Doody*

Osran, Hadley, Ph.D., psychologist: State expert in *State v. Doody*

Silberman, Al, Ed.D., psychologist: Defense expert in *State v. Doody*

Streib, Victor L., professor of law: Defense expert re juvenile death penalty cases in *State v. Doody*

Warner, James, firearms identification and ballistics specialist: Defense expert in *State v. Doody*

Audio, Video, and Multimedia Materials

MCSO tapes: audiotapes of Bruce, Caratachea, Doody, Garcia, McGraw, Nunez, Parker, Peterson, and Zarate interrogations; videotapes of Armstrong interrogation

Peter Balkan: CD-ROM containing all documents and reports initially provided by MCSO and county attorney's office in *State v. Doody*, plus experts, witnesses, consultants, and trial records

Russ Kimball: audio- and videotapes, photos, notes

TV coverage: ABC, CBS, NBC affiliates in Phoenix, video footage of crime scene, Tucson suspects, arrests, release from jail, and interviews; ABC

Nightline with Ted Koppel program re Tucson suspects, false confessions, and the MCSO; Discovery Channel program re temple murders, arrests, and interrogations

SECONDARY SOURCES

Important Legal Opinions and Statutes

Anti-Terrorism and Effective Death Penalty Act (AEDPA), 28 U.S.C. & 2254(d)

Overview: A defendant can prevail in federal court on appeal of a state court murder conviction only if he can show that the state court's adjudication of his claim (1) resulted in a decision that was contrary to, or involved an unreasonable application of, clearly established federal law, as determined by the Supreme Court of the United States; or (2) resulted in a decision that was based on an unreasonable determination of the facts in light of the evidence presented in the state court proceeding.*

Ariz. Rev. Stat. & 13-1105(A) (1991)

Overview: Under Arizona law, a person commits first-degree murder if (1) intending or knowing that his conduct will cause death, such person causes the death of another with premeditation; or (2) acting alone or with one or more persons such person commits or attempts to commit . . . robbery . . . and in the course of and in furtherance of such offense or immediate flight from such offense, such person or other person causes the death of any person.

Arizona v. Doody, 930 P.2nd 440 (Ariz. Ct. App. 1966)

Overview: The court found no legal error or constitutional violation in the taking of Doody's confession. It determined that the lower court ruling declining to suppress the confession was correct, that the giving of *Miranda* warnings to Doody was legally proper, and that Doody knowingly and voluntarily waived his constitutional rights prior to confessing.

Arizona v. Edwards, 111 Ariz. 357, 529 P.2d 1174 (1974), Arizona Supreme Court

Overview: In Arizona, confessions are prima facie involuntary, and the burden is on the State to show that the confession was freely and voluntarily made. If the defendant's will has been overborne, and his capacity for decision diminished, then the use of his confession is violative of the principles of due process.

Arizona v. Fulminate, 499 U.S. 279 (1991)

Overview: Juvenile confessions, obtained during custodial interrogation, are inherently suspect and must be carefully assessed for voluntariness.

Berkemer v. McCarty, 468 U.S. 420 (1984)

Overviews in this section, with some modification, are from the LexisNexis database, www.lexis-nexis.com

Overview: *Miranda* warnings and the suspect's waiver of rights do not dispense with the voluntariness inquiry which must be conducted by courts prior to admitting an inculpatory statement.

Brown v. Mississippi, 297 U.S. 278 (1936)

Overview: Confessions procured by means revolting to the sense of justice cannot be used to secure a conviction in a court of law.

Bruton v. United States, 391 U.S. 123 (1968) (White, J., dissenting)

Overview: A confession is like no evidence and is probably the most probative and damaging evidence that can be admitted against a defendant. In the case of a coerced confession, the risk that the confession is unreliable, coupled with the profound impact that the confession has upon the jury, requires a reviewing court to exercise extreme caution before determining that the admission at trial was harmless.

Colorado v. Connelly, 479 U.S. 157 (1986)

Overview: Coercive police activity is a necessary predicate to a finding that a confession was not given voluntarily.

Cooper v. Dupnik, 963 F.2d 1220 (9th Cir., 1992, on appeal from U.S. District Court for the District of Arizona)

Overview: Extraction of a statement under physical or psychological coercion violates due process and the right to remain silent. Law enforcement officers must not deliberately turn *Miranda* warnings into mere formalities or deliver them as a psychological ploy designed to make the suspect ignore the warnings. Nor may they comply with *Miranda* in form only, while ignoring its spirit and substance.

Culombe v. Connecticut, 367 U.S. 568 (1973)

Overview: Confessions must be the product of an essentially free and unconstrained choice by the suspect. If not, the suspect's capacity for self-determination has been critically impaired and the use of his confession offends due process of law.

Dickerson v. United States, 530 U.S. 428 (2000)

Overview: The historic *Miranda* decision is a "constitutional decision" of the Supreme Court, and as such, it cannot be abrogated by state legislatures or the federal congress. A coerced confession is an involuntary confession; accordingly its admission in evidence against the accused is a due process violation under the Fourteenth Amendment.

Gallegos v. Colorado, 370 U.S. 49 (1962)

Overview: A teenager may not on his own be able to fully appreciate what is at stake when the police seek to question him.

Gilbert v. Merchant, 488 F.3rd 780 (7th Cir. 2007)

Overview: Even where juvenile suspects agree to custodial interrogation without the presence of a parent or friendly adult, the absence of a friendly adult is a factor in assessing the voluntariness of a juvenile's confession.

Haley v. Ohio, 332 U.S. 596 (1948)
Overview: Numerous cases recognize the coercive potential in unbroken hours of custodial interrogation of a juvenile, particularly when they take place overnight.

In Re Gault, 387 U.S. 1 (1967)
Overview: The Supreme Court has long recognized that admissions and confessions by juveniles require special caution.

Miranda v. Arizona, 384 U.S. 436 (1966)
Overview: In order to combat the inherent pressures in custodial interrogation, and to permit a full opportunity to exercise the privilege against self-incrimination, suspects must be adequately and effectively apprised of their rights and the exercise of those rights must be fully honored. These rights include the right to counsel and the right to remain silent. The warning that a suspect has a right to remain silent is an absolute prerequisite in overcoming the inherent pressures of the interrogation atmosphere. It is not just the subnormal or woefully ignorant who succumb to an interrogator's imprecations, whether implied or expressly stated, that the interrogation will continue until a confession is obtained.

Missouri v. Seibert, 542 U.S. 600, plurality opinion (2004)
Overview: Giving the *Miranda* warnings and getting a waiver from the suspect has too often produced a virtual ticket of admissibility because state courts rarely find a confession inadequate or involuntary following adequate warnings.

Moore v. Czerniak, 534 F.3rd 1128 (9th Cir. 2008)
Overview: A taped recording of a defendant's confession, taken with all the requisite formalities by police officers, and played to a jury that hears the defendant's confession in the defendant's own words, and from his own lips, will have a particularly prejudicial impact on the defendant.

Oregon v. Elstad, 470 U.S. 298 (1985)
Overview: *Miranda* established an irrebuttable presumption of coercion for statements made during custodial interrogation by suspects who were not given the *Miranda* warnings.

Roper v. Simmons, 543 U.S. 551 (2005)
Overview: Juvenile suspects have unique vulnerabilities and must be treated with special caution when assessing statements made during custodial interrogation.

Schneckloth v. Bustamonte, 412 U.S. 218 (1973)
Overview: The due process protection is embodied in a voluntariness inquiry that asks whether a defendant's will was overborne by looking at the totality of circumstances surrounding the taking of a confession.

Withrow v. Williams, 507 U.S. 680 (1993)
Overview: Assessing the totality of the circumstances surrounding the taking
of a suspect's confession should include consideration of the length and
location of the interrogation; evaluation of the maturity, education, physical
and mental condition of the suspect; and the fundamental determination of
whether he was properly advised of his *Miranda* rights.

Books

Brandt, Charles. *The Right to Remain Silent*. New York: St. Martin's, 1988.
Chodron, Pema. *Comfortable with Uncertainty*. Boston: Shambhala, 2002.
Cook, Thomas H. *The Interrogation*. New York: Bantam, 2002.
Cray, Ed. *The Big Blue Line: Police Power vs. Human Rights*. New York: Coward-
McCann, 1967.
Edds, Margaret. *An Expendable Man: The Near Execution of Earl Washington Jr.*
New York: New York University Press, 2003.
Frank, Gerold. *The Boston Strangler*. New York: Signet, Penguin Group, 1966.
Fritz, Dennis. *Journey toward Justice*. Santa Ana, CA: Seven Locks Press, 2006.
Grisham, John. *The Innocent Man: Murder and Injustice in a Small Town*. New
York: Doubleday, 2006.
Gudjonsson, Gisli H. *The Psychology of Interrogations and Confessions: A
Handbook*. Hoboken, NJ: Wiley, 2003.
Guiora, Amos N. *Constitutional Limits on Coercive Interrogation*. New York:
Oxford University Press, 2008.
Heaton-Armstrong, A., E. Shepherd, G. Gudjonsson, and D. Wolchover.
Witness Testimony: Psychological, Investigative and Evidential Perspectives.
New York: Oxford University Press, 2006.
Inbau, Fred E. *Lie Detection and Criminal Interrogation*. 2d ed. Baltimore:
Williams and Wilkins, 1948.
Inbau, Fred E., and John E. Reid. *Criminal Interrogation and Confessions*. 2d ed.
Baltimore: Williams and Wilkins, 1967.
Inbau, Fred E., John E. Reid, Joseph P. Buckley, and Brian C. Jayne. *Essentials of
the Reid Technique: Criminal Interrogations and Confessions*. Sudbury, MA:
Jones and Bartlett, 2005.
Kamisar, Yale. *Police Interrogation and Confessions: Essays in Law and Policy*.
Ann Arbor: University of Michigan Press, 1980.
Kamisar, Yale, Wayne R. LaFave, and Jerold Israel. *Basic Criminal Procedure:
Cases, Comments, and Questions*. 4th ed. St. Paul, MN: West Publishing,
1974.
Kaufman, Fred. *Admissibility of Confessions in Criminal Matters*. Maplewood,
NJ: Carswell, 1974.
Kelleher, Michael D. *Flash Point: The American Mass Murderer*. Westport, CT:
Praeger, 1997.

Leo, Richard A. *Police Interrogation and American Justice.* Cambridge, MA: Harvard University Press, 2008.

Lyon, Kathryn. *Witch Hunt: A True Story of Hysteria and Abused Justice.* New York: Avon Books, 1998.

Macdonald, John M., and David Michaud. *Criminal Interrogation: The Confession, Interrogation and Criminal Profiles for Police Officers.* Denver: Apache Press, 1992.

McCrary, Gregg O., with Katherine Ramsland. *The Unknown Darkness: Profiling the Predators among Us.* New York: HarperTorch, 2003.

O'Hara, Charles E. *Fundamentals of Criminal Investigation.* 3d ed. Springfield, IL: Charles C. Thomas, 1973.

Royal, F. Robert, and Steven R. Schutt. *The Gentle Art of Interviewing and Interrogation: A Professional Manual and Guide.* Englewood Cliffs, NJ: Prentice-Hall, 1976.

Sager, Mike. *Scary Monsters and Super Freaks: Stories of Sex, Drugs, Rock 'n' Roll and Murder.* New York: Thunder Mouth Press, 2003.

Scheck, Barry, Peter Neufeld, and Jim Dwyer. *Actual Innocence: Five Days to Execution and Other Dispatches from the Wrongly Convicted.* New York: Doubleday, 2000.

Stuart, Gary L. *Miranda: The Story of America's Right to Remain Silent.* Tucson: University of Arizona Press, 2004.

Sullivan, Timothy. *Unequal Verdicts: The Central Park Jogger Trials.* New York: Simon and Schuster, 1992.

Taylor, John. *The Count and the Confession: A True Mystery.* New York: Random House, 2002.

Vadackumchery, James. *Police Interrogation: Dos Which the Police Do Not Do.* New Delhi: APH Publishing, 1998.

White, Welsh. *Miranda's Waning Protections: Police Interrogation Practices after Dickerson.* Ann Arbor: University of Michigan Press, 2001.

Selected Articles and Websites

Bedau, Hugo Adam, and Michael L. Radelet. "Miscarriages of Justice in Potentially Capital Cases." 40 *Stan. L. Rev.* 21 (1987).

Blum, George J. "What Constitutes 'Custodial Interrogation' within *Miranda v. Arizona* Requiring that Suspect Be Informed of Federal Constitutional Rights." 38 *A.L.R.* 6th, 97.

Dwyer, Jim. "Cornered Minds, False Confessions." *New York Times,* December 9, 2001.

Forrest, Krista D., Theresa A. Wadkins, and Richard L. Miller. "The Role of Preexisting Stress on False Confessions: An Empirical Study." *Journal of Credibility Assessment and Witness Psychology* 3, no. 1 (2002): 23.

Hirsch, Alan. "Why the Innocent Confess." *Los Angeles Times,* April 25, 2006.

Innocence Project, http://www.innocenceproject.org

Kassin, Saul M. "On the Psychology of False Confessions: Does Innocence Put Innocents at Risk?" *American Psychologist* 60 (2005): 215.

Leo, Richard A., and Steven A. Drizin. "Bringing Reliability Back In: False Confessions and Legal Safeguards in the Twenty-First Century." *Wis. L. Rev.* 479 (2006).

Leo, Richard A., and Richard J. Ofshe. "The Consequences of False Confessions: Deprivations of Liberty and Miscarriages of Justice in the Age of Psychological Interrogation." 88 *J. Crim. L. & Criminology* 429 (1998).

———. "The Decision to Confess Falsely: Rational Choice and Irrational Action." 74 *Denv. U. L. Rev.* 979 (1997).

Taylor, B. Don, III. "Evidence beyond the Confession." *Arizona Attorney* (May 2006): 22.

White, Welsh S. "Confessions in Capital Cases." *Univ. Ill. L. Rev.* 979 (2003).

Wisconsin Criminal Justice Study Commission, Position Paper on False Confessions, available at www.wcjsc.org.

Expert Witnesses

Bayless, Brad, Ph.D., psychologist
   State expert in *State v. Doody*
Durand, Mary, death-penalty mitigation specialist
   Defense expert in *State v. Doody* and *State v. Hoover*
Esplin, Phillip, Ed.D., psychologist
   Defense expert in *State v. Doody*
Green, Jordan, criminal lawyer
   Defense expert re plea bargains and prosecutorial discretion in *State v. Doody*
Hale, John, handwriting analyst
   Defense expert in *State v. Doody*
Jayne, Richard, consultant, John E. Reid and Associates
   Defense consultant in *State v. Doody*
Lanyon, Richard I., Ph.D., psychologist
   Defense expert in *State v. Garcia*
Martig, Roger, Ph.D., psychologist
   State expert in *State v. Doody*; evaluated both Garcia and Doody
Menendez, Kathryn, Ph.D., psychologist
   Psychological profile of Garcia in *State v. Garcia*
Moerman, Michael, Ph.D., anthropologist
   Defense expert in *State v. Doody*
Osran, Hadley, Ph.D., psychologist
   State expert in *State v. Doody*
Silberman, Al, Ed.D., psychologist
   Defense expert in *State v. Doody*

Strieb, Victor L., professor of law
  Defense expert re juvenile death penalty cases in *State v. Doody*
Warner, James, firearms identification and ballistics specialist
  Defense expert in *State v. Doody*

Index

Riley, Pat, 23, 119, 143, 204, 219, 231, 248, 260; crime scene report by, 274–75; and internal affairs investigation, 175–76, 177; interrogation of Caratachea, 145–46; interrogation of Doody, 128–31, 133–34, 139, 235; interrogation of Nunez, 59–60, 67–69, 73–74, 81–82, 87–89; interrogation of Parker, 64–65, 71–72, 77–78, 84–85, 104, 109–10; interrogation of Zarate, 66–67, 78–81, 106, 107, 112; interviews with McGraw, 25–30, 32–33, 36–38, 123, 272
Roberts, David, 215–16
Rogers, John W., 278
Rohlwing, Gary, 237
Romley, Richard, 170, 182, 186, 218, 278, 279, 298; dismissal of charges against Tucson Four, 171–72, 173, 174, 272–73
Rosenblatt, Paul, 279
Rowlett, Angel, 135, 227, 229

Sager, Mike, 201, 207; on Doody trial, 231, 232; Garcia interview, 268–69
saliva samples: from Doody, 159
Salp, Tom, 14
Sanchez, G., 5
Sands, Brian, 160, 276; interrogation of Garcia, 138–39, 143
Scoville, Wayne: interrogation of Parker, 64–65, 71–72, 84–85, 104, 109–10; interrogation of Zarate, 66, 79–81
Scull, K. C., 181, 257, 274; and Cameron murder confession, 182, 183–86; and Garcia's mitigation and sentencing process, 263–65, 268; prosecution of Doody, 218, 222–28, 230–36, 243–46, 251–52, 252
search warrants, 32, 206; for Tucson suspects, 118–20, 142–43, 276

sentencing process: Doody's, 255–62; Garcia's, 263–70; Hoover's, 207–16
Sheraton Hotel: task force use of, 38, 39, 99, 104, 109, 113, 115, 117
Sherfield, Patrick "Peter," 31, 32, 33, 34, 35, 36, 37, 39, 92, 100; implication of, 103, 104–5, 109–10; as suspect, 57–58
Sherfield, T. C., 92, 93
Shorts, Tom, 118; interviews McGraw, 25–30
shotgun, 8–9, 140, 143, 149
Sinsabaugh, Rick, 18, 112, 119, 219, 247, 248; on Caratachea's rifle, 19, 125, 187, 231; and internal affairs investigation, 176, 177; interrogation of Caratachea, 126–28, 131–33, 134–36, 153–54; interrogation of Doody, 136–37, 139–42, 144, 157–59, 235, 236; interrogation of Parker, 85, 92–93, 103–5
skin samples: from Zarate, 120
Slonaker, Stanley, 117, 118
Sopha, Somsak, 2, 223–24, 252
South Tucson residents, 114–15, 122
Sripanprasert, Foy, 2, 3, 10, 16, 223, 244–45, 251–52, 253
Starr, Brad, 20
State v. Doody: closing arguments in, 243–52; defense case in, 228–30, 236–41; Doody tapes played at, 233–36; exhibits presented at, 42(fig.), 43(fig.); jury deliberation and verdict in, 252–54; pretrial issues in, 219–21; prosecution's case in, 222–28, 230–36, 241–43; sentencing process in, 255–62
Streib, Victor, 257–58
suspects, 90, 291; Bruce as, 61–64; Nunez as, 59–60; Parker as, 64–65, 67–68; Sherfield as, 57–58; task

About the Author

Gary L. Stuart earned degrees in business and law at the University of Arizona, graduated in the top 10 percent of his law school class, and served as an editor of the *Arizona Law Review*. He was a partner in Jennings, Strouss, & Salmon, one of Arizona's largest law firms, for thirty years. Early in his career, he began to teach, write, and lecture at both the local and national levels. Along the way, he acquired professional recognition by making the hallmark lists at the top of his profession, including *Who's Who in American Law* (1st ed.), Martindale-Hubbell's *Preeminent American Lawyers*, Woodward/Whites' *Best Lawyers in America*, and *Arizona's Finest Lawyers*. He tried more than one hundred jury cases to a conclusion and earned the rank of advocate as a juried member of the American Board of Trial Advocates. The Arizona State Bar certified him as a specialist in trial practice. The National Institute of Trial Advocacy honored him with its Distinguished Faculty designation in 1994. Stuart completed an eight-year term on the Arizona Board of Regents and served as its president from 2000 to 2005.

He has written scores of law review and journal articles, op-ed pieces, essays, and stories, as well as over fifty Continuing Legal Education (CLE) booklets and six books: *The Ethical Trial Lawyer* (State Bar of Arizona, 1994); *Litigation Ethics* (Lexis-Nexis Publishing, 1998); *The Gallup 14*, a novel (University of New Mexico Press, 2000); *Miranda: The Story of America's Right to Remain Silent* (University of Arizona Press, 2004); *AIM for the Mayor: Echoes from Wounded Knee*, a novel (Xlibris Publishing, 2008); and *Innocent until Interrogated: The True Story of the Buddhist Temple Massacre and the Tucson Four* (University of Arizona Press, 2010).

He is the Senior Policy Advisor and Adjunct Professor of law at ASU's Sandra Day O'Connor College of Law, practices law part time, and is a frequent CLE lecturer in ethics and legal writing.